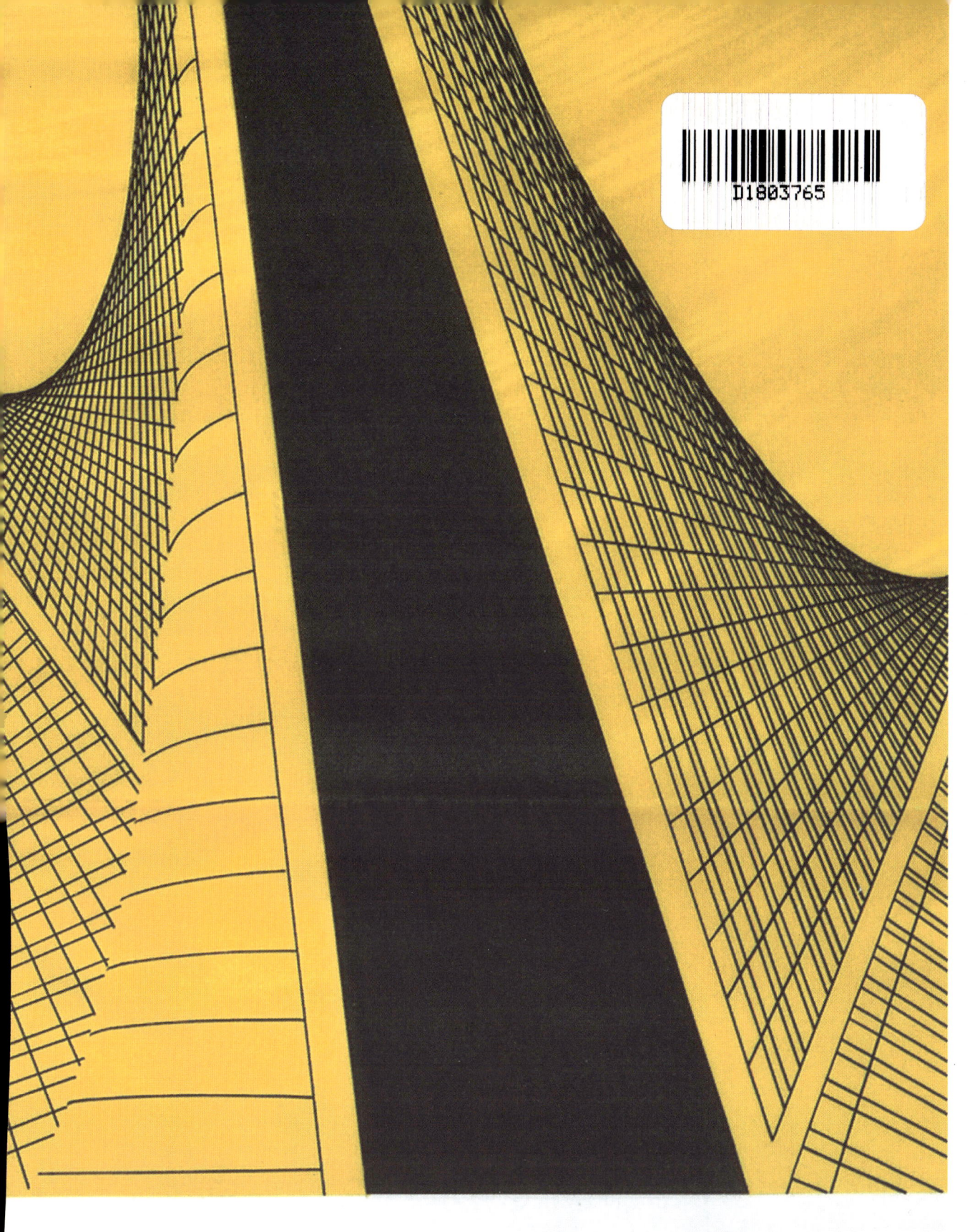

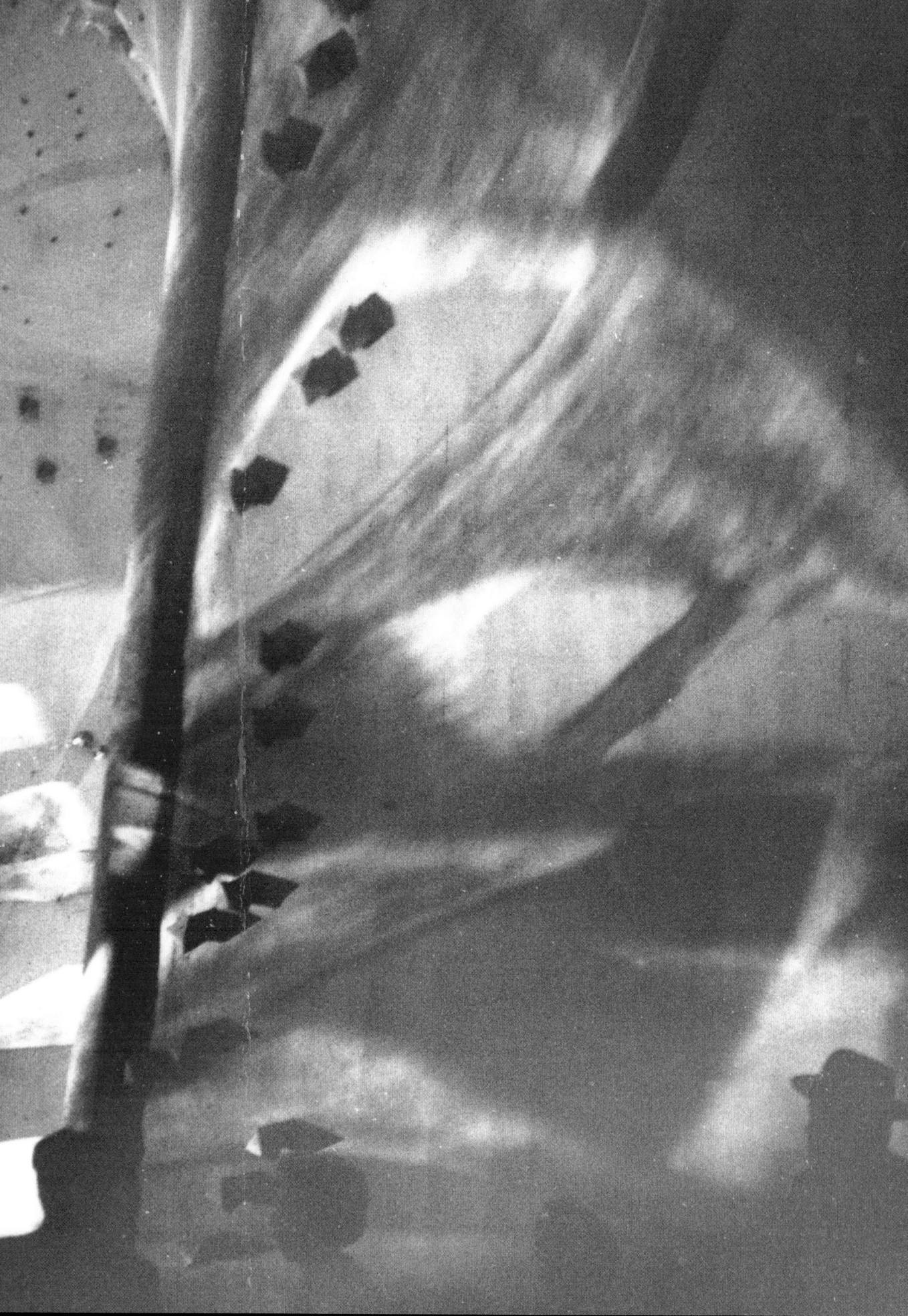

Inside Le Corbusier's Philips Pavilion

A Multimedial Space at the 1958 Brussels World's Fair

Peter Wever

nai010 publishers

Contents

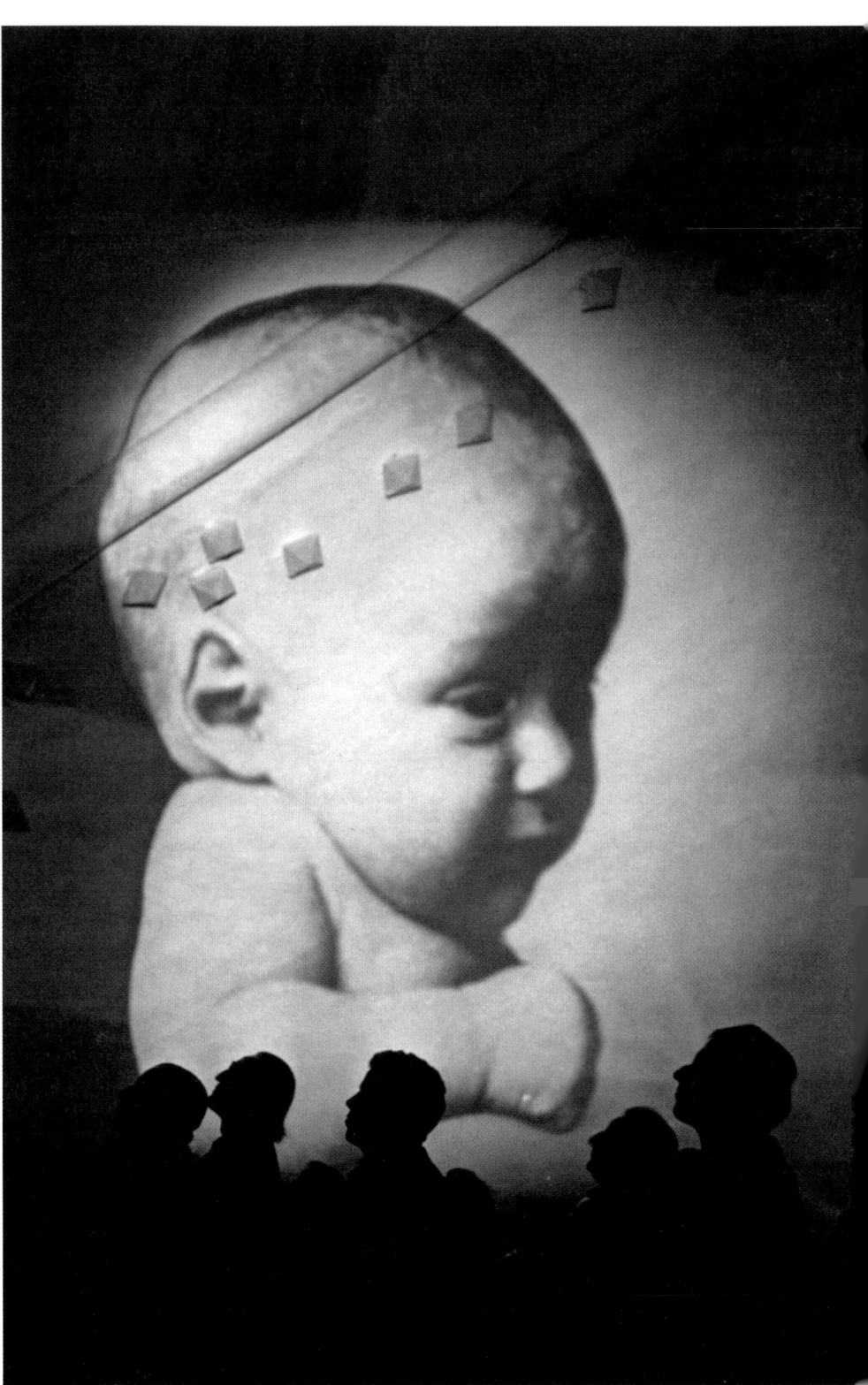

Visitors inside Le Corbusier's Philips Pavilion experience the performance *Le poème électronique.*

	Preface Peter Wever	4
	Introduction Ludo van Halem	8
1	**Pavilion without a Façade** *Le Corbusier Versus Gerrit Rietveld* Peter Wever	14
Text Box I	**Woman's Hairpins Help to Build Architecture of the Future** *An Unlikely Tale of the Conception of the Philips Pavilion*	34
2	**Colour in the Philips Pavilion** *Le Corbusier's Use of Types Couleurs* Peter Wever	36
3	**The Decorators** *Creation of the Light Effects in Le poème électronique* Peter Wever	48
4	**Shadowplay** *Pierre Arnaud's Replacement Show for the Philips Pavilion* Pierre Arnaud and Peter Wever	74
5	**An Austrian in Eindhoven** *Anton Buczynski and the Recording of Le poème électronique* Kees Tazelaar	82
6	**Inside the Philips Pavilion** *Personal Stories from Those Who Operated Le poème électronique* Peter Wever	90
7	**That's Entertainment** *Publicity for the Philips Pavilion* Peter Wever	100
Text Box II	**The 'Electronic Poem' in the Philips Pavilion** *A Rich and Rare Experience of a World of Wonder*	114
8	**Like Ants in a Hurricane** *One and a Half Million Visitors to the Philips Pavilion* Peter Wever	122
9	**Beyond the Final Performance** *Demolition of the Philips Pavilion* Peter Wever and Kees Tazelaar	138

Notes	151
Bibliography	163
Image Credits	165
Name Index	166
Credits	168

Preface

Dedicated to Pepita Eijkman-de Nerée tot Babberich, Pierre Arnaud, Theo Boesveld, Wiel Cox, Max Naveaux and Paul Vancoppenolle. Without their memories this book would not have been written.

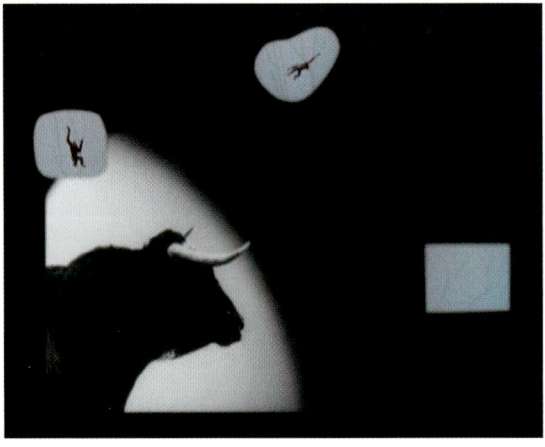 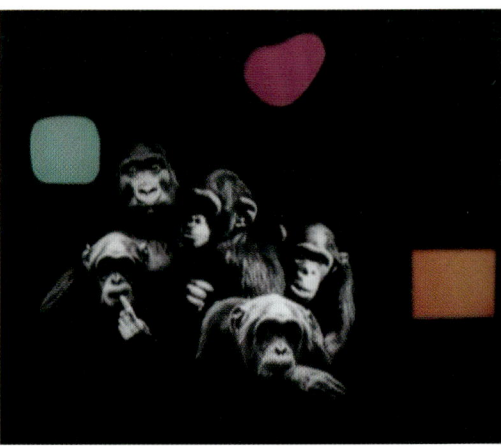

Chronological stills from a montage in which the *écran* and *tri-trous* film images of the performance *Le poème électronique* are superimposed depicting the composition by which these images were actually projected on the walls of the Philips Pavilion. The retrieved *tri-trous* film images were shown to the public for the first time again at the Rijksmuseum in Amsterdam on 12 September 2014 as part of this montage.

The idea of writing a book about Le Corbusier's Philips Pavilion for the 1958 Brussels World's Fair developed in August 2008. It seemed the next logical step following the publication of a book about the adjacent Dutch pavilion earlier that year, which marked the fiftieth anniversary of the World's Fair. It was clear that the same approach should be taken as in the previous book, using former employees' stories and anecdotes, especially as previous publications about the Philips Pavilion had mainly been based on archive material rather than oral history. It therefore came as a particularly welcome surprise when two former employees from the Philips Pavilion were introduced to me in response to a 2008 exhibition about the Dutch pavilion at Zoetermeer's Stadsmuseum.

Nelly Boesveld-Oosterom had worked at the Netherlands and the Benelux pavilions at the World's Fair, and she introduced me to her husband Theo Boesveld, one of the technicians at the Philips Pavilion. His fascinating memories form an important part of this book. Unfortunately, Nelly and Theo did not live to witness the book's publication. Theo had provided me with the correct spelling of Wiel Cox's name, another Philips technician, which made it possible for me to contact him via the Internet. His memories, too, play an important role in this book.

I was also contacted by Pepita Eijkman-de Nerée tot Babberich, the daughter-in-law of Christiaan Eijkman, who was awarded the 1929 Nobel Prize in Physiology or Medicine. She introduced herself as a former hostess at the Philips Pavilion. Although the Philips pavilion did not have an official hostess, her colleagues' stories make it clear that she certainly fulfilled her duties at the pavilion with all the grace and aplomb associated with the World's Fair's renowned hostesses. Unfortunately, I met Pepita only shortly before she passed away. She had kept a book with handwritten farewells from her Philips Pavilion colleagues. Using their names as well as the Internet, it was possible to contact the Belgian Paul Vancoppenolle, one of

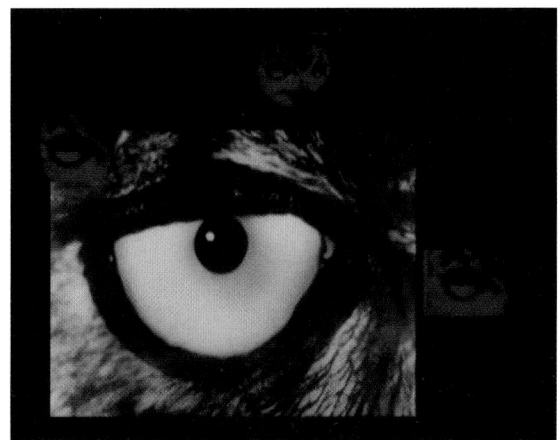

the pavilion's projectionists. Paul's memories were particularly valuable for writing this book. It also appeared that Paul was still in contact with projectionist Max Naveaux and technicians Michel Cools and Michel Soete, all of them Belgians. Subsequently, in August 2009, during a reunion held in the shadow of the Brussels Atomium, five former Dutch and Belgian employees of the Philips pavilion met each other again, in some cases for the first time in more than fifty years.

Besides their personal stories and anecdotes, some former employees had also kept tangible reminders of the pavilion. Of priceless cultural value was the rediscovery of Le Corbusier's film with *tri-trous* images, which was part of the performance *Le poème électronique* that was presented in the Philips pavilion. This film, long considered lost, had been stored for fifty-one years by Max Naveaux. It is now in the safekeeping of the EYE Film Institute Netherlands in Amsterdam. The film was digitzed by the Cineric film laboratory in New York and shown to the public for the first time again at the Rijksmuseum in Amsterdam in September 2014. Paul Vancoppenolle's and Max Naveaux's amateur films and Theo Boesveld's and Wiel Cox's personal photographs provided a picture of the day-to-day activities at the Philips pavilion.

It gradually became clear that enough new aspects of the Philips Pavilion could be revealed to justify writing this book. Furthermore, in 2009, I made contact with the Frenchman Pierre Arnaud, who had created a replacement show for the Philips Pavilion that was to be implemented if the performance created by Le Corbusier and Edgard Varèse turned out to be a failure. A separate chapter is dedicated to his story.

I am indebted to all those mentioned above, for sharing their memories and kindly presenting me with objects from or related to the Philips Pavilion. It became clear to me that 1958 was a very special year for all those involved.

This book is not aimed at investigating the pavilion's architecture or elucidating the meaning of Le poème électronique. Instead, each chapter of the book is intended to shed light on an unknown aspect of the pavilion, based on former employees' recollections, objects, and 'new' archive material. Researching this archive material took me further and further away from home, to institutes in Eindhoven, Rotterdam, Amsterdam, The Hague, Brussels, Paris and Los Angeles. The fact that various national and international museums, institutes and archives preserve material relating to the Philips Pavilion confirms the building's unique cultural significance. Although I was warmly received everywhere I went, I would particularly like to acknowledge the generous support provided by the following people: Gerard Verhoogt (Art Committee of the Eindhoven University of Technology), Frans Wilbrink (Stichting tot Behoud van Historische Philips Producten, Eindhoven), Olga Coolen (Philips musum, Eindhoven), Hetty Berens (Het Nieuwe Instituut, Rotterdam), Carolien Provaas (Nederlands Fotomuseum, Rotterdam), Mark Paul Meyer (EYE Film Institute Netherlands, Amsterdam), Harm Stevens (Rijksmuseum, Amsterdam), Lutgart Janssens-De Cupere (Corporate Communication & Public Affairs, Philips Belgium, Brussels), Arnaud Dercelles (Fondation Le Corbusier, Paris), Jeanette Clough, Sally McKay and Teresa Mesquit (Getty Research Institute, Los Angeles).

While writing this book, I also had the privilege of drawing on the expertise of Rika Devos (1958 Brussels World's Fair architecture), Bart van den Berg and Leendert de Jong (World's Fairs), Jan de Heer (Le Corbusier), Emiel de Jong (film projection), Wim Langenhoff (Philips), Sven Sterken (Iannis Xenakis) and Wijnand and Mieke Plaizier (friendship). I would like to thank them all.

Kees Tazelaar, head of the Institute of Sonology at the Royal Conservatoire in The Hague, deserves special mention. I approached him after his lecture about the Philips Pavilion at the Van Abbemuseum in Eindhoven during the 2006 'Kalff Day' [De Dag van Kalff]. An intensive and inspiring contact developed as we worked towards the publication of Kees' doctoral thesis and this book, for which the role of Kees has been infinitely more than merely a co-author.

A special word of thanks to Ludo van Halem, curator of 20th-Century Art at the

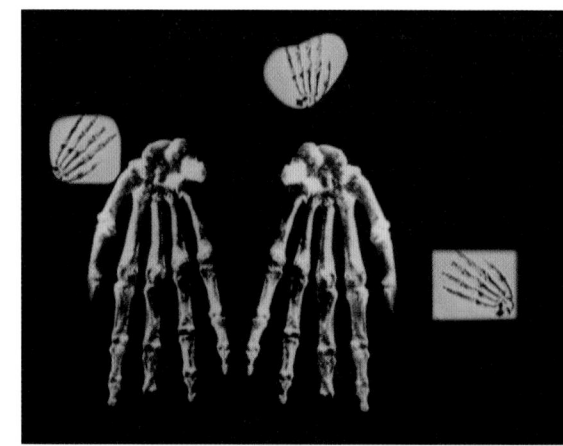

Chronological stills from the same montage as mentioned on p. 4.

Rijksmuseum in Amsterdam, for his continued enthusiasm and efforts on behalf of this book, for his careful reading of chapters, for writing the introduction, and for putting me in contact with nai010 publishers.

I shared my initial idea for this book with art historian André Koch. I am indebted to him for casting his critical eye over each chapter and for his constructive comments.

I would also like to express my gratitude to Eelco van Welie and Marcel Witvoet of nai010 publishers for their confidence in the project, for their dedication and cooperation, and to Peter Kingma of Joseph Plateau graphic designers for the book's fine layout. This book could not have been published without the generous financial support of the heirs of Theo A. Boesveld-Oosterom, Stichting Charema, Fonds voor Geschiedenis en Kunst, the Geoffrey Donaldson Institute, the Prof. Dr. H.F.J.M. van den Eerenbeemtfonds (Erfgoed Brabant), the De Gijselaar-Hintzenfonds, the Meulensteen Art Centre and the Prins Bernhard Cultuurfonds.

Finally, I would like to thank Chaja, Lisa and Haye for their love and support. I promise it will take some time before I venture into another project like this.

Peter Wever
February 2015

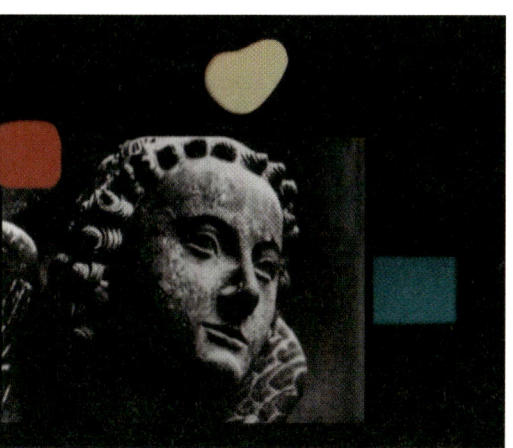
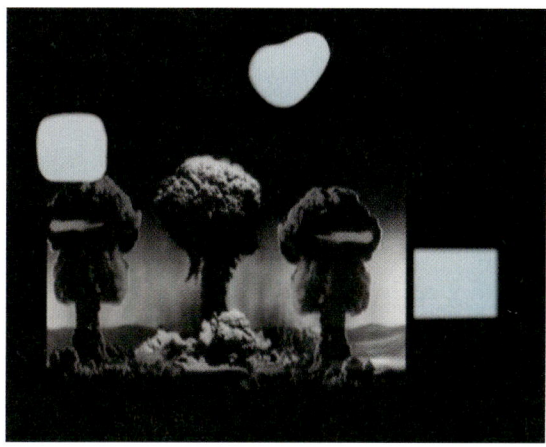

Introduction

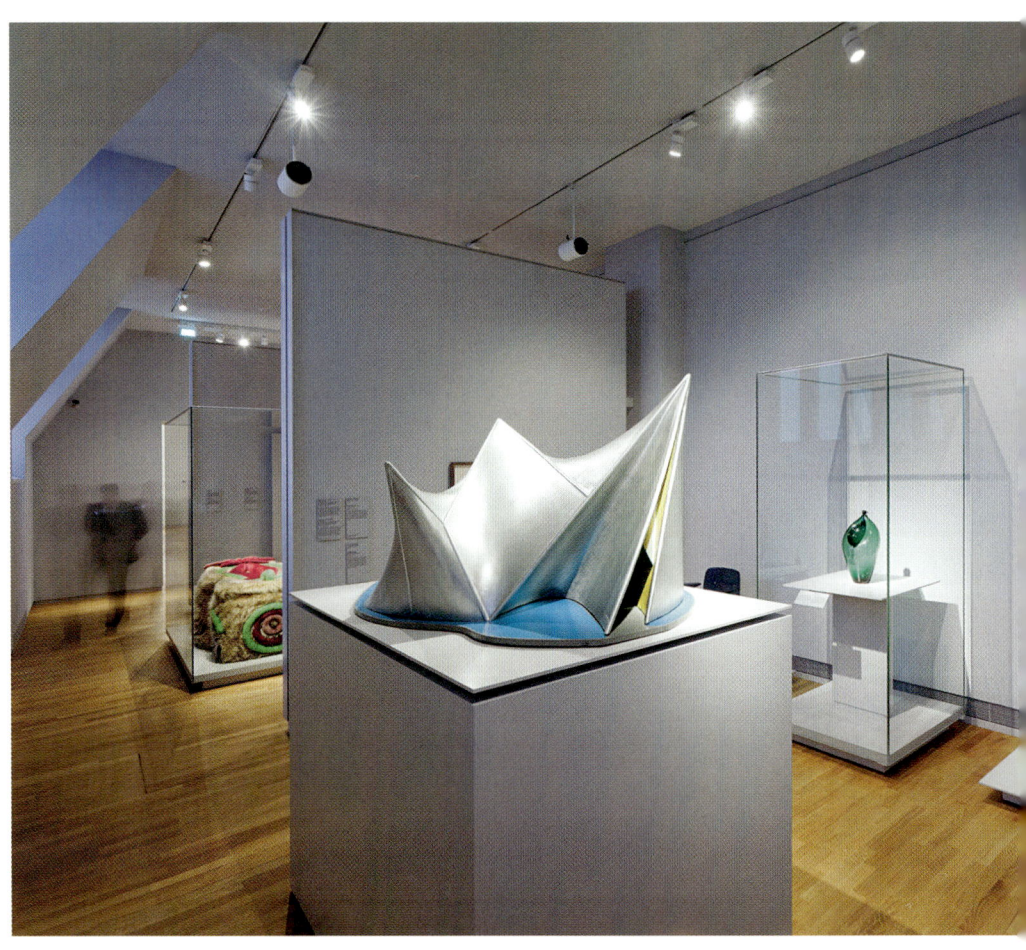

Scale model of the Philips Pavilion on display at the 20th-Century Galleries of the Rijksmuseum in Amsterdam.

When the journalist Bibeb interviewed the architect Gerrit Rietveld for the weekly magazine *Vrij Nederland*, shortly before the official opening of the 1958 Brussels World's Fair, she elicited some striking comments about his confrère Le Corbusier. As one of the five architects of the 'Architect Group Brussels 1958', Rietveld had played a key role in the design and realization of the Dutch pavilion at this World's Fair. In the interview, however, he roundly admitted that he had been swept aside by Le Corbusier in the design of the adjoining corporate pavilion of the Philips Lightbulb Factories Ltd. This electronics concern had been the only Dutch company to respond to the organization's invitation to represent the country's industry by putting up their own pavilion. For this prestigious assignment, Philips had managed to secure the services of the esteemed architect Le Corbusier. To preserve a certain unity in the Dutch section, the original idea was that Rietveld would design the exterior and Le Corbusier the interior of the Philips Pavilion,

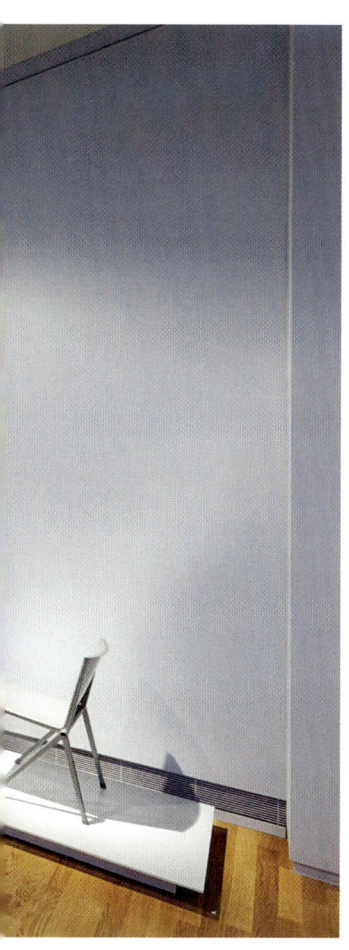

he told Bibeb. 'But Le Corbusier said, "Rietveld, I am making an interior that does not have an exterior." . . . I had the design in my pocket. But, well, he's a hard nut to crack. He just bulldozes his way through everyone. An extraordinary fellow, though . . . No, it's a good thing that he exists, especially for the more accommodating architects of this world.' Rietveld concluded, with gentle self-mockery: 'I'm a bit accommodating myself. I try to be as accommodating as possible.'

Le Corbusier's assertion to Rietveld that he wanted a structure with only an interior was a cryptic way of saying that he was more interested in what happened inside the Philips Pavilion than in the architectural impact of the building itself. He was happy to leave the latter to his energetic assistant, Iannis Xenakis, who, acting on the basis of Le Corbusier's simple sketch of the floor plan – shaped like a stomach – designed an audacious, inimitable building. With its unique shape, the aluminium-coloured building could easily vie with the much larger Atomium, the figurehead of the 1958 Brussels World's Fair. Together, these pavilions made the futuristic tone of this first World's Fair after the Second World War visible and tangible to all.

Le Corbusier's emphasis on an 'interior without an exterior' perplexed friends and foes alike. The board of the 'Foundation World Exhibition Brussels 1958 Netherlands Section', which was responsible for the Dutch contributions, wondered in desperation if the by then world-famous architect should be taken seriously. These doubts led to an effort to hem Le Corbusier in, quite literally, by proposing that a rectangular outer frame be erected around the Philips Pavilion. This would give the tent-like concrete structure, with peaks sticking out wildly in all directions, an austere frame that would match the restrained rhythm of the Netherlands' main pavilion. But Le Corbusier, who was just then building an entire city in India and was used to brushing off much greater opposition than this, had powers of persuasion that no one in the Dutch camp was able to withstand. He insisted on his concept and was left to carry on with his plans, but he left behind him a trail of resentment among his Dutch fellow workers.

Notwithstanding the awkward communication between Le Corbusier and Xenakis on the one hand and the Dutch organizers on the other, described in the first chapter of this book, the splendid *Gesamtkunstwerk* that eventually rose on the site reached an enormous public. One and a half million people attended the multimedia performance *Le poème électronique*, which was presented in the Philips Pavilion in the six months of the World's Fair. That performance, that 'interior', had been Le Corbusier's chief concern. But even the 'exterior' that Xenakis had devised for the structure, which was presented quite casually as a sort of by-product, turned out to have such remarkable visual and formal qualities that half a century after its demolition in 1959, people were still urging that it be rebuilt. Very few pavilions erected for the numerous World's Fairs have commanded such enthusiasm.

When the Philips Pavilion was destroyed on 2 February 1959, the blast effectively signalled the beginning of a myth that has since been nourished for decades by a plethora of publications, exhibitions, reconstructions, and rebuilding plans. The first in-depth publication about the pavilion and *Le poème électronique*, by the Dutch architecture critic Bart Lootsma, appeared in January 1984, twenty-five years after the demolition, in the Dutch magazine *Wonen-TA/BK*. This publication coincided with an exhibition about the pavilion at Eindhoven College of Technology, as it was then, and a performance, by the AKSO ensemble, of the electronic composition that Edgard Varèse wrote as part of *Le poème électronique*. Twelve years later, in 1996, the American architecture professor Marc Treib published the book *Space Calculated in Seconds: The Philips Pavilion, Le Corbusier, Edgard Varèse*.

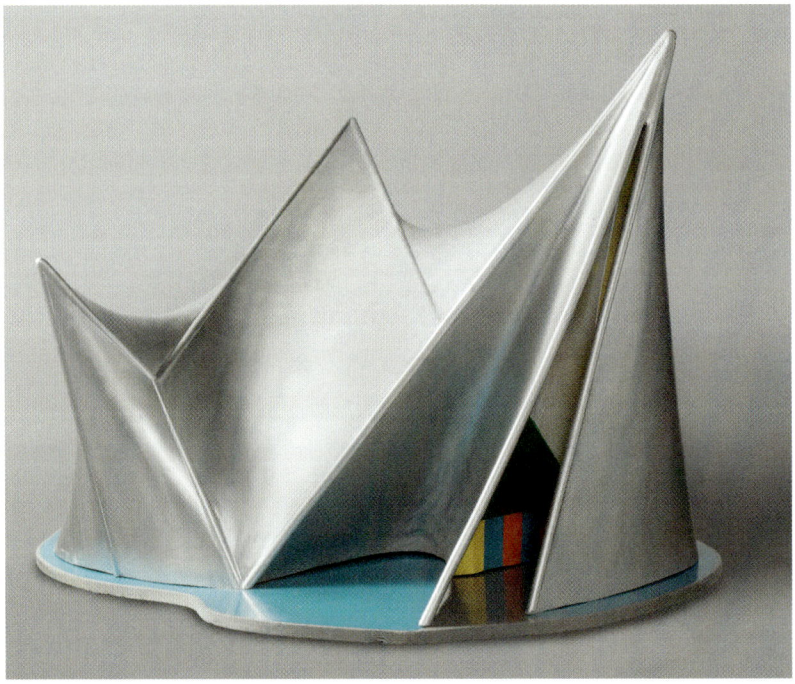

Scale model of the Philips Pavilion on display at the 20th-Century Galleries of the Rijksmuseum in Amsterdam. Left: the polychrome entrance to the pavilion; right: the exit.

This book grew to a large extent from research into archival material about the Philips Pavilion from Louis Kalff, the former General Art Director of Philips, which had been purchased by the Getty Research Institute in Los Angeles. Kalff had not only initiated the project within the company but was also responsible for implementing it.

After that, in 2000, the book *Le Corbusier Padiglione Philips: Bruxelles* by the Italian architect Alessandra Capanna appeared in the series *Universale di architettura*; and six years later, in connection with an exhibition about Edgard Varèse in the Museum Tinguely in Basel, came the book *Edgard Varèse und das Poème électronique: Eine Dokumentation*. At the time of this exhibition, but as a separate initiative, an international symposium took place in Eindhoven on 18 June 2006, at which the results were presented of a study conducted by the Alice Foundation [Stichting Alice] into the feasibility of reconstructing the building at Strijp S, a former industrial site of Philips that is under redevelopment. The Alice Foundation recorded the background history and the findings of this feasibility study in 2007 in the book *Make it New: Le poème électronique*. The reconstruction did not happen, but neither were the plans shelved. The Foundation for the Reconstruction of the 1958 Philips Pavilion [Stichting Reconstructie Philips Paviljoen 1958], as successor to the Alice Foundation, still cherishes the hope that the pavilion may be rebuilt in Eindhoven in the near future.

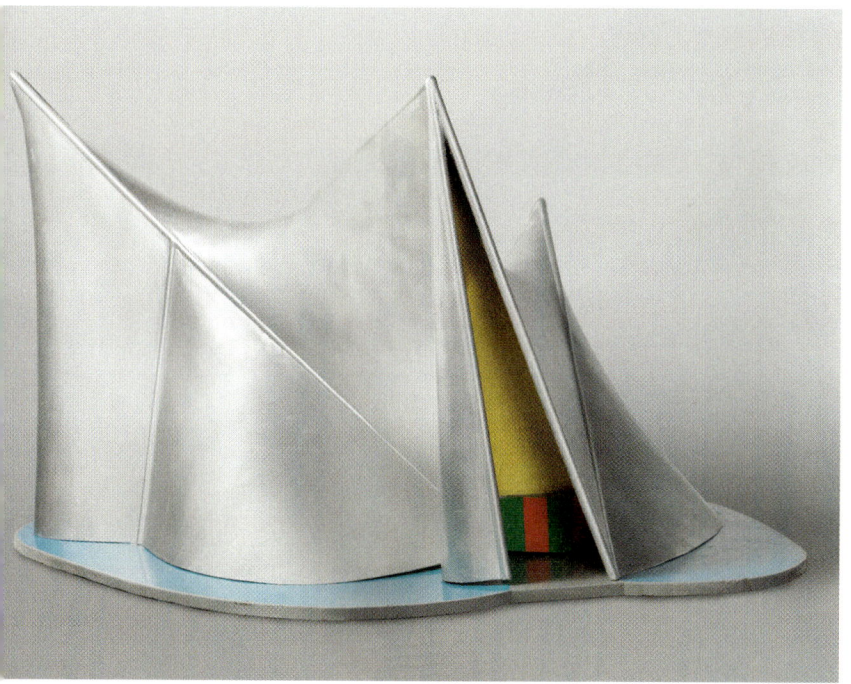

Since 2013, the Rijksmuseum has possessed in its collection an original scale model of the Philips Pavilion, as a striking example of the commissions given by leading Dutch companies to artists, architects and designers in the twentieth century. Around this scale model, visitors can hear a reconstruction by Kees Tazelaar of Varèse's electronic composition. The genesis and performance of this composition had already been the subject of a long television documentary, broadcast in 1998, by Willem Hering and Hank Onrust, and are described in detail in Kees Tazelaar's book *On the Threshold of Beauty: Philips and the Origins of Electronic Music in the Netherlands, 1925–1965*, published in 2013.

The initiator and primary author of the present book, Peter Wever, has also published on the Philips Pavilion before, in *Dichtbij klopt het hart der wereld. Nederland op de Expo 58*, which appeared in 2008 on the occasion of the fiftieth anniversary of the 1958 Brussels World's Fair. It includes a discussion of the antagonism that Le Corbusier aroused among his Dutch colleagues, an account that formed the prelude to this book. Unlike the above-mentioned publications and plans, which dwell largely on the parts played by Le Corbusier, Iannis Xenakis, and Edgard Varèse, the present book focuses on the supporting cast. For in the design he conceived for the Philips Pavilion, Le Corbusier presented the support staff with a fiendishly difficult project to bring to fruition. The building was very far from being an ideal theatre that could effortlessly accommodate a multimedia performance. Quite the opposite: it could be said that Xenakis' extreme design for the exterior took little or no account of the technical requirements that might be needed for the different multimedia components of *Le poème électronique*. Consequently, the combination of the different parts of the *Gesamtkunstwerk* – the building, the projection and sound technology, and the facilities needed for the audience –

generated a dizzying array of problems. It was primarily the support staff who had to solve these problems.

On the basis of a renewed study of the accessible archive material, Peter Wever describes in details the problems that arose in creating the building and the performance, as well as in the operational aspects of publicity and visitor support. By now, this archive material has become dispersed to different parts of the world: to the Getty Research Institute in Los Angeles, the Fondation Le Corbusier in Paris, and the Philips Company Archives in Eindhoven. The latter archives, unfortunate enough, were not open for public research. This hiatus was amply offset, however, by the use of alternative material that generally remains under the radar of art-historical research, such as that used for promotion and publicity, and amateur footage. This material, trivial and ephemeral though it may be, nonetheless constitutes an important visual source for understanding certain aspects of the Philips Pavilion and *Le poème électronique* that have never before been described so clearly, such as the polychrome decorations at the building's entrance and exit and the alternating colour projections during the performance.

In addition, interviews were conducted with numerous people who had been directly involved in making the project a reality and running it on a day-to-day basis, such as technicians and publicity officers. Besides a treasure trove of data and insights that were passed on orally and have been recorded for posterity in this publication, these contacts also led to the discovery of Le Corbusier's original film material that had been presumed lost and that is of considerable cultural-historical importance. This material enables us to gain a far more accurate picture of the performance of *Le poème électronique* than was possible hitherto.

Unlike earlier publications, this book is also the record of a quest: not into features that only contribute to the mythical dimensions of the Philips Pavilion, but rather into everyday life at the pavilion, what took place behind the scenes. The numerous details that Peter Wever was able to unearth therefore restore the Philips Pavilion and *Le poème électronique* to the proportions of a human enterprise, with all the false starts, irritations, and doubts that go along with it. One of the most striking examples is the manifest lack of confidence in Le Corbusier, even at Philips. It was not previously known that the persistent problems and changes had prompted the company, acting in the utmost secrecy, to order a backup performance from Pierre Arnaud, a French producer who specialized in sound and light spectacles. This 'shadow' performance, however, was never performed in its entirety.

This new information combines with numerous hitherto unknown details to produce a richly-nuanced picture of the goings-on at the world's first ever major multimedia performance for a mass audience. Even so, how those visitors experienced it, what it was like to enter that completely disorienting space and to be immersed for eight minutes in a bath of changing coloured lights emanating from dozens of fluorescent light tubes, what it was like to be surrounded by waves of electronically-manipulated sound coursing through the air from hundreds of loudspeakers, while being simultaneously bombarded with images representing tens of thousands of years of human culture, we cannot know: no historical study can bring that eight-minute experience back to life. Le Corbusier's stated aim was to fundamentally alter the members of the audience: the stomach-shaped

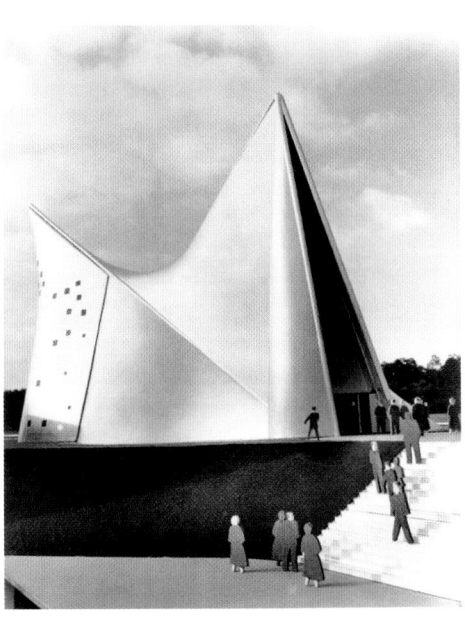

Publicity photographs of a presumed lost 1:12.5 scale model of the Philips Pavilion constructed around April 1957.

floor plan is a metaphor for this transformation process. In the interview with Bibeb, Rietveld recalled Le Corbusier's remarks, imagining the flow of visitors: 'It must feel as if they're entering a slaughterhouse. In: bang, a blow to the head, and out.' It is highly unlikely that the 'accommodating' Rietveld would ever have dreamed of regarding his public as cattle led to slaughter, but Le Corbusier possessed sufficient self-importance to disregard the unsavoury implications. The parameters of that transformation are naturally impossible to gauge unequivocally; many interpretations are possible.

Peter Wever also describes the blanket incomprehension that greeted the performance, both among the employees within the building – even after experiencing it over 3,000 times – and in a veteran art critic like Willem Sandberg, director of the Stedelijk Museum in Amsterdam, who wondered in despair: 'does it satisfy le corbusier's imagination? does it satisfy ours? i don't know . . .' For Philips too, the project was fairly unsatisfying and not something the company wanted to repeat. The costs had spiralled out of control and the project generated a multitude of problems. The solutions to those problems, such as the appointment of an Austrian recording technician who, in contrast to Philips' own technicians, worked amicably alongside Edgard Varèse, increased the costs still further. True, its contribution to the 1958 Brussels World's Fair endowed the electronics company with a cultural-historical myth, but whether the project had helped to sell a single extra television set or light bulb, no one could say. And in the long term, it was Le Corbusier who got all the credit, even though the pavilion bore the name of Philips.

Ludo van Halem
Curator of 20th-Century Art, Rijksmuseum, Amsterdam
February 2015

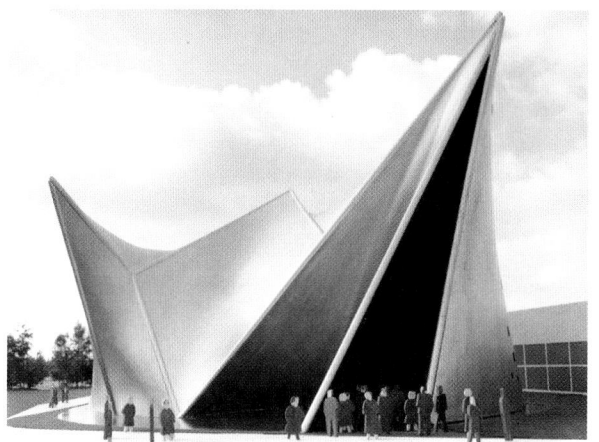
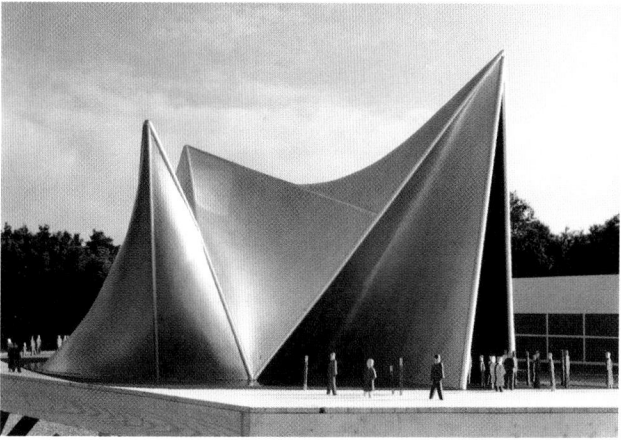

1 Pavilion without a Façade
Le Corbusier Versus Gerrit Rietveld
Peter Wever

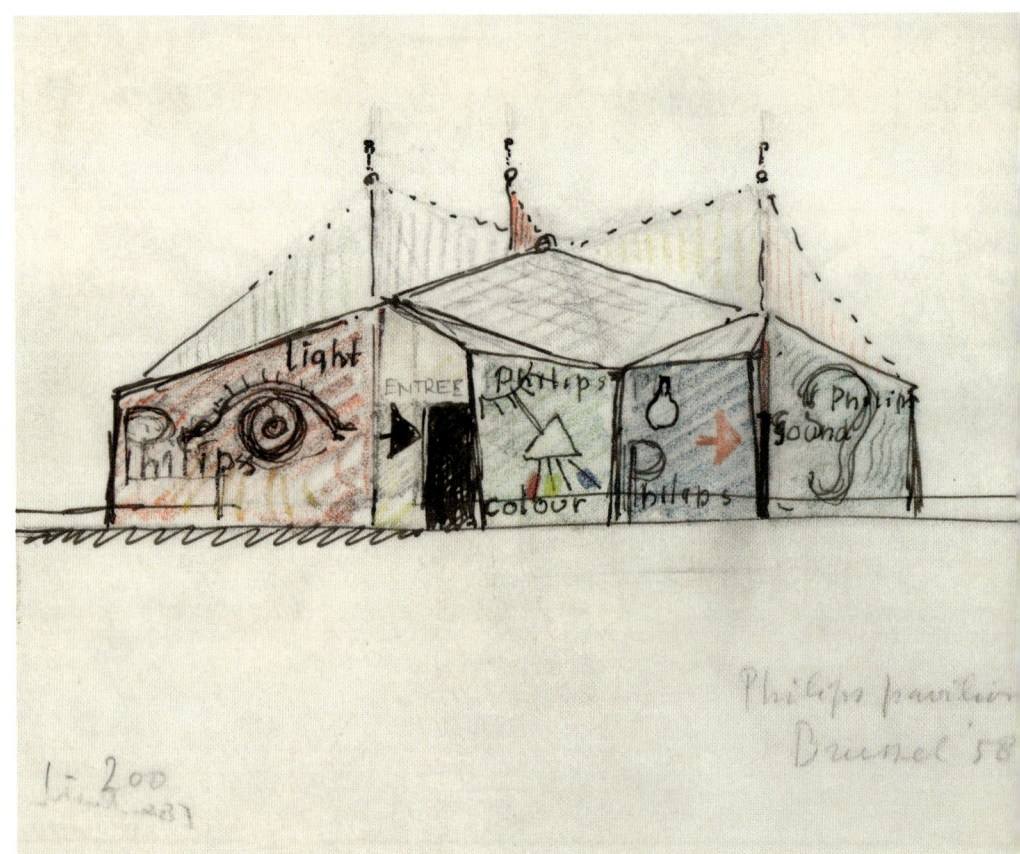

1.1
On the left is an image of Gerrit Rietveld's sketch for the front of the Philips Pavilion. On the right is an image of the sketch model of the design. Rietveld had presumably brought this sketch and sketch model to the meeting with Le Corbusier in Paris on 8 June 1956.

In Louis Kalff's original plan, Le Corbusier would design the interior of the Philips Pavilion at the 1958 Brussels World's Fair, with Gerrit Rietveld designing the exterior. Although Rietveld had already made a design for the pavilion, Le Corbusier did not allow any kind of architectural form to be given to the pavilion's appearance. This made any form of cooperation between the two architects impossible. For J.J.P. Oud, this was an unacceptable development, which caused him to consider resigning as the supervising architect of the Dutch pavilion. Below, a portrait is painted of this tumultuous period in Dutch architectural history.[1]

Philips' Participation in the 1958 Brussels World's Fair

In September of 1954, the Netherlands accepted the Belgian government's invitation to participate in the 1958 Brussels World's Fair. This led, in August of 1955, to the establishment of the 'Foundation World Exhibition Brussels 1958 Netherlands Section', which had the aim of organizing, furnishing, maintaining, and liquidating a Dutch section at the World's Fair. The chosen theme for the Dutch pavilion was 'water', the ally and the enemy of the Dutch people. The four architectural firms of Ir. Joost Boks (Rotterdam), Prof. Ir. Jo van den Broek and Jaap Bakema (Rotterdam), Ir. Frits Peutz (Heerlen), and Gerrit Rietveld (Utrecht) joined forces as the 'Architect Group Brussels 1958',

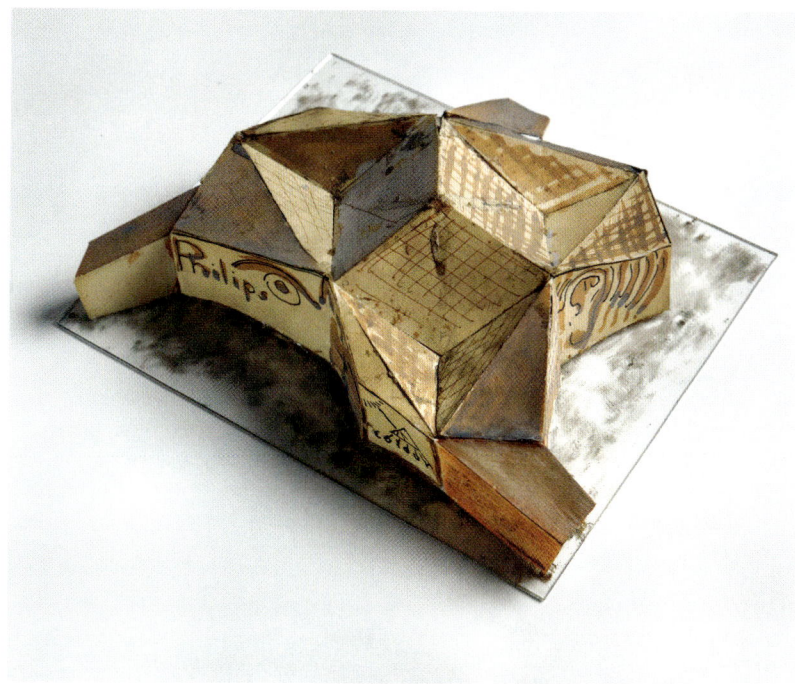

and were responsible for creating the design of the Dutch pavilion under the supervision of the architects Dr. Jacobus (J.J.P.) Oud and Ben Merkelbach. The final plan for the Dutch pavilion included a water basin with an artificially generated wave on the upper part of the assigned area, and a polder landscape defended by a dike on the lower part. Exhibition halls and a model farm were to be placed around this construction of water, dike, and polder. The board of the Foundation offered Dutch companies the opportunity to present themselves on the site of the Dutch section with their own pavilion, under the conditions that such a pavilion would have to be fully justified aesthetically, and that the exhibition would be technically spectacular. The N.V. Philips' Gloeilampenfabrieken [Philips Lightbulb Factories Ltd.] was the only company that responded and received permission to rent a piece of property on the site of the Dutch section.[2]

On 23 March 1956 Philips' General Art Director Ir. Louis Kalff officially requested space for a pavilion at the Dutch site. Philips intended to fill this pavilion with an unprecedented synthesis of light, space, colour, and sound, in a demonstration that was less based on displaying the Philips products themselves than on showing what could be achieved with these products. To ensure that this demonstration be at the highest possible international artistic level, Philips had secured the cooperation of the Swiss-French architect Le Corbusier to

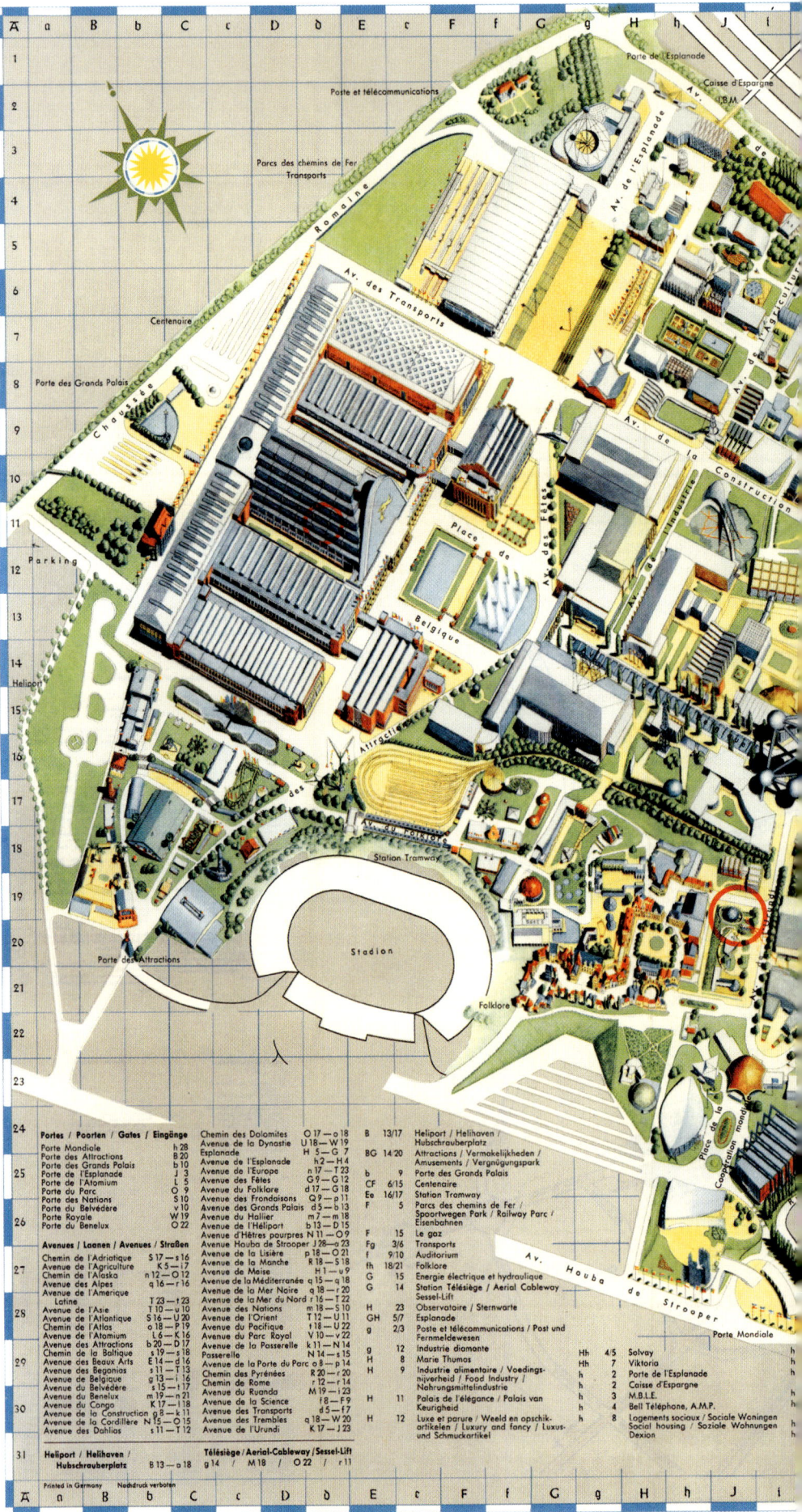

1.2
Overview of the site of the 1958 Brussels World's Fair. The Dutch section, with the Philips Pavilion, is located to the west of the large butterfly-shaped French pavilion.

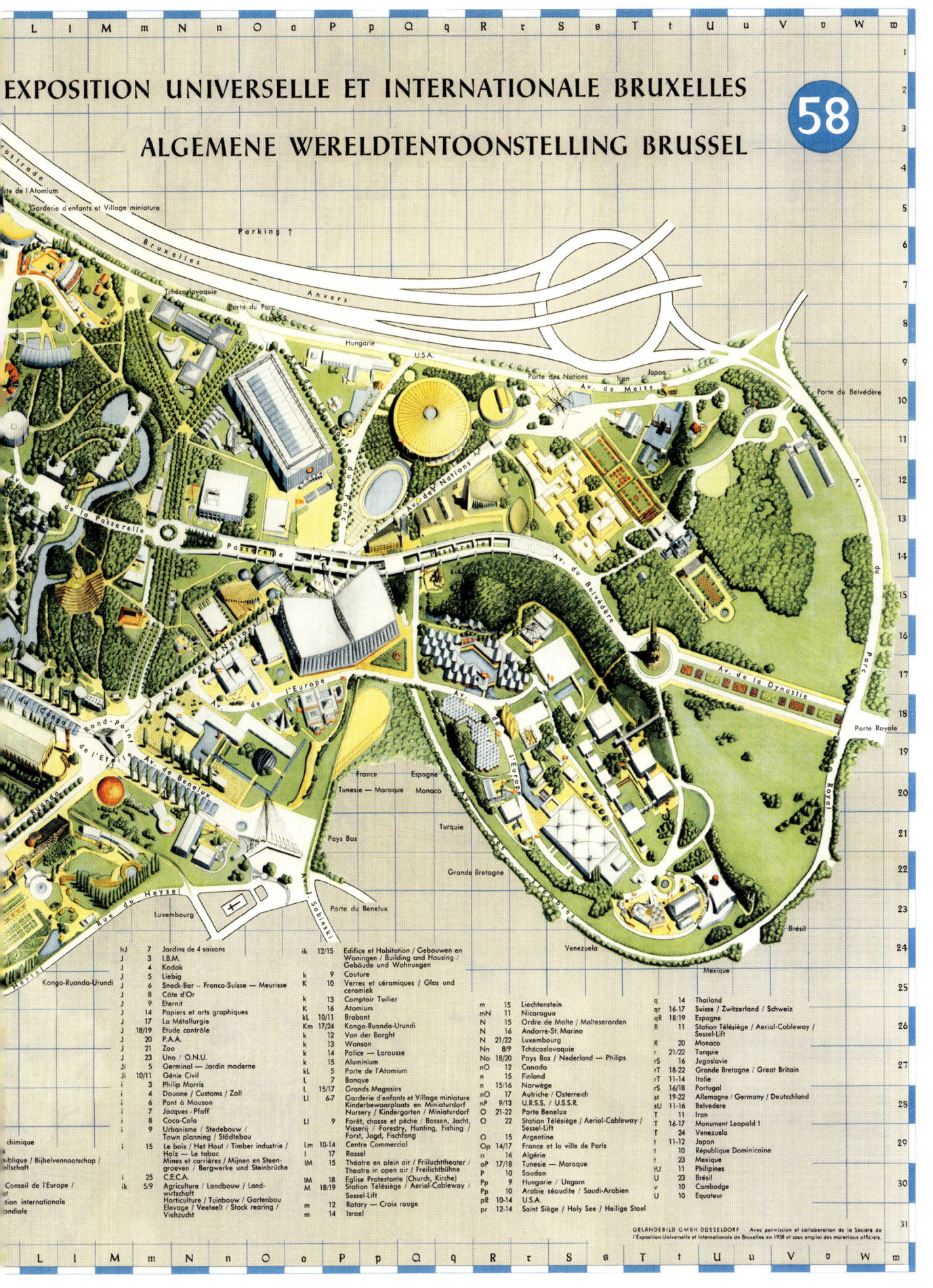

design the pavilion's interior. In order to maintain a sense of harmony with the adjacent Dutch pavilion, Philips assumed that it was desirable to have the exterior of the pavilion made by one of the members of the Architect Group Brussels 1958. Le Corbusier had essentially agreed to this. Regarding the choice of the architect for the exterior, it was indicated that Philips 'would in principle want the architect Rietveld to oversee the exterior, meaning that the Philips entry would be created via a collaboration between Le Corbusier for the interior, Rietveld for the exterior, and the undersigned [Kalff] for the coordination and implementation of the plan'.[3]

In response to the official application, the architects Boks, Bakema, and Rietveld, together with the Dutch exhibition organizer Jac. Kleiboer, were designated by the Foundation's governing board to enter into talks with Kalff.[4] In these discussions, a number of agreements were made with regard to restrictions and limitations on the pavilion.[5] It was agreed, for example, that the pavilion would be approximately 15 meters tall.[6] In late April of 1956, Rietveld indicated that he would soon need to have a general picture of the Philips Pavilion in order to arrive at an overall composition for the buildings of the Dutch section in Brussels.[7] A meeting between Kalff, Rietveld, and Le Corbusier was then arranged.

Gerrit Rietveld's Design for the Philips Pavilion

Kalff and Rietveld visited Le Corbusier in his studio in Paris, on Rue de Sèvres 35, on the morning of 8 June 1956.[8] During the meeting, Le Corbusier showed 'a small photo of a rather modernist-looking model, and an elegant floor plan'. Rietveld had also brought along 'a design and a small sketch model' for the exterior of the Philips Pavilion. But he soon realized that his design would not be suitable, and decided not to show it.[9] A crucial moment in the meeting proved to be Le Corbusier's remark, 'Rietveld, I am making

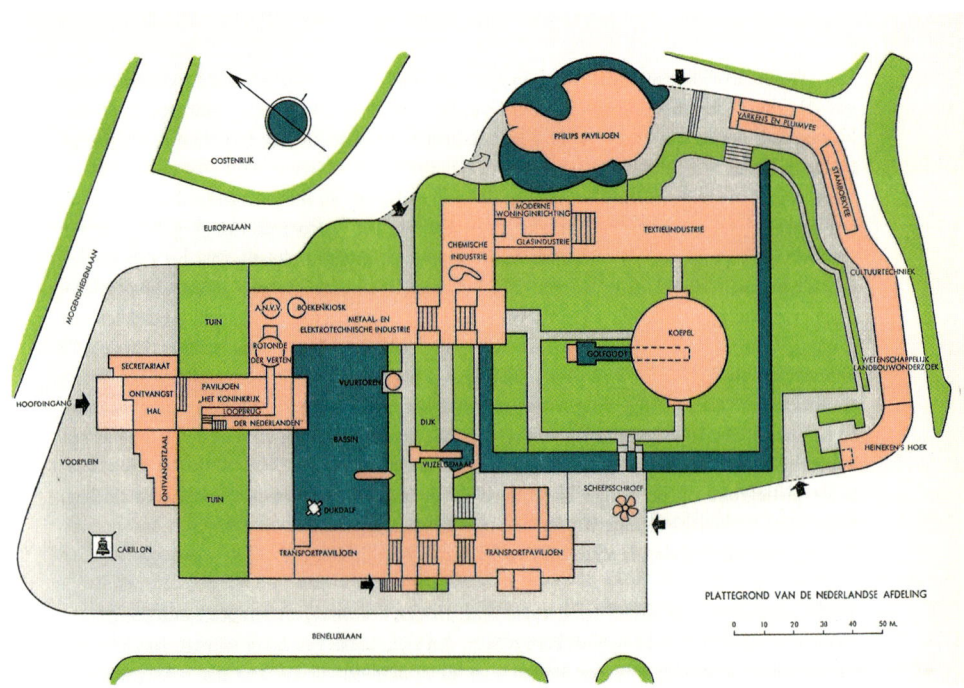

1.3
Map of the Dutch section at the 1958 Brussels World's Fair. The Philips Pavilion is situated on the eastern side of the Dutch pavilion.

1.4
Gerrit Rietveld on the site of the Dutch pavilion, which was then still under construction, in around October of 1957.

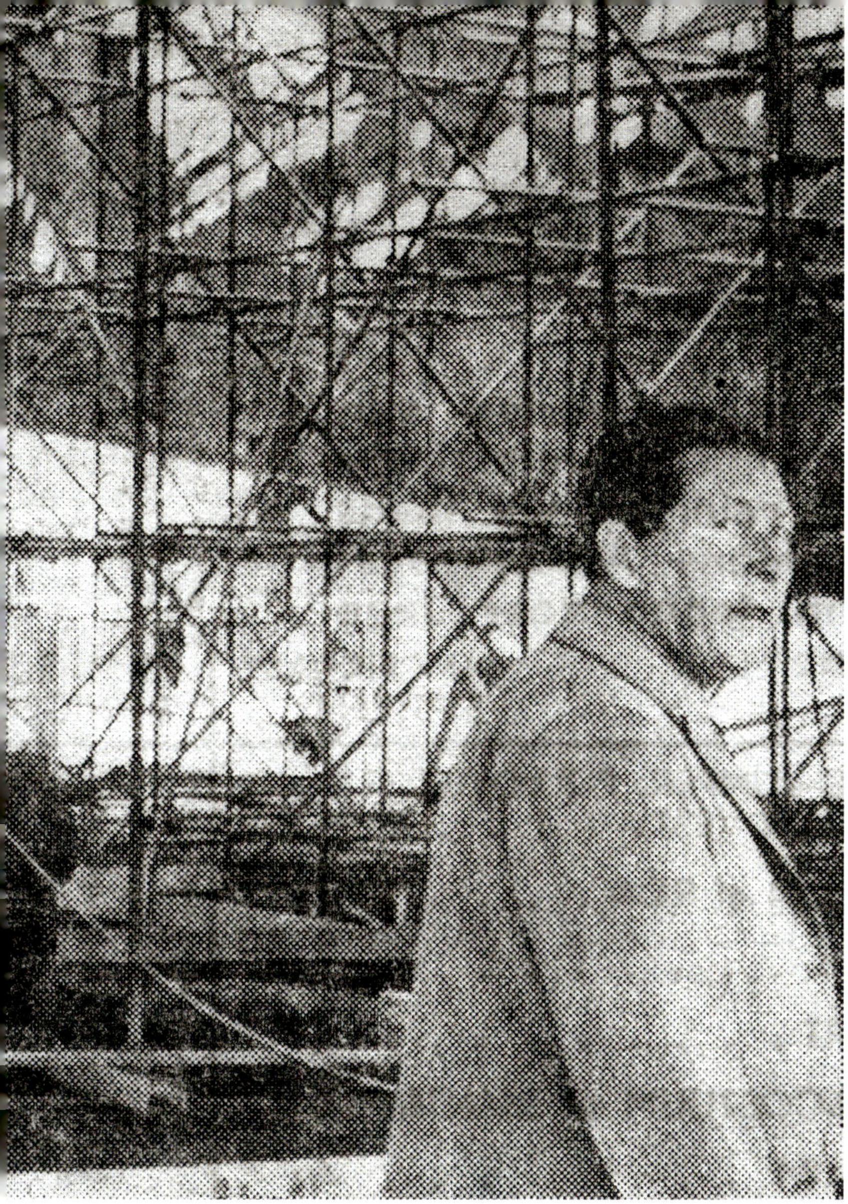

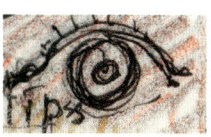
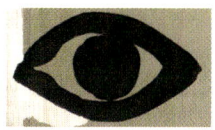
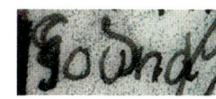
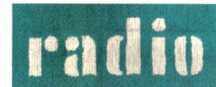
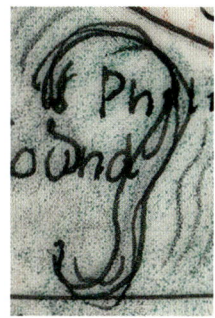
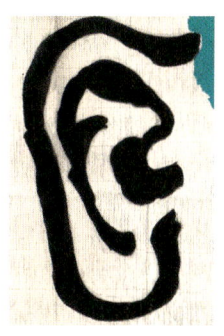
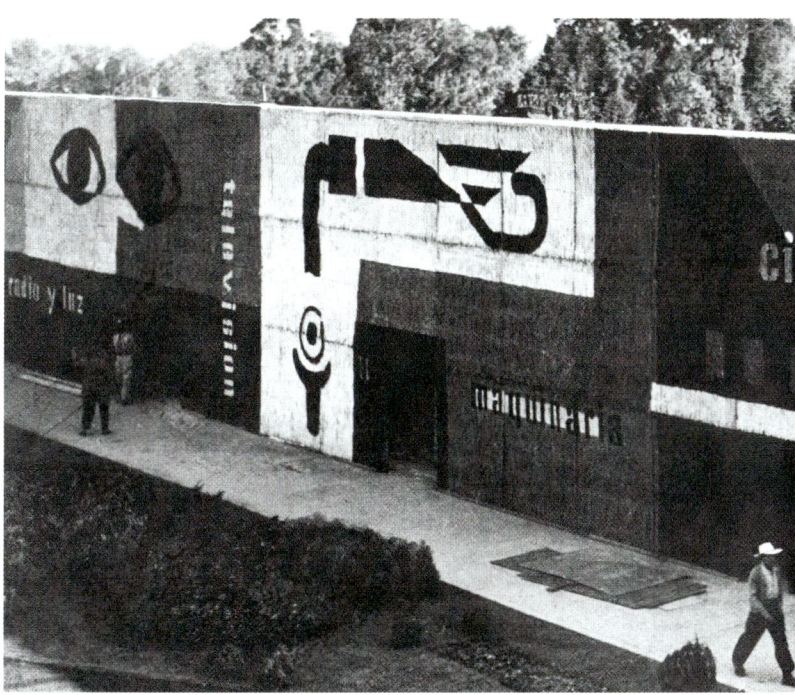

1.5
Part of the mural that Gerrit Rietveld had commissioned Jan Bons to make for the exhibition *Asi es Holanda* in 1952 in Mexico City, Mexico.

1.6
A comparison between some figurative elements and text elements in Gerrit Rietveld's sketch design for the Philips Pavilion (left), and the mural that Rietveld commissioned Jan Bons to make for the exhibition *Asi es Holanda* (right).

an interior that does not have an exterior.'[10] This ruled out any possibility of a collaboration. Rietveld described the meeting as 'a disappointment'. His description of Le Corbusier's attitude was telling: 'Thinking that he is the only one who knows best is something he shares with other greats in our profession (e.g. Fr. Lloyd Wright), but that he does so to such a degree makes him a small man in my eyes.'[11] According to Rietveld, everything would have turned out differently if only 'le Corb were a man who could allow himself to be subordinate'.[12] In retrospect, Rietveld said about the meeting: 'I found it unpleasant, but it didn't hurt me. I already knew that it would be Corbusier's pavilion, even if they had accepted my design.'[13]

Rietveld's design for the Philips Pavilion shows a tent-like structure with coloured walls, covered by a roof with a prism structure. On the walls are large figurative elements (eye, prism, lightbulb, ear) and text elements (Philips, light, colour, sound) that refer to Philips, and to the sound and light show that was to take place inside the pavilion.[14] Noteworthy is the apparent influence of the graphic designer Jan Bons on Rietveld's design. The large figurative elements and texts on the coloured walls of the Philips Pavilion strongly resemble the mural that Rietveld had commissioned Bons to make in 1952 for the exhibition *Así es Holanda* in Mexico City, Mexico. The representations and texts on Bons' mural for *Así es Holanda* refer to the various exhibitors in the rear exhibition spaces, one of which was a Philips

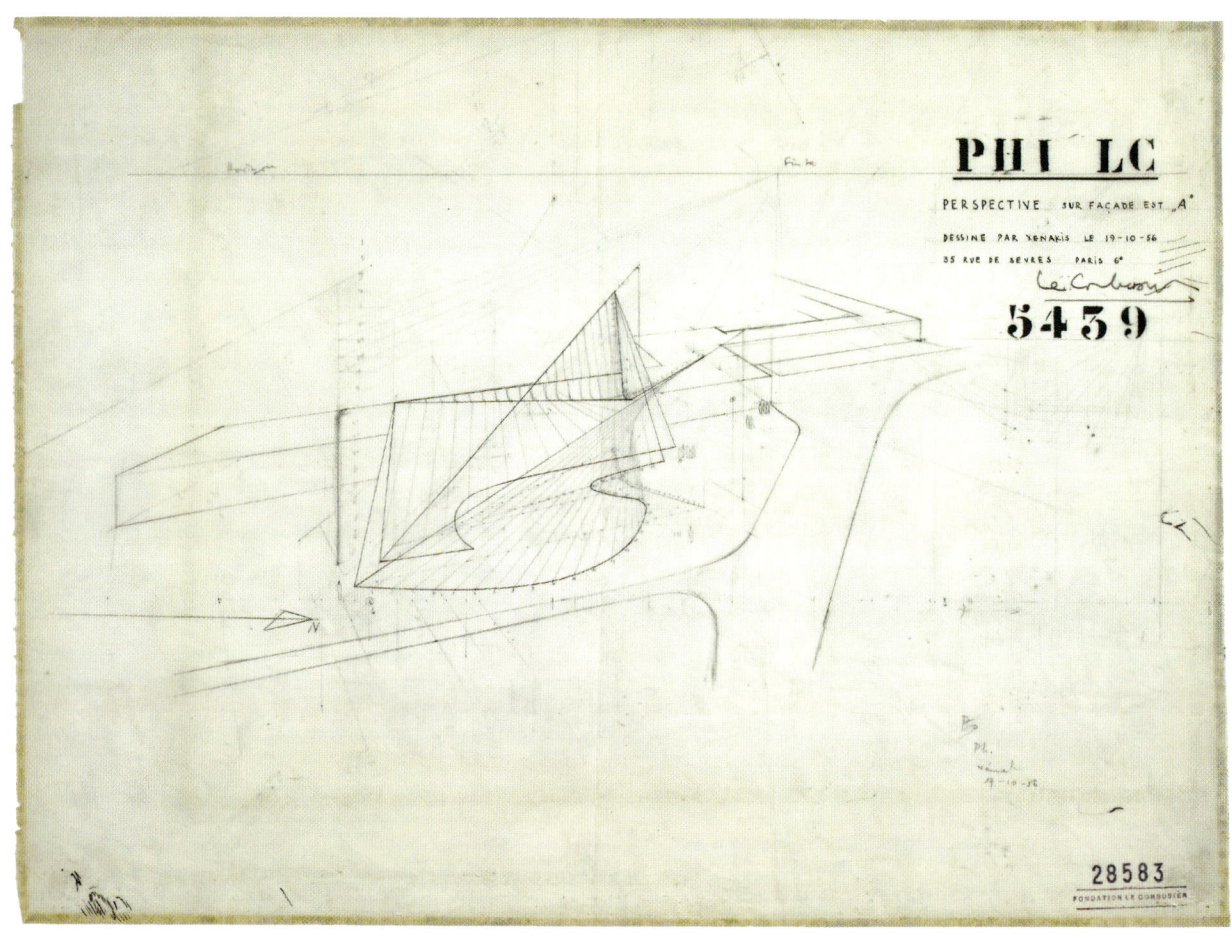

space.¹⁵ Rietveld and Bons had met in 1946, and then began a long-term cooperation.¹⁶ Both men also worked together closely on the realization of the textile section at the Dutch pavilion at the World's Fair.¹⁷ Bons was also responsible for designing the logo for the Dutch pavilion, after a unanimous recommendation by the Architect Group Brussels 1958 in April of 1956.¹⁸

It remains unclear whether any other people had also seen Rietveld's sketches for the Philips Pavilion, and whether these sketches would have withstood the test of criticism. The main criticism of Le Corbusier's design was that it did not match the relatively austere architecture of the Dutch pavilion¹⁹, although that argument could also be applied to Rietveld's design.

Pavilion without a Façade

In the months following the meeting in Paris, the architects of the Dutch pavilion and the Philips team were anxiously awaiting a definitive description of the pavilion.²⁰ In July of 1956, Kalff had urged Le Corbusier to contact the architects Van den Broek and Bakema during the *Congrès Internationaux d'Architecture Moderne* in Dubrovnik, Yugoslavia, for an exchange of ideas on the pavilion's exterior. Kalff would then bring up these ideas in a discussion with Rietveld about the exterior and the lighting.²¹ Apparently, Kalff still entertained the hope that some form of collaboration between Le Corbusier and Rietveld was possible.

More clarity finally came in October of 1956. Kalff informed Bakema about the state of affairs: 'As far as we can currently see, the pavilion of Le Corbusier will indeed only have an interior (...) and Le Corbusier is therefore against the idea that any kind of architectural form whatsoever should be given to the exterior appearance. In itself, we find this an original way of thinking, and we also believe that this exterior-less pavilion could be more or less sensational. Of course, we quite regret that this essentially precludes any form of cooperation with Mr. Rietveld (...). Nonetheless, we now hope that the ideas of Le Corbusier will lead to a form that is bound to strongly contrast with its surroundings, but that will also be so different (…) that it will lead to a more satisfactory solution than if one were to attempt to reach a certain harmony by enlisting the assistance of one of your architects.'²² On the one hand, the Foundation responded with amazement: 'In our opinion, the idea that this pavilion will only have an interior and no shell can hardly be taken seriously.' On the other hand, the Foundation sent out a clear message that it would not be accepted if Le Corbusier were to develop a plan that did not fit in with the rest of the Dutch section.²³

On 13 October 1956 the commission for the design of the Philips Pavilion and a sound and light show was officially given to Le Corbusier.²⁴ Around that time, his assistant Iannis Xenakis, a Greek-French composer and architect, began to elaborate on Le Corbusier's sketch plans. Xenakis designed a structure whose shape was dictated by saddle-shaped mathematical figures called hyperbolic paraboloids. His first drawings were made between 16 and 23 October, and were presented to Philips on 24 October.²⁵ Shortly thereafter, the design was submitted to the Architect Group Brussels 1958, and was by and large accepted.²⁶ The architects had resigned themselves to the idea that Le Corbusier would also provide the exterior of the pavilion.²⁷ Yet, the supervising architects Oud and Merkelbach found it very inappropriate that they had not been consulted in this decision. Oud in particular could not accept the fact that Le Corbusier would provide the exterior of the pavilion.²⁸

The issue was discussed by the Foundation in an emergency meeting held on 17 December 1956. This meeting resulted in Mr. Herman Van Walsem, the Commissioner General of the Dutch pavilion, writing in a letter to Kalff that it would still not be allowed 'to let the Philips Pavilion "mess up" the Dutch section'. Apparently, the criticism had since become more focused on the design of the pavilion, and less on the fact that Le Corbusier would provide its exterior. Commissioner General Van Walsem indicated that the

1.7
Perspective drawing PHI LC 5439 of the Philips Pavilion, by Iannis Xenakis, dated 19 October 1956.

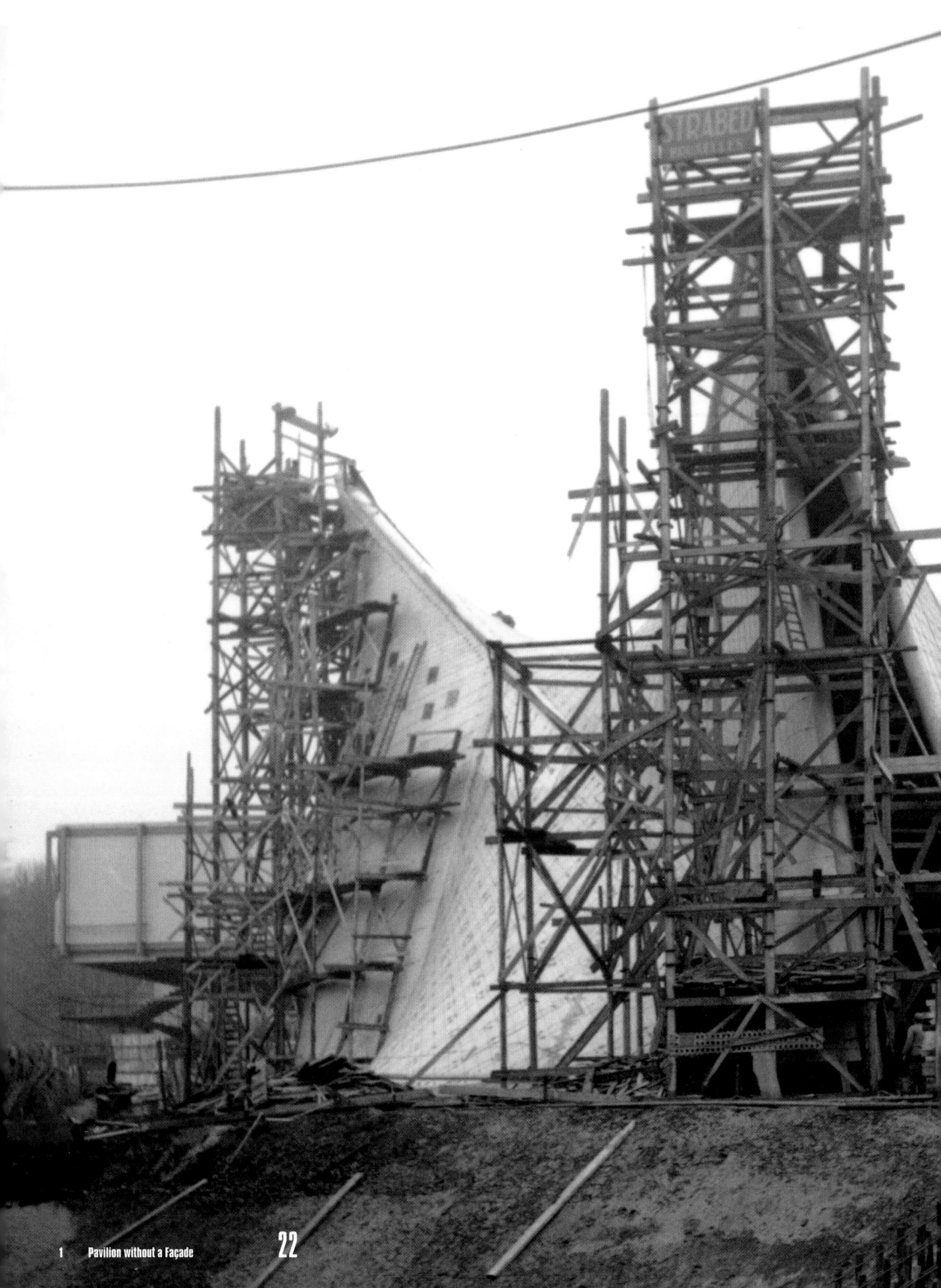
1 Pavilion without a Façade

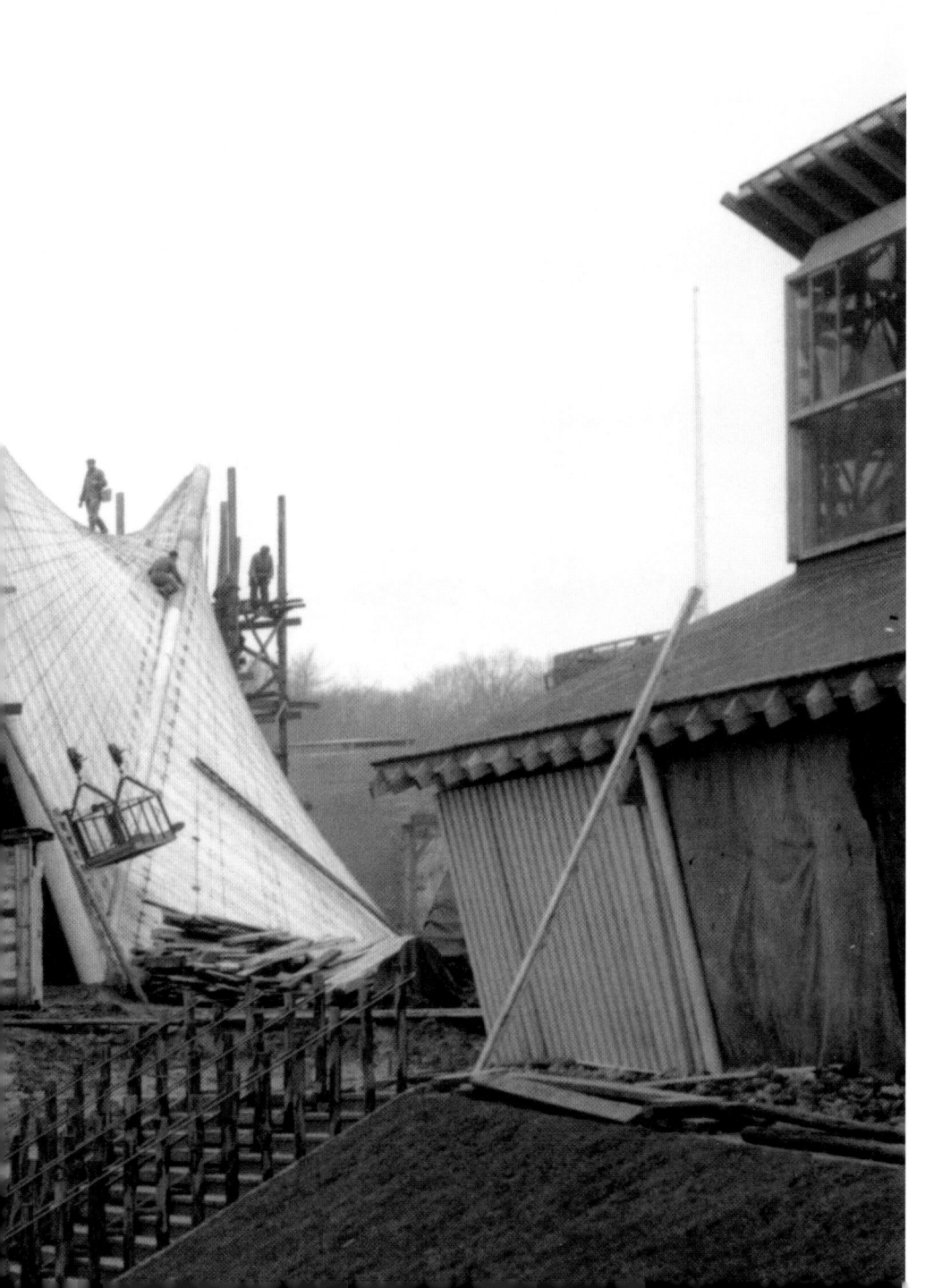

1.8
The Philips Pavilion under construction at the site of the 1958 Brussels World's Fair.

Foundation had decided that the Philips Pavilion had to meet a number of requirements, including being bordered by an open rectangular skeleton with a maximum length, width, and height of 33, 20, and 13 meters respectively.[29]

It has been suggested that these requirements came from Rietveld.[30] Yet, no evidence for this suggestion was found in the investigated archival material. Rietveld himself was not present at the emergency meeting.[31] Shortly before this meeting, and probably because of his absence, Rietveld had reported to the Foundation that he considered it possible that Le Corbusier's design could be 'a living part of the Dutch section'.[32] It seems more likely that Oud played a major role in drafting the design requirements. From the outset, Oud had opposed any form of Le Corbusier's

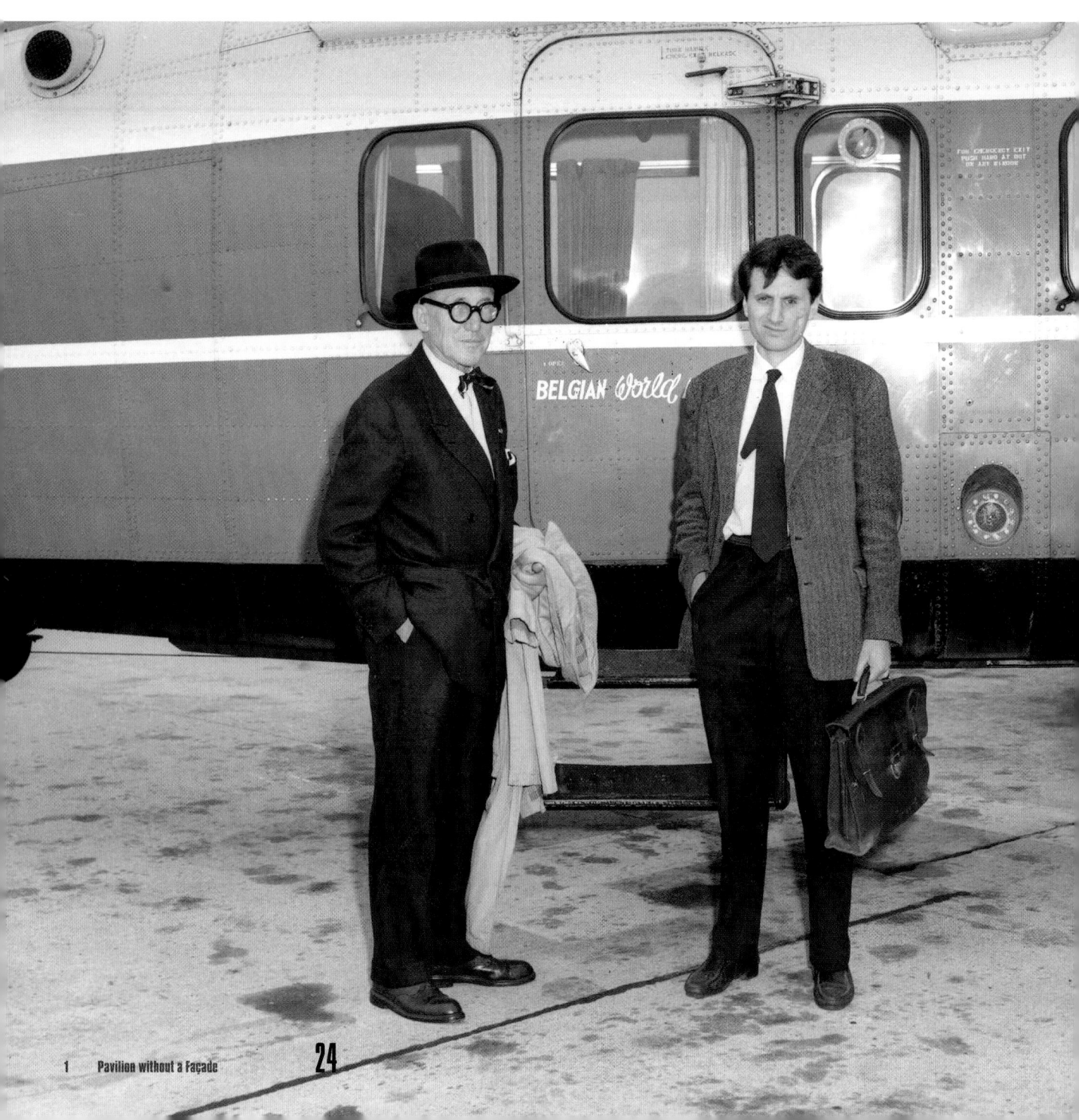

1   Pavilion without a Façade

participation in realizing the Philips Pavilion. In early March of 1956, Oud had already indicated that he regretted that no attempt had been made to find a Dutch architect to provide the interior of the pavilion, because he feared that, in relation to the Philips Pavilion, only Le Corbusier's name would be mentioned.[33] The assumption that Oud played a key role in conceiving the skeleton structure is supported by the reaction of Kalff, in which he refers to the 'recommendation of the Dutch supervisors'.[34]

Kalff reacted furiously to the plan to surround the Philips Pavilion with 'a kind of cage with certain limited dimensions'. 'No architect of any standing, let alone a man as internationally renowned as Le Corbusier, would allow such bullying, nor would the architects of the Dutch pavilion. (...) The entire world would then be made aware of the not very collegial attitude of the otherwise so skilful Dutch architects toward their French colleague.' Kalff again expressed regret that it had not been possible to have Rietveld provide the exterior of the pavilion. He gave the Foundation a clear message: 'If one is (...) to keep to the requirements, then Le Corbusier will stop his work. (...) We should like to point out to you (...) that if Le Corbusier, as a result of this unfortunate history, were to not realize the pavilion, he will undoubtedly publish the reasons for this throughout the world, because he would consider himself insulted and harmed as a result. We doubt that this would benefit the reputation of the Dutch architects, and wonder whether this will create the impression that they are not very progressive, and are averse to modern ideas.'[35]

Confrontation in Brussels

Following Kalff's letter, the Foundation decided that the issue would be discussed again on 9 January 1957, during a meeting of its governing board, in which a final decision would have to be made on whether or not to approve the design for the Philips Pavilion.[36] Kalff had increased the pressure on the Foundation by stating that a decision had to be made before 10 January, as on that date a discussion would take place between Philips, Le Corbusier, and the French engineering company Anciens Établissements Eiffel about the granting of the construction assignment.[37] During the meeting of the governing board, the architects Van den Broek, Bakema, and Rietveld, as well as the two supervisors Oud and Merkelbach, were also present. In view of the precarious nature of the agenda item relating to the Philips Pavilion, it was decided not to include the opinions expressed at the meeting verbatim in the meeting's minutes. Nonetheless, the minutes indicate that the criticism focused not only on the design of the pavilion, but also on the person of Le Corbusier himself. Particular points of criticism included 'the absolute inadequacy of the (...) extremely scant sketch of his project' and the fact that 'this architect has not even bothered to pay a visit to the site of the Dutch section (...)'. Conversely, Dr. Barend van Spaendonck, the representative for industrial businesses in the governing board made it clear that it would be most regrettable if a decision were to be taken that would lead to Philips forgoing its participation. Eventually, it was decided to postpone the final decision and to invite Kalff and Le Corbusier very soon for a discussion about the pavilion at the exhibition site in Brussels.[38]

On the morning of 19 January 1957 a meeting was held at the offices of the Dutch section on the exhibition site in

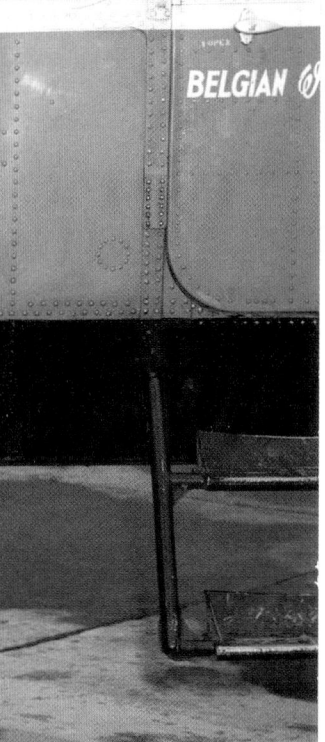

1.9
Le Corbusier and Iannis Xenakis in front of a helicopter of the Belgian airline Sabena during a 1957 trip to the site of the World's Fair.

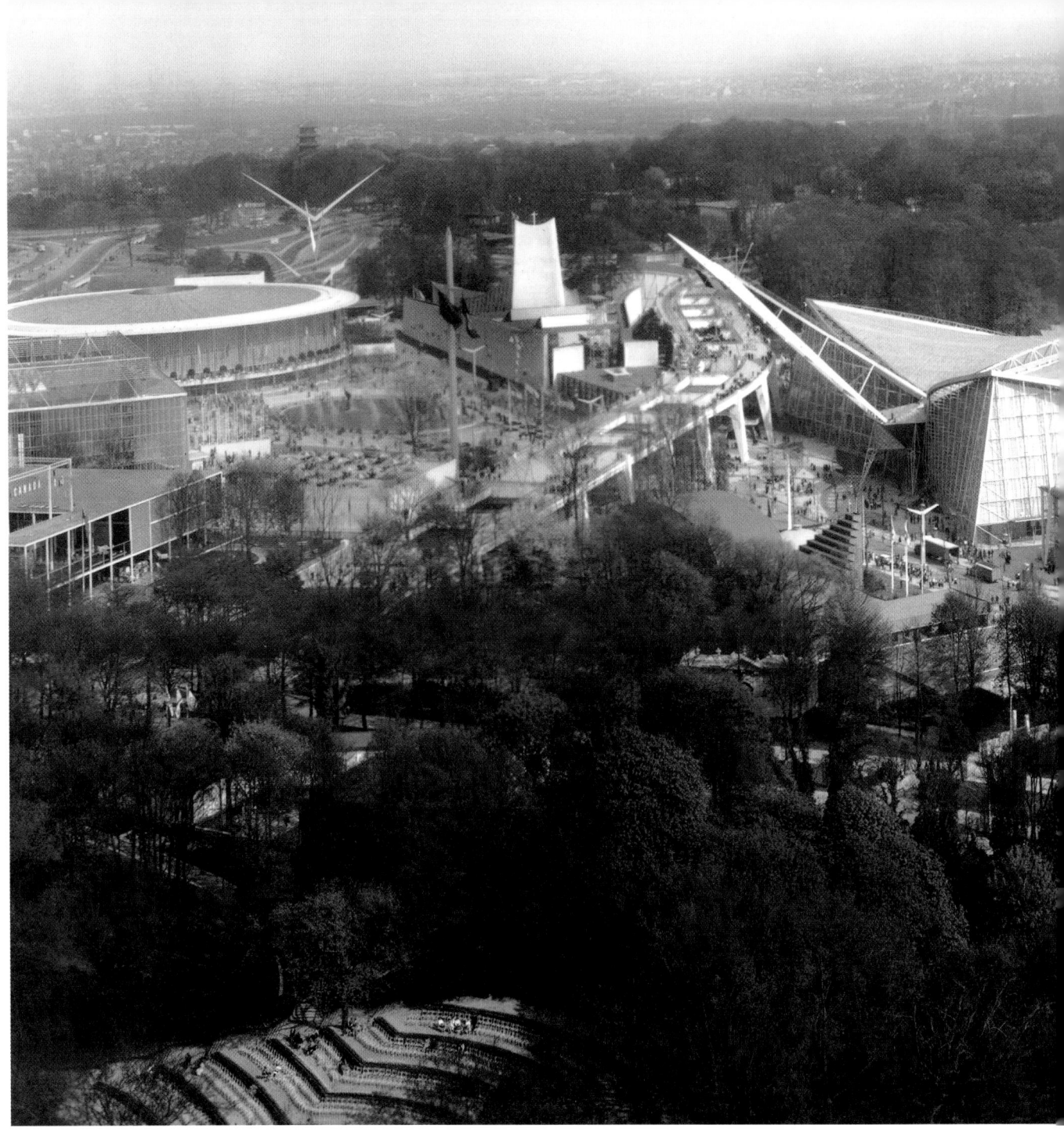

1 Pavilion without a Façade

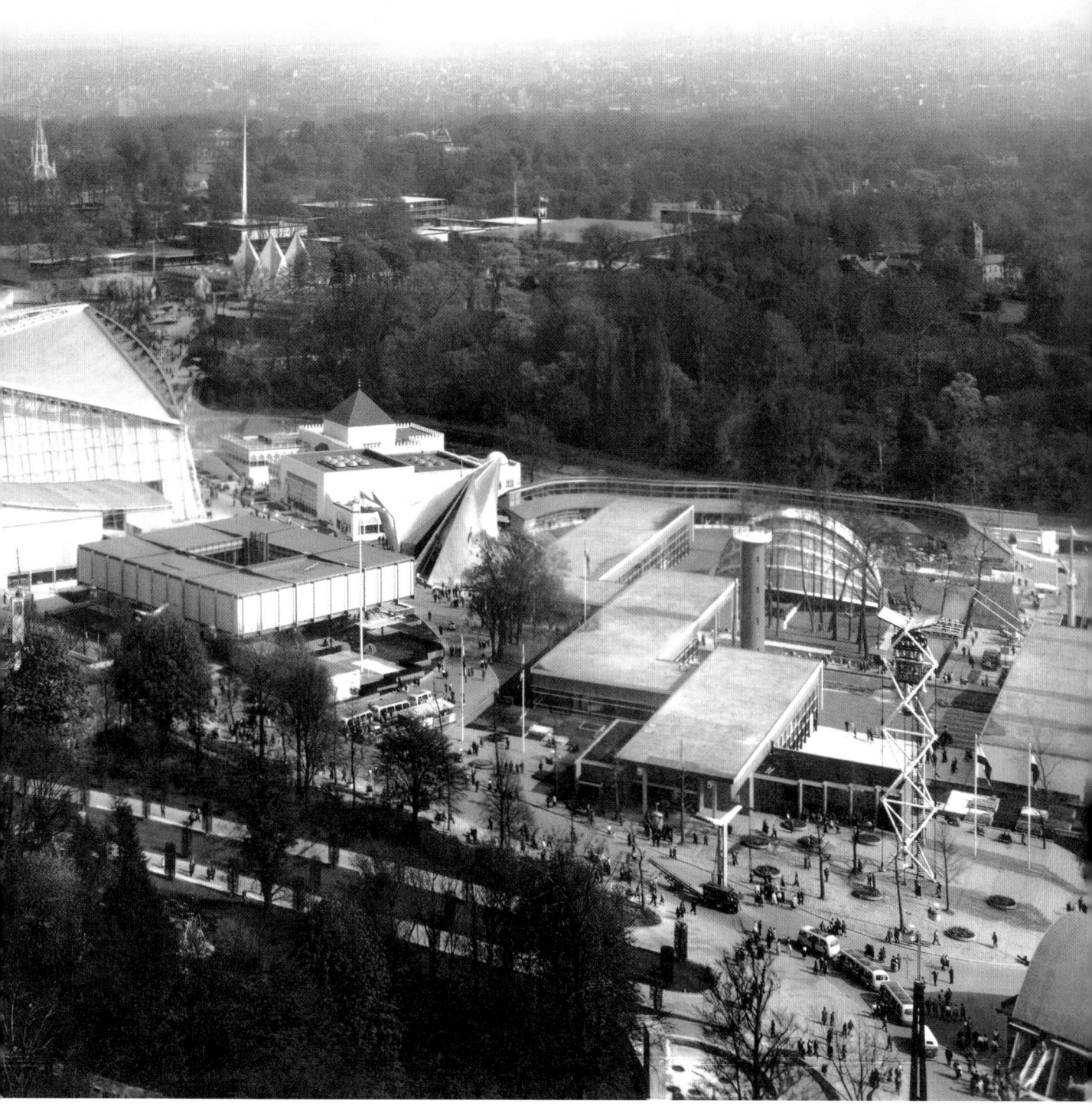

1.10
Aerial photo of the site of the 1958 Brussels World's Fair. The Philips Pavilion was sandwiched between the Dutch pavilion (on the right and rear sides), the Austrian pavilion (front side), and the Tunisian pavilion (left side). To the left of the Austrian pavilion were the pavilion of the city of Paris, and the huge French pavilion.

Brussels.³⁹ Oud was unable to attend, meaning that the supervisors would be represented by Merkelbach only. Merkelbach wanted conditions to be imposed on Philips, rather than directly on Le Corbusier, which would prevent the Philips Pavilion from having an effect that was 'by nature and character disparaging or destructive' to the Dutch pavilion. Philips would then have to add these conditions to Le Corbusier's assignment.⁴⁰ Merkelbach also sent a letter to Le Corbusier himself, in which he expressed the hope that a solution could be reached that would be to everyone's satisfaction.⁴¹ Commissioner General Van Walsem felt 'that the best tactic would be to play to Corbusier's vanity' by asking if he could provide a solution, and could change his design so that it would better fit in with the Dutch pavillion.⁴²

The situation was further clouded by an incorrect statement in the Dutch national newspaper *De Telegraaf* of 11 January 1957: 'There is still no agreement about the execution of the Philips Pavilion. This pavilion, which was designed by the Dutch group of architects, was not approved by the famous modern French architect Le Corbusier, who had been expressly invited by Philips.'⁴³ The report gave the impression, to the regret of Merkelbach, that Le Corbusier had the jurisdiction to decide on the execution of the Dutch entry.⁴⁴

On 19 January 1957, Le Corbusier and Xenakis flew from Paris to the Melsbroek airport near Brussels.⁴⁵ A meeting was held at the exhibition site; present were Commissioner General Van Walsem, architect Bakema,

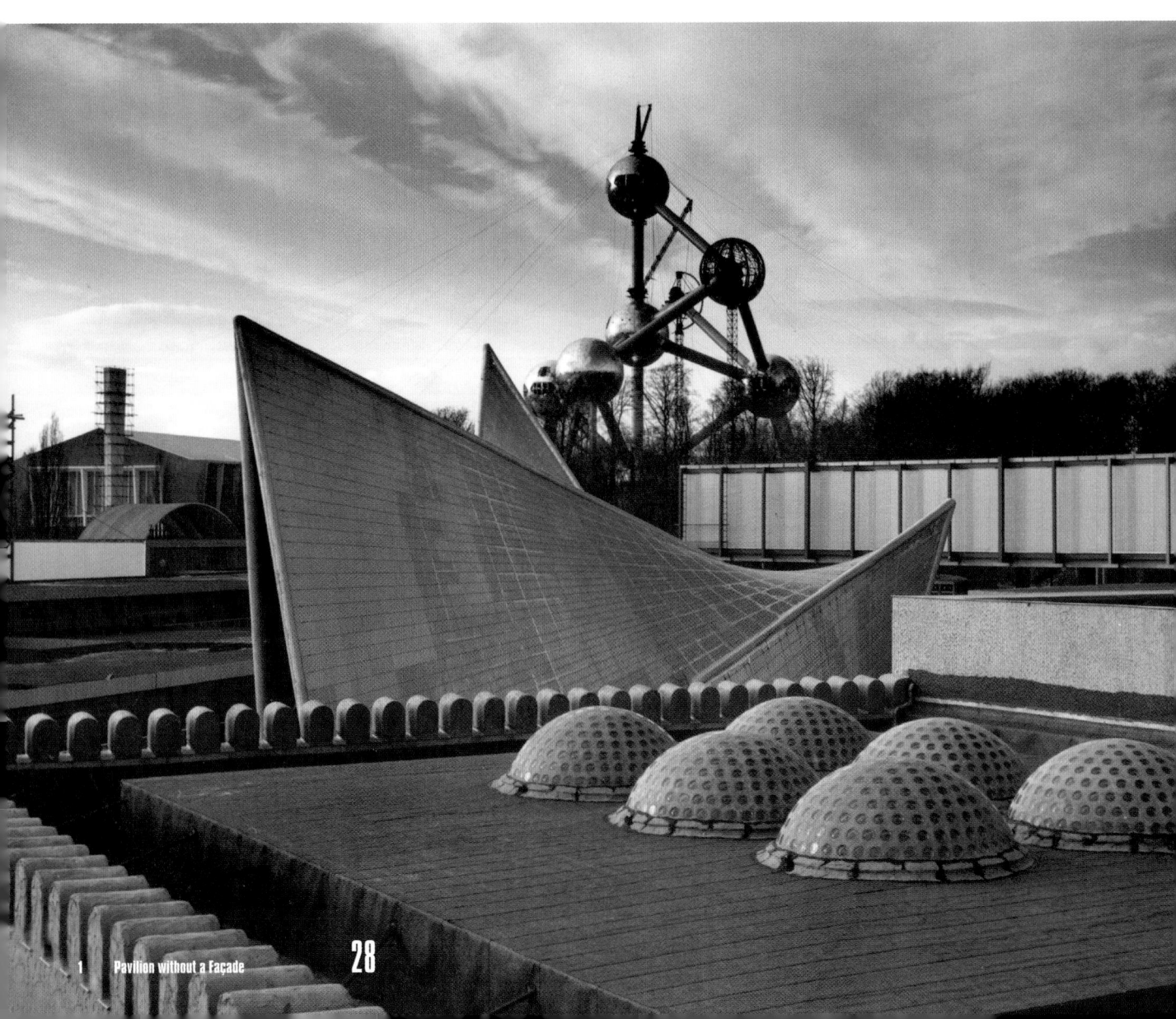

supervising architect Merkelbach, Van Spaendonck as the representative of the governing board, engineer Kalff, and Marcel van Goethem, the Belgian chief architect of the exhibition. At the site, models of the Dutch pavilion and the Philips Pavilion were placed side by side. The pros and cons were then discussed.[46] The Foundation had already listed the advantages and disadvantages of the Philips Pavilion in a memo. The main drawbacks they cited were that the extravagant design did not fit in with the relatively austere architecture of the Dutch entry; that the Philips Pavilion would belittle the Dutch section; and that visitors would be more likely to visit the Philips Pavilion than the Dutch pavilion, out of curiosity. In terms of benefits, it was mentioned that the Philips contribution would bolster Dutch prestige; that the bizarre shape of the pavilion would attract visitors to the Dutch entry; and that Philips would contribute approximately one hundred thousand guilders for the rental of the property.[47]

During the discussion, it was Le Corbusier who said that he feared competition from the Dutch pavilion.[48] He also expressed the opinion that the Philips Pavilion would be compromised by the various national pavilions surrounding it. He praised the Dutch pavilion several times as particularly successful, and thought that the contrast with the Philips Pavilion would ensure a successful entry.[49] Le Corbusier was clearly trying, in keeping with the Dutch strategy, to appeal to the vanity of the Dutch architects. In consultation, an agreement was reached regarding the restrictions placed on the pavilion. It is noteworthy that the restrictions had less to do with the design itself, and more with the size of the building and its distance from the Dutch pavilion.[50] During the discussion, the representatives of the Foundation had recognized that the design of the Philips Pavilion was mainly a consequence of what would take place within the pavilion.[51] The idea of surrounding it with an open rectangular skeleton was abandoned. When all parties, Bakema on behalf of the architects and Merkelbach on behalf of his colleague Oud, had agreed, a lunch was shared.[52] Le Corbusier and Xenakis flew back to Paris that same afternoon.[53]

J.J.P. Oud Considers Withdrawal

Oud, however, proved to be extremely unhappy with the agreement, and considered withdrawal.[54] In a rather unfortunate move, a few days after the meeting with Le Corbusier in Brussels, Commissioner General Van Walsem invited the entire group of architects and the two supervisors to a dinner at the Hotel Des Indes in The Hague.[55] Oud considered the dinner to be a festive ending to the conflict surrounding the Philips Pavilion, and declined the invitation. He did use this opportunity to express his displeasure in writing: 'Since about 1920, Dutch Architecture has taken on an important role in the development of architecture throughout the world. By bringing together four leading architects, we have managed to bring this kind of architecture to the forefront at the 1958 Brussels World's Fair as a complete and unified entity. I suspect that no other country will be able to achieve this kind of unity. (...) The demonstration of this Dutch cultural unity is being significantly harmed by the foreign element that the Philips Pavilion will be.'[56]

Commissioner General Van Walsem pointed out to Oud the proxy he had given Merkelbach to settle the matter in his name. Van Walsem decided to postpone the dinner, and expressed the hope that Oud's reluctance would dissipate.[57]

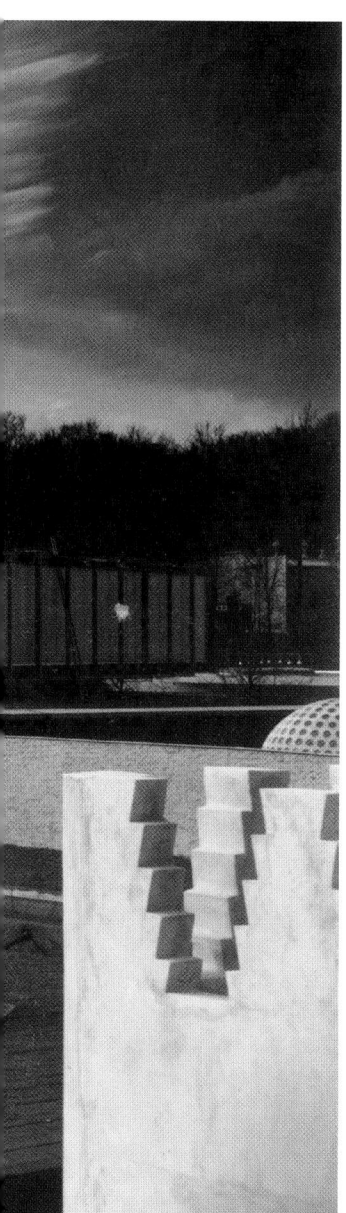

1.11
A view from the roof of the Moroccan pavilion shows that the Philips Pavilion was compromised by various national pavilions surrounding it.

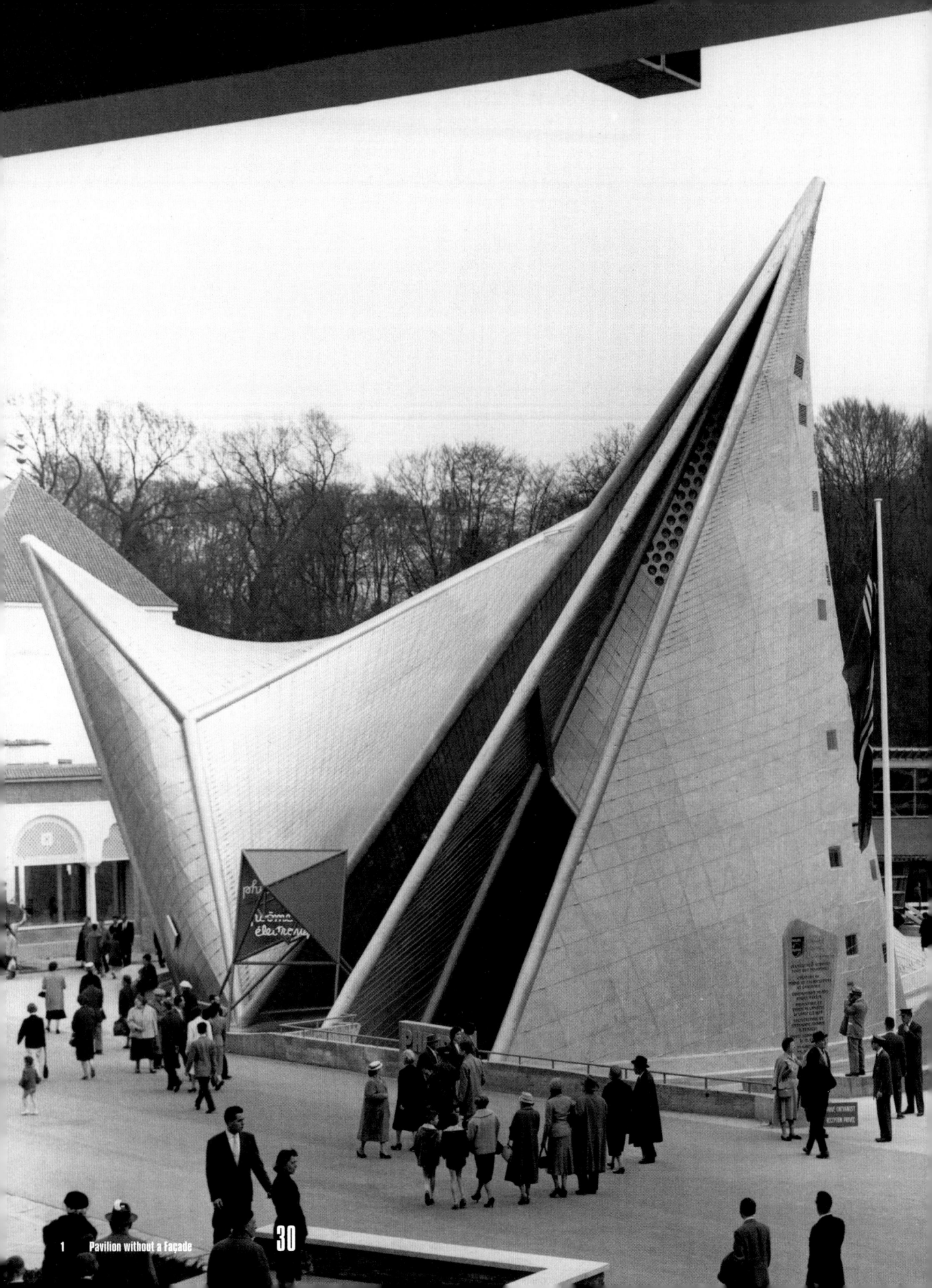
1 Pavilion without a Façade

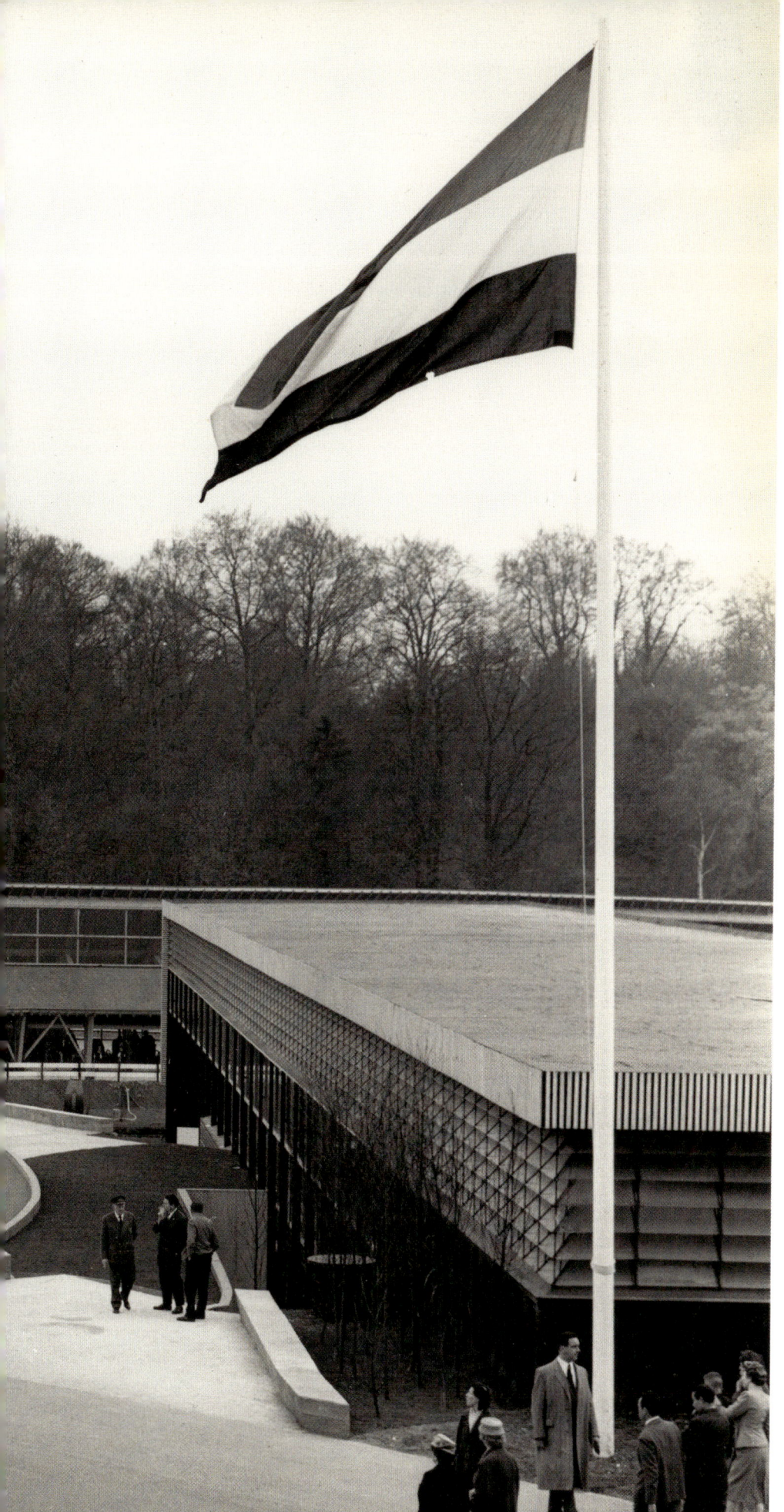

1.12
The extravagant Philips Pavilion flanked by the austere Dutch pavilion.

This was by no means what happened. Oud again brought the matter up in writing: 'Seeing as this Pavilion falls outside of the architectural spirit, outside of the composition, and outside of the proportions of the exhibition's design, there is in my opinion nothing to be achieved by any kind of compromise. (...) The only compromise that seemed acceptable to me was the plan that had originally been agreed upon: to have Rietveld work on the exterior, and Le Corbusier on the interior. Because I do not easily abandon an assignment that I have taken on, I will continue on, despite Philips. (...) However, I now consider this to be a duty, whereas at the beginning it was very much a pleasure.'[58] Oud's inflexibility can be explained by the fact that he had been campaigning against the person of Le Corbusier since the 1920s, as he had against his work and his writings. In a 1927 letter to the Czech-Swiss architectural historian Sigfried Giedion, Oud described Le Corbusier as 'unlikeable because day by day he whips himself into a greater sense of virtuosity', and as 'the biggest disappointment of the past few years'.

In addition to a heartfelt disagreement in terms of theoretical ideas about architecture, the vehemence with which Oud confronted Le Corbusier in those years can be attributed to having lost a competition, with Le Corbusier being suspected of having derived some of his principles from the architectural ideas of *De Stijl*.[59] For Oud, the great amount of attention paid to Le Corbusier as a painter was occasion to write an article in 1938 for *De 8 en Opbouw,* in which he said that 'for the development of the new architecture, it is extraordinarily regrettable to us that Le Corbusier has been held up for so long as an example to Dutch architects'.[60] Also decisive for the relationship between the two men was the decimating evaluation that Le Corbusier issued in 1939 about Oud's (anonymized) entry to a competition for a new city hall in Amsterdam.[61]

Although Oud stayed on as architectural supervisor for the Dutch pavilion, the conflict surrounding the Philips Pavilion was reason enough for the architect Peutz to withdraw from the Architect Group Brussels 1958. Even before the discussion of 19 January in Brussels, Peutz had requested this in part because he no longer wanted to participate in the 'advertising' that Le Corbusier was generating for himself.[62] He found it unacceptable that an architect other than Rietveld would design the Philips Pavilion, although at the same time he felt that Le Corbusier should have complete freedom if he were given the assignment. Peutz considered Le Corbusier's design to be 'less like architecture' and more like 'mathematical niceties'.[63] But the Foundation indicated that it would be very unfortunate if, at that particular moment in the conflict, it became known that Peutz wanted to withdraw.[64] Peutz then stayed on as a passive member of the architects group until his honourable discharge in December of 1957.[65] The controversial dinner organized by Commissioner General Van Walsem finally took place in mid-March of 1957, in the absence of Oud and Peutz.[66]

The ground-breaking ceremony for the foundation of the Philips Pavilion took place on 6 May 1957.[67] The Foundation urged Philips to let the Dutch architects be represented at the ceremony by Boks.[68] In retrospect, the Foundation wrote in its report on the 1958 Brussels World's

1.13
Amateur Kodachrome color slide of the Philips Pavilion in operation.

Fair that the architect group's fear about the Philips Pavilion dominating the rest of the Dutch section turned out to be completely unfounded.[69] Rietveld said of the Philips Pavilion: 'the stand is a stunt, even though it has very little to do with architecture.'[70] After the 1958 Brussels World's Fair, its organization awarded Le Corbusier an honorary diploma with a gold medal. None of the architects of the Dutch pavilion received this token of appreciation.[71]

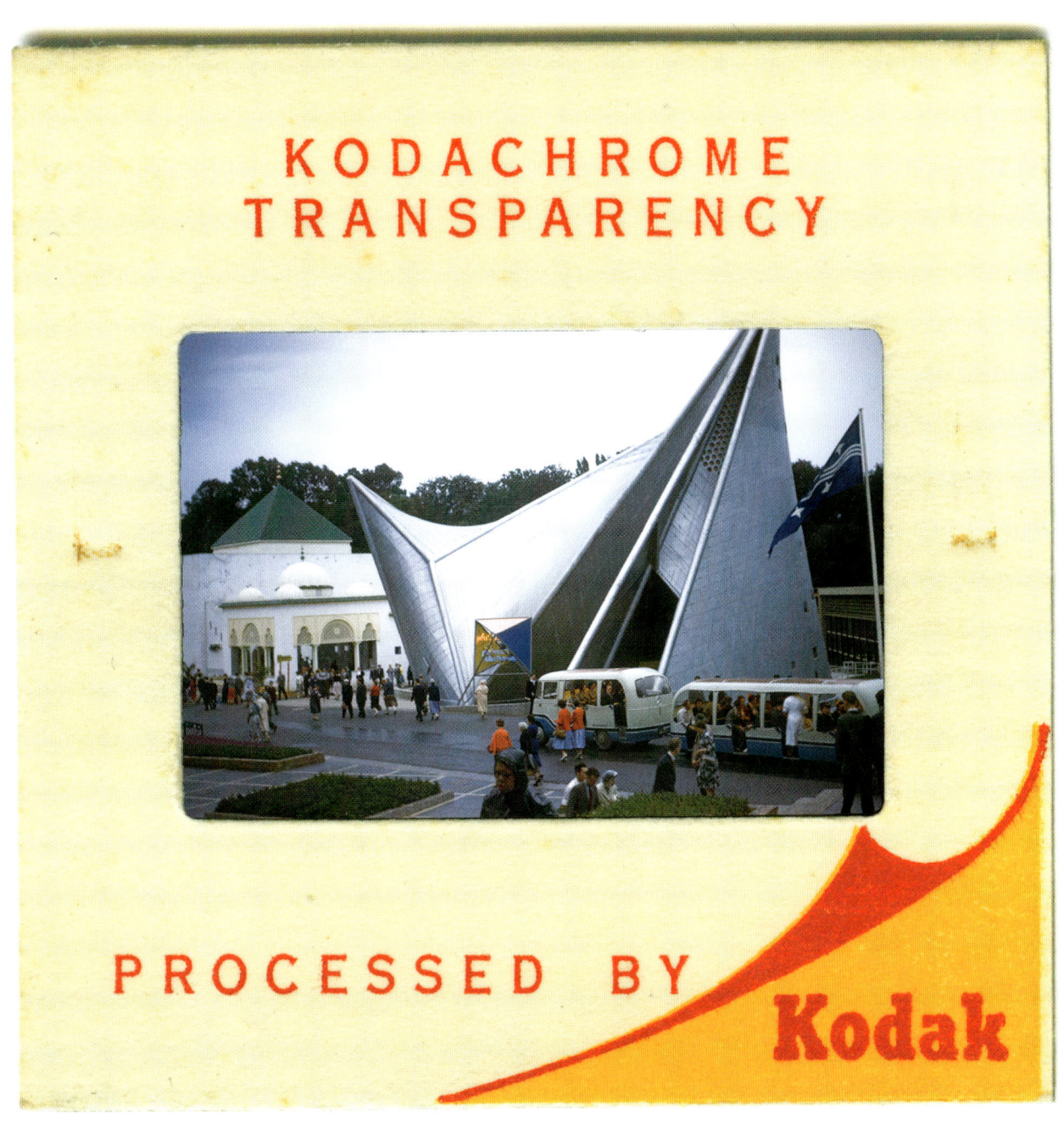

Text Box I

Woman's Hairpins Help to Build Architecture of the Future

An Unlikely Tale of the Conception of the Philips Pavilion

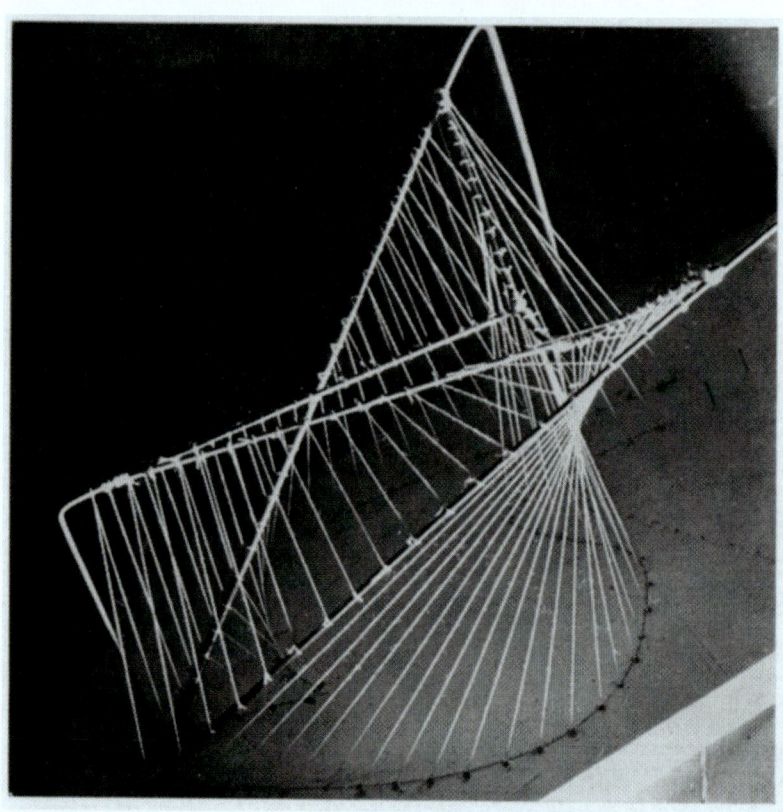

I.1
The first scale model of the Philips Pavilion, which Iannis Xenakis made at Le Corbusier's request using strings and piano wire on a wooden surface. Lucien Hervé photograph, undated.

The design of the Philips Pavilion is surrounded by misconceptions and myths. For example, the New York newspaper *New York World-Telegram and the Sun* published a column by Inez Robb in April of 1958 that refers to a highly unlikely occurrence.[1] It suggests that Le Corbusier created the first model of the Philips Pavilion using his maid's hairpins, and that the Belgian contractor then carefully transported this model to Brussels to be further worked out in detail. The column is printed below in its entirety.

This fair is full of avant-garde architecture and usually, after a second look, I like it fine. The French pavilion, for instance, is going to be a dilly when it's done.

But there is a building that stumps me, and it is by the man long hailed as the mentor, prophet and granddaddy of modern architecture, France's le Corbusier. This Gallic Frank Lloyd Wright has designed for the staid Philips Electronic Co. of the Netherlands a building that looks like an unsolved problem in plane – or do I mean solid? – geometry. Every time I go past it I want to exclaim, 'Dig that crazy Euclid.'[2]

It's hard to explain what the building looks like, because it doesn't look like any other building I've ever seen – or you, either. It's a series of cones and triangles glued together at odd angles so that the apex of the cones (does a cone have an apex? I flunked math) and triangles all stick out hither and yon in space.

But if I don't understand the building, I am privy to a briefing on the masters and how he works that may make a footnote for history, since Mr. le Corbusier is certain of a niche. When the Philips firm decided to go all-out and hire the legendary le Corbusier (he had a hand in planning the United Nations buildings in New York), it hired a Belgian builder and sent him to France to consult with the architect. 'Well, we might as well begin with a circle,' Mr. le Corbusier said, according to my informant who carried a spear in this scene. Thereupon Mr. le Corbusier drew a circle.

'Then we shall have to let the people in,' he continued, and drew a door. 'Next we shall have to let them out,' he added, and drew another door in the circle opposite the first.

At that critical moment, Mr. le Corbusier's maid came into the room. The woman wore her hair in a chignon, pinned up with old-fashioned bone hairpins. These apparently were just the building material the master was looking for.

He stopped the woman and took the pins out of her hair, first trying a pin this way, and then that, on the circle. After thrusting a pin through the paper at one angle, Mr. le Corbusier would study it for a moment before deciding to move it or let it remain.

Eventually, he pulled the last hairpin from the chignon, and hair cascaded over the woman's shoulders. The master regarded the pin thoughtfully, made a final thrust and handed the astounded Belgian builder the piece of paper studded with bone hairpins.

'Here is your building,' said Mr. le Corbusier.[3]

And there indeed it was. The builder returned to Brussels, guarding the paper and the hairpins as if they were jewels, and set to work. The result is the most unusual building in a fair distinguished by the architecture of tomorrow.

In fact, the building belongs to that category of objects that people, buffaloed for a better descriptive phrase, call 'a conversation piece.' It certainly is making conversation at the fair. And I am thinking of letting my hair grow and laying in a gross of hairpins, just in case.

2

Colour in the Philips Pavilion
Le Corbusier's Use of *Types Couleurs*

Peter Wever

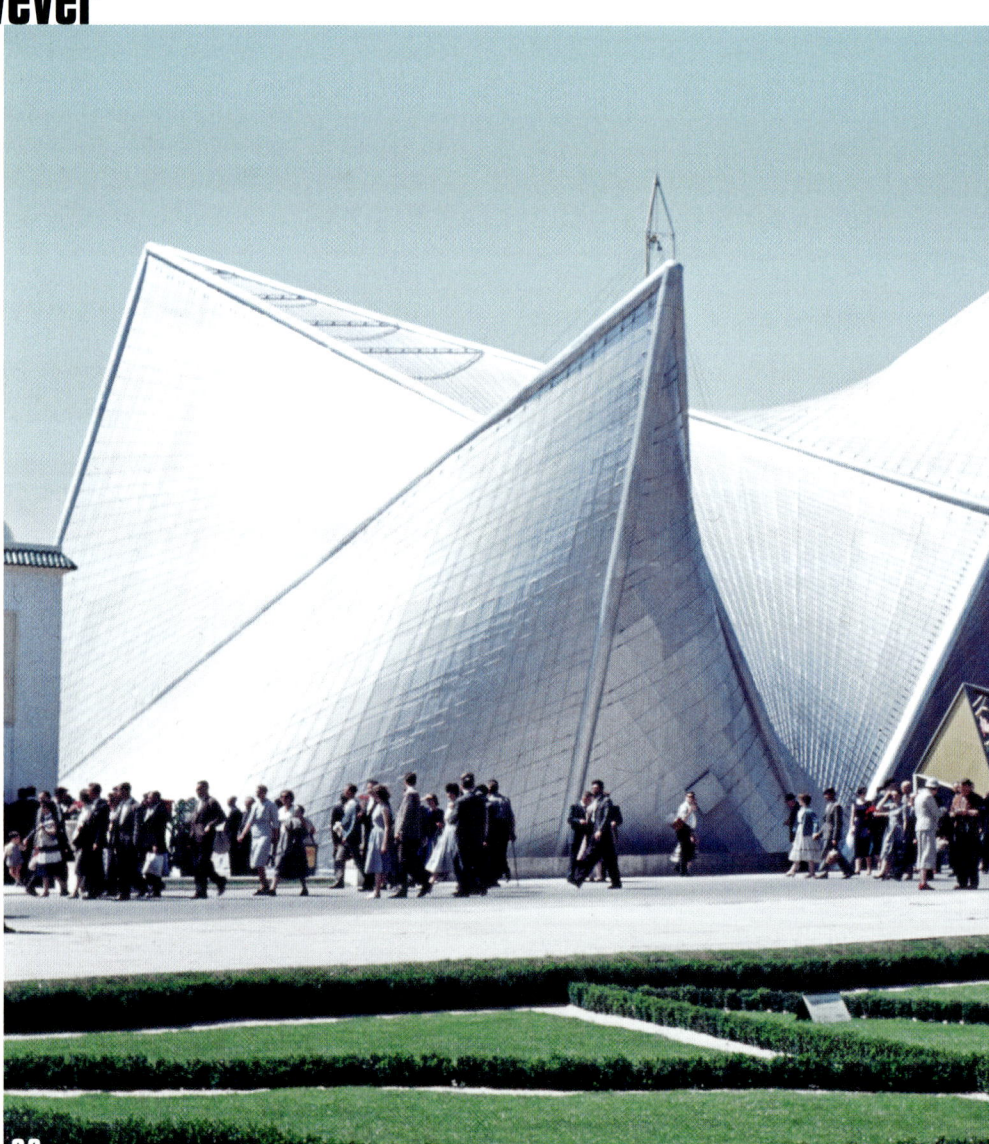

2.1
'The silvery and lustrous Philips Pavilion looms before the visitor to the Brussels' International Exhibition.'

Polychromy, the multi-coloured painting of buildings and sculptures, is an important aspect in Le Corbusier's work. At first glance, the Philips Pavilion, with its aluminium-coloured exterior, does not come across as an example of polychrome architecture. But the Philips Pavilion, along with the chapel of Notre-Dame-du-Haut in Ronchamp, the Zürich exhibition pavilion, and the buildings in Chandigarh are all mentioned as examples of Le Corbusier's post-war use of *types couleurs*. In the Philips Pavilion, polychromy was used modestly in both the entrance and the exit of the pavilion, with the colours, especially in the entrance, largely hidden from the view of visitors to the World's Fair.[1]

Le Corbusier's Concept of Polychromy

In 1956, Le Corbusier expressed the core of his post-war concept of polychromy in the foreword to the book *Art in European architecture. Synthèse des arts* by Paul Damaz. 'Architecture (...) is primarily a confrontation of materials, each material having its own potential, its power of action and reaction. Thus it is, in the first place, an expression of the interplay of materials or a choice to be made of a material. This is preponderant. Immediately afterwards the phenomenon of colour follows, but not as yet the work of the painter or the sculptor. It is one of the exteriorizations of the architectural

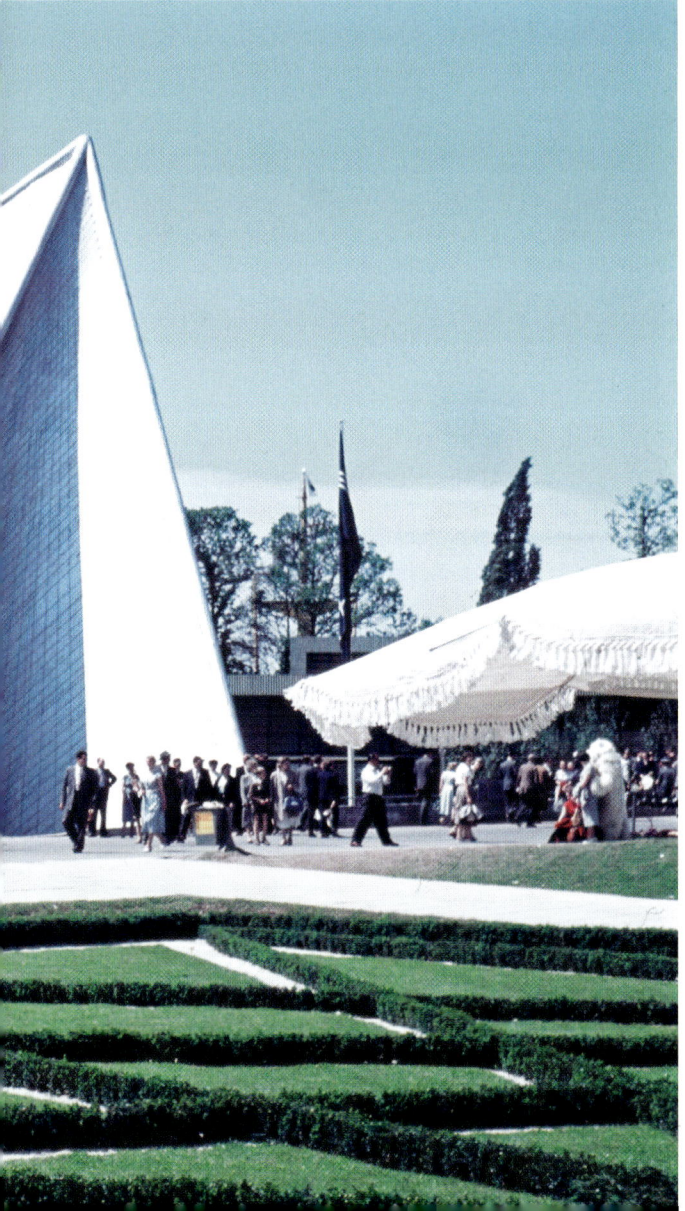

will that manifests itself and flares up through polychromy, meaning that, in conjunction with forms, circulations and light, coloured harmonies may emerge, whose power of action on our sensitivity is enormous.' In this argument, Le Corbusier expresses a preference for natural polychromy, the colour of the material, instead of painted polychromy. Yet polychrome painting could still play a modest but nonetheless powerful role as an ornamental form.[2]

With its aluminium-coloured exterior, the Philips Pavilion does not seem to be an example of polychrome architecture. But colours were indeed used, to a modest extent, in both the entrance and the exit of the pavilion.

The Aluminium-coloured Exterior

On 19 January 1957, a meeting was held on the site of the 1958 Brussels World's Fair between Le Corbusier, Iannis Xenakis, and Louis Kalff on one side, with the other side represented by several delegates from the governing board and the group of architects from the Dutch pavilion. Marcel van Goethem, the Belgian chief architect of the exhibition, was present as a third party. The aim of the meeting was to find a solution to the conflict between the parties regarding the contrast between the extravagant architecture of the Philips Pavilion and the austere Dutch pavilion.[3]

A few days earlier, Herman Van Walsem, the Commissioner General of the Dutch pavilion, had prepared several suggestions for the proposed agreement. His fourth point concerned the colour of the Philips Pavilion's exterior: 'The exterior of the Philips Building, including all of its protrusions, will be kept to a neutral colour, e.g. aluminium or greyish.'[4] In Brussels, agreement was reached on all of the matters discussed. With regard to the colour of the exterior, the official memo of the discussion indicated that the Philips Pavilion would be in an aluminium or copper colour.[5]

In Paris on 1 June 1957 Kalff and Le Corbusier discussed the use of high-gloss aluminium paint for the exterior. Although Le Corbusier did not agree immediately at that moment,[6] the aluminium colour was ultimately chosen. First, the concrete exterior of the pavilion was covered with a special waterproof paint, which also covered the bracing wires. An aluminium finishing paint was then applied to this waterproof primer.[7] In this way, the exterior of the Philips Pavilion gave the impression of having a silver colour. In its press kit, Philips described the pavilion as follows: 'The silvery and lustrous Philips Pavilion looms before the visitor to the Brussels' International Exhibition.'[8] The international press also highlighted the silver nature of the exterior. *The New York Times* wrote about 'a building that looks like an improbable and gigantic seashell frozen into silvered concrete'.[9] The *Frankfurter Allgemeine Zeitung* described the pavilion as *Der zeltähnlich geschwungene Bau von Le Corbusier im silbern glänzenden Schalenbeton* [The tent-like meandering structure of Le Corbusier with silver shiny concrete slabs].[10]

Inside the pavilion, the public area was the largest space. For acoustic reasons, the walls of the public space were coated with a sprayed asbestos (known as Limpet asbestos, a mixture of asbestos and cement), and then painted white.[11]

The Use of *Types Couleurs*

In the travel report of his 15 November 1957 visit to Le Corbusier's studio in Paris, Kalff wrote that Le Corbusier himself wanted to choose the colours of the entrance and exit only after the scaffolding had been removed from the Philips Pavilion.[12] In January of 1958, Philips drew up a list of questions to be posed to Le Corbusier regarding the pavilion and *Le poème électronique*. The three-page list mentioned as item 9 'Colour of the entrance blue, optical adaptation', and as item 10 'Colour of the exit yellow, idem reversed,

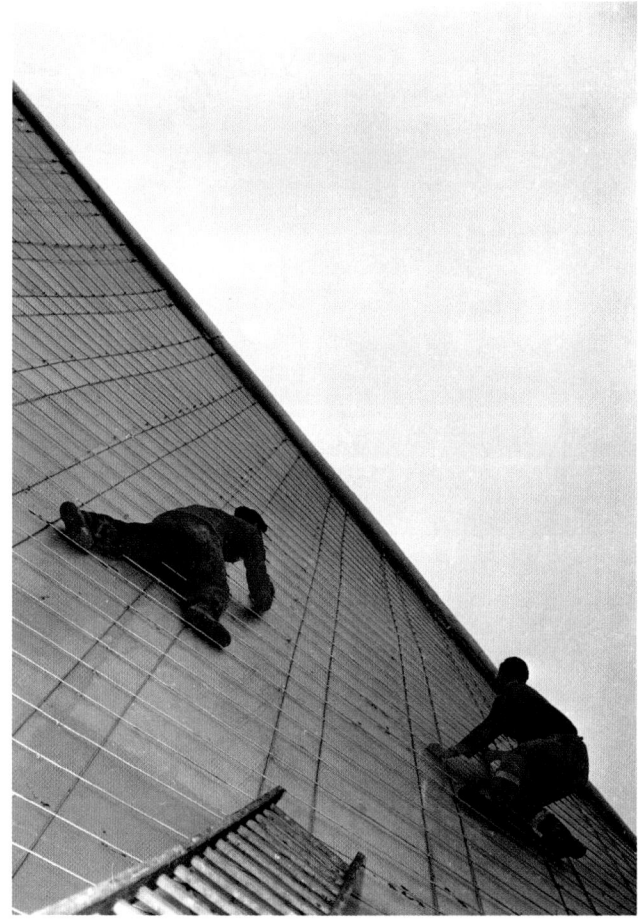

2.2
Workers balancing on bracing wires during the construction of the Philips Pavilion.

2.3
View of the exterior of the Philips Pavilion during the application of the aluminium-coloured finishing paint, on top of the waterproof undercoating.

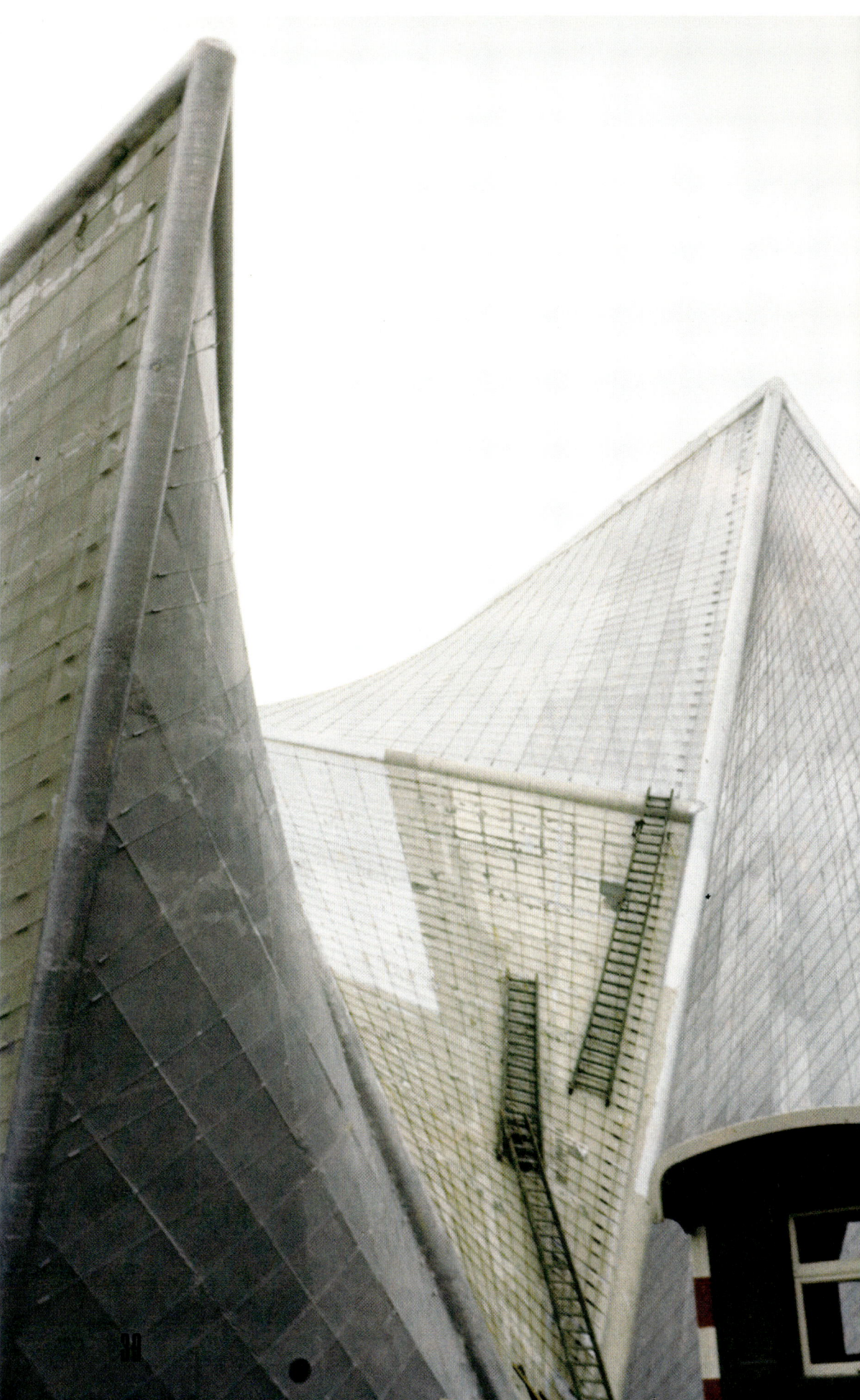

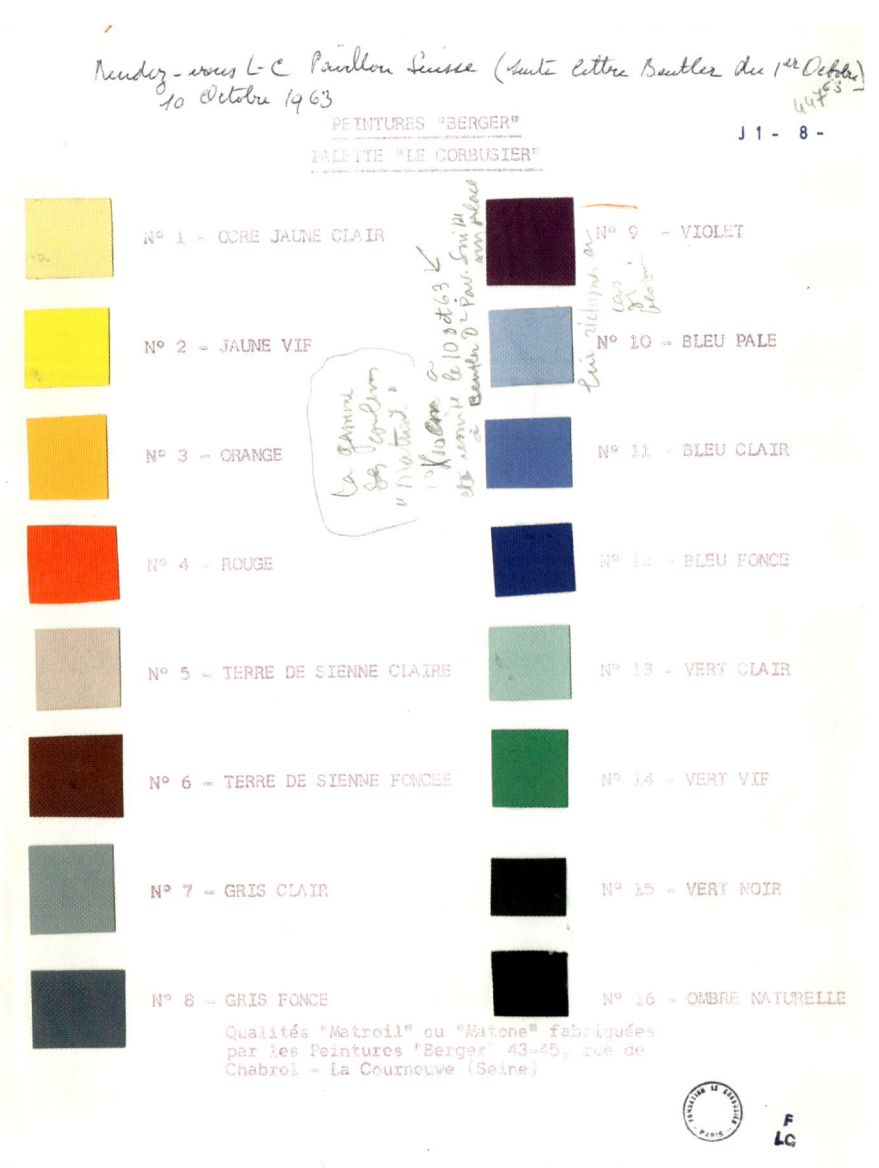

2.4
Colour samples featuring the *types couleurs*, consisting of sixteen colours that Le Corbusier derived in 1951 from Newton's colour spectrum.

2.5
An original scale model of the Philips Pavilion shows the four colours used for the pavilion's entrance and exit. The top image shows the entrance to the pavilion. The two folding doors consisted of alternating blue and red panels, above which was a green canopy ceiling. On either side of the folding doors was a yellow plane that continued on the right side on the wall of the control room. The bottom figure shows the pavilion's exit, where there were two folding doors with alternating green and red panels, above which was a yellow canopy ceiling.

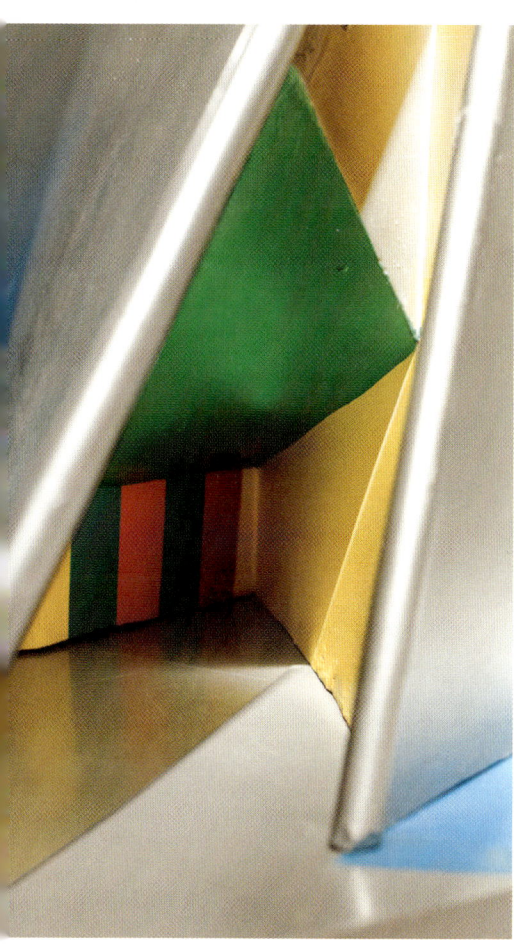

and in harmony with the colour of the sky'.[13] Clearly, this involved a suggestion to Le Corbusier regarding the colours of the pavilion's entrance and exit. 'Optical adaptation' referred to the eye's sensitivity adjustment in the transition from light to darkness, or from darkness to light. The colour blue would provide a gradual transition from light to dark, and thus allow for better adaptation to the dark when entering the pavilion. Conversely, using the colour yellow for the exit would achieve a better adaptation to the light by gradually transitioning from darkness to light.

On 18 February, Kalff sent a letter to Le Corbusier, again inquiring about the intended colours for the entrance and exit.[14] On 11 March, five weeks before the opening of the World's Fair, Kalff was informed by Xenakis that there was still no decision about the colours of the entrance and exit, as Le Corbusier had not found the time to decide. Xenakis suggested that Kalff make the choice himself if he could no longer wait.[15]

On 13 March 1958 Kalff replied to Xenakis that Philips would indeed decide on the colours of the entrance and exit, partly because the pavilion's scaffolding was to be removed within ten days. During an earlier visit to Brussels, Le Corbusier had allegedly given some indication about the choice of colour. Kalff's plan was to paint the panels of the folding doors in alternating blue and red, and to paint the canopy ceilings above the doors white. The walls that ran into the entrance doors, located deeper in the pavilion, were to be painted in the same aluminium colour as the exterior, except for the control room's wall with windows, which was to remain unpainted ['*brut*'].[16] Yet, one of Le Corbusier's sketchbooks contains an undated sketch in which he indicated in words (*jaune, vert, bleu*) and with letter codes (j, v, r and al, corresponding to *jaune, vert, rouge,* and *aluminium*) what colours were to be used for the pavilion's entrance and exit.[17] Examination of an original scale model, as well as original colour photographs, colour slides, and colour cine-films of the Philips Pavilion, reveals that Le Corbusier's choice of yellow, red, blue, and green was actually used.[18]

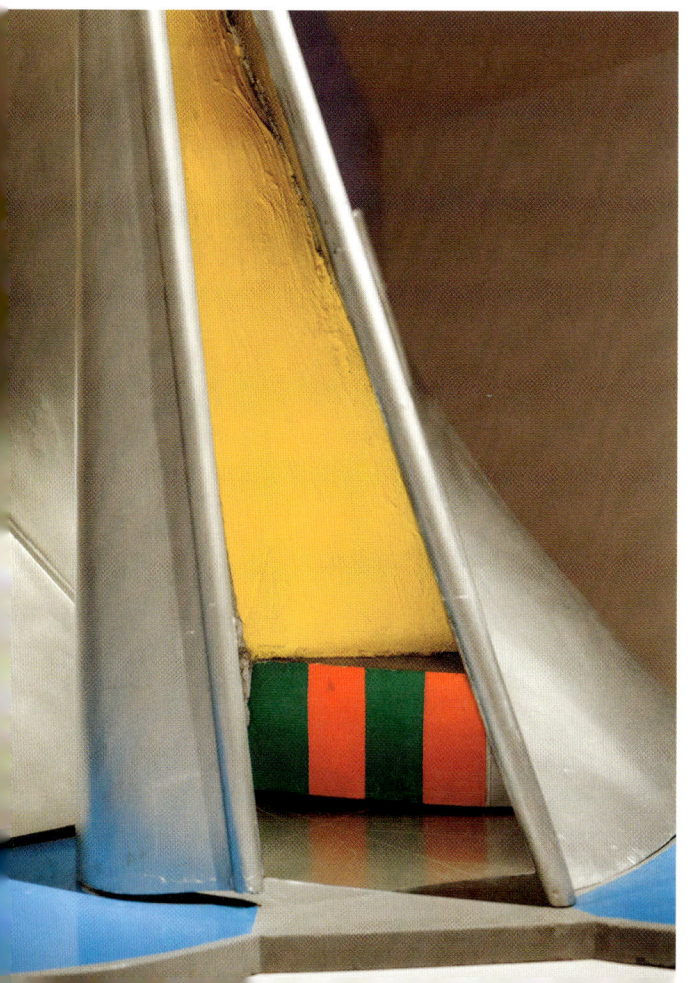

The two folding doors at the entrance to the Philips Pavilion consisted of alternating blue and red panels. The canopy ceiling above the folding doors was coloured green. On either side of the folding doors, a yellow surface had been added that continued on the right-hand side on the wall with the windows of the control room. The two folding doors of the pavilion's exit consisted of alternating green and red panels, with a yellow canopy ceiling overhead.[19] Because the doors of the entrance, and to a lesser extent the doors of the exit, were located deep inside the pavilion, the polychrome painting was not easily visible. The colours of the entrance in particular were only visible to visitors when entering the pavilion.

It is likely that the four colours used come from the standardized colour palette known as *types couleurs*. This colour palette consists of sixteen different colours, and represents Newton's colour spectrum. In 1951, Le Corbusier developed this palette for the Unite d'habitation in Marseilles, and thereafter used it in almost all of his projects. Other examples of the use of *types couleurs* in Le Corbusier's post-war architecture include the chapel of Notre-Dame-du-Haut in Ronchamp, the Zürich exhibition pavilion, the renovation of the Pavillon Suisse in Paris, and the buildings in Chandigarh, India.[20]

Objet mathématique

In the travel report of his visit to Le Corbusier's studio on 15 November 1957, Louis Kalff wrote about Le Corbusier's desire to place a mathematical sculpture in the water around the pavilion.[21] It is assumed that the idea for this so-called *Objet mathématique* came from Le Corbusier, and that Xenakis was responsible for its development.[22] In a letter dated 18 February 1958, Kalff asked Le Corbusier about the further development of the idea.[23] A week later, on 25 February, a sketch design of the *Objet mathématique* was made.[24] The final design drawings, with colour indications, were the work of Xenakis, and dated from 3 and 4 March 1958, when the colours of the pavilion's entrance and exit had not yet been determined. The metal structure consisted of three interlocked geometric figures, in colours from the *types couleurs* palette. The outermost and largest figure, an octahedron, was made of grey tubes in which three of the eight planes were filled with a triangular panel in the colours blue, red, and yellow. The middle figure, a cuboctahedron (the figure created when a cube and an octahedron cross each other exactly at the half-way point of their ribs), was comprised entirely of yellow tubes. The innermost and smallest figure was an octahedron that was filled with eight green planes. Inside the structure, the word 'philips', written in Le Corbusier's handwriting, was displayed in a pink-red neon light tube, and the words 'poème électronique' in light blue neon light tubes.[25] The *Objet mathématique* was fabricated in the Philips machine shop in Eindhoven,[26] and had an impressive height of five meters and twenty centimeters.[27] It was located on the left of the entrance in a pond, behind a low concrete wall on the street-facing side of the Philips Pavilion.[28] A common feature of the Philips Pavilion and the *Objet mathématique* was that matching colours were used in the polychrome painting, and that both designs consisted of geometric elements.

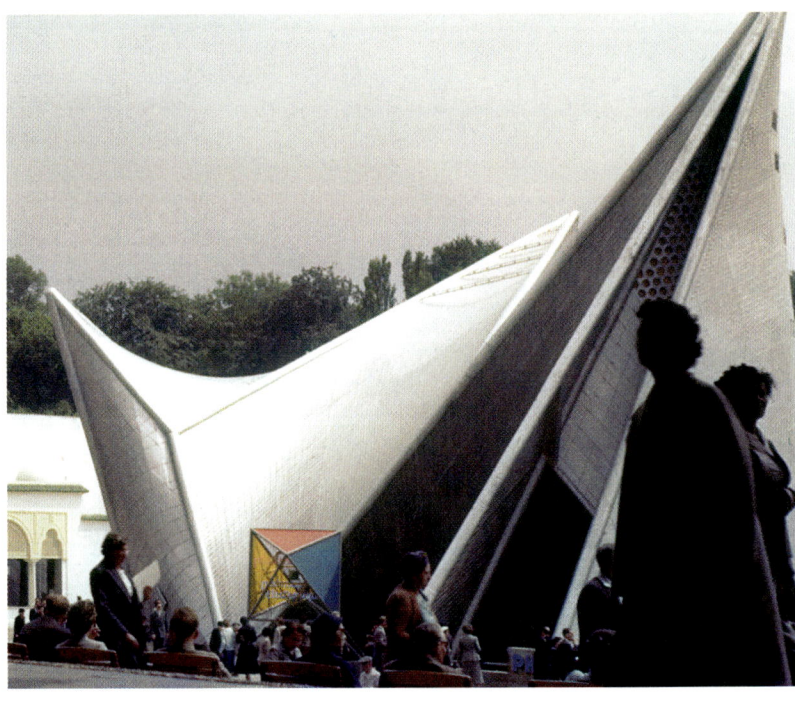

2.6
The polychromy of the Philips Pavilion. The left image shows the vestibule of the pavilion's entrance, with a green canopy ceiling and a yellow wall next to the (not visible) folding doors. The right image shows the folding doors of the exit, with alternating green and red panels, above which was a yellow canopy ceiling.

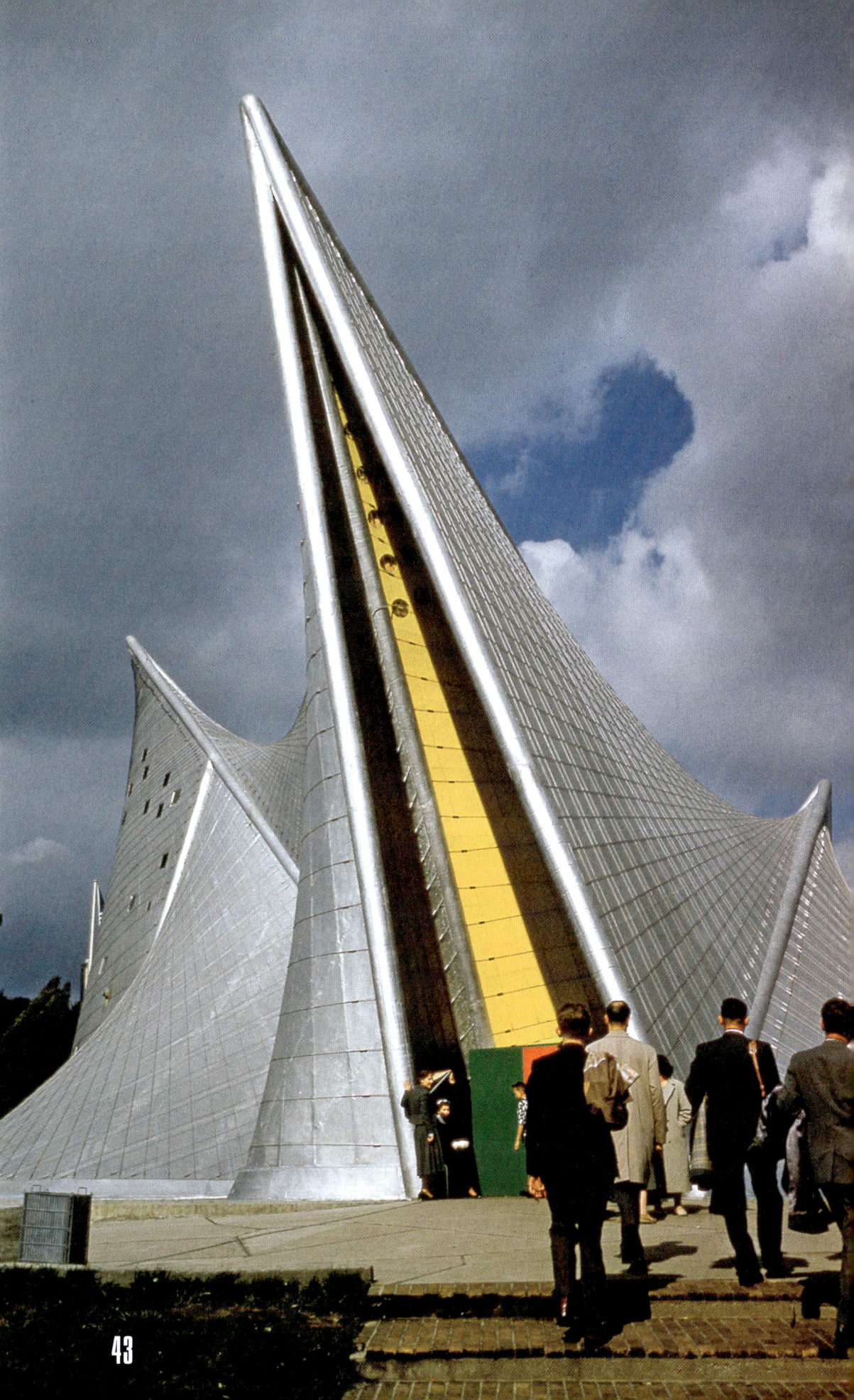

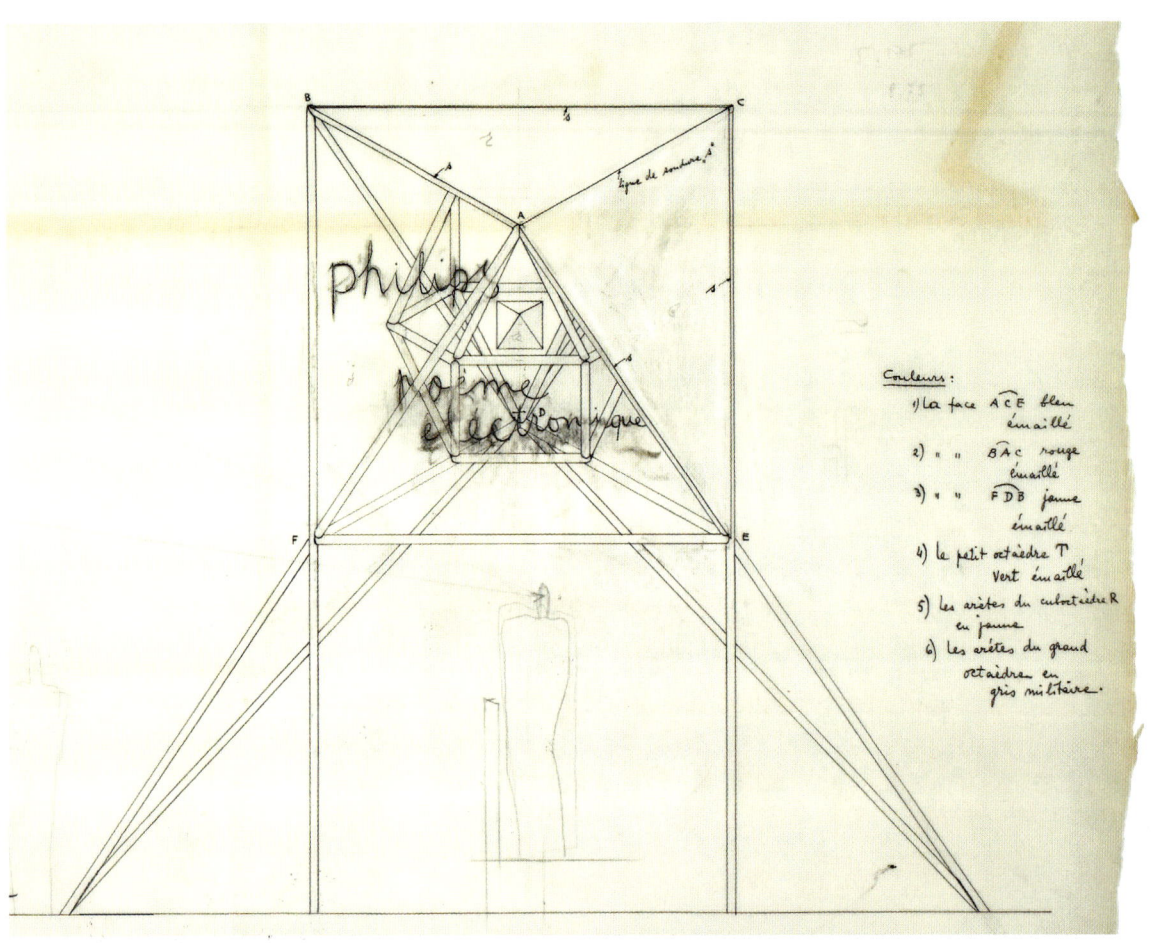

2.7
Front view of the *Objet mathématique* in the design drawing PHIL.-L.C. 5548, with colour designations for the various metal pipes and plates from which the sculpture was to be manufactured.

2.8
The *Objet mathématique* consisted of a large outer octahedron made of grey tubes, in which three planes were filled with a blue, a yellow, and a red panel. Inside was a cuboctahedron consisting of yellow tubes. The innermost and smallest figure was an octahedron of green planes. Inside of the structure, the word 'philips', written in the handwriting of Le Corbusier, was displayed in a pink-red neon light tube, and the words 'poème électronique' in light blue neon light tubes.

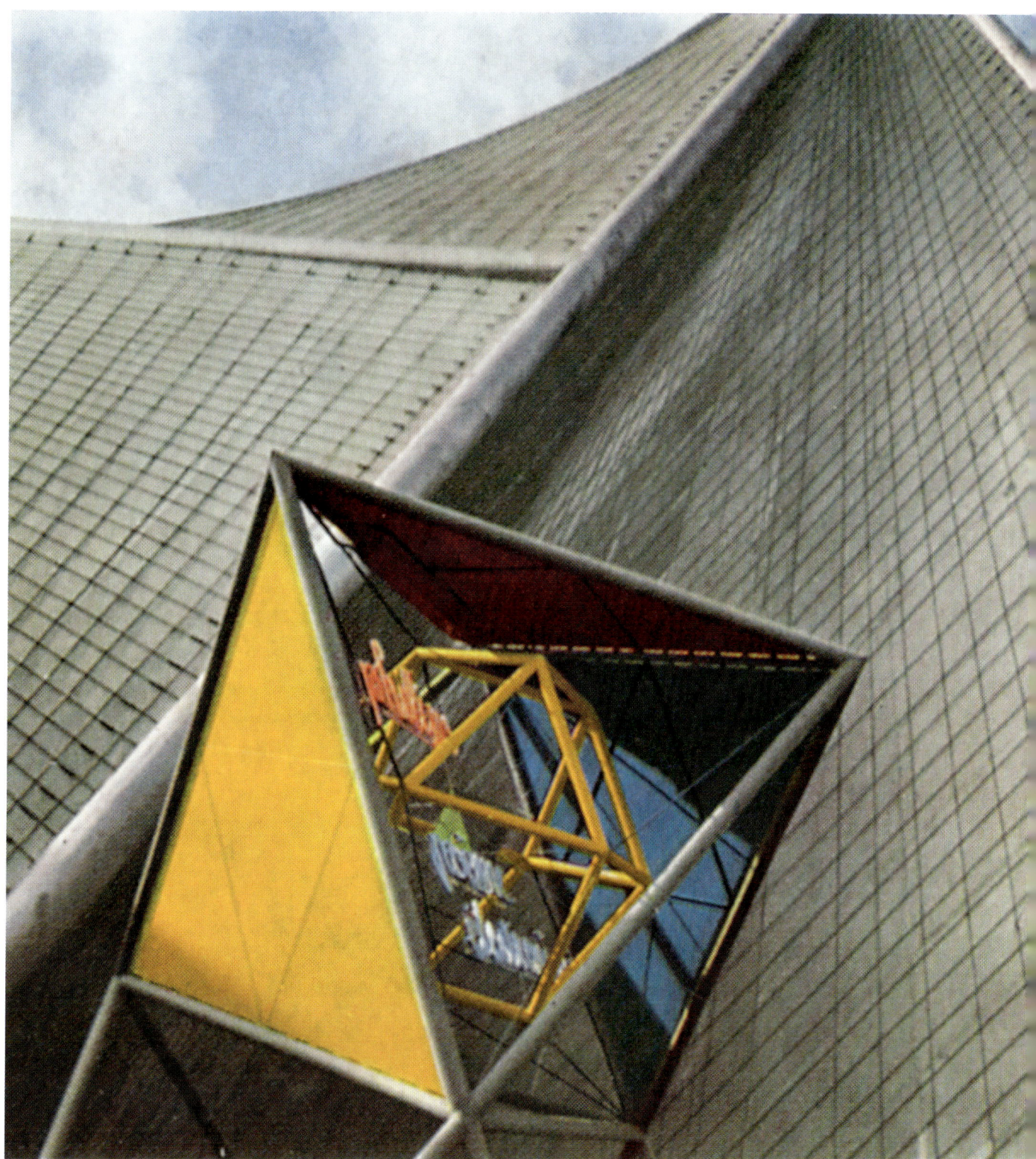

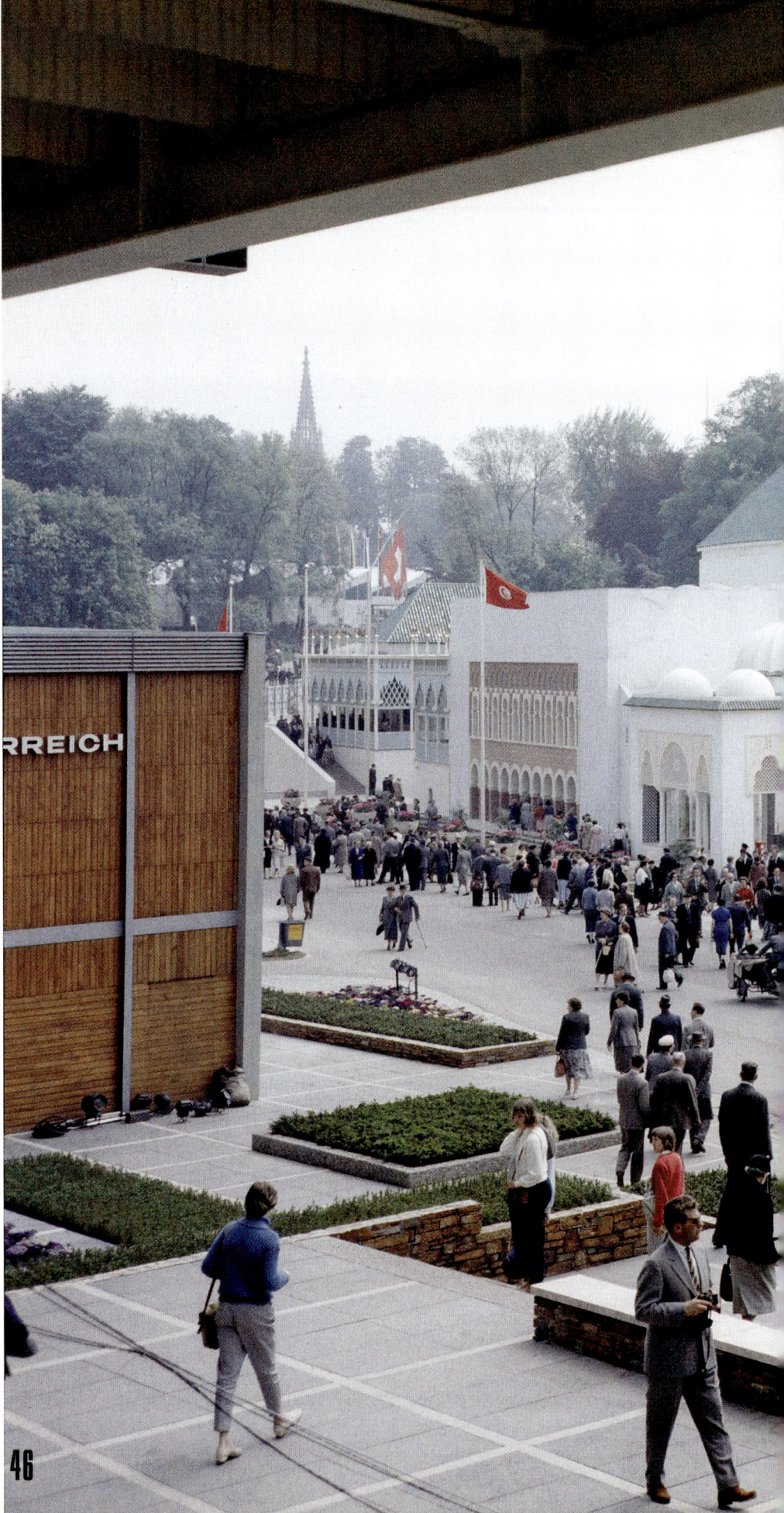

2.9
The *Objet mathématique* was placed to the left of the entrance, in a pond behind a low concrete wall on the street-facing side of the Philips Pavilion.

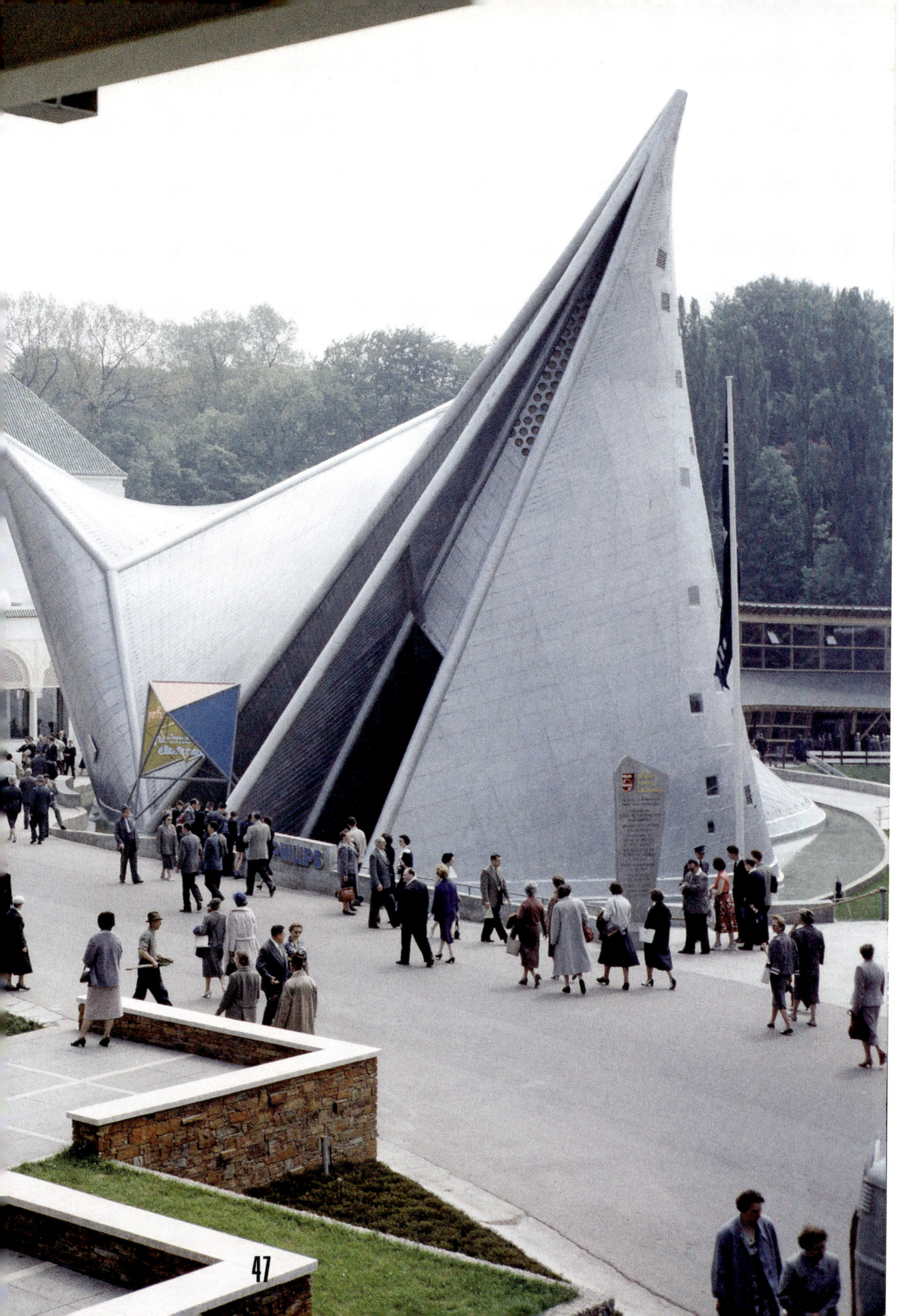

3 The Decorators
The Creation of the Light Effects in *Le poème électronique*

Peter Wever

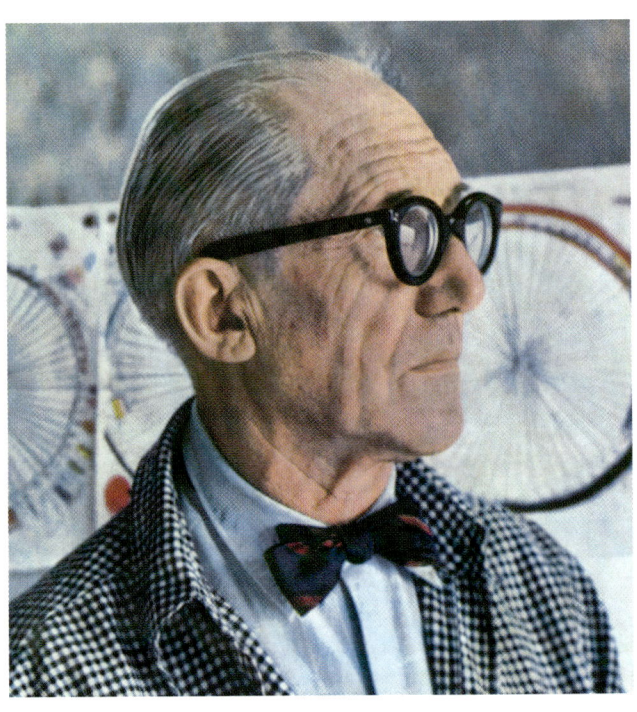

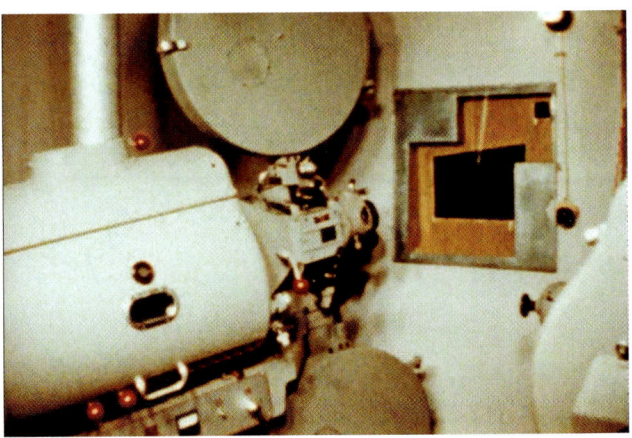

3.1
On the left, Le Corbusier, with sheets of paper with circles in the background, part of an early version of the *minutage*. Each circle represents one minute, divided into 60 seconds, which specifies from one second to the next what should be on view during *Le poème électronique*. On the right, the first minute of this *minutage*, which is also visible to the left of Le Corbusier.

3.2
One of the two Philips FP56 projectors in the projection booth on the ground floor of the Philips Pavilion.

A range of light effects were used in the performance *Le poème électronique*. Prominent among them were so-called *écran* and *tri-trous* film images that were projected onto the walls of the Philips Pavilion. In conjunction with the film images, areas of colour or *ambiances* were projected, the aim being to heighten the psycho-physiological sensations that Le Corbusier sought to induce in visitors. Two employees from the Office of Lighting Advice [Lichtadviesbureau] at Philips were put in charge of creating the light effects, and others working at the Philips Pavilion soon took to calling them 'the decorators'. They were responsible for projecting the *tri-trous* films and *ambiances* onto the pavilion's walls. The efforts to create the light effects in line with Le Corbusier's intentions ran up against serious technical problems. When Philips' General Art Director, Louis Kalff, later wrote, looking back at the event, that the combination of the photographic images with colour and light had been 'only partly successful', it was something of an understatement.

The Performance *Le poème électronique*

What Philips Lightbulb Factories Ltd. sought to achieve in the Philips Pavilion at the 1958 Brussels World's Fair was a synthesis of light, space, colour, and sound, such as never seen before, in a demonstration that would focus less on exhibiting Philips' products themselves than on showing what could be achieved with them.[1] The architect Le Corbusier accepted the commission for the pavilion and the demonstration mainly because of the opportunity it gave him to design a totally new sound and light show, thus creating a *Gesamtkunstwerk*: an artwork that would be a synthesis of different art forms. Le Corbusier made his acceptance conditional on the participation of the experimental composer Edgard Varèse – a Frenchman living in the United States – whom he wanted to provide the musical part of the performance.[2] The performance staged by Le Corbusier and Varèse became known as *Le poème électronique*. It consisted of an eight-minute musical composition by Varèse combined with light effects designed by Le Corbusier, which included film images and colour projections. Le Corbusier's script, with its detailed instructions on which film images and projections were to be shown for each second of *Le poème électronique*, was dubbed the *minutage*.[3]

Le Corbusier's ambitious plans created a plethora of technical difficulties for Philips.[4] In the end, it was the light effects of the performance *Le poème électronique*, rather than the architecture and the music, that caused most problems for the lightbulb company in its presentation.

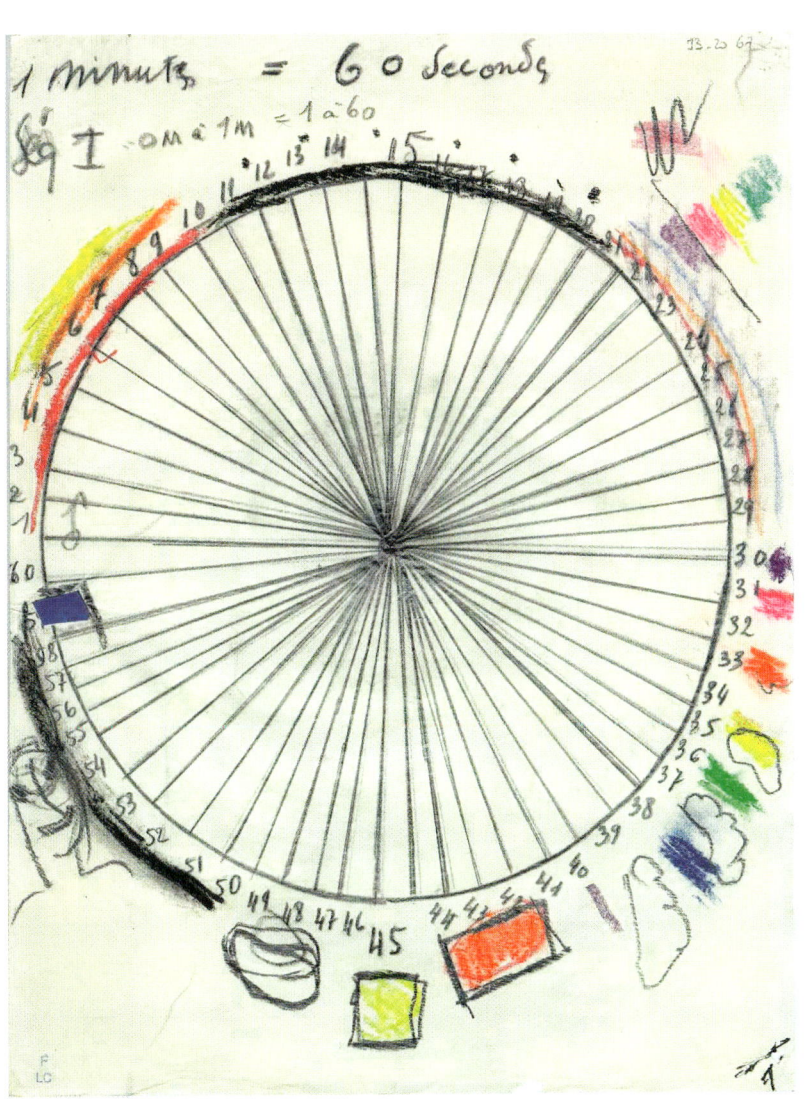

The *Écran* and *Tri-trous* Films

Film images constituted a prominent part of *Le poème électronique*. The Philips Pavilion had two projection booths from which film images were projected on the opposite walls. Each one had two projectors for the simultaneous projection of two different 35-mm films that had been given the names *écran* and *tri-trous*.

The *écran* [screen] can be seen as the main film, consisting of black-and-white images illustrating the theme of *Le poème électronique*,[5] which was to show 'our civilization [setting] out to conquer modern times'.[6] The first part of the *écran* film showed images of cultures from the past, while the second part showed images of contemporary science, which – in the form of engineers, atom bombs, telescopes and architecture – had supplanted the old icons.[7] The film was a collaborative venture involving Le Corbusier, the author, editor, graphic designer, and publisher Jean Petit,[8] the filmmaker Philippe Agostini, and Jan Coolen, art director at Joop Geesink's Dollywood Studios.[9] Working on the basis of Le Corbusier's script, Petit collected the photographic documentation that Agostini used to make the film.[10] At a later stage, the actual making of the film was handed over to the Dollywood Studios in Duivendrecht, near Amsterdam.[11] Some of the images for the film, most notably those depicting sculptures from different cultures, were taken from the books *Le musée imaginaire de la sculpture mondiale* by André Malraux and *L'esprit des formes* by Élie Faure. Others derived from various museums, such as the Musée de l'Homme and the Musée d'Histoire Naturelle.[12]

The *tri-trous* film was recorded at a late stage as part of *Le poème électronique*. On 1 June 1957, Le Corbusier had met with Louis Kalff in Paris and explained that he envisaged a film consisting largely of black-and-white photographs enclosed by areas of colour linked to coloured light on the surrounding walls.[13] It was in a letter of 26 October to Kalff that Le Corbusier first mentioned that the performance needed to include a *tri-trous* (derived from 'trois trous', meaning three holes), without illuminating the term at all.[14] During a subsequent visit to Paris on 15 November, Kalff began to get a clearer picture of the *tri-trous*, which Le Corbusier described as an extremely important new element of *Le poème électronique*. It consisted of 'projected images, largely black-and-white, but in some cases simple coloured filters, which constantly appear and disappear in three places on both sides of the pavilion'. This was theoretically to be achieved by setting

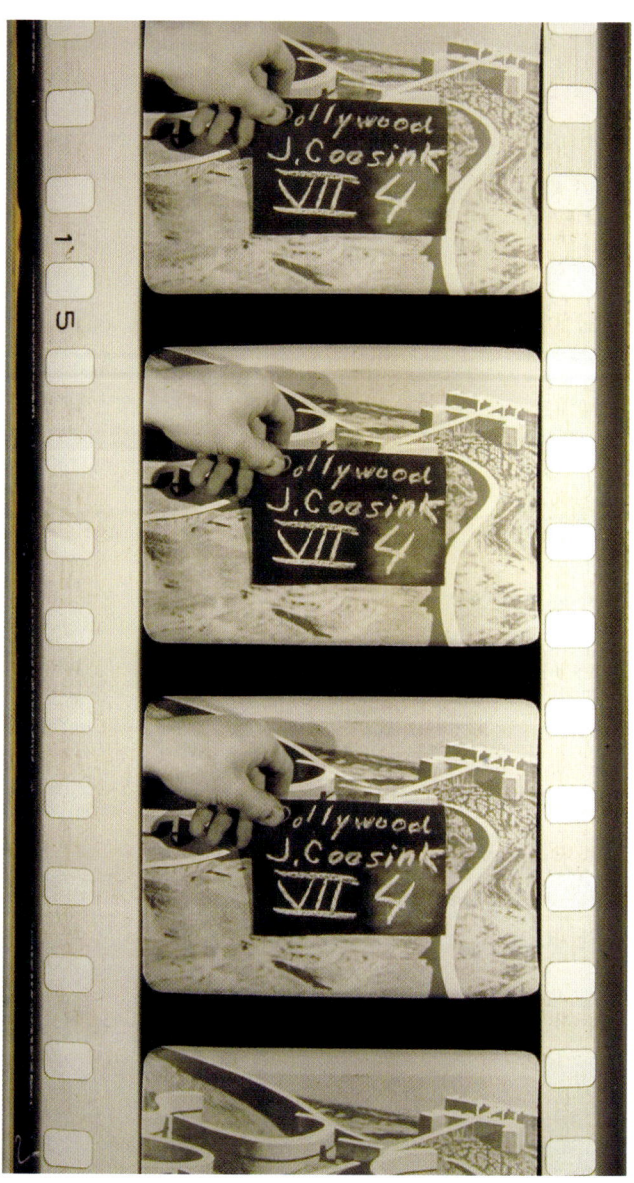

3.3
Three images from a 35-mm strip rush print of the *écran* film. This is the first positive copy of an original camera negative. The name 'J. Coosink' on the blackboard is probably a composite name formed from Joop Geesink and Jan Coolen, founder and art director, respectively, of the Dollywood Studios. The code 'VII 4' indicates a recording of an image for the seventh sequence, *To all mankind*, of *Le poème électronique*. This image is a model of Le Corbusier's Plan Obus for the city of Algiers.

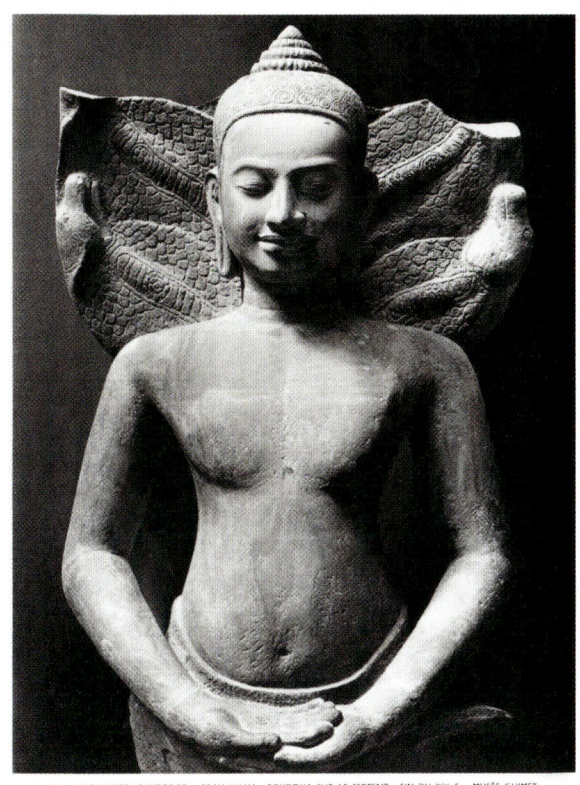
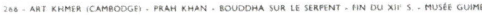
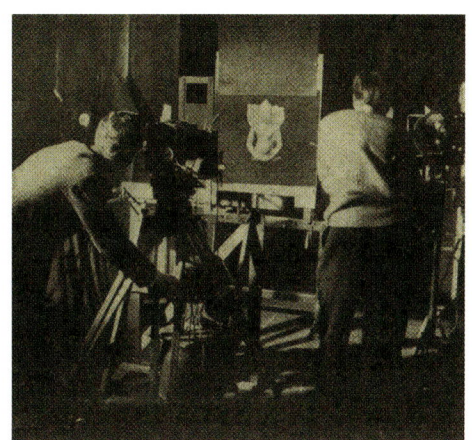
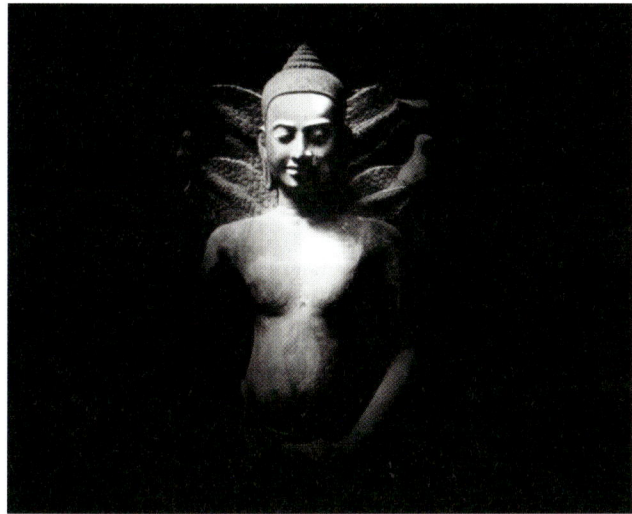
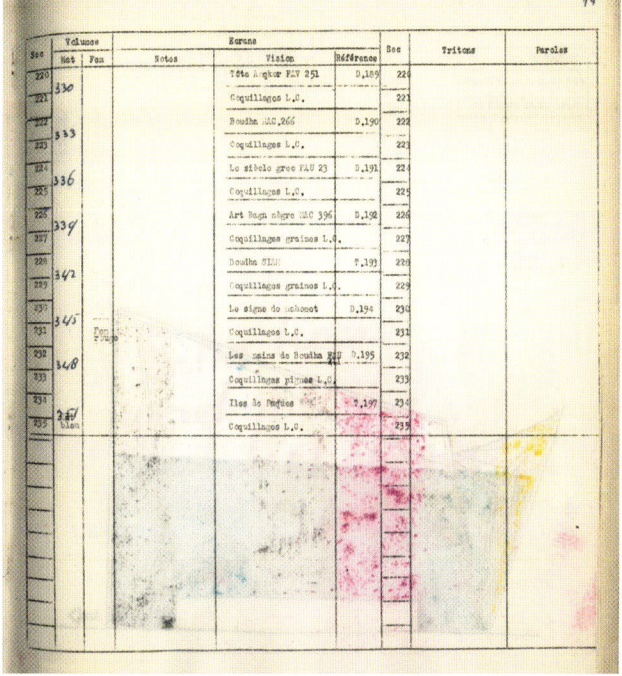

3.4
A picture from the book *Le musée imaginaire de la sculpture mondiale* by André Malraux (top left) is converted into film in Joop Geesink's Dollywood Studios (top right). According to the *minutage définitif* of *Le poème électronique* (bottom right) the image appears by the name *Boudha* at the 222nd second in the fourth sequence, *Man-made gods*, in the *écran* film (bottom left).

up an automatic operating system that would project slides through different diaphragms which might be circular, square, or triangular, for instance – with a maximum diameter of three metres per projection.[15] Le Corbusier initially thought that the desired effect could be achieved using six 16-mm projectors.[16] In January 1958, Philips suggested to Le Corbusier that the *tri-trous* could be achieved using light projections or with a separate colour film. Although the latter option meant that both reserve projectors in the booths would have to be used for the projection of the *tri-trous*,[17] this solution was nonetheless adopted. A strip of film was made, also at Dollywood Studios,[18] that was completely opaque, with the exception of three places in which images and colours had been added. A four-mirror construction on the outside of the projection booth apertures made it possible to project the *tri-trous* images around the *écran* images on the opposite walls.[19] These mirrors had to be adjusted with great precision, which was one of the tasks of J.A.M. Binnendijk and J. van Eeghen of Philips' Office of Lighting Advice who were usually dressed in white dustcoats. The two were nicknamed 'the decorators' by the pavilion manager, Simon de Bruin.[20]

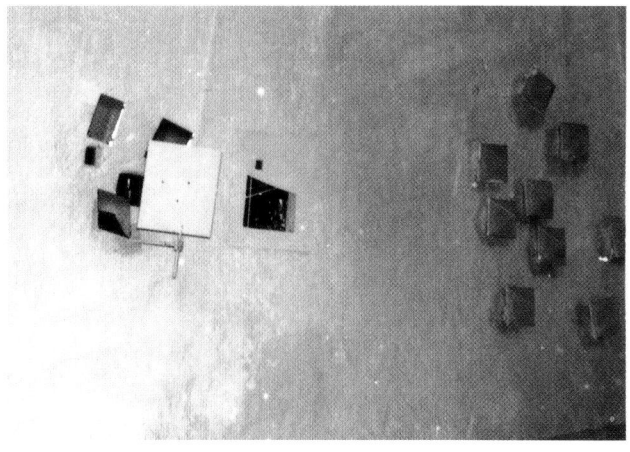

3.5
View of the two projection apertures in the projection booth on the first floor of the Philips Pavilion. On the right, the aperture for the projector of the *écran* film can be seen. In front of the projection aperture on the left, the four-mirror construction is visible that was used to project the three *tri-trous* film images around the *écran* image on the opposite wall. On the far right, a group of loudspeakers is visible.

3.6
One triangular and one square *tri-trous* projection on the walls of the Philips Pavilion; the *écran* projections from both projection booths are visible. Lucien Hervé photograph, 1958.

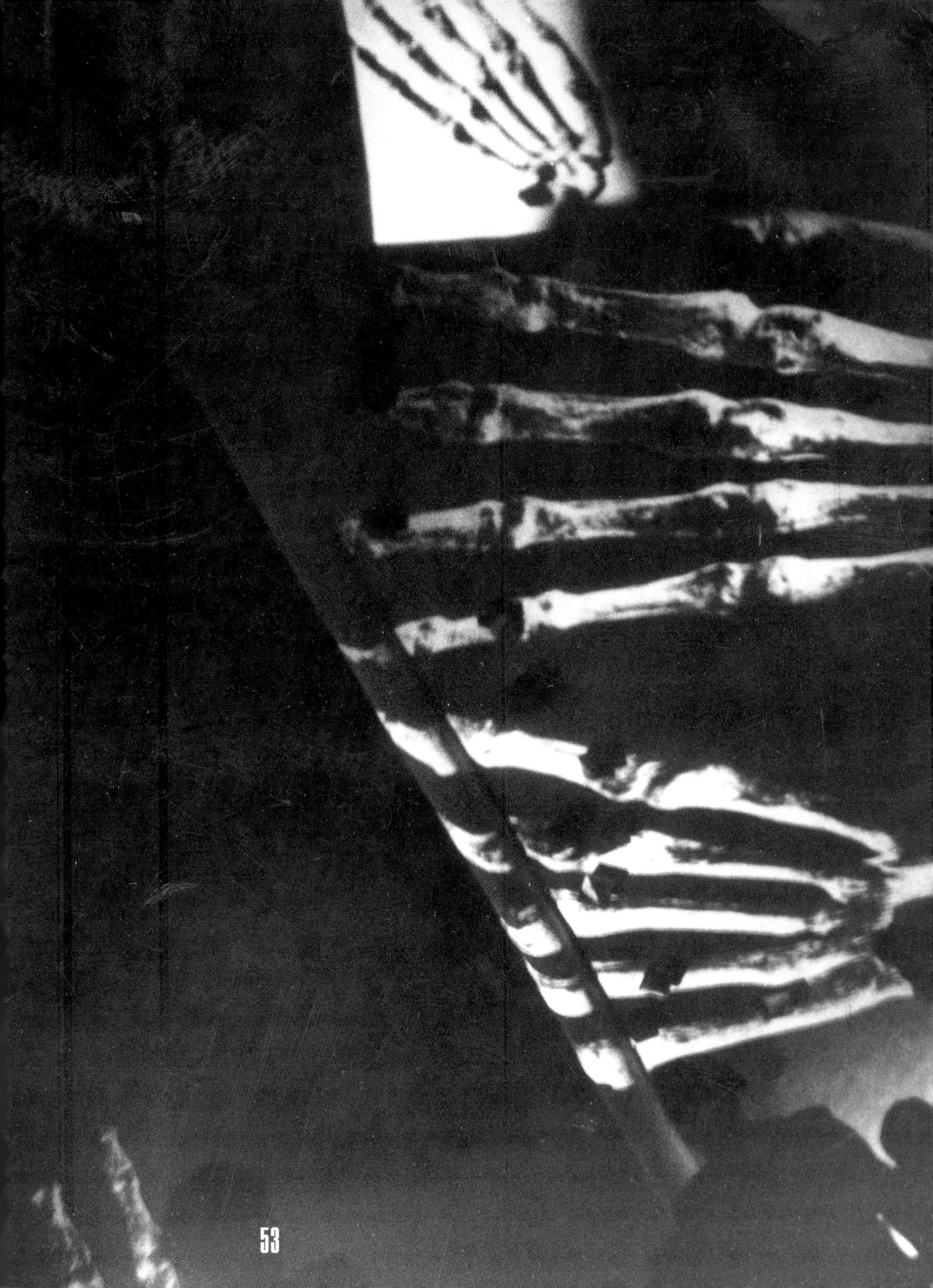

Retrieval of the *Tri-trous* Film

A 35-mm negative copy and a positive copy of the *écran* film have been preserved in the archives of the EYE Film Institute Netherlands, Amsterdam, for many years.[21] The original material of the *tri-trous* film was assumed to have been lost.[22] In the spring of 2009, however, it turned out that after the end of the World's Fair, the projectionist Max Naveaux had been given permission to take positive copies of both the final *écran* film and the *tri-trous* film from the Philips Pavilion home with him. Through the mediation of projectionist Paul Vancoppenolle, both films have since been handed over to the author, who has transferred them to the EYE Film Institute Netherlands for safekeeping in its storage facility. EYE has had the *tri-trous* film digitized by Cineric film laboratory in New York, as far as possible restoring the original colours. The images on the original *tri-trous* film show that the makers adhered, to some extent, to the original idea of using circular, square and triangular projections. Within the three *tri-trous* frameworks, black and white alternate with several hues of red, blue, yellow, green and purple. This corresponds to the colours specified for the *tri-trous* film images in Le Corbusier's final *minutage* of 2 March 1958, which is known as the *minutage définitif*.[23] In addition, the *tri-trous* frames show a range of partly coloured images, some of which corresponded to the *écran* film images.

The *minutage définitif* describes in detail the seven consecutive sequences of *Le poème électronique*: *Genesis*, *Spirit and Matter*, *From darkness to dawn*, *Man-made gods*, *How time moulds civilization*, *Harmony*, and *To all mankind*.[24] The first film images of the performance *Le poème électronique*, which appear, according to the *minutage définitif*, at 0'31", are *tri-trous* images, which are described as *La danse des singes* [Dance of the Apes].[25] In the original film material, this appears to be a rather naïve-looking animation of apes swinging from branches. This animation does not occur in the *écran* film, and therefore does not feature in present-day reconstructions of *Le poème électronique* that are based solely on the *écran* images.[26] It confirms that the *tri-trous* film should be regarded as a fully-fledged element of *Le poème électronique*. In this context, the *tri-trous* is described on the one hand as images engaging in a 'conversation' with the *écran*,[27] and on the other hand as images with 'the power

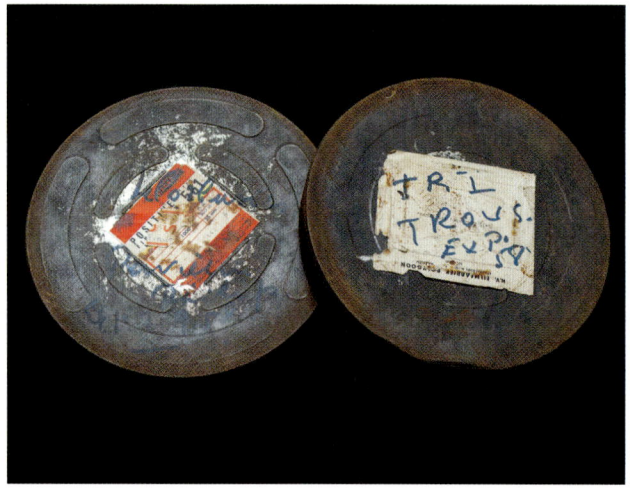

3.7
The film canisters in which the projectionist Max Naveaux kept the original *écran* and *tri-trous* films from the Philips Pavilion for 51 years.

3.8
The first film images of *Le poème électronique*, which according to the *minutage définitif* appear at 0'31", are *tri-trous* images described as *La danse des singes* [Dance of the Apes].

3.9
The first images of the *écran* film, which according to the *minutage définitif* appear at 0'40", are consecutive projections of a bull and a toreador.

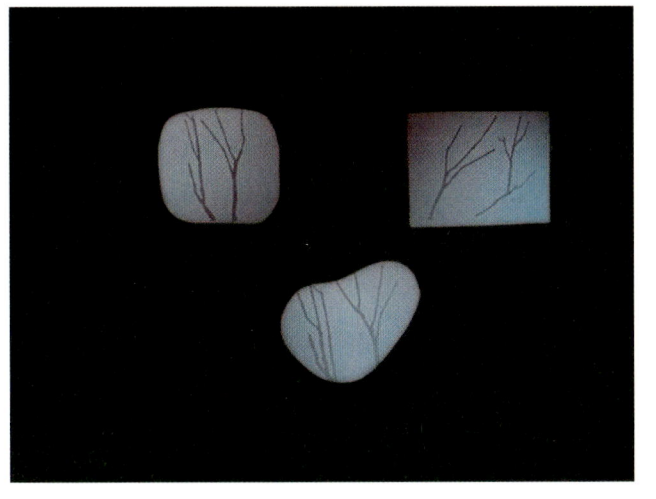
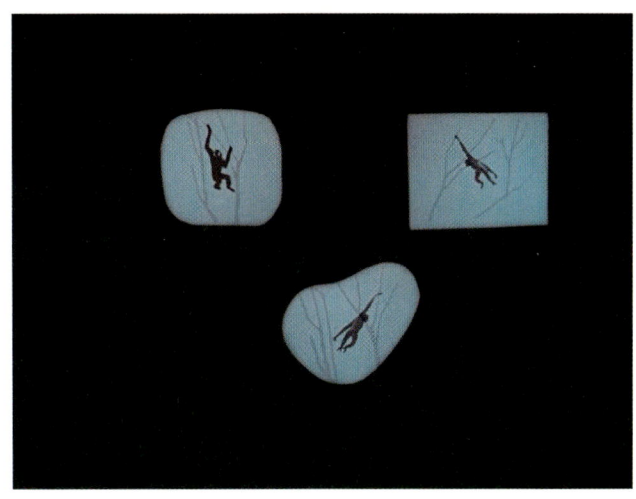
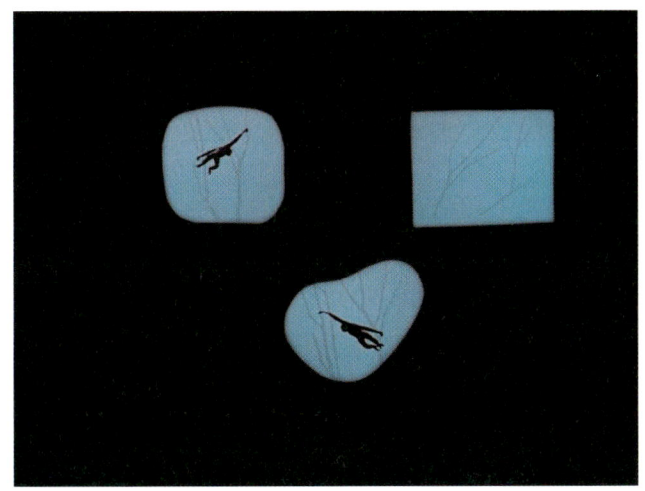
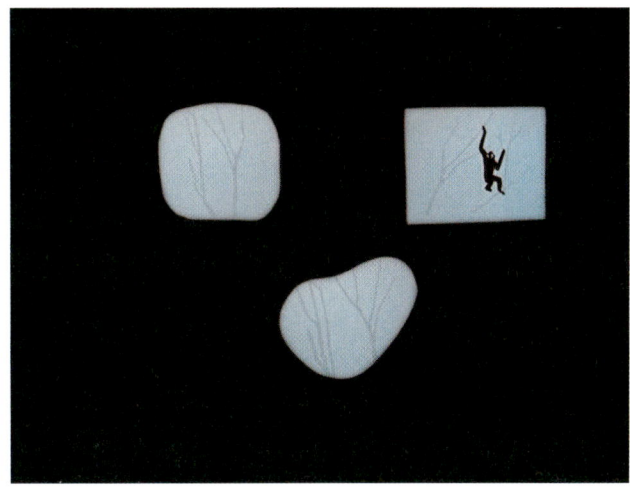
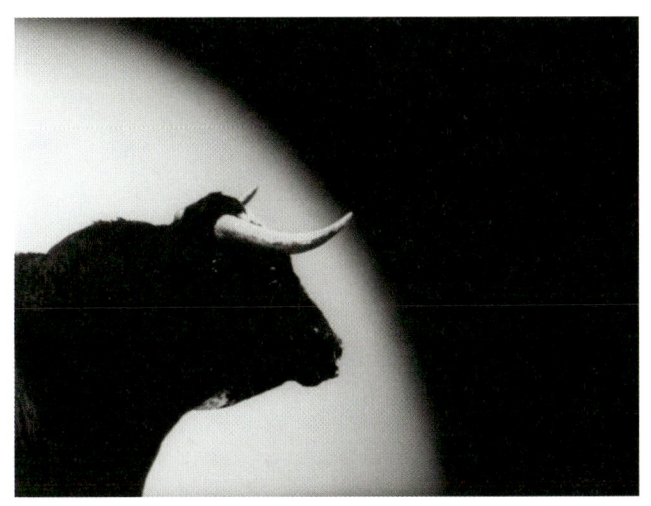
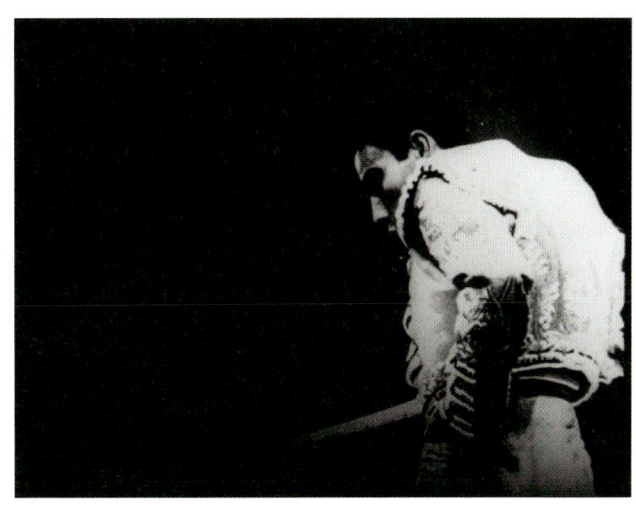

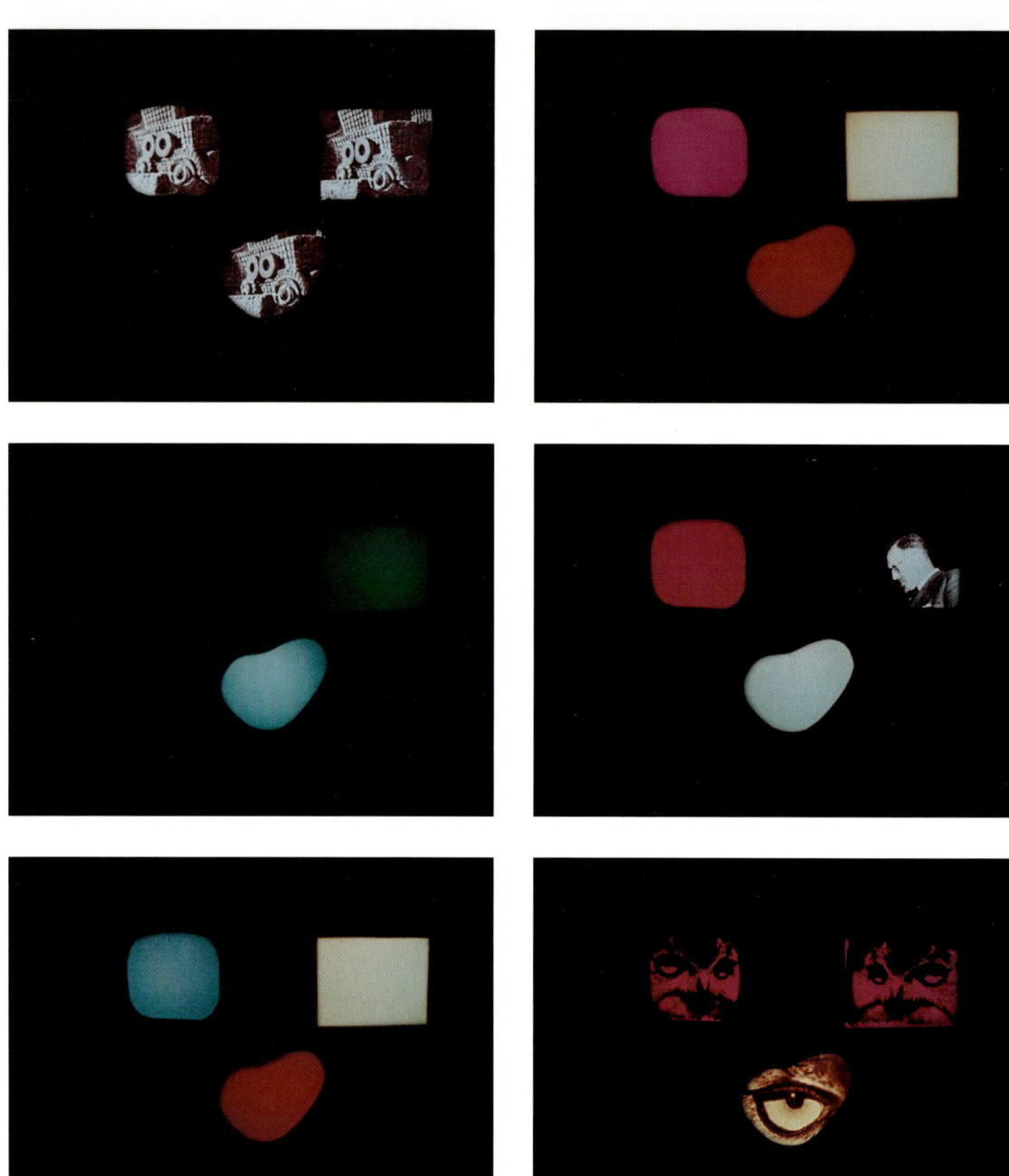

3.10
Different chronological images from the *tri-trous* film. Within the circular, square or triangular frameworks, different images were shown alternately, and black and white alternated with different hues of red, blue, yellow, green and purple.

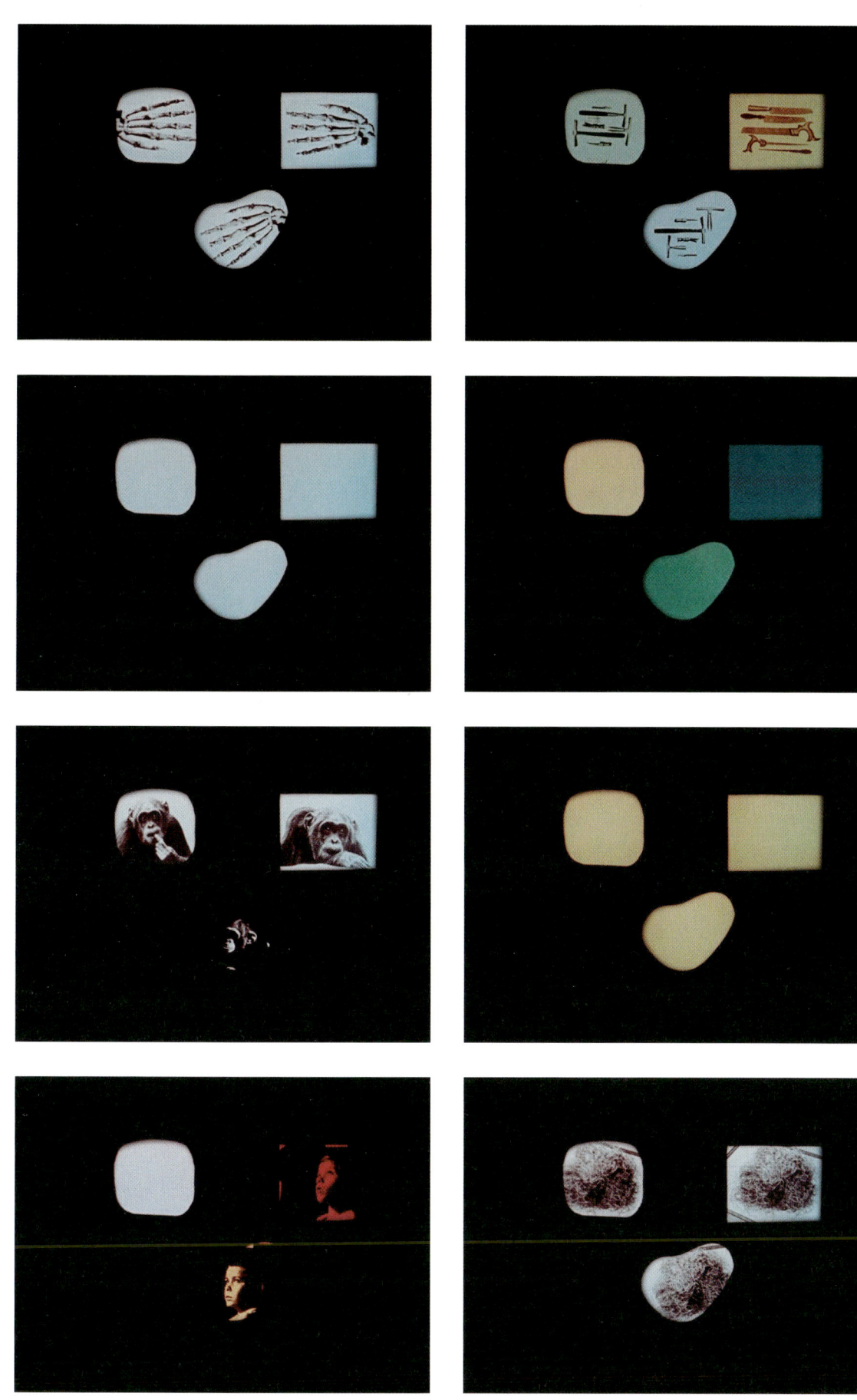

57

to override the narrative of the *écran* images'.²⁸ The first film images of the *écran*, which appear, according to the *minutage définitif*, at 0'40", are consecutive projections of a bull and a toreador. For four seconds, these images were to be projected simultaneously with *La danse des singes*.²⁹ One may easily posit a relationship between the *tri-trous* film images of apes and the subsequent *écran* images of a human being (the toreador) dominating nature (in the form of the bull) – a relationship that would fit well into *Genesis*, the first sequence of *Le poème électronique*. The images also correspond to the overall theme of the performance, which is to show 'our civilization [setting] out to conquer modern times'.³⁰ However, in this context, it is interesting to note that the *minutage définitif* contains a note stating that the images of the bull and the toreador bear no relation to the apes of the *tri-trous*.³¹

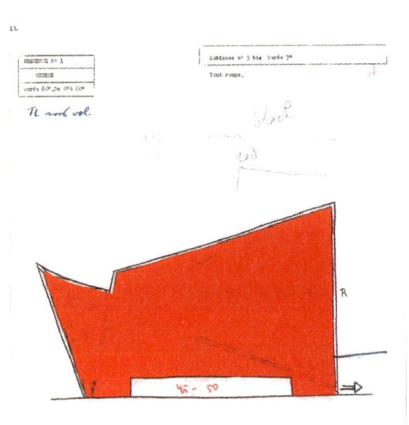 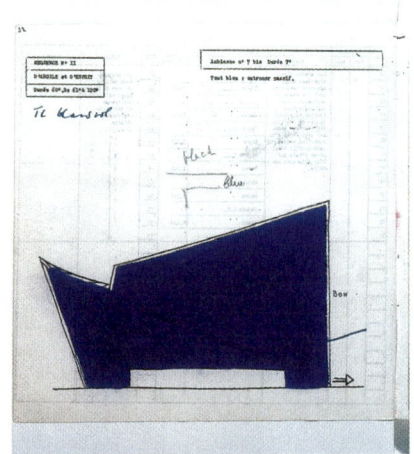 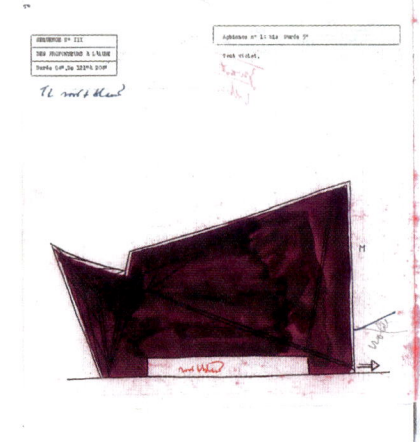

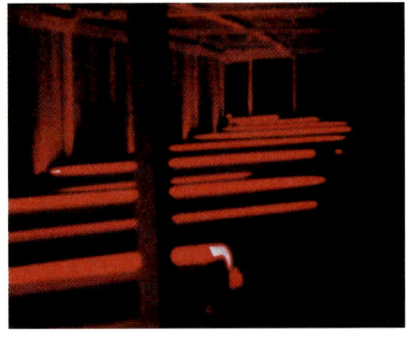 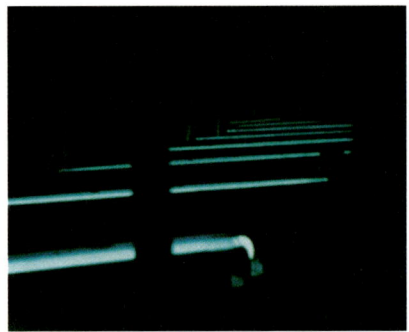 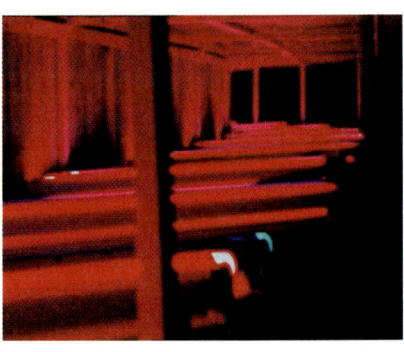

3.11
Three of the pages of Johan Jansen's personal copy of the *minutage définitif*, noting (from left to right) that red fluorescent light tubes, blue fluorescent light tubes, and a combination of the two should be used to create *ambiance* no. 5 bis, *ambiance* no. 7 bis, and *ambiance* no. 14 bis, which would flood the entire public area in red, blue and violet monochrome light, respectively.
Le Corbusier, *minutage définitif*, 1958.

3.12
View behind the balustrade in the public area during the performance of *Le poème électronique* for which (from left to right) red fluorescent light tubes, blue fluorescent light tubes, and a combination of the two were used.

Lighting in the Creation of the *Ambiances*

As far as the light effects in the performance of *Le poème électronique* are concerned, Le Corbusier distinguished – besides the *écran* and the *tri-trous* – elements he called *ambiances* and *volumes*. In addition, a red sun, a moon, stars, clouds, and lightning had to be conjured up during the performance. The *ambiances* were defined as areas of light designed to evoke a specific atmosphere. They were created by projecting coloured light onto the pavilion walls, with a distribution into zones that at times accentuated the architectural contours of the building. The *volumes* consisted of a female figure and a geometrical object composed of metal tubes, which hung opposite each other in the pavilion's apexes. Both *volumes* were coated with fluorescent paint. Under ultraviolet light, the human figure lit up in red, while the geometrical object appeared greenish-blue. The human figure symbolized matter and the geometrical object represented spirit. The red sun, the moon and the clouds were to be produced using projectors, the lightning with a lightning projector, and the stars with 50 lightbulbs distributed around the top of the pavilion walls.[32]

Two types of *ambiances* can be distinguished. The first category consisted of those that were largely associative in nature, in which the pavilion's walls were construed as a kind of sky in which sun and moon, stars, clouds and lightning, dawn, sunset and night appeared. The combination of these elements with the *écran* and *tri-trous* films can be read as images from the human world overlaid on a celestial surface. A second category of *ambiances* was that in which the entire pavilion was illuminated in one or more colours, thus immersing the public in a kind of colour bath. In this connection, Le Corbusier himself wrote that the colour environment – the red, black, yellow, green, white, blue – was intended to induce certain psycho-physiological sensations in the pavilion's visitors.[33]

The *ambiances* had to be created with the aid of fluorescent light tubes, floodlights, and projectors. Forty groups of five fluorescent light tubes were placed behind a 1.85-metre high balustrade in the public area, which followed the contours of the pavilion floor.[34] The 'decorators' had wrapped four fluorescent light tubes in each group in red, blue, yellow or green cellophane, cut to size.[35] The fluorescent lighting was strong enough to illuminate the entire space, or, with diminished current, to create the illusion of a luminous horizon.[36]

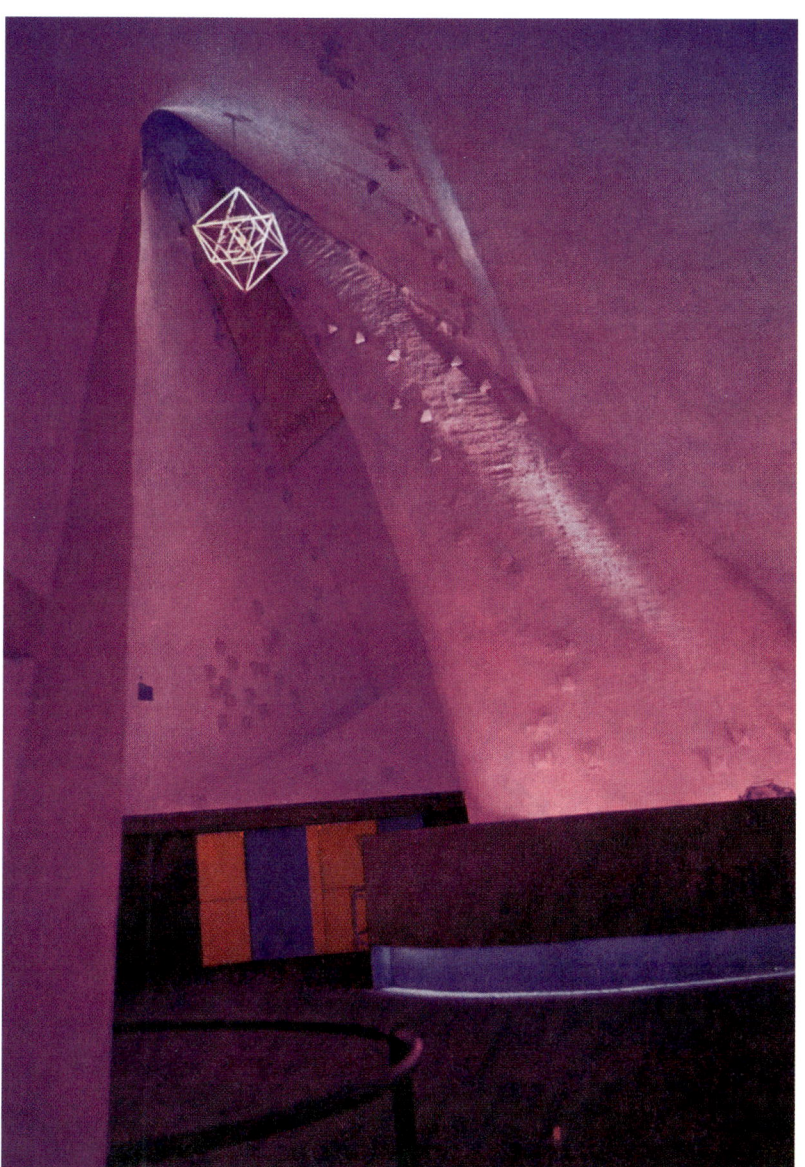

3.13
The public area of the Philips Pavilion, with a view of the closed entrance doors. Here, an *ambiance* **in the colour violet was created using fluorescent light tubes wrapped in coloured cellophane behind the balustrade.**

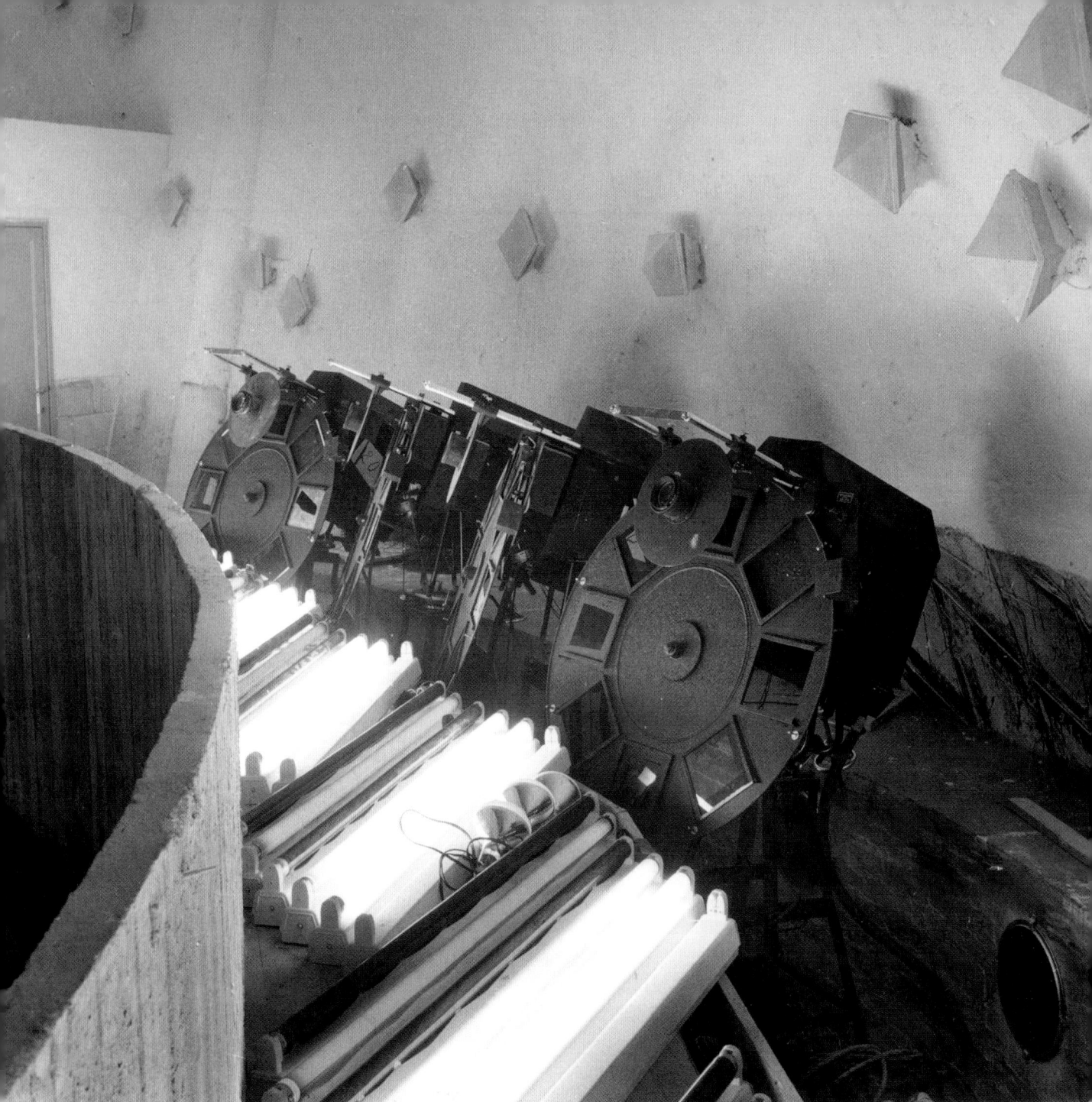

3.14
View behind the 1.85-metre high balustrade to the right of the projection booth in the public area, behind which several groups of fluorescent light tubes and four Reiche & Vogel projectors are visible.

3.15
A drawing of *ambiance* no. 9 on a page from Johan Jansen's personal copy of the *minutage définitif*. His notes make it clear that the glowing border was to be created by using a low current in green fluorescent light tubes. The red colours in the apexes of the pavilion were to be produced using floodlights that Jansen indicated with the letters VC. The red sun was to be produced using a projector. Le Corbusier, *minutage définitif*, 1958.

3.16
View behind the balustrade to the left of the projection booth in the public area in which twelve floodlights wrapped in coloured cellophane can be seen that were used to project specific colours in the apexes of the pavilion. Also visible are two Tovèrli projectors, several groups of fluorescent light tubes, and in the foreground four spotlights.

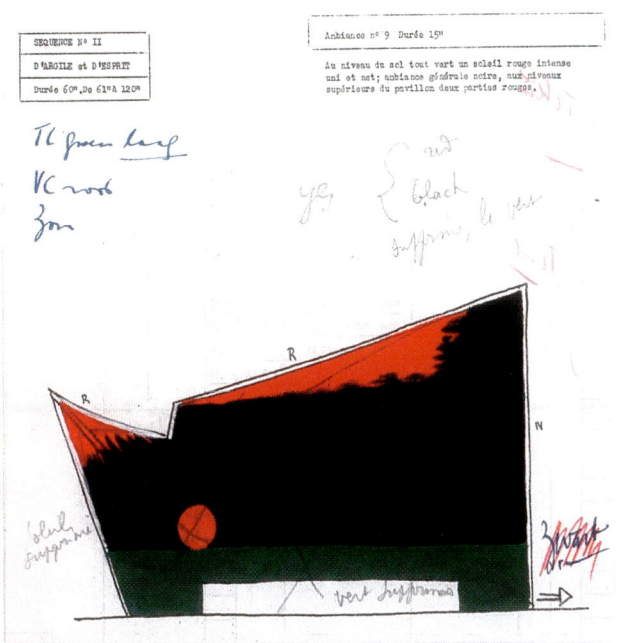

61

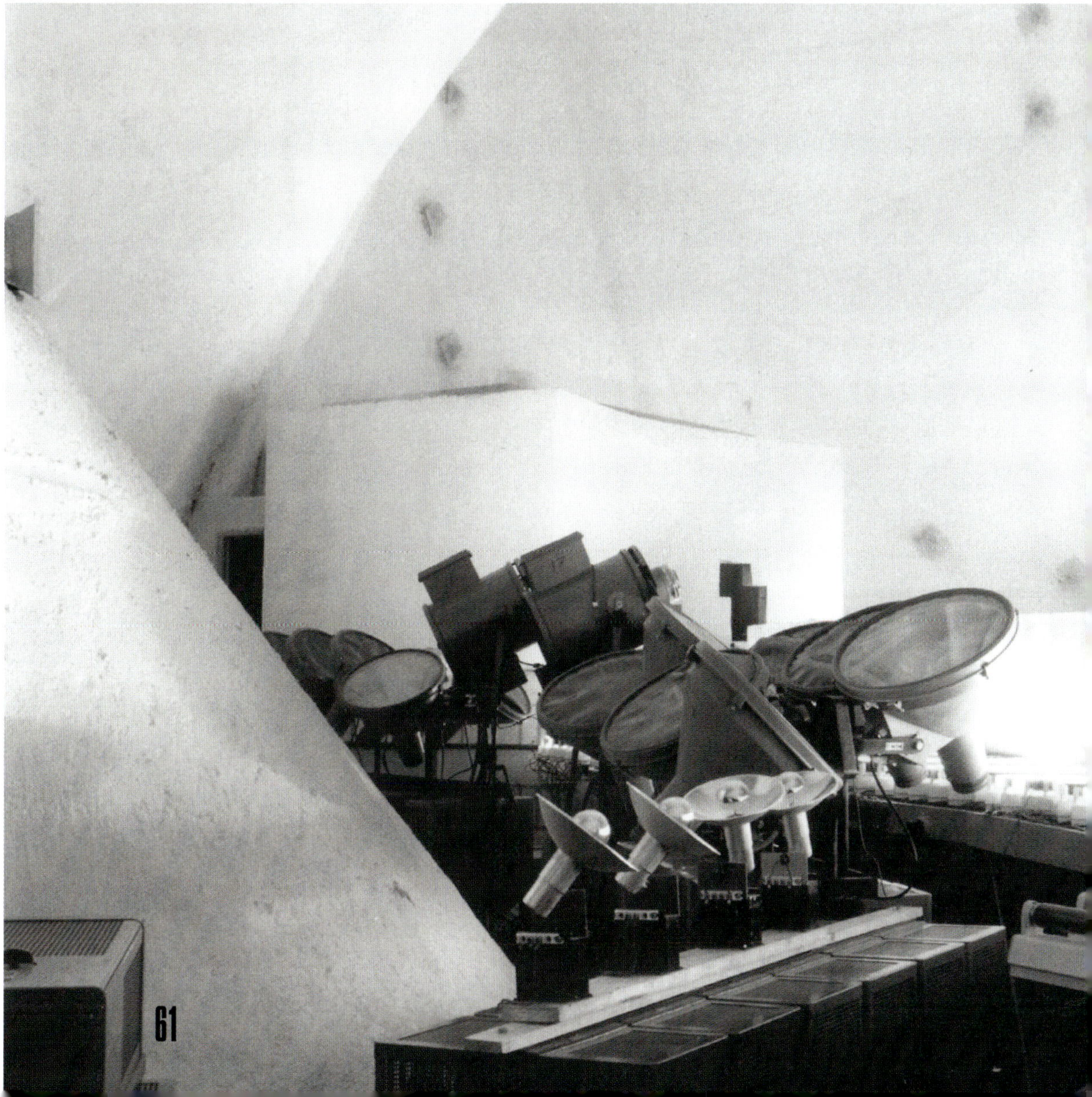

The Getty Research Institute possesses Johan Jansen's personal copy of the *minutage définitif*. Jansen was a lighting expert attached to the Office of Lighting Advice, and had been sent to Brussels in the capacity of 'overall troubleshooter'.[37] The copy contains his notes on the use of the different light sources, which helps to clarify how specific *ambiances* could be achieved. For instance, next to an *ambiance* that would flood the entire space with red light, Jansen wrote 'TL [=fluorescent lighting] red, full'. Next to a similar light effect in the colour violet, his note reads 'TL red + blue', indicating that he used additive colour mixing of two primary colours to produce a secondary colour.[38]

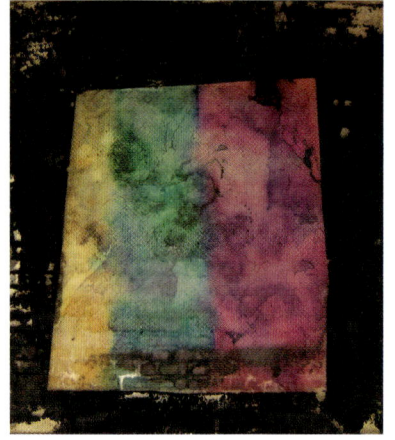
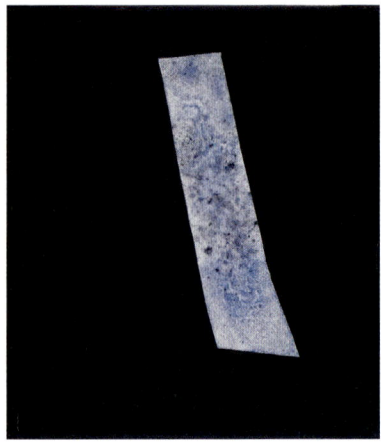

The floodlights were equipped with 500-watt lightbulbs that could project red, yellow and blue colour accents on the walls. They were installed in three places behind the balustrade in the public area. The decorators wrapped the glass covers of the floodlights, like the fluorescent tubes, in coloured cellophane, and they were also responsible for directing the light beams.[39] It is assumed that these beams were used to achieve the specific colours in the apexes of the pavilion, which were present, according to the *minutage définitif*, in five *ambiances*.[40] The number of floodlights installed in the pavilion was increased several times during the World's Fair.[41]

Projection in the Creation of the *Ambiances*

The *ambiances* were in part created by the projection of coloured glass slides for which a total of eight projectors were installed at various places in the Philips Pavilion.[42] Four 3,000-watt projectors made by the German manufacturer Reiche & Vogel could be used to project a series of 18x18 cm square glass slides on the pavilion walls. To achieve this, each projector was equipped with a rotating disk accommodating eight slides.[43] In the collections of the Art Committee of Eindhoven University of Technology and the Getty Research Institute, a total of 26 different glass slides are preserved that were used with the Reiche & Vogel projectors in the Philips Pavilion. Some of these slides are monochrome, while others have horizontal or vertical coloured strips, which correspond, in part at least, to colour patterns in the *minutage définitif*.[44] Some of the slides have been badly damaged or have become discoloured. This, combined with the fact that the surviving slides are probably not a

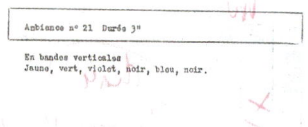
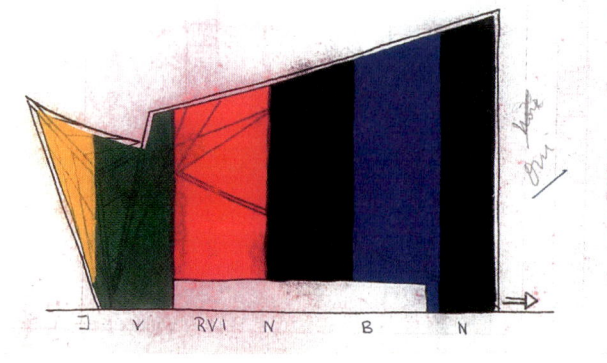

3.17
By projecting the two glass slides, shown at the top, side by side, using Reiche & Vogel projectors, it was possible to produce ambiance no. 21, shown at the bottom, as depicted in the ambiances. Philips, glass slides for *ambiances*, 1958; Le Corbusier, *minutage definitif*, 1958.

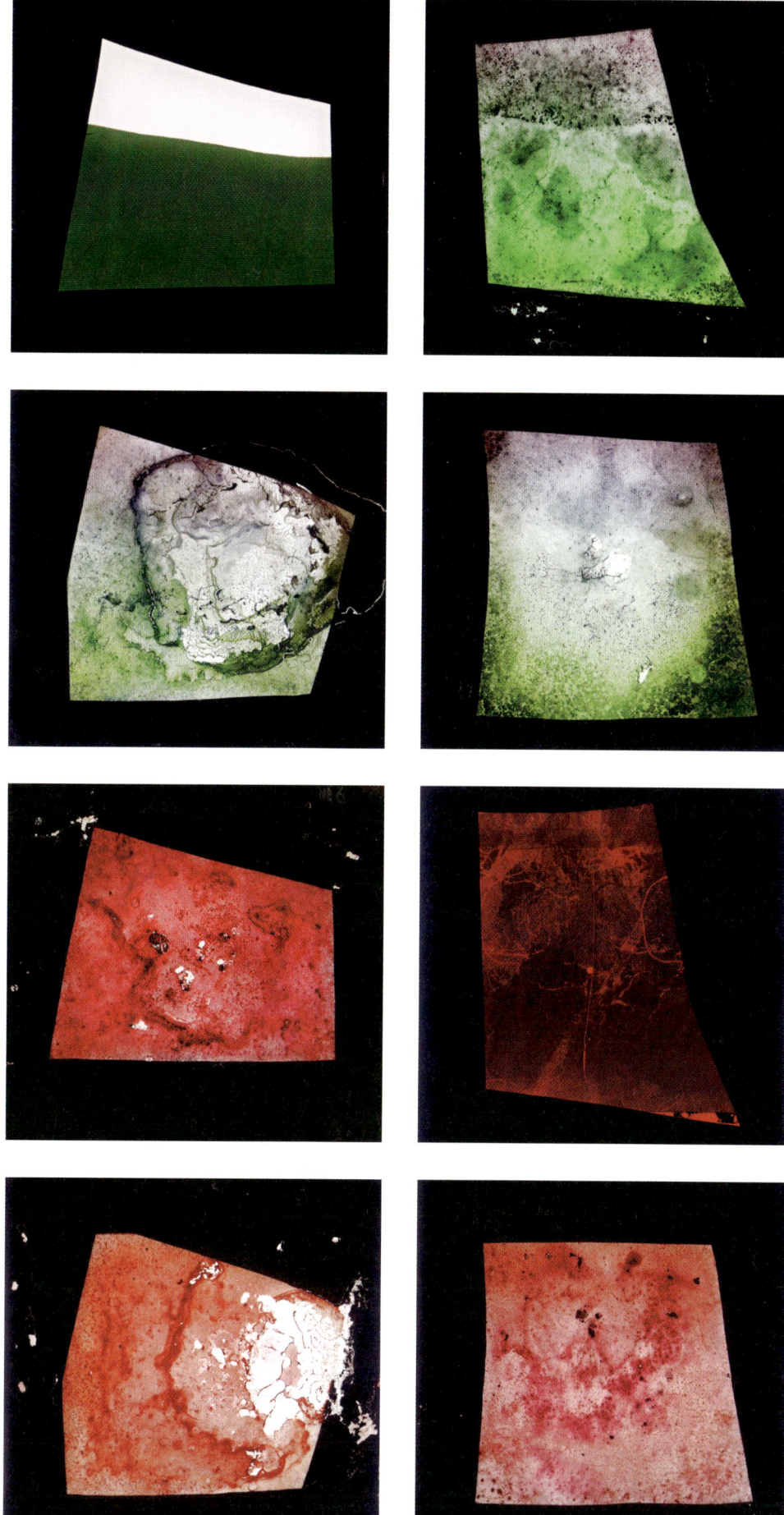

3.18
Two sets of four glass slides for the Reiche & Vogel projectors, in which the four different contours can be recognized that are found in the majority of the glass slides. These contours probably corresponded to the shape of the walls on which the glass slides were projected. Philips, glass slides for *ambiances*, 1958.

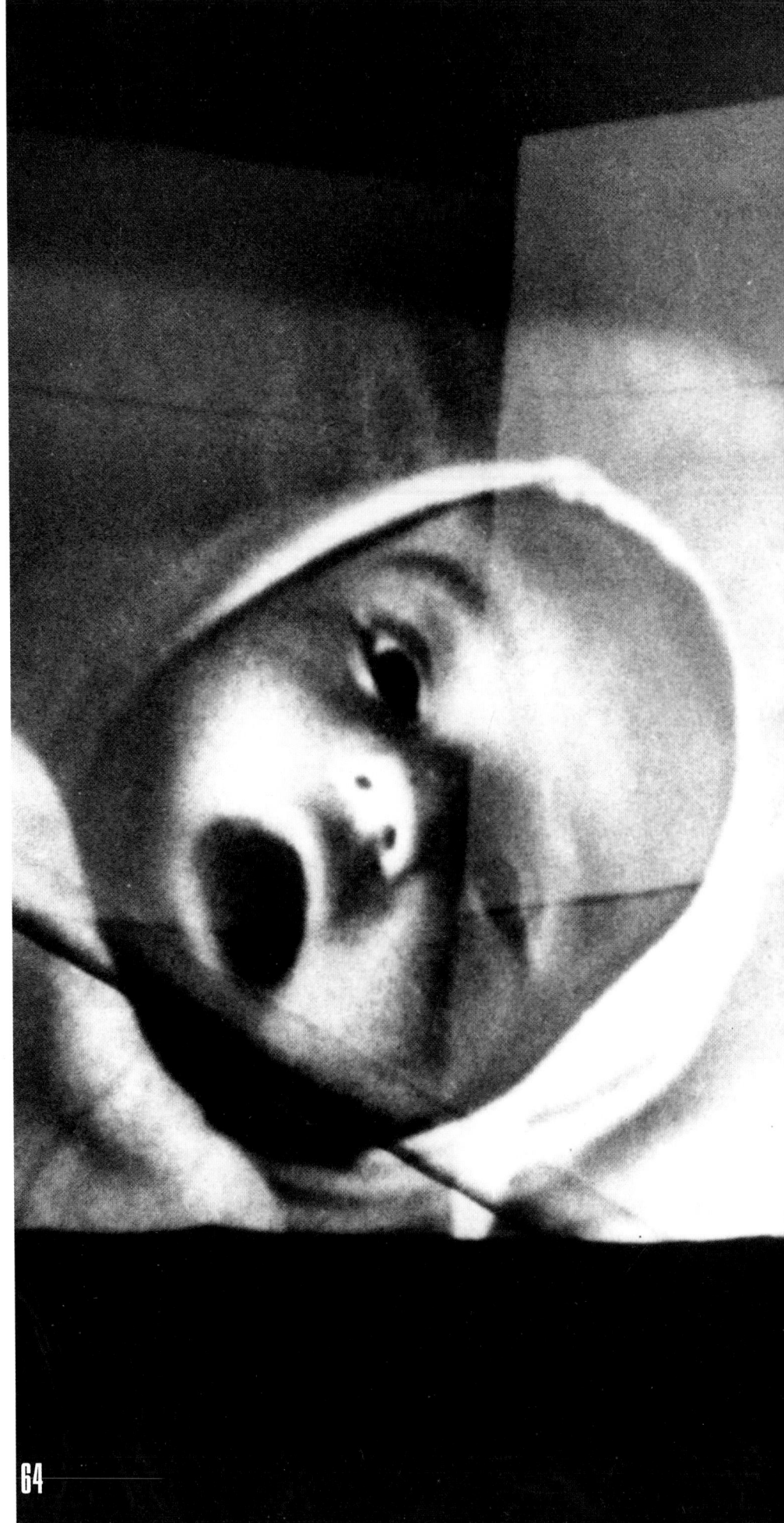

3.19
To the right of the *écran* image, the projection – using a Reiche & Vogel projector – of a glass slide with horizontal strips is visible.
Lucien Hervé photograph, 1958.

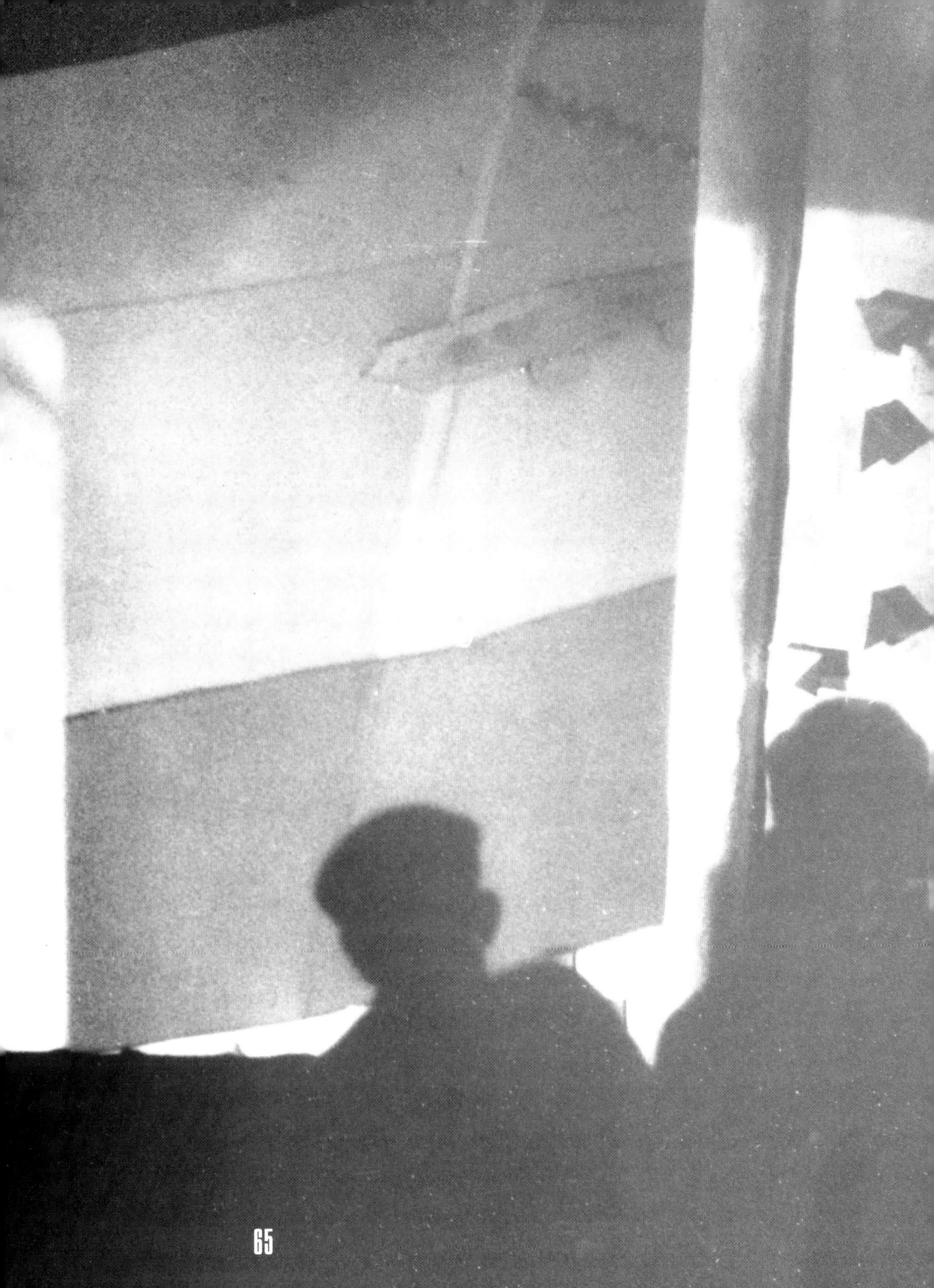

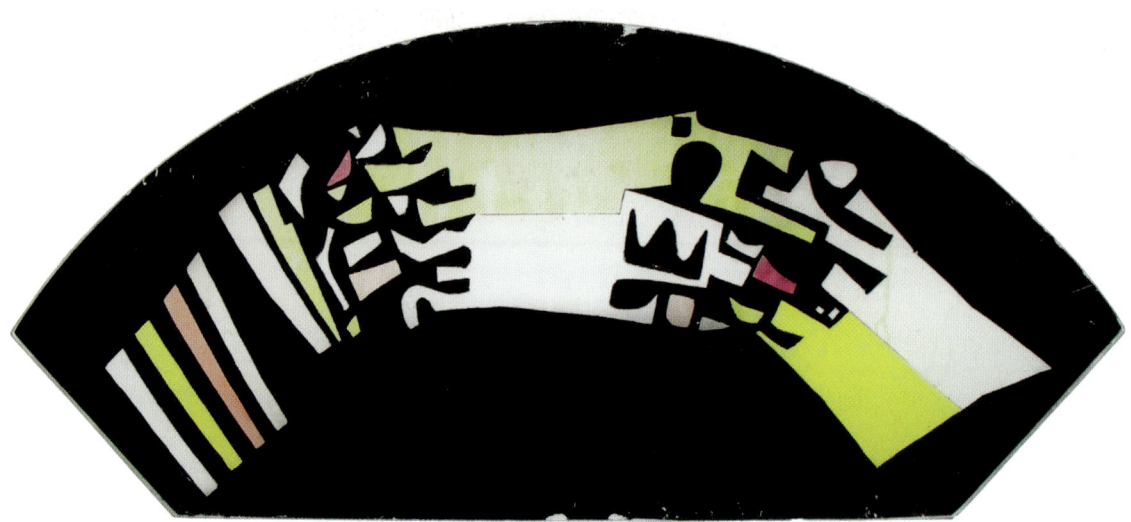

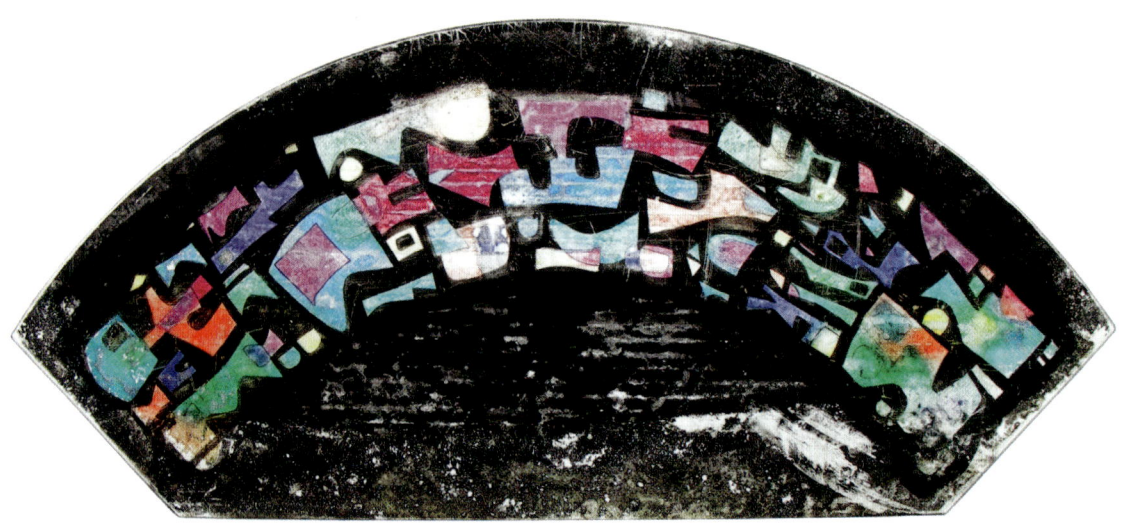

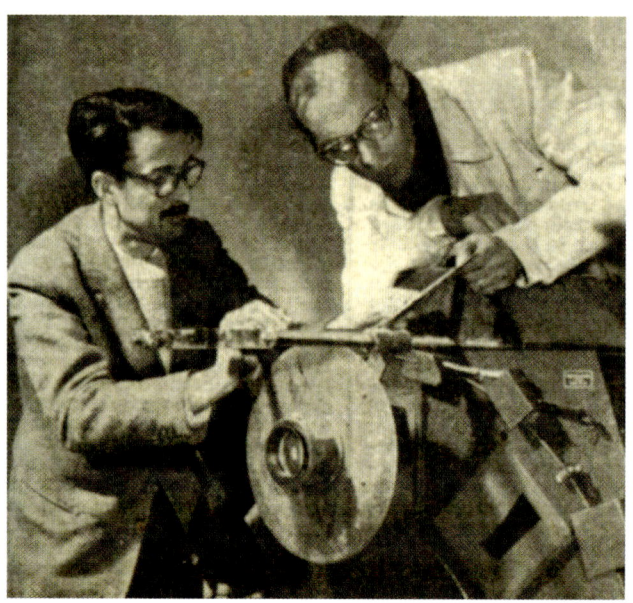

3.20
The two employees from Philips' Office of Lighting Advice who were known as 'the decorators', J. van Eeghen (left) and J.A.M. Binnendijk (right), studying a glass slide beside a Reiche & Vogel projector.

3.21
Two fan-shaped glass slides for the Tovèrli projectors in the Philips Pavilion, the figurative patterns of which are representative of the twelve surviving specimens.

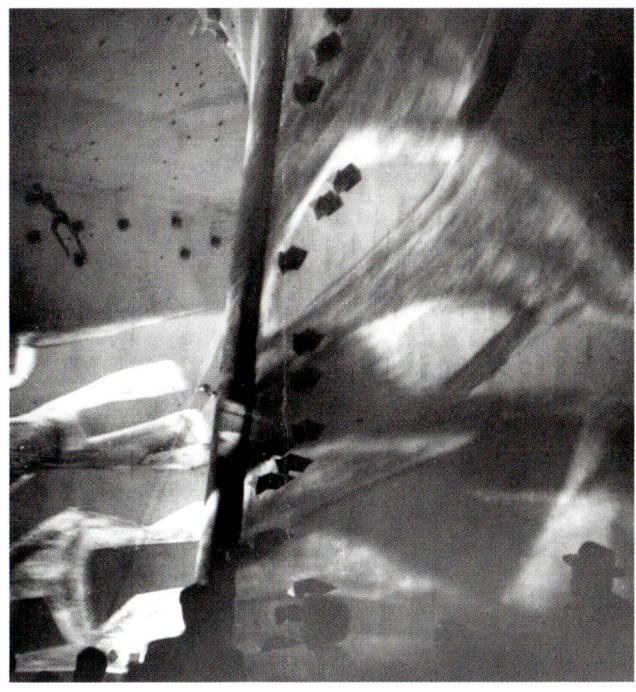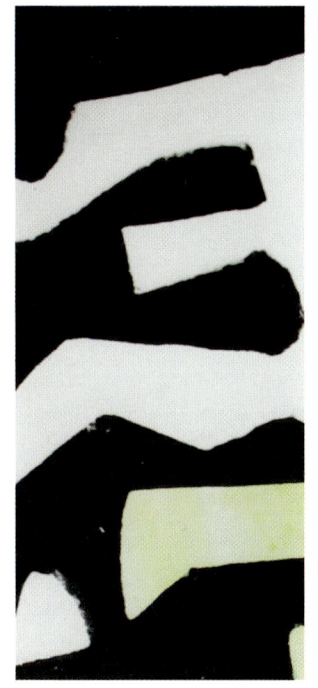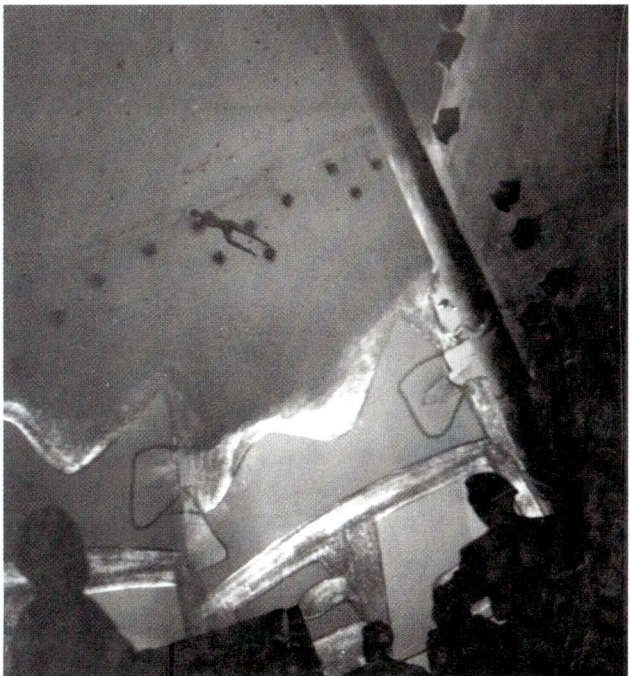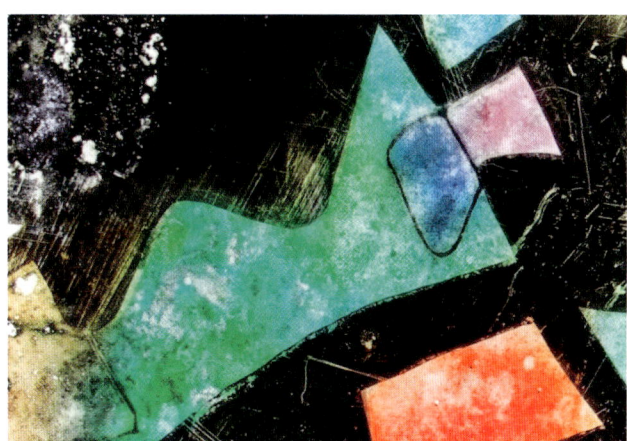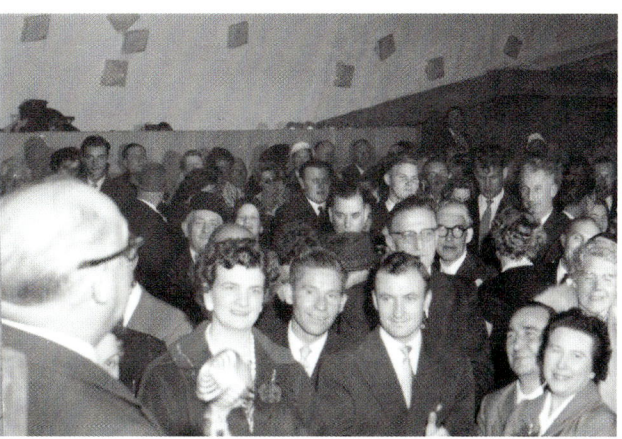

3.22
In the top left picture, a projection of a fan-shaped glass slide beamed by a Tovèrli projector is visible on the wall of the Philips Pavilion. In the bottom left picture, two identical images beamed by two Tovèrli projectors are visible, side by side. To the right of these pictures, the cut outs show the specific detail of the fan-shaped glass slide that was projected.
Lucien Hervé photographs, 1958.

3.23
Set up on the left behind the balustrade in the public area of the Philips Pavilion is a Tovèrli projector. This was a modified theatre spotlight which had been fitted with a lens to project images from a rotating disc.

complete set, means that it is not easy to fathom how and where they were used in the performance.

Since the film images of *Le poème électronique* were projected from two projection booths on the facing walls within the pavilion, it may be assumed that the Reiche & Vogel projectors beamed their images to the same walls. Since there were four Reiche & Vogel projectors, this suggests that it was possible to project glass slides from two projectors on each of these two walls, side by side. This would make it possible, for instance, to use two slides to produce *ambiance* no. 21 of the *minutage définitif*, which consisted of vertical stripes of different colours: these were (from left to right) yellow, green, violet, black, blue, and black.[45] In most of the glass slides, one of four distinct contours can be made out, which were probably intended to accentuate the architectural contours of the pavilion.[46] These contours probably corresponded to the shapes of the walls on which they were projected. The slides were made in the pavilion itself, by Binnendijk, one of the decorators, who used Ecoline in the colours red, yellow, green, orange, and black.[47] The decorators were also responsible for adjusting the direction of the projectors.[48]

In the collections of the Art Committee of Eindhoven University of Technology and the Getty Research Institute, there are also twelve fan-shaped glass slides, which are 75 cm wide and 32 cm high. On the basis of the figurative patterns on these slides, they can be divided into two sets of six with roughly identical motifs in each set.[49] There is a striking resemblance between these slides and Le Corbusier's paintings.[50] It has been speculated that the fan-shaped slides may be the remnants of an early attempt to project the *ambiances* that was subsequently abandoned.[51] However, several photographs from the collection of the Fondation Le Corbusier, as well as an 8-mm amateur film that was shot by projectionist Max Naveaux in the Philips Pavilion, show that these slides were in fact used at some point during the performance of *Le poème électronique*. For instance, in the 8-mm film it can be seen that a fan-shaped slide was projected between the last *écran* film images of the fourth sequence, *Man-made gods*, and the first *écran* images of the fifth sequence, *How time moulds civilization*. At this point the figurative patterns of the slide move across the pavilion wall, indicating that the slide was turned in front of a lens during projection.

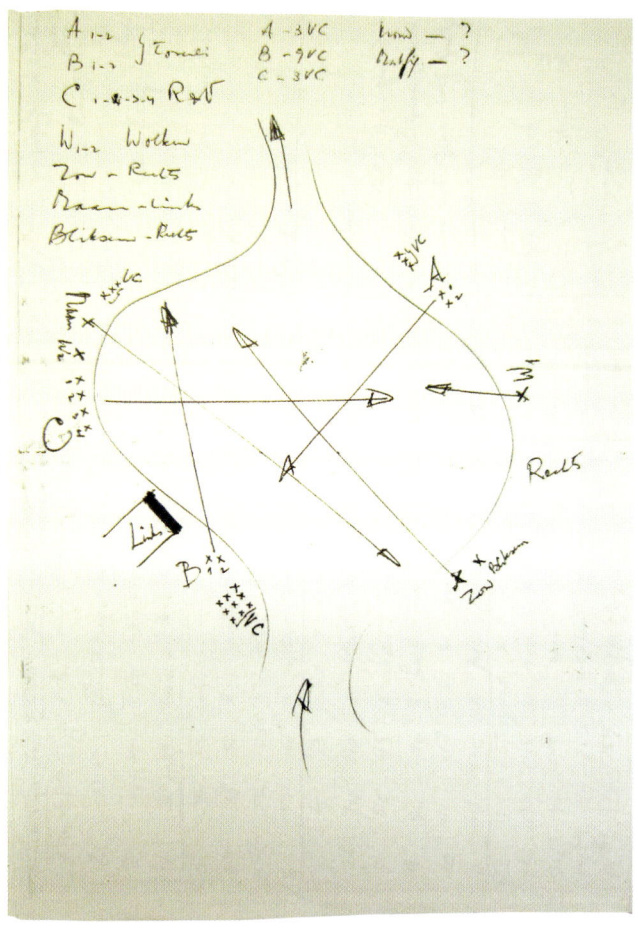

3.24
An undated sketch-like floor plan of the Philips Pavilion, probably made by Johan Jansen, states that four projectors made by the Dutch manufacturer Tovèrli were installed (labelled A 1-2 and B 1-2) as well as four from the German manufacturer Reiche & Vogel (labelled C 1-2-3-4).

3.25
The handwriting in different colours, with several deletions, in Johan Jansen's personal copy of the *minutage définitif* indicate the difficulties of creating the various ambiances. It appears that in *ambiance* no. 10, the top picture, the green light and the red sun were omitted, and in the end only red fluorescent lighting was used. Ambiance no. 29 in the bottom picture was omitted altogether. Le Corbusier, *minutage définitif*, 1958.

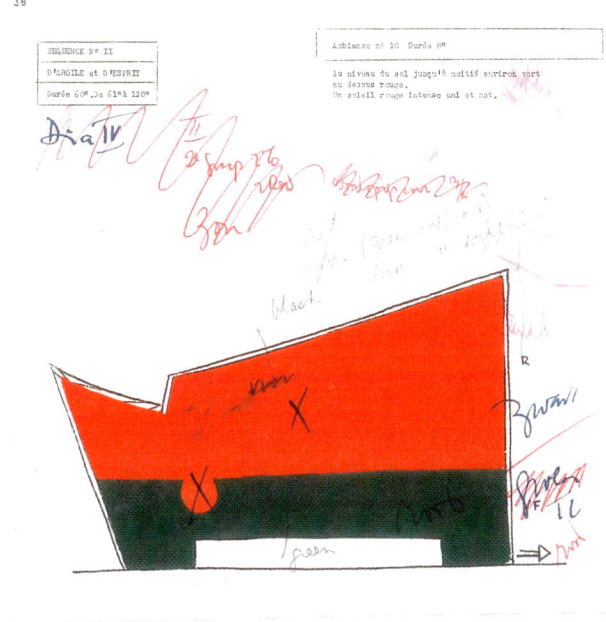

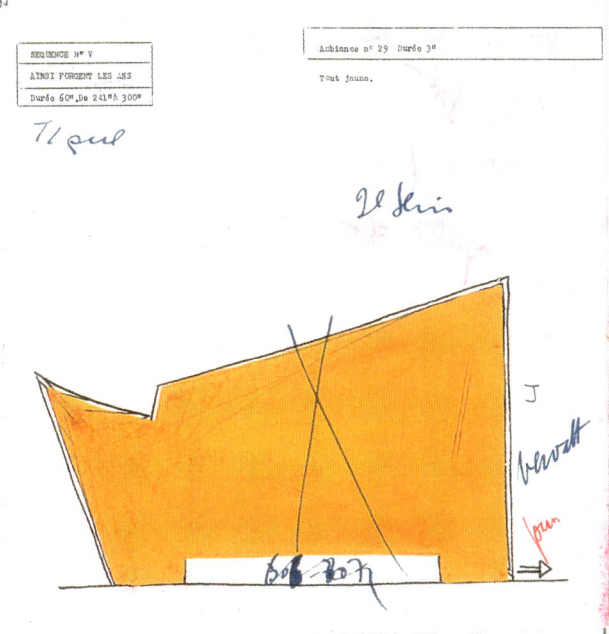

The fan-shaped slides were projected using four projectors produced by the Amsterdam-based manufacturer Tovèrli.[52] Founded in 1947, Tovèrli was mainly active in making and selling theatre and projection lighting. Its range included a modified theatre spotlight – known as the Tovèrli projector – which had been fitted with a lens to project images from a rotating disc. These discs – presumably the fan-shaped slides – were custom-made and generally designed by third parties.[53] Both in photographs of the interior and on floor plans of the Philips Pavilion, it is clearly visible that the Tovèrli projectors were placed side by side in twos.[54] In line with this set-up, photographic material of the performance clearly shows that identical images were projected next to each other on the pavilion's wall using two Tovèrli projectors.[55]

Demise of the *Minutage Définitif*

Le Corbusier's *minutage définitif* of 2 March 1958 turned out not to be the final script of the performance. As far as the light effects were concerned, the final version was the one drawn up by the lighting expert Johan Jansen on 24 June 1958.[56] The efforts to create the intended light effects ran into numerous problems. It proved to be extremely difficult to define the external contours of the projected light sharply enough. The projections and lighting on both sides of the public area generated a considerable quantity of diffuse reflected light. As a result, the colour effects and contrasts were weaker than expected. The problem was solved by minimizing light intensities, avoiding large white areas, and using the right colour combinations. The latter point meant avoiding combinations of complementary colours, since when these were mixed, the result was either white or far less strongly saturated colours.[57]

Kalff visited the Philips Pavilion with the acoustics expert Willem Tak on 23 May, three days after the first public performance of *Le poème électronique*. He reported that a two-minute strip of black was missing from the beginning of the *tri-trous* film, as a result of which it was out of sync with the *écran* film. He also observed that the clouds were not shown at all, the stars were illuminated far too infrequently, and the red sun projection was too weak. Kalff concluded that the script performed at that time was a pale reflection of Le Corbusier's intentions. He instructed Johan Jansen to make a new *minutage* for the *ambiances* as soon as the definitive *écran* film had been delivered.[58]

Jansen's subsequent struggle to create the different *ambiances* using the available light sources and projectors is clear from his personal copy of the *minutage définitif*. His notes on *ambiance* no. 10, for instance, show his handwriting in three different colours and with several deletions, outlining the various ways he was considering of creating the horizontal red and green stripes with a red sun.[59] It seems that he decided to omit the green light and the red sun,[60] possibly because red and green produced an undesirable colour when mixed. Another example was *ambiance* no. 29, which for some unknown reason was left out altogether.[61]

In Jansen's final *minutage* of 24 June for the lighting, the positioning in time deviates from Le Corbusier's *minutage définitif* from the very first *ambiances*. Moreover, the figurative patterns of the fan-shaped slides for the Tovèrli projectors are completely absent from the *minutage définitif* and were supposedly introduced by Jansen. The clouds that are present in four *ambiances* in the *minutage définitif* occur in only one *ambiance* in the *minutage* of 24 June.[62] Furthermore, it can be inferred from the available photographic material that the initial set-up, with on the one hand two Reiche & Vogel projectors and on the other two Tovèrli projectors side by side, was abandoned at some point, and the projectors set up separately instead.[63]

Jansen gave his new *minutage* to pavilion manager De Bruin on 27 June. After visiting the Philips Pavilion on 26 August, however – a date that was closer to the end than the beginning of the World's Fair – Jansen reported that the

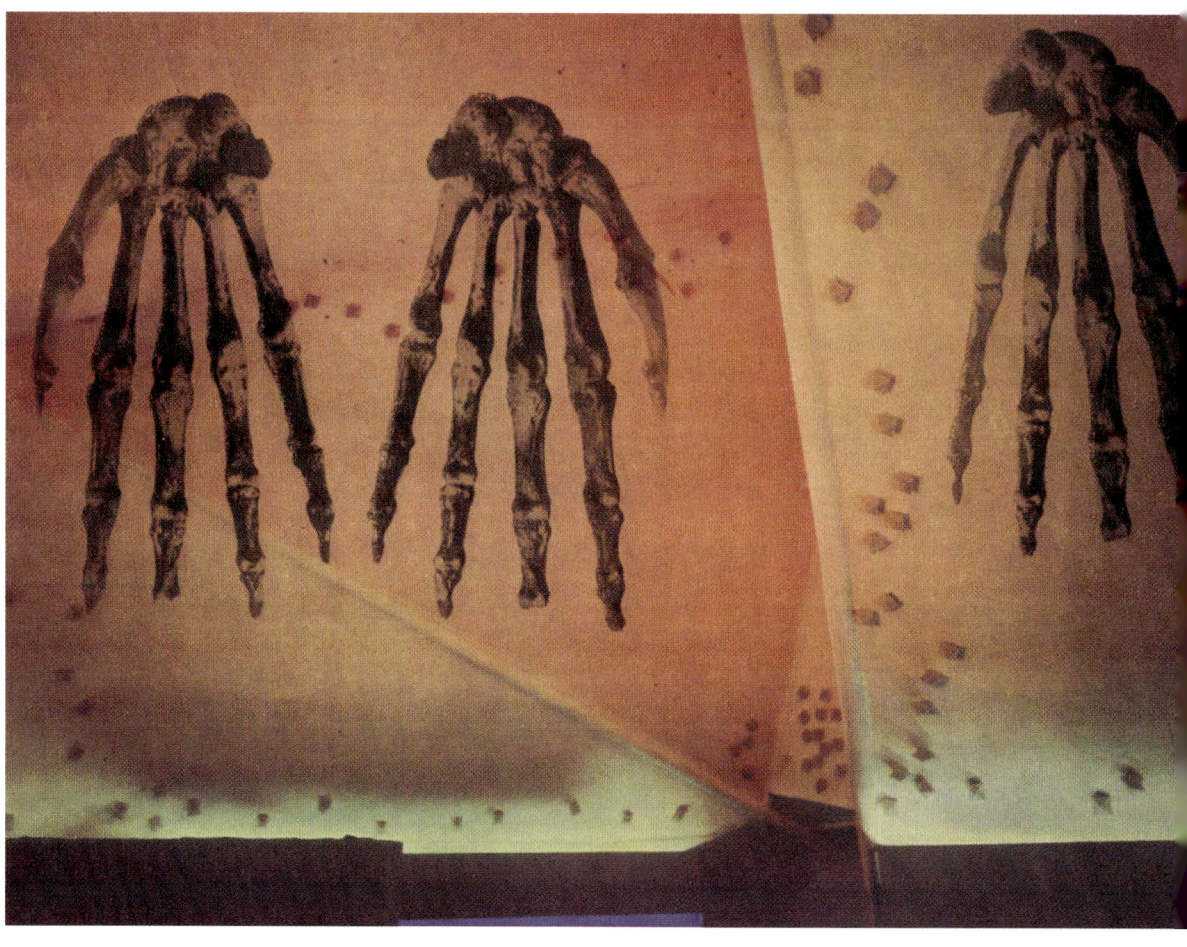

3.26
Écran film images surrounded by an *ambiance* projected onto the walls of the Philips Pavilion on which several groups of loudspeakers are clearly visible.

3.27
Floor plan of the Philips Pavilion with simplified schematic indications of the light sources. The arrows on the left and right denote the entrance and exit, respectively. The top of the floor plan represents the side facing the street.

3 The Decorators

signals for the light effects of his *minutage* had not been recorded on the revised control tape. In addition, the lightning projector, the components of which were scattered around in disarray, had not been used.[64]

All in all, the light effects in Jansen's final *minutage* for the lighting differed substantially from those that Le Corbusier had intended. After visiting the pavilion at the end of September 1958, Le Corbusier referred in his sketchbook to *ambiances* having regrettably been left out.[65] When Louis Kalff later wrote, looking back at the event, that the combination of the photographic images with colour and light had been 'only partly successful', it was something of an understatement.[66]

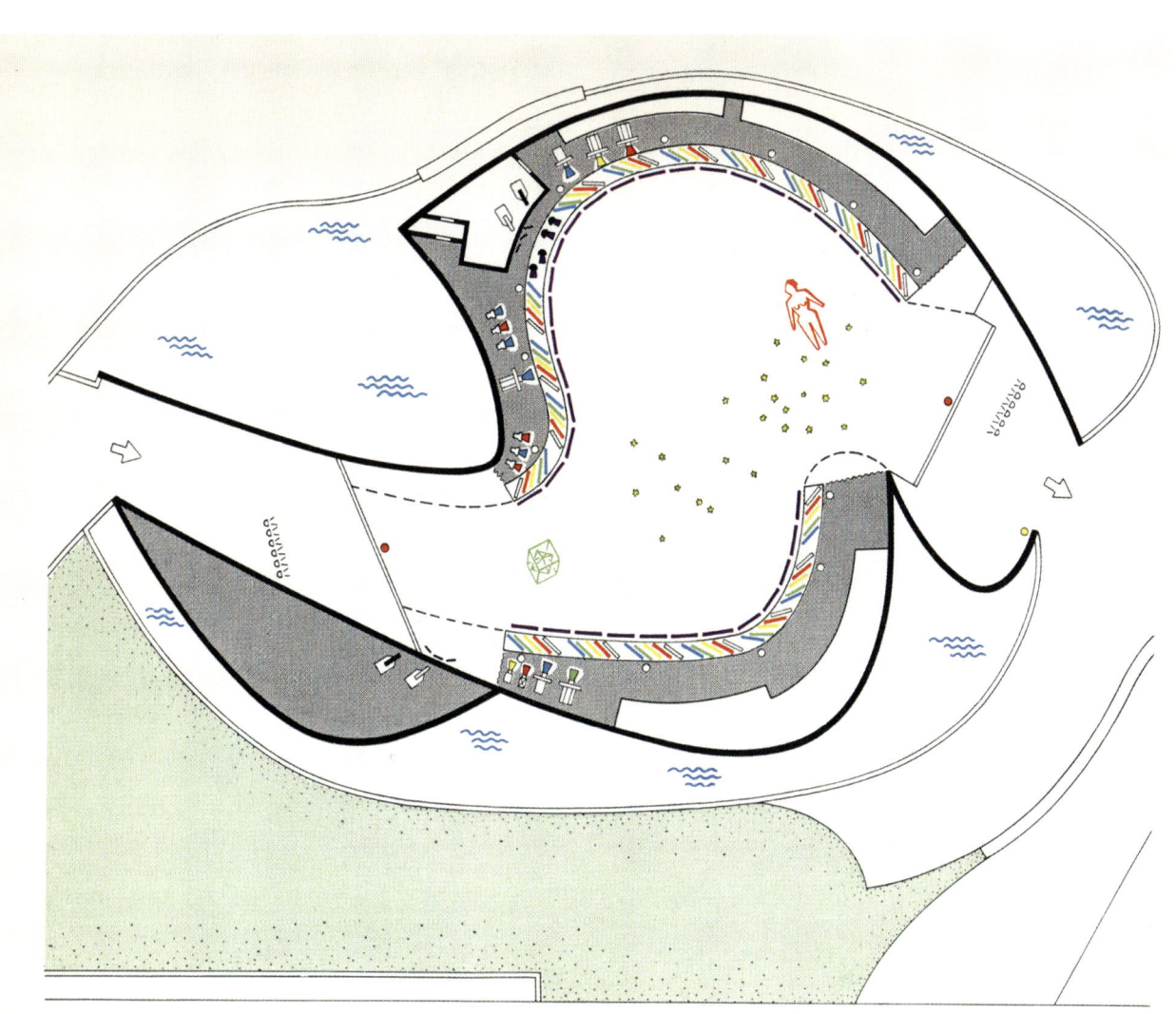

- Film projector (for "écrans")
- Film projector (for "tritrous")
- Projector (for "ambiances")
- Projector (clouds)
- Projector (sun)
- Projector (moon)
- Spotlight (coloured patches)
- U-V source ("volumes")
- Filament lamps (stars)
- Fluorescent lamps ("TL" M), white and coloured
- U.V. source (floor-tiles)
- Emergency lighting (white)
- Emergency lighting (red)
- Panic lighting
- Mirrors for directing "tritrous" beams
- Yellow fluorescent lamps ("TL" M) in exit porch.

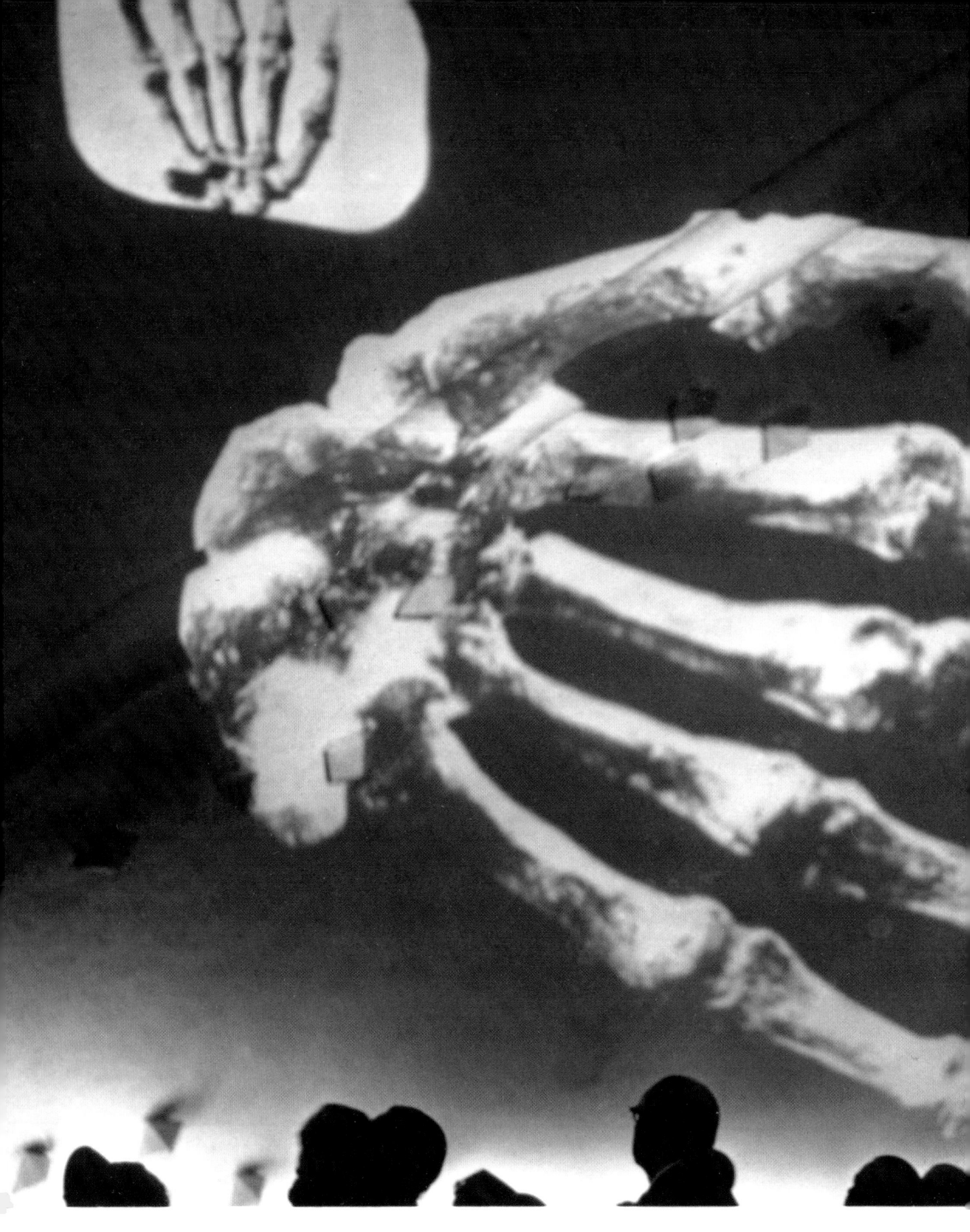

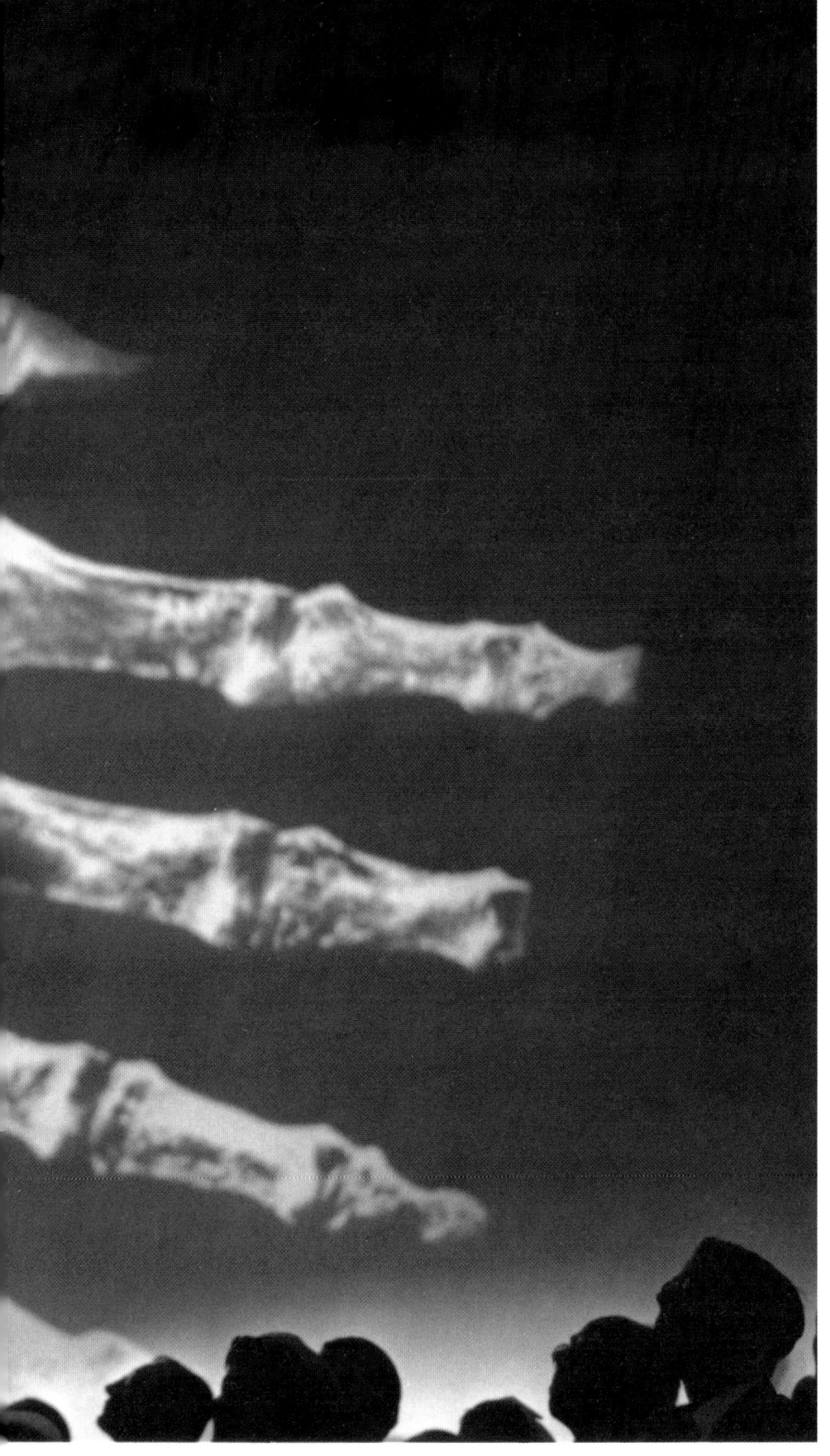

3.28
Visitors to the Philips Pavilion witness the projection of *écran* **and** *tri-trous* **film images during a performance of** *Le poème électronique.*

4 Shadowplay
Pierre Arnaud's Replacement Show for the Philips Pavilion

Pierre Arnaud and Peter Wever

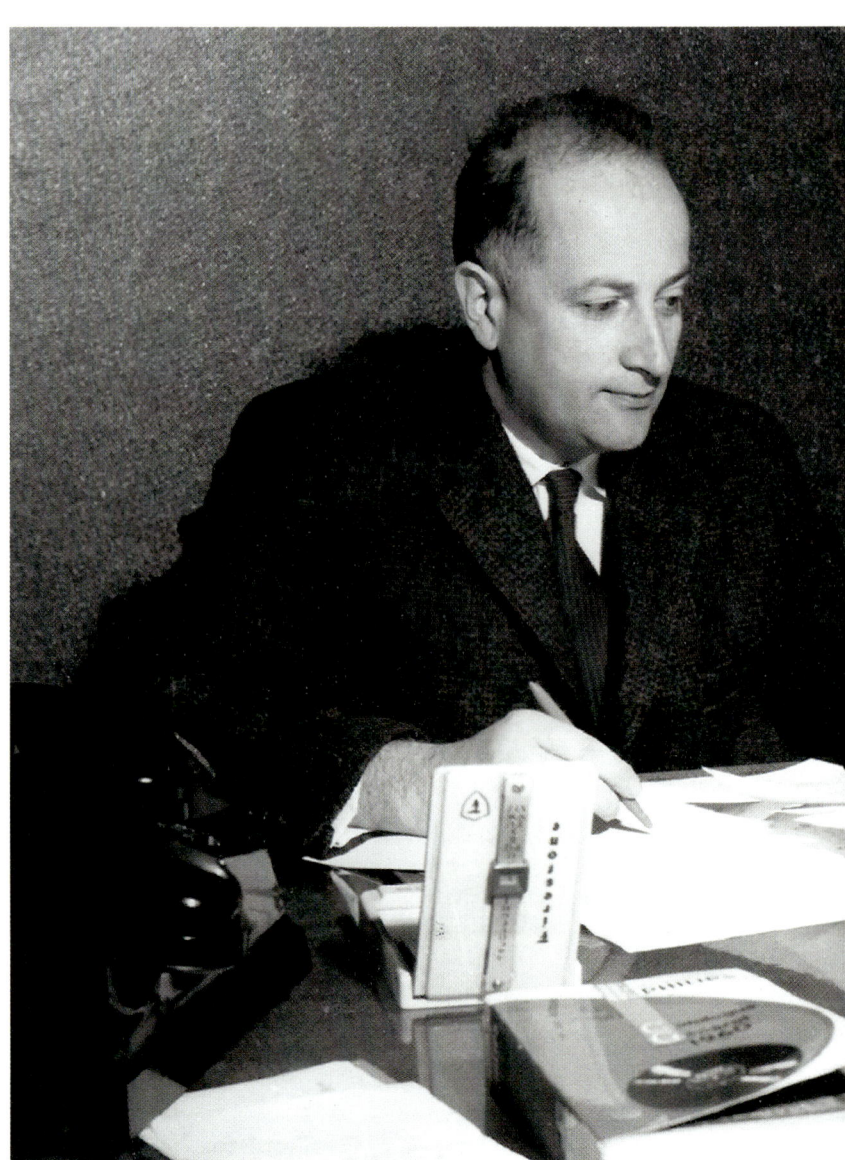

4.1
Pierre Arnaud in his office at the *la Diffusion Magnétique Sonore* **studio in Paris.**

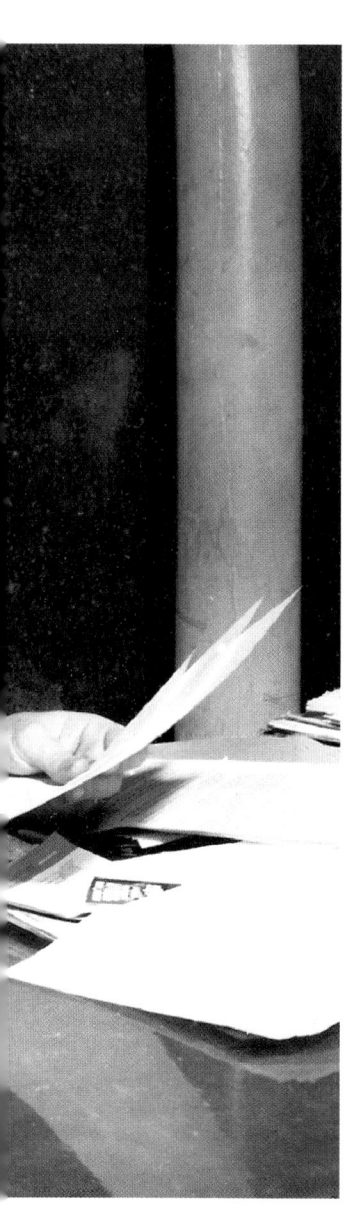

In late 1957, Pierre Arnaud was asked, under conditions of utmost secrecy, to make a 'replacement show' for the Philips Pavilion in case the performance created by Le Corbusier and Edgard Varèse turned out to be a failure.[1] Out of respect for Philips, Pierre Arnaud kept his story to himself for more than fifty years. In 2009, a search into the background of the expense item called 'Reserve program P. Arnoud (special budget)', listed on an overview of the Philips Pavilion's budgetary developments, led to Pierre Arnaud. Confronted with questions about the content of this 'reserve program', Pierre Arnaud decided to break his silence, and put his story in writing.[2]

. . . At the time that we were in discussions with Philips France about the sale of our *studio la D.M.S.*,[3] I was informed of a visit by the general manager of Philips France, Mr. Haver Droeze.[4] When I put down the phone, he was already there. During a short tour of the studio, he seemed interested, but he quickly changed the topic. He told me that he wanted to offer my services to a certain Mr. Hartong, and introduced me to him.[5] Hartong was the multinational's global commercial director, and he had a top-secret project that he wanted to discuss with me.[6] I would have to meet with him a few days later in Eindhoven. It was expressly mentioned that I was not to speak to anyone else about this. Hartong sounds a bit like 'pay attention' [*Achtung*] in German, even though the spelling is a bit different. This name was well suited to the man I met, for two reasons. First, he looked like Chancellor Adenauer, who, at that time, was trying to become friends with his arch-enemy De Gaulle.[7] And, like the characters from the books of John le Carré, he seemed to blend into the décor; you wouldn't notice anything about this man if you ran into him on the street. But when his gaze crossed yours, which only happened when he wanted to speak to you, you had better be on guard!

Right at the beginning of my visit to Eindhoven, Hartong explained that our meeting was unrelated to the possible purchase of *studio la D.M.S*. He asked me again not to talk to anyone about what he was going to tell me, not before the end of the 1958 Brussels World's Fair. I promised, and was extremely curious about the secret. He began to talk about the plan to build a Philips Pavilion at the World's Fair, in which absolutely no devices would be displayed, and in which no use would be made of any of the propaganda or publicity that could already be seen on every street corner. The Philips name had to be linked to something surprising, something new, something that had never been seen before. Something that visitors would never forget, and that at the same time would give Philips, in their subconscious, the image of modernity, development, and innovation. They had decided to invite the architect Le Corbusier for this pavilion, because his work had always been controversial, and always led to spirited discussions. A budget of about 250 million francs had been made available to him to create a structure that would radiate Philips' innovative character.[8] Le Corbusier had been given complete freedom, and no one would know what he was planning until he himself decided to present his project. Nobody from Philips was allowed to meddle, express their opinion, or disapprove of the design. If this clause was violated, Le Corbusier would immediately have 25 million francs transferred to his bank account as compensation. Because none of the company's divisions was willing to risk having to pay this fee, Le

Corbusier's creative freedom was guaranteed.[9] The pavilion that Le Corbusier had designed was somewhat reminiscent of a large asymmetrical circus tent with two masts. It was strange, but that was not a problem. Le Corbusier had asked Edgard Varèse, a famous composer of *Musique concrète*, to compose an eight-minute piece of music. Another artist, whom Hartong did not name, was to supply film footage that would be projected onto the interior walls of the pavilion, via hidden film projectors. Varèse and the filmmaker were not allowed to exchange information. The only requirement that Le Corbusier had given to both of them was that the music and the projections had to begin and end at the same time.[10]

Hartong then indicated that people at Philips had been doing their best not to worry, and that they still stood behind the idea of not interfering with the project. Hartong then introduced me to Mr. Kalff, Philips' General Art Director, who until then had been sitting quietly on a chair. Kalff was responsible for the supervision of the project, and the support of the artists. He asked me to follow him to the 'scene of the crime'. Along the way, Kalff told me that Varèse had come to Eindhoven eight months earlier.[11] He had been given access to a large warehouse, where many speakers had been installed on the walls.[12] Varèse was supported by a number of Philips engineers whose boss, a certain Mr. Tak – he was a kind of cowboy, a Gary Cooper type – followed us during the visit.[13]

After visiting the warehouse, we returned to Hartong's office, where we drank cups of coffee with milk that were served all day long (this was new to me, because it was my first visit to the Netherlands, and I had not yet been to the United States). Hartong began to speak, and said that Philips did not want to run any risk of failure. That is why he asked me, in the deepest secrecy, to prepare a replacement show that would be set up under the pretext that auxiliary equipment needed to be installed at the pavilion in Brussels. If, for some reason, Le Corbusier's 'happening' might jeopardize Philips' reputation, then my show would replace his. At the same time, Le Corbusier would receive a check in the amount of 25 million francs as compensation. I had every reason to be astonished, but the conversation continued on in the same tone and at the same pace. Hartong indicated that Philips would cover all the costs for the realization of the project, and asked about the fee I would

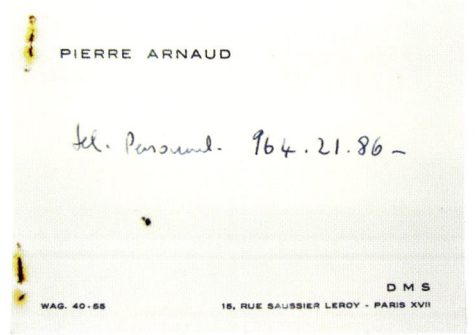

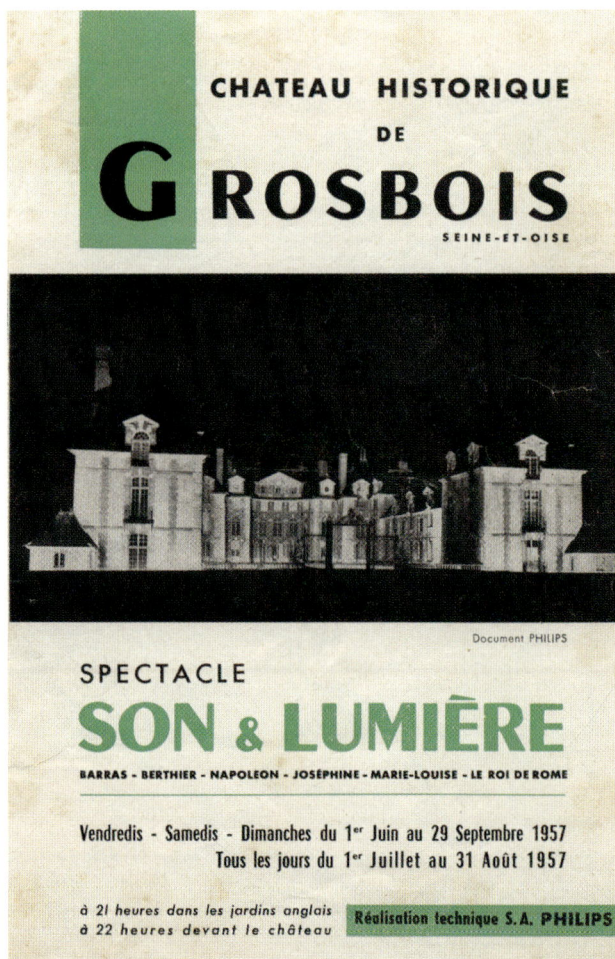

4.2
Business card, with handwritten private phone number, that Henk Hartong received in about August of 1957 from Pierre Arnaud, which was then forwarded to Louis Kalff.

4.3
Information brochure from 1957 for the *spectacle Son & Lumière* [sound and light show] of Grosbois Castle near Paris, developed at Pierre Arnaud's *la Diffusion Magnétique Sonore* studio.

want for the show. I was caught off guard, but then heard myself in a firm voice mentioning the amount of five million francs. Hartong immediately responded with a counter-offer of two and a half million francs, which was ten per cent of the compensation that would be paid to Le Corbusier. I later learned that this was customary for Philips, but not sacred. They always asked for half of the requested amount, and if negotiations stalled, they could agree on 75 per cent. That meant that I could have earned one and a quarter million francs more, but I was still very happy with the amount that I had accepted.[14]

I had to decide what kind of show I would create, and tried to give shape to my ideas. Because Le Corbusier had made a show that lacked any cohesion or subject, I proposed to do the opposite, and create a presentation full of symbolism for Philips, although it would still be abstract in terms of images and music. I decided to create a symphony of sound and image, in three parts and a coda. To determine the theme, I asked Hartong to summarize, in a few words and without having to think too much, what Philips meant to him. I got an admirable answer. Without thinking about it for even a moment, he said it was very easy for him. Philips had the duty to ensure, on all levels within the company, that profits would accrue to the shareholders. But once this basic duty had been satisfied, it was the personal responsibility of all of the company's employees to promote the progress of mankind, if only for a few minutes, or even for a few seconds. That is why I suggested, in line with Hartong's description, to depict the evolution of man and technology.[15] He simply said that I could go my own way. The visit was then quickly concluded, as we had agreed on all matters.[16]

Back in Paris, but still dumbstruck, I further developed my ideas for the replacement show into a scenario that shows a continuous evolution.

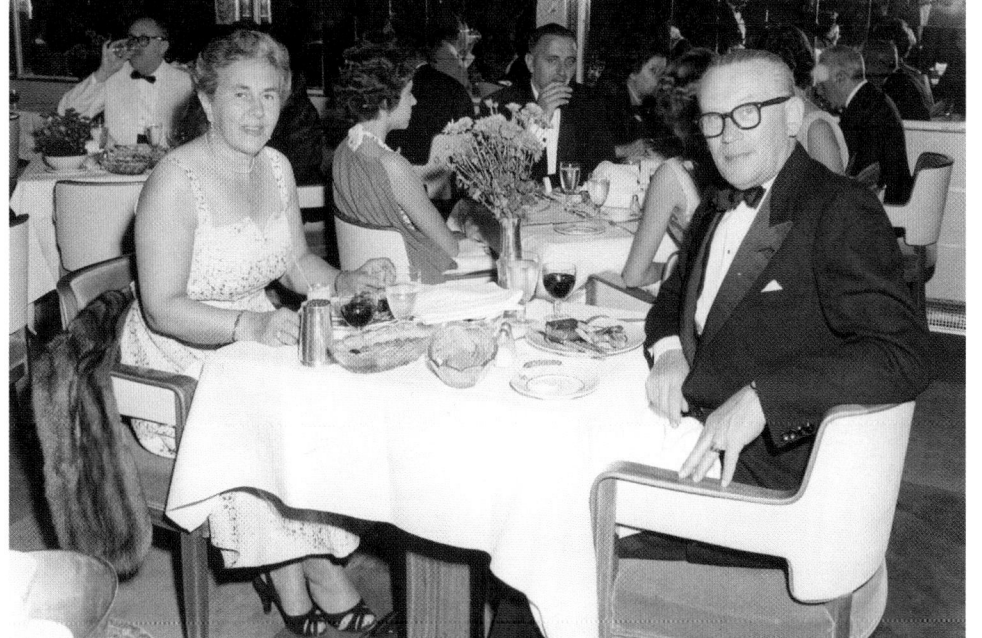

4.4
On the right, Henk Hartong, member of the Board of Directors of Philips Lightbulb Factories Ltd.

First part.

As faint and vague light projections in white and blue form and transform on the walls of the pavilion that surrounds the audience, the soft and pure Gregorian chanting of a single male voice begins. Then multiple voices can be heard in perfect harmony. They then merge into a polyphonic choir, while the footage on the walls also begins to divide at the same time. The theme then evolves into a classical style, until it has become a gigantic mixed choir. At the same time, the blue shapes become clearer and more prominent, and the voices that began on one side now fill the entire space.

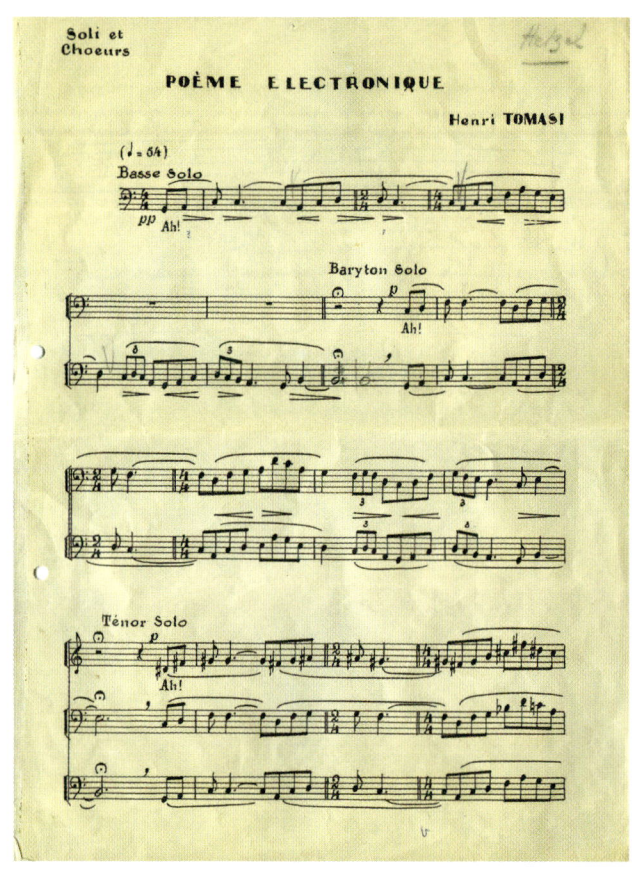

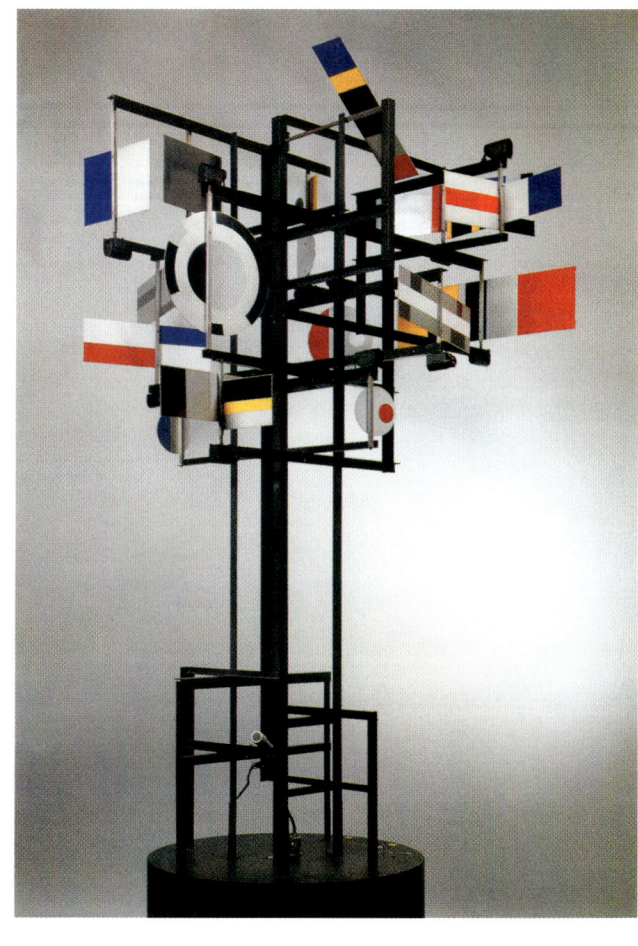

4.5
Sheet music for soloists and choirs [*soli et choeurs*] of the composition *Le poème électronique* that Henri Tomasi created as part of the replacement show for the Philips Pavilion.

4.6
The cybernetic artwork 'CYSP 1' by Nicolas Schöffer. Pierre Arnaud filmed coloured shadows that were created by colour projections onto this moving artwork, and then used this as film footage in the replacement show for the Philips Pavilion.

Second part.

The various voices change into the instruments of a large orchestra: the sopranos become flutes, the altos become clarinets, the tenors violins, the baritones cellos, and the basses become double basses. The white and blue colours transform into the various pure colours of the colour spectrum. A rhythm is created that is also echoed in the film footage.

Third part.

Then there is a second transformation in the continuous development of the theme. The instruments of the orchestra are replaced by the sounds of modern appliances: boat sirens, train whistles, the sound of jet engines racing through the air, and the thumping of industrial sounds. The image at this point only consists of black, white, and grey, but the movements have become faster and more mechanical.

Coda.

And then the finale, which begins with a big, powerful chord by all the voices, supported by projections of blue light. This is followed by a second chord from the orchestra, which is backed by light projections in all colours. Eventually we hear the closing chord, in which all of the sounds – voices, orchestra and mechanical sounds – are united, backed by light projections in all colours.

At my request, my friend Henri Tomasi composed the musical piece, which was recorded with the Orchestra Lamoureux at the Salle Apollo in Paris. The vocals were recorded in our studio, and the mechanical sounds in the control room. After the mixing, the whole was transferred to two tape recorders, each with two synchronized stereo tracks. The tape recorders, which at that time were the most advanced in Europe, were built especially for the occasion by one of our friends. For the film footage, we filmed colour projections that were created by a cybernetic artwork made by Nicolas Schöffer, with whom I had already been working for some time on coloured shadows that were shaped by his moving structures. So the film images were animated, but still abstract.[17]

Despite having all the paperwork that Philips France had prepared, my car with the secret production was nonetheless stopped for hours at the border between Belgium and the Netherlands. It appeared that the tape recorders were not on the list of customs items. We were held there until Kalff, who had been alerted by telephone, had Hartong intercede on our behalf. During the night, we transferred the film footage and the audio tapes to the warehouse with reserve equipment in Eindhoven.[18]

The World's Fair opened a few weeks later.[19] The work of Le Corbusier

4.7
Letter dated 15 February 1958, in which Pierre Arnaud explains to the involved parties, point by point, the elements that the replacement show consisted of. This letter was delivered to Eindhoven together with the film footage and the audio tapes that were to be used for the replacement show.

was discussed in many newspapers, magazines, and broadcasts. As expected, his spectacle generated a huge amount of interest and received a lot of – sometimes excessive – praise. There were some chuckles from the audience, which was typical of performances of *Musique concrète*. But there was no reason to interrupt the show.

The existence of the replacement show remained a secret during the World's Fair.[20] In October, I attended presentations, in the presence of Mr. Hafkemeijer and Mr. Tak, of both the replacement show and the performance created by Le Corbusier and Varèse.[21] The presentation of the replacement show consisted of the music by Henri Tomasi and the film footage by Nicolas Schöffer. The light projections were missing, because, in the case of emergency, these were to have been installed overnight at the pavilion in Brussels. But I still got a good impression of what the show might have looked like.

What ever became of the replacement show? Chris van Lummel, who at the time was responsible for Philips' *Son et Lumière* service in Eindhoven, combined the film footage and Varèse's score into a documentary, but few people have seen it.[22] Both the original films as well as the working copies from Brussels have been lost. But I have kept the original music in our studio. A few years ago, we re-synchronized the recordings using modern equipment. That recording was presented on the radio station *France Culture* by the *Comité d'Honneur des Amis d'Henry Tomasi*, of which I was a member.[23]

Our involvement with the Philips Pavilion had a few other consequences for our company. For the opening of the World's Fair, Hartong wanted to have an interview with Le Corbusier, in which he presented his project. I was asked to record this interview in my studio in Paris. At no time was the great architect informed, by me or by anyone else, of our 'secret' engagement with his work.[24]

Another coincidence brought Iannis Xenakis to our studio. Le Corbusier had Xenakis, a brilliant composer and architect, make the drawings for the Philips Pavilion. Kalff had sent Xenakis to our studio to record a piece of music that Xenakis had composed. This piece was to be played in the pavilion in Brussels as intermission music. Xenakis had decided to use the

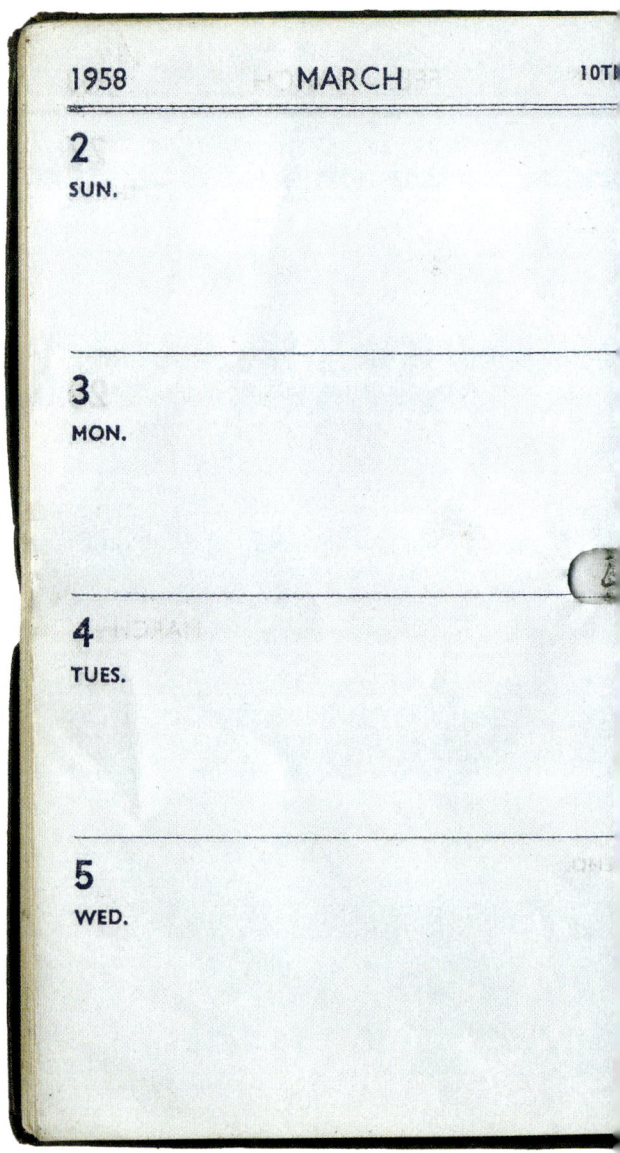

sound of burning charcoal as the basis for this music. Because this sound itself was very weak, we had to amplify it. Then it was merged and mixed, under the directions of Xenakis. The basic sound of burning charcoal was a surprisingly crystal-clear tone of charcoal particles shattering and exploding into flames. Some ingenuity was required to make this recording, and we nearly set the studio on fire and died of asphyxiation. The editing was even more difficult. Xenakis had our sound engineer Georges Chottin chop up the recording into five or six different small sounds. These small pieces of tape were then edited and mixed. The end result sounded almost identical to the original recording, with the only difference being that now everything had been calculated, and nothing more was left to chance.[25]

There is no evidence to support the veracity of the story told here.[26] Even our invoice to Philips Eindhoven lacks any details that could confirm any of this. But I am left with an excellent memory of my encounter with Le Corbusier and the amazing Philips Pavilion, and in no way do I regret this unforgettable experience.

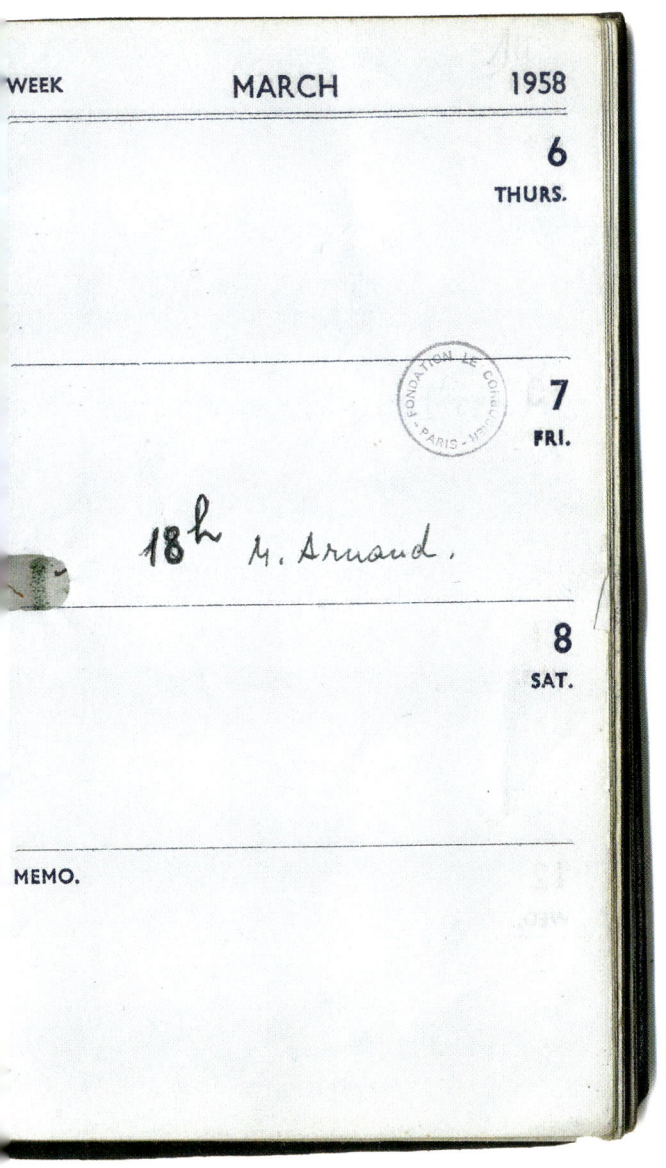

4.8
Le Corbusier's agenda includes a first appointment with 'M. Arnaud' on 7 March 1958.

5 An Austrian in Eindhoven

Anton Buczynski and the Recording of *Le poème électronique*

Kees Tazelaar

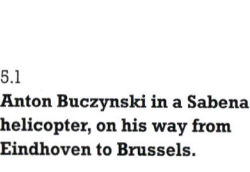

5.1
Anton Buczynski in a Sabena helicopter, on his way from Eindhoven to Brussels.

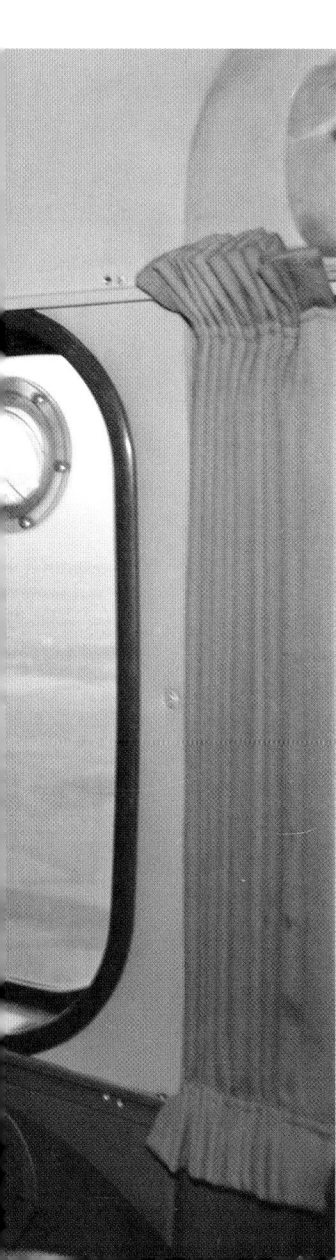

In February 1958, the Austrian recording technician Anton Buczynski was asked to go to Eindhoven to help Edgard Varèse produce the music for *Le poème électronique*. Tensions between Varèse and the other technicians were running high, but Varèse and Buczynski soon established a relationship of trust. The composition (especially the second half) contains sounds that Buczynski produced on the basis of Varèse's instructions. Without the Austrian's help, it is questionable whether the music would have been finished in time for the opening of the World's Fair. In 2004, the year before his death, Anton Buczynski gave an interview in which he recalled his trials and tribulations in Eindhoven in 1958.[1]

The avant-garde nature of the multimedia performance in the Philips Pavilion was very remote from the original intentions of Philips, which initially envisaged a far more mainstream kind of presentation. The plans for the music, in particular, were a good deal more conservative. The initiators had toyed with the idea of incorporating music by the British composer Benjamin Britten, along the lines of his *The Young Person's Guide to the Orchestra*, a recording of which would be perfect for demonstrating the company's audio equipment, besides which it would have broad appeal to the general public.

Understandably, then, when Philips' Board of Directors were given a demonstration of a fragment of *Le poème électronique* on 6 February 1958, in the presence of Le Corbusier, Edgard Varèse, and Iannis Xenakis, the views regarding the work's suitability for presentation at the World's Fair were sharply divided. Varèse's contribution, in particular, attracted fierce criticism. Was this actually music at all? Doubts of this kind had already led to a plan to commission a different composition in secret so as to have something else in reserve.[2] This certainly did not mean, however, that Philips was assuming at that point that the performance including images designed by Le Corbusier and music by Varèse and Xenakis was going to be jettisoned. On the contrary, every effort was made to ensure that this performance would be ready in time for the opening. This is clear, for instance, from the fact that shortly after the demonstration on 6 February, an extra recording technician was added to the team working with Varèse in a Philips truck garage at the Strijp III premises in Eindhoven, which had been converted into a test workshop and studio. That technician was Anton Buczynski.

Anton Buczynski started out at the company Wiener Radiowerke, where he had been working since 1952 on the development of the Philips series 10000 professional tape recorders. When a vacancy arose within the company a few years later, he was called in and quizzed about his musical background. It emerged that Buczynski had sung in the Wiener Sängerknaben [Vienna Boys' Choir] until his voice broke, and had received a sound musical training there. He was adept at reading musical scores, and the company decided to appoint him as recording technician for classical music at Philips Austria.

Buczynski never figured out why Philips should have cast its net as wide as Austria in its quest to boost the production team in Eindhoven in 1958.[3] Buczynski was a good recording technician but had no particular experience with contemporary music, let alone electronic music. Furthermore, Philips had a recording company in the Netherlands – Philips' Phonographic Industries in Baarn – with recording technicians of its own, and maintained good ties with the Nederlandse Radio Unie [Netherlands Radio Union; NRU].[4] Whatever the

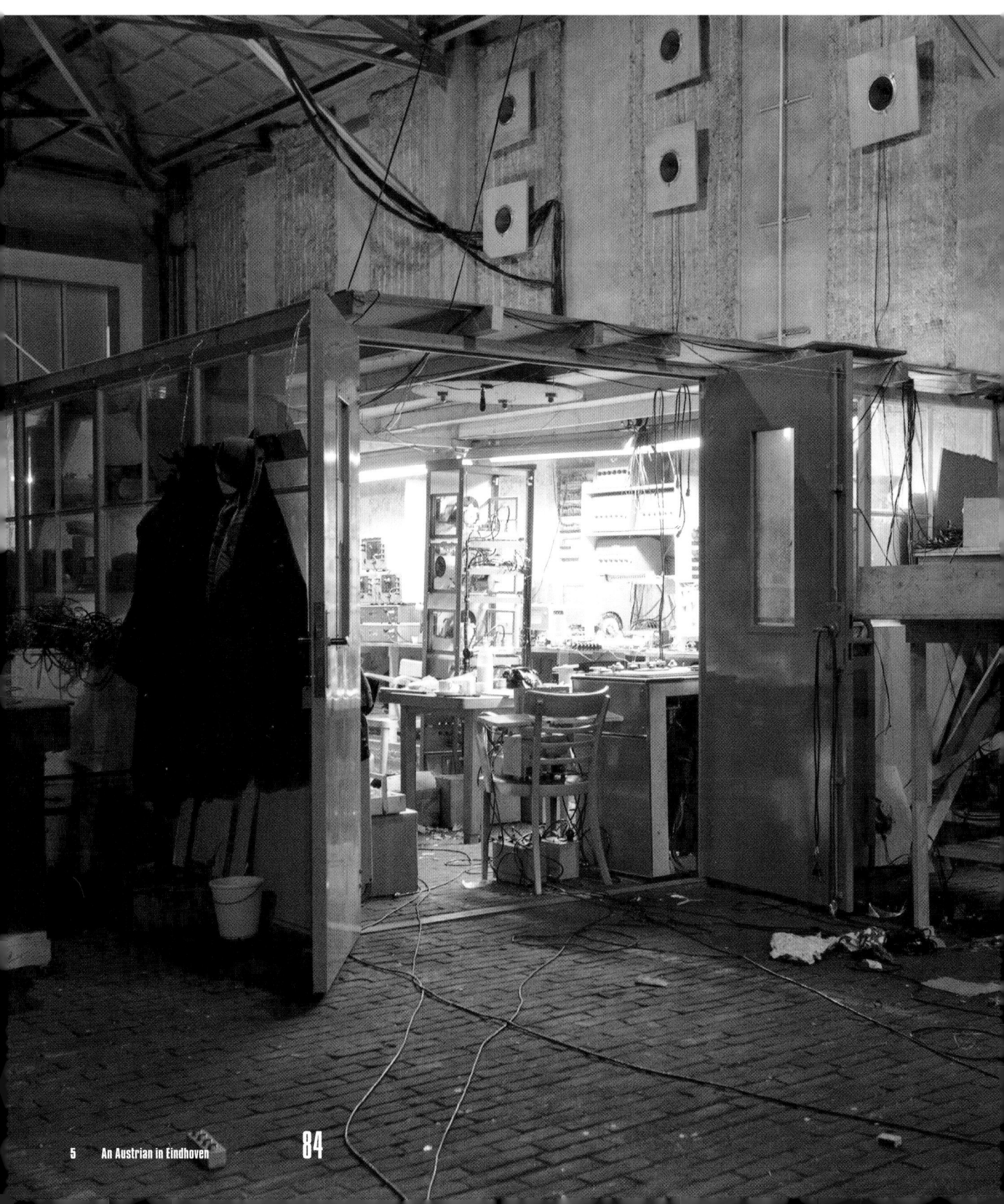

case may be, Buczynski accepted the offer to go and work for Varèse in the capacity of 'editor-recorder', arriving in Eindhoven on 19 February 1958.[5]

Edgard Varèse had already been in the Netherlands since 2 September 1957, and had hoped to be finished within a few weeks. But five and a half months later, when Buczynski arrived, he had completed only about half of the eight-minute musical composition for Le poème électronique,[6] with less than two months to go before the opening of the World's Fair. What made matters worse was that the tension between Varèse and the technicians Willem Tak and Jan de Bruyn had reached boiling point. Varèse felt that they did not take him seriously, and he had become convinced – not entirely without justification – that his work was being deliberately undermined.[7] Tak, for his part, gradually had to accept a completely different role in the production process from what he had been led to expect, and regarded the musical demands of Varèse, who was constantly racked by doubts and technically inept, as quite absurd.[8] Varèse dismissed echo and reverberation effects – in which Tak was an expert – as Walt Disney clichés, while viewing audio distortion, an effect that trained sound technicians will bend over backwards to avoid, as highly desirable.

Buczynski immediately sensed that Varèse felt extremely isolated in Eindhoven. He felt that the composer and the other technicians 'had not hit it off', but decided to keep out of the conflict. After all, he was a guest, seconded from Vienna, and it was none of his business. Buczynski was unfamiliar with Varèse's music, and found the score Varèse was using completely unintelligible: 'It was a piece of brown paper, wrapping paper, with lines, zigzag figures and waves drawn on it. I was mystified. And whenever a new sound had been created, he would rub something out and draw something else in its place.'

As time went on, however, Buczynski found himself becoming impressed by Varèse as a composer. Initially their exchanges were rather stilted, partly because Buczynski could not speak good English or French. But he had

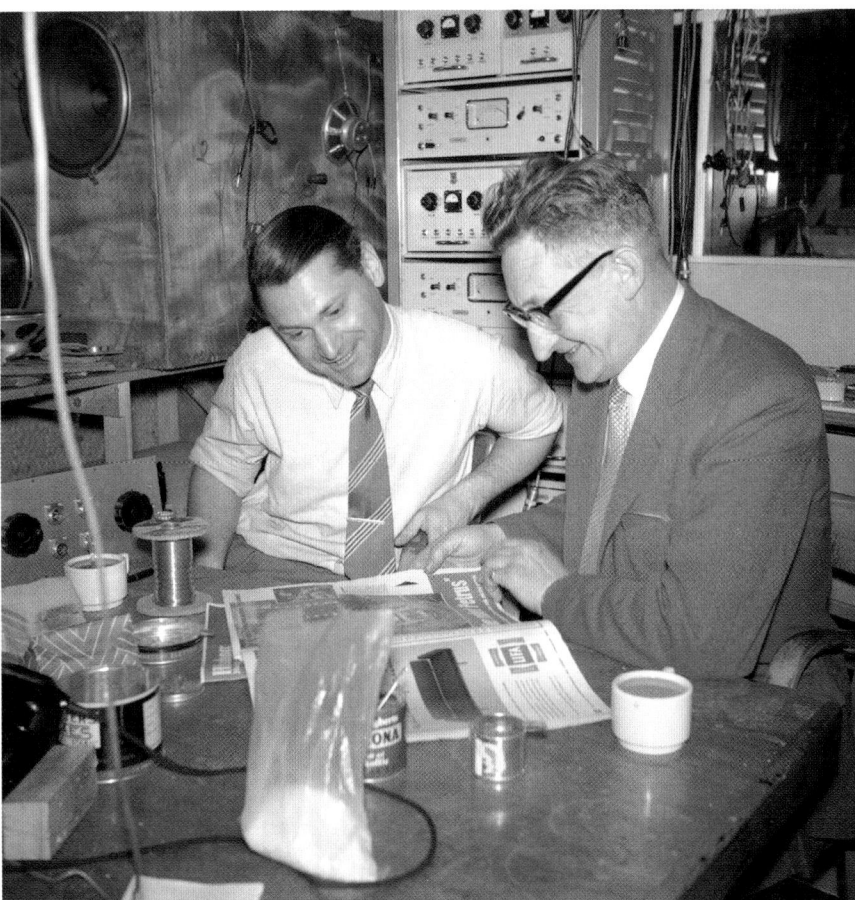

5.2
View of the studio in the converted Philips truck garage on the Strijp III premises in Eindhoven, where Anton Buczynski worked from February to April 1958.

5.3
Anton Buczynski (left) and the acoustics expert Willem Tak (right) enjoying a coffee break in the studio on the Strijp III premises.

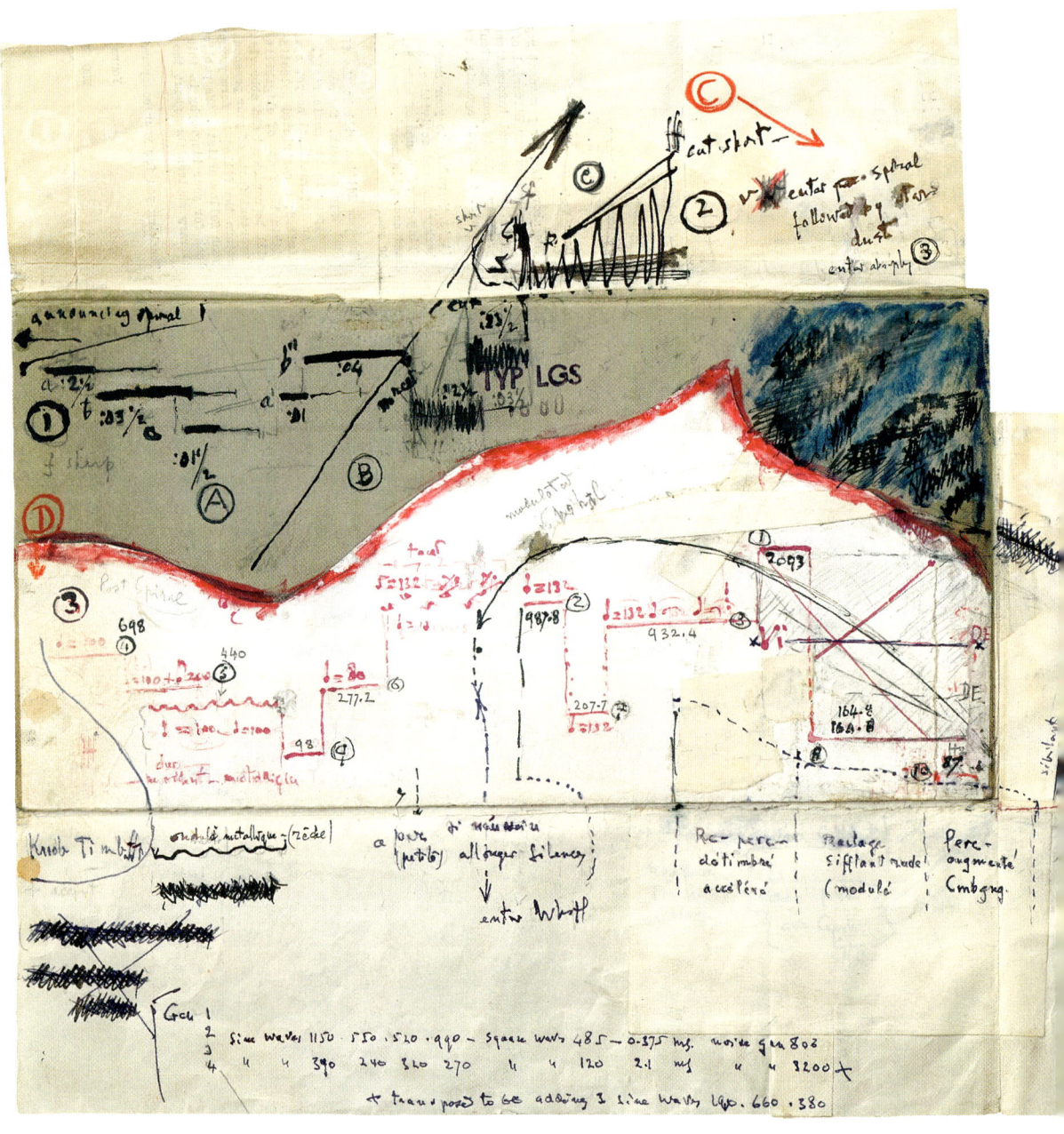

done a lot of work in Italy, and one day when something kept going wrong he started cursing in Italian, assuming that no one would understand. Varèse heard him, and cried in surprise: '*Ah… Lei parla Italiano!*'[9] From then on, they spoke Italian to each other, which had the added advantage that Varèse could say things to Buczynski without anyone else being able to understand. A relationship of trust developed. Varèse in particular was delighted by this, since he had often felt excluded during the long discussions in Dutch that Tak and De Bruyn used to conduct in his presence.

Besides editing the sounds already recorded, Buczynski's work included making new sounds. Varèse's music for *Le poème électronique* – especially the second part – includes sounds produced by Buczynski on Varèse's instructions. For instance, Buczynski made the footsteps we hear from 4'40" to 5'34" with a trick often used in radio plays, which involves placing a little wooden cigar box and shaking it in front of the microphone. From [...]" and from 7'32" to 7'41" we hear the sound of a fighter jet. The [...] to imitate this sound, by mixing electronic static with a whining [...] not satisfy Varèse. Buczynski recalls: 'For the apotheosis of Le [poème élec]tronique, Varèse wanted fighter jets flying through the pavilion, [...] speaking. So we had to get the noise of fighter jets from some[...] it wasn't possible to synthesize it. We had to record it. Tak [...] commander of the airbase at Eindhoven, and asked if he could [...] a couple of fighter jets to perform a nose dive over Strijp III, [g]arage, so that we could record it. Well, we were still hauling the [microphone]s up to the roof and there they came, three of them! Too early. So Tak got them on the line again but they couldn't do it again because of the fuel, it was too expensive. So we just left the microphones on the roof, with an umbrella protecting them, and waited for the wind to change, so that the pilots would have to fly over Strijp III when coming in to land at the airbase.[10] A few days later, we were able to record the sound after all.'

Perhaps the most remarkable passage of Le poème électronique is the soprano solo (6'44" to 7'02"). Although Buczynski cannot remember the soprano's name, the voice is thought to be that of the opera star Cristina Deutekom. She was still a student in Amsterdam's opera class at the time, and she was the only person for many miles around who could reach the top F prescribed by Varèse's score.[11]

Buczynski's other activities, besides editing and producing sounds, included making and mending equipment on the spot. It was not always easy to procure the necessary parts. On one occasion, Buczynski had to wait a very long time for an electrolytic capacitor he needed for a repair job. After he had threatened to pack up and go back to Vienna, he was finally given a sheaf of papers and sent to the nearby Philips Research Laboratories or 'NatLab'.[12] Papers notwithstanding, he was not allowed to pass beyond the porter to the 'top-secret' NatLab. So he never saw the inside of the NatLab's electronic music studio, and all he knew of the music that Henk Badings was making there he gleaned from Jan de Bruyn, who had been Badings's assistant at the NatLab before starting work for the Electroacoustics Main Industrial Division [Hoofdindustriegroep Elektroakoestiek; ELA] as Varèse's technician.

Most of the equipment that Buczynski had to develop related to the spatial effects that had to be added to Varèse's music. Long before it had been decided to use electronic music for the performance in the Philips Pavilion, and before Varèse had received the commission, a demonstration of Philips' expertise in spatial sound had been part of the plans. In the years before, Philips had developed groundbreaking electroacoustic equipment that could be used to vary the reverberation time in theatres and concert halls. The Teatro alla Scala in Milan was one of the theatres that had installed such a system, celebrating its arrival with a festive production of Mozart's opera Die Zauberflöte [The Magic Flute] on 7 December 1955, conducted by Herbert von Karajan.

The initial plans for the Philips Pavilion included one of

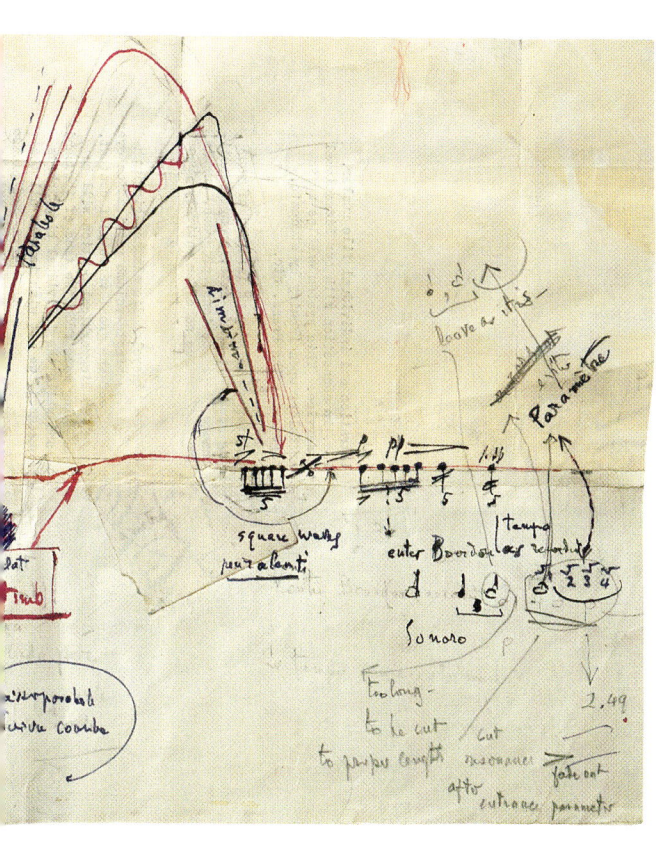

5.4
The collage-like graphic score of Le poème électronique, on wrapping paper, which Varèse produced in Eindhoven.

these reverberation systems, but this idea was later dropped for practical reasons. Instead, these reverberation effects – with which the music could be made to sound claustrophobically dry one minute and endowed with cathedral-like reverberations the next – were integrated into the audio tape of the music itself. To achieve this, the technicians used a Philips reverberation system that was part of the equipment in the garage at Strijp III. There was also a need to enable virtual, fluid movements of sounds between the outermost loudspeaker clusters, that is, those above the entrance and exit of the Philips Pavilion.[13]

Accustomed as we are to today's sophisticated audio technology, we can scarcely imagine how complicated it was in those days to integrate these effects into the recording of Varèse's music. Philips' resources were advanced for the time, but even so, Buczynski had to design and build the necessary equipment on the spot. He ended up constructing a device with two large dials, one of which regulated the spatial movement of the sound while the other controlled the amount of reverberation. The sounds processed by these means were recorded using a stereo tape recorder that was borrowed from Philips' Phonographic Industries especially for this purpose.

Varèse left for Brussels on 8 April 1958, even before the final touches had been made to the music master tape, leaving Buczynski to finish his work on *Le poème électronique* without him. Then Buczynski too went to Brussels, where he had a new job working in the Austrian Pavilion, opposite the Philips Pavilion. There, in a custom-equipped auditorium, Austria's leading music educationalists gave courses in musical interpretation. These courses often expanded into real concerts, and attracted large audiences. The public did not occupy the same space as the musicians; they were separated from the studio by an enormous sound-proofing glass partition and listened to the musical performances over loudspeakers. Buczynski belonged to a team of technicians who took turns at the audio panel. This sound installation too was supplied by Philips.

While he was working in the Austrian pavilion, Buczynski occasionally crossed the Avenue de l'Europe to listen to the results of his work in Eindhoven. Once his job at the Austrian Pavilion was finished he returned to Vienna, after which his contribution to *Le poème électronique* was largely forgotten.

Some time after his return to Vienna, he was asked to take on a new job in the Netherlands, this time for a year working as a classical music recording technician. He and his wife moved to Baarn, where they purchased a painting featuring Dutch windmills, with the idea of taking it back to Vienna to remind them of their time in the Netherlands. But one year turned into two, two years became five, five became ten, and the sound technician ended up working in the Netherlands until his retirement in 1983 and indeed until his death. All those years, the painting with the windmills hung on the wall of the Buczynski home in Baarn.

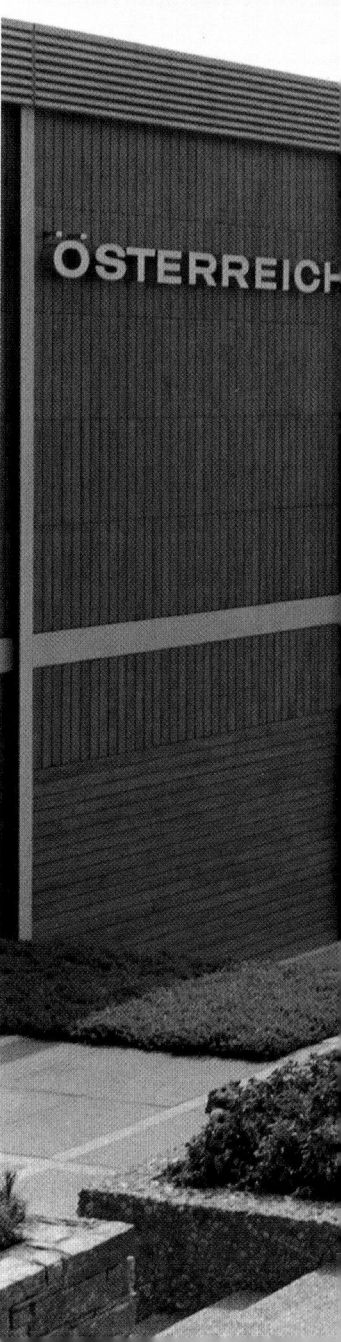

5.5
View of the Avenue de l'Europe and the Philips Pavilion opposite the Austrian Pavilion in which Anton Buczynski worked as a sound technician during the 1958 Brussels World's Fair..

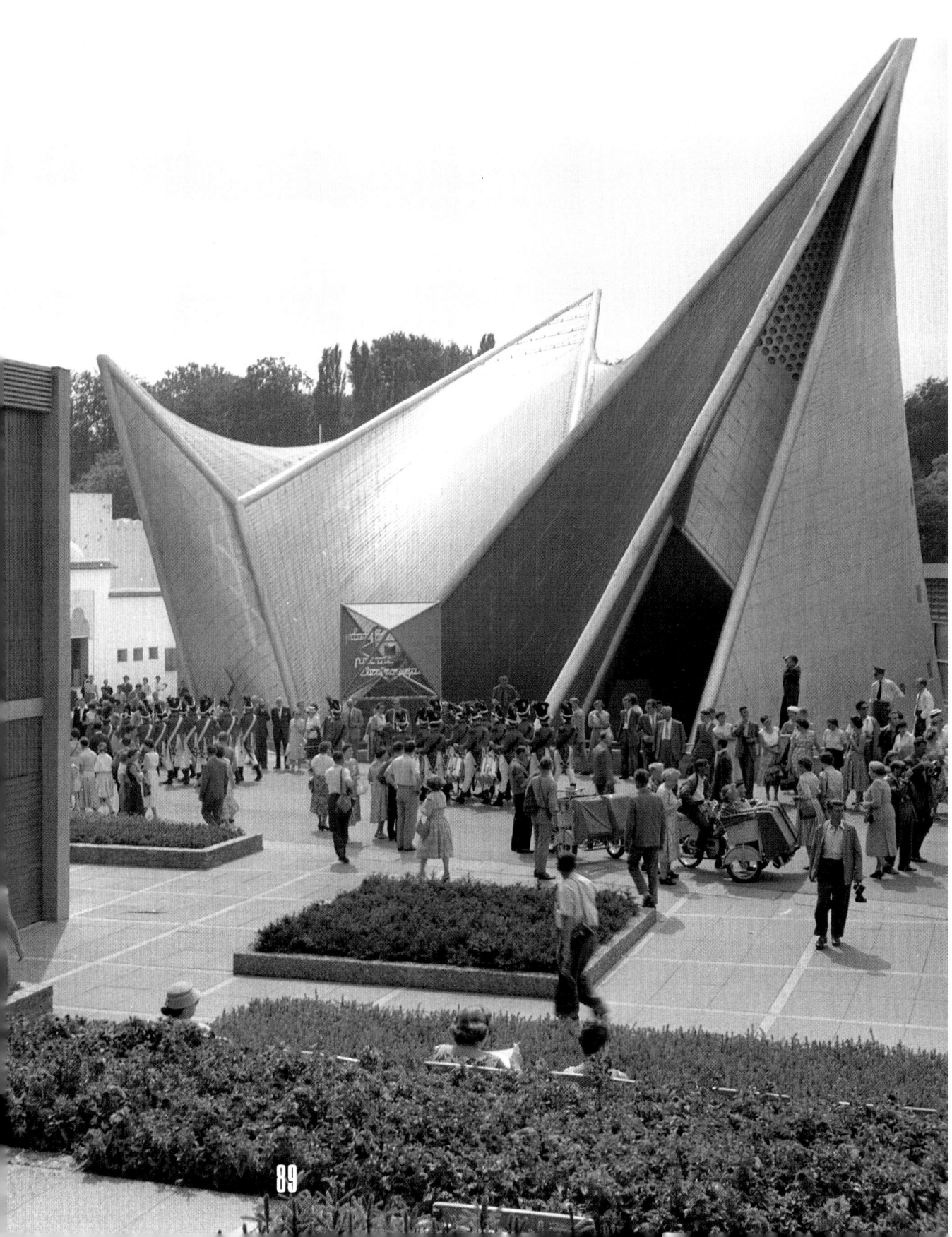

6 Inside the Philips Pavilion
Personal Stories from Those Who Operated *Le poème électronique*

Peter Wever

6.1
Arrival of the equipment and apparatus racks for the Philips Pavilion at the 1958 Brussels World's Fair. From left to right, technicians Pierre Losange, Wiel Cox and Michel Cools.

The daily performances of *Le poème électronique* and the publicity for Philips during the 1958 Brussels World's Fair were in the hands of a close-knit, permanent group of at least nineteen Dutch and Belgian technical and publicity staff. More than fifty years later, a number of former employees have recounted their memories of the pavilion. These personal stories reduce the mythical Philips Pavilion to more earthly proportions.[1]

Delayed until Further Notice

On Thursday 17 April, the 1958 Brussels World's Fair opened to a public that would eventually number 41 million visitors.[2] The Philips Pavilion remained closed to the public that day: the building itself had been completed, save for a few details,[3] but *Le poème électronique* was nowhere near ready to be performed.[4] Embarrassed Philips representatives made it known that the pavilion would open on 22 April regardless of any further changes Le Corbusier wanted to make to the performance.[5] Although an opening ceremony took place that day, including the premiere of an incomplete *Le poème électronique*, the actual performances for the public did not start until later.[6] Everyone worked tirelessly until late at night to get the complete work ready for performance. Various people, including acoustics expert Willem Tak and acoustics technician Jan de Bruyn of the Electroacoustics Main Industrial Division, were sent from Eindhoven to the pavilion in Brussels.[7] During this period, the staff at the Philips Pavilion were asked to be especially vigilant to ensure that no journalists or photographers entered the pavilion before the opening. Projectionist Paul Vancoppenolle saw an elderly man wearing a hat, thick-rimmed spectacles and a bow tie approach the entrance to the pavilion. He was about to confront the man but a sixth sense stopped him; when he asked one of his colleagues about the man, he discovered that he had nearly denied Le Corbusier access to the Philips Pavilion.[8] The opening of the pavilion was delayed yet again after rats chewed through the insulation of the electricity cables, leading to a short-circuit in the electrical system.[9] In the end, the first public performance of *Le poème électronique* took place on 20 May.[10]

The In-crowd

When the Philips Pavilion was actually operational, a close-knit, permanent group consisting of at least nineteen employees was responsible for the daily running of *Le poème électronique* and the publicity for Philips. The day-to-day management of the pavilion was in the hands of the Dutchman Simon de Bruin, whose portliness earned him the nickname 'Dikke De Bruin' [Fatty De Bruin]. At Philips De Bruin worked for the exhibition department of the Main Industrial Division Products for Industrial Applications [Hoofdindustriegroep Produkten voor Industriële Toepassingen].[11]

Performances of *Le poème électronique* were directed from the control room by a group of five Philips technicians: the Dutchmen Theo Boesveld, Jan van Hoof and Wiel Cox, and the Belgians Pierre Losange and François Vanderschrick. Theo Boesveld and Jan van Hoof worked for the department of Electronic Company Mechanization [Elektrische Bedrijfsmechanisatie] of the Main Industrial Division Products for

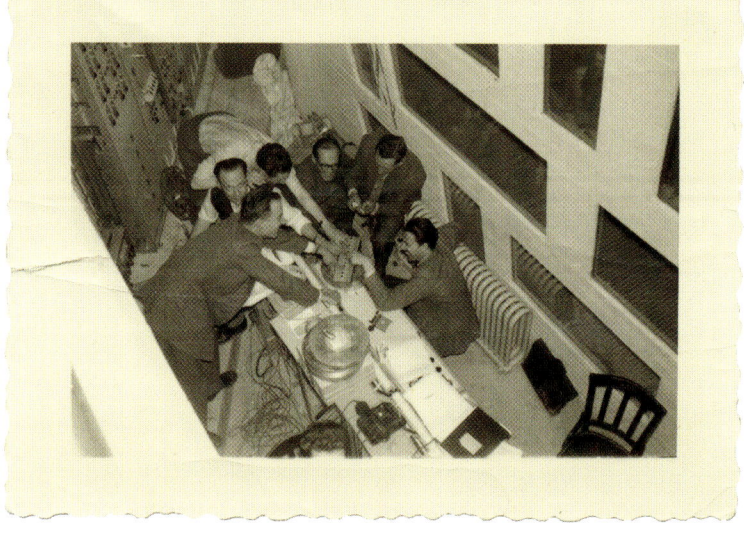

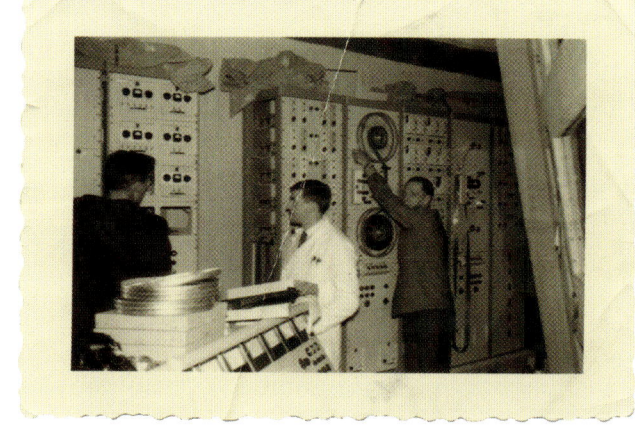

6.2
Job advertisement in the Belgian French-language newspaper *Le Soir*, dated 27 February 1958, for two projectionists and five pavilion attendants for the Philips Pavilion.

6.3
Staff-member pass for technician Wiel Cox, permitting access to the Dutch pavilion and the adjacent Philips Pavilion.

6.4
Night work in the Philips Pavilion control room to get *Le poème électronique* ready to be performed. The photograph at the top shows, clockwise from the left, acoustics technician Jan de Bruyn, technicians Jan Brouwer and Wiel Cox, lighting technician J.A.M. Binnendijk, acoustics expert Willem Tak and, probably, lighting technician J. van Eeghen. The men's hands are on the device that was used for encoding the command tape on which the control signals for the light and sound effects were recorded. The photograph was taken from a narrow, balustraded passageway on the first floor of the pavilion that provided a view of the control room. The photograph at the bottom shows, from left to right, Jan de Bruyn, and technicians Theo Boesveld and Jan Brouwer. It is clear that one of the perfotape machines for scanning the audiotapes and the control tapes with control signals for the sound and light effects had not been installed yet.

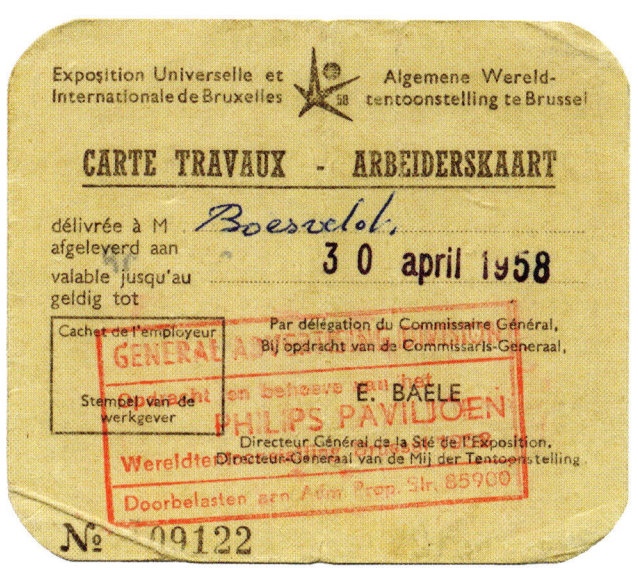

Industrial Applications, where equipment for Philips' own production lines and some of the equipment for the Philips Pavilion was made. Wiel Cox worked for the Electroacoustics Main Industrial Division, where he had earlier been closely involved in realizing Varèse's music in Eindhoven. François Vanderschrick and Pierre Losange were part of a group of four Belgian technicians who were made available for the pavilion by the Service Department at Philips Brussels.[12]

The Belgians Paul Vancoppenolle and Max Naveaux had temporary contracts with Philips, working as projectionists in the projection booths on, respectively, the ground floor and the first floor. They were assisted by Michel Cools and Michel Soete, respectively, who were among the four Belgian technicians seconded by the Service Department at Philips Brussels. They had initially been made available to assist the Dutch technicians install the cables between the different pieces of equipment in the pavilion, and François Vanderschrick was their team leader. When this work had been completed, the four were assigned tasks in operating the performances for the duration of the World's Fair.[13]

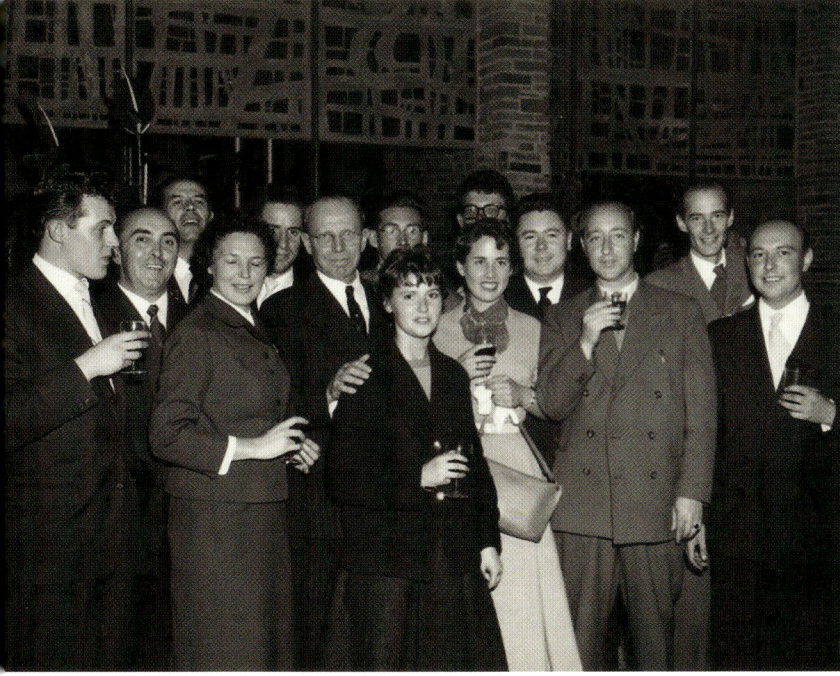

Pepita de Nerée tot Babberich from the Netherlands and Annie de Potter and Robert Sterneberg from Belgium were in charge of on-site sales of the book about the pavilion and *Le poème électronique*. The Belgian pavilion attendants, Jaak Derijcke, Paul Gellens, Julien Huyghe, Raymond Médard and a certain Mr. Vanden Bossche, ensured the efficient flow of visitors in and around the pavilion. Stef Niamonitakis, a Belgian electrotechnician of Greek parentage, worked for Electro Naval in Antwerp; he was on standby in the pavilion throughout the Word's Fair in case any of the electrical equipment installed by his company failed. To help him combat boredom, he was taught how to operate the film projectors, and he often helped in one of the two projection booths.[14]

A number of on-call employees were occasionally present in the Philips Pavilion. In his absence Simon de Bruin was replaced by the Belgian Marcel Desqueper, head of the Service Department at Philips Brussels.[15] Visiting dignitaries were given a guided tour by Frans Heukensfeldt Jansen, head of the Public Relations/Guided Tours department in Eindhoven, and his colleague Therus van Andringa de Kempenaer, who both travelled to Brussels when their services were required.[16] John Hafkemeijer of the General Advertising Division in Eindhoven was in charge of publicity for the Philips Pavilion and was therefore often in Brussels.[17] And lastly, the half-Russian Sonja Bootz worked as an interpreter at the Canadian pavilion but also provided guided tours of the Philips Pavilion in Russian upon request.[18] Dutch was, of course, the official language

6.5
Worker's pass for technician Theo Boesveld, authorizing him to enter the grounds of the World's Fair during the period when the Philips Pavilion had still not opened to the public.

6.6
Some of the Philips Pavilion employees attending a reception at the Dutch pavilion on 30 September 1958. From left to right, technician Jan van Hoof, publicity officer Robert Sterneberg, head of the Service Department at Philips Brussels Marcel Desqueper, secretary Ton Vervoort of the Dutch pavilion, technician Wiel Cox, President of the Board of Directors Frans Otten, technician Pierre Losange, publicity officer Annie de Potter, technician Michel Cools, publicity officer Pepita de Nerée tot Babberich, projectionist Paul Vancoppenolle, unidentified man, acoustics technician Jan de Bruyn, and technician François Vanderschrick.

spoken in the pavilion; the entire Belgian team, including the pavilion attendants, was bilingual but among themselves, the Belgians mainly spoke French. Despite the ever-present linguistic conflict in Belgium, language was never a problem at the Philips Pavilion.[19]

Behind the Scenes

The work spaces for the Philips Pavilion were located immediately to the right behind the entrance to the building. In the vestibule leading to the public area was a wall that had numerous windows, and double doors that provided access to a central area. From there, the tiny control room could be accessed. With the exception of the loudspeakers, all the electroacoustical equipment in the pavilion was installed two-fold. In the centre of the control room were two identical control desks, while perfotape machines, racks containing control-signal amplifiers, and racks with loudspeaker relay systems were located along the walls. Upon entering the pavilion, visitors could look through the windows in the wall and see the technical equipment in the control room. Two lavatories, a workshop and a spiral staircase leading upstairs were also located on the ground floor. A hatch provided access to a very narrow passage under the public area. The spiral staircase led to the first floor, 3.20 metres above ground floor level, opening onto a landing where a kitchenette with a sitting area ('the coffee room') was located, complete with a larder, a bench with a boiler and coffee-machine, and a fridge that was restocked with soft drinks every day. A door to the left of the spiral staircase provided access to an area with rectifiers and a narrow, balustraded passageway that provided a view of the control room, while to the right a door provided access to projectionist Max Naveaux's projection booth. The two film projectors for the écran and the tri-trous films were located in the projection booth. On the second floor, 6.20 metres above ground floor level, the spiral staircase opened onto a landing with a workbench where equipment could be repaired. To the left, a door provided access to a technical area where control units had been installed, and a door to the right provided access to showers and a changing room. The ventilators for air circulation were located on the third floor, 9.20 metres above ground floor level.[20]

Projectionist Paul Vancoppenolle's projection booth

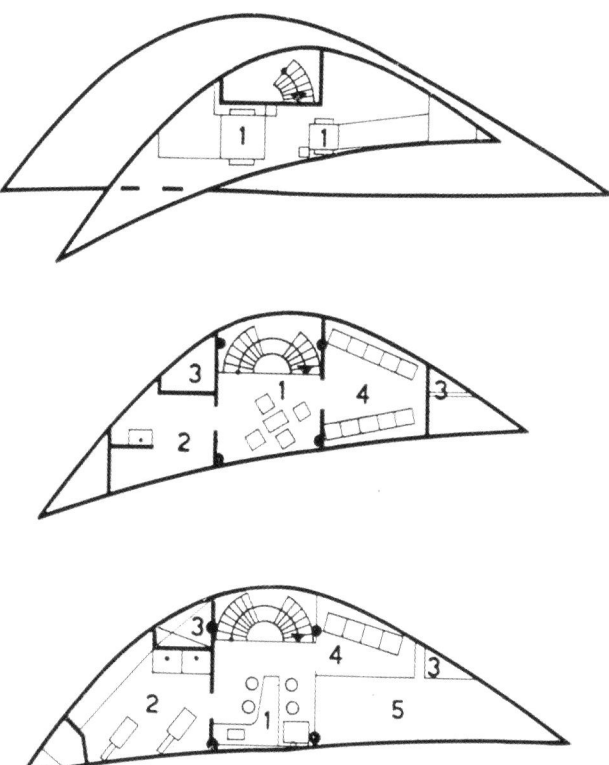

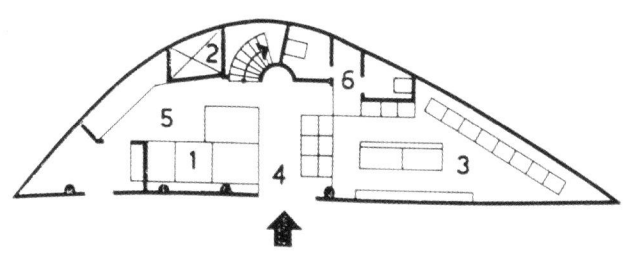

6.7
Floor plans, from top to ground level, of the Philips Pavilion (based on sources mentioned in note 20).

plan at 9.20 metres
1   ventilators
plan at 6.20 metres
1   landing with workbench
2   showers and changing room
3   ventilation ducts
4   apparatus racks

plan at 3.20 metres
1   kitchenette with sitting area
2   projection booth
3   ventilation ducts
4   apparatus rack
5   open space
plan at ground level
1   transformer
2   ventilation duct
3   control room with two control desks and apparatus racks
4   entrance
5   workshop
6   lavatories

6.8
Publicity photographs of the tiny control room in the Philips Pavilion. The photograph on the left shows technician Jan Brouwer standing in front of the wall with perfo tape machines, holding a reel of perfo tape in his hands. The photograph on the right shows technician Wiel Cox and pavilion manager Simon de Bruin sitting behind the two identical control desks.

with two film projectors for the *écran* and *tri-tous* films was located behind the balustrade in the public area on the ground floor. The gases generated by the lamps of the two projectors were extracted via a flue that led from the projectors to a hole in the pavilion's exterior wall. To conceal this flue hole, which was located at eyelevel on the pavilion's street side, a square tile was placed on the exterior wall, leaving a 10-centimetre gap between the tile and the wall. However, the flue proved inadequate to the task of extracting the gases and as a result, Paul Vancoppenolle and his colleague Michel Cools developed terrible headaches. For this reason, pavilion manager Simon de Bruin had a Philips vacuum cleaner complete with suction and blow nozzles brought in from Eindhoven. It was attached vertically to the inside wall of the projection booth, under the flue. The end of the vacuum cleaner hose was placed in the flue via a hole and pushed towards the outside. When the vacuum cleaner was switched on to the blow position, the air at the end of the flue was blown out, sucking out the gases produced by the projector lamps. The system was very effective. In practical terms, it meant that every time a performance of *Le poème électronique* started, a vacuum cleaner was switched on first.[21]

'Continuez à la Main...'

Le poème électronique contained a number of instances where Le Corbusier's images and Varèse's composition were linked. This was partly why it was essential that every aspect of the performance be controlled automatically. To achieve this, an interlock system was installed in the pavilion to make sure all equipment relating to images, sound and light would start synchronously by pressing a button on the control desk. At the moment this button was pressed, the audiotapes, control tape and film reels all had to be positioned at the correct starting point. When the equipment was activated, synchronous motors supplied from the same generator ensured a constant playback time for the different tapes.[22] Only the projector lamps had to be switched on manually prior to a performance, so a 'Lanterns on!' command would first be issued from the control room.[23]

In August 1958 a paraphrased interview with technician François Vanderschrick about operating this 'fully automated show' appeared in the Dutch regional newspaper *Eindhovens Dagblad*: "'Look, this is how I switch on the

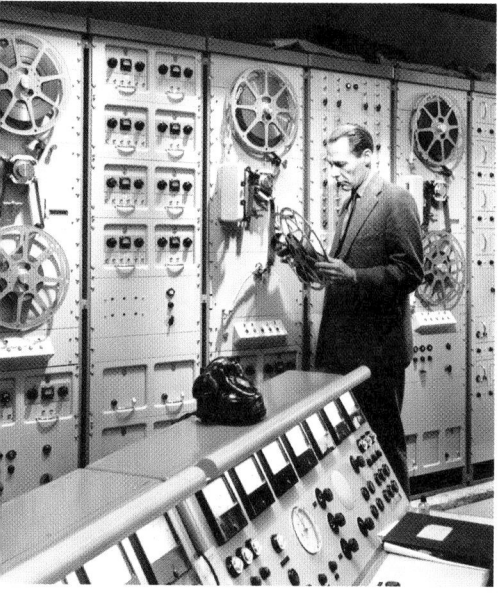
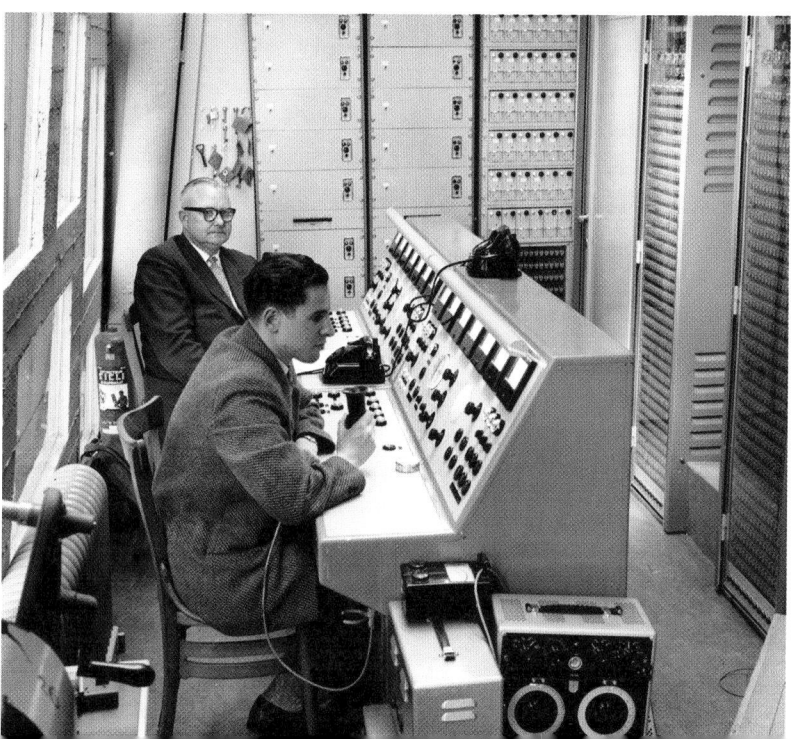

Electronic poem," and he presses the "On" button and then the "Go" button. "Now we've started, from now on everything will happen completely automatically, no one can change a single thing, the human hand plays no further role, only those two reels," as he points to two strangely striped film reels that are slowly turning on one of the impressive grey machines. "One is an audiotape, the other is the command tape, which conducts the hundreds of loudspeakers, projectors, spotlights, all the instruments, which, inside the Stomach, produce and combine the hundreds of darting and changing images and sounds of the Electronic poem." Proudly, he adds that "It's perfect every time. We've now given more than 1,500 performances and only twice had a slight hitch, when one of the tapes snapped – after all, they are subject to wear and tear"'[24]

Projectionist Paul Vancoppenolle emphasized that the interlock system was switched on for all performances. As far as he could recall, the interlock system failed only once: Pierre Losange was at the control desk at the time, and when he became aware that something was going wrong he used a loudspeaker to instruct the projectionists to start the four film projectors manually: '*Continuez à la main . . .* ' [continue manually].[25]

Light, Colour, Rhythm, Image, Sound . . . Smell

Light, colour, rhythm, image and sound were the merged phenomena that turned *Le poème électronique* into the first multimedia performance for the masses.[26] A sixth, unforeseen, phenomenon, however, also contributed to the multi-sensory experience of the performance: to put it frankly, the pavilion sometimes stank, and this was exacerbated when some visitors were so petrified or suddenly got such a fright during the performance that they wet themselves. On one occasion a heavily pregnant woman's waters even broke. There was no air conditioning in the Philips Pavilion but the

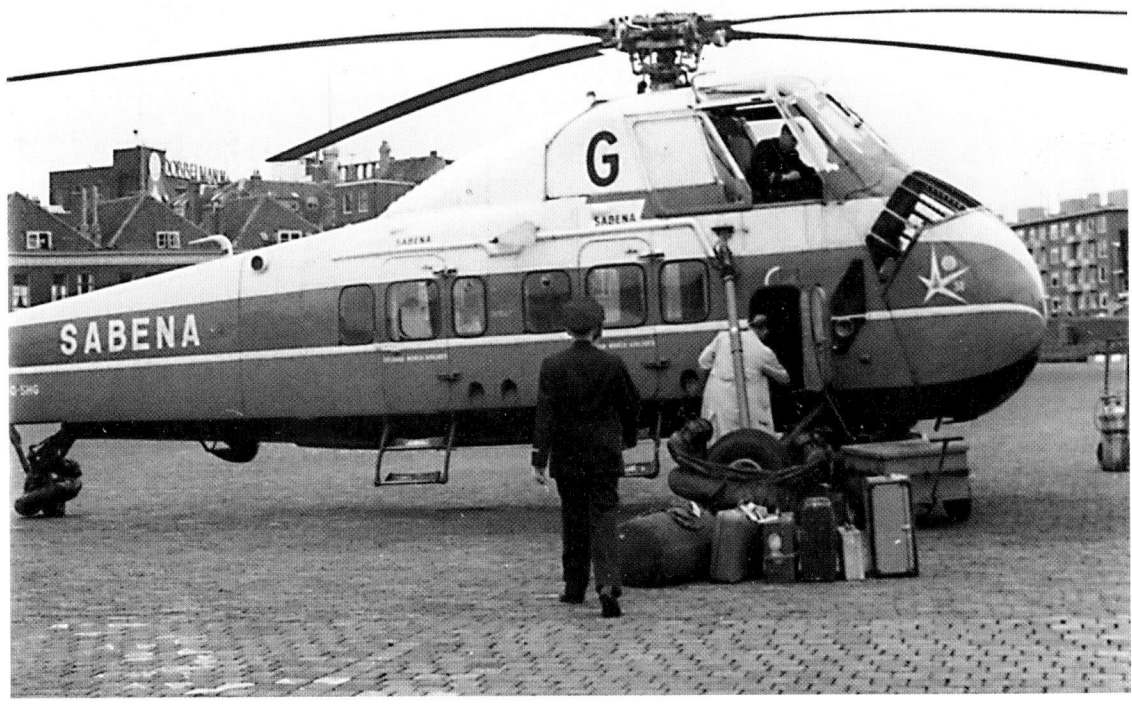

public area was supplied with fresh air from vents placed high in the building's facade: from here, the air flowed to a crawl space under the public area through a ventilating duct via powerful ventilators on the third floor of the work areas. This crawl space, which the technicians called *le caniveau* [the gutter], led the air to the public area via gaps in the balustrade along the pavilion's inside wall. Several times a day, approximately a quarter of a litre of undiluted fluid citronella was poured through a hatch into the crawl space to mask unpleasant odours in the public area. Generous amounts of citronella were also used when the building was cleaned every evening. In fact so much citronella was used in the pavilion that employees could still smell it when they returned to their hotel in the evenings.

When the weather was warm, the public area was sometimes cooler than the outside temperature because of the ventilation system. But the unventilated projection booth on the ground floor sometimes became unbearably hot, partly because of the heat released by the two projectors – technician Michel Cools sometimes had both feet in a bucketful of cold water while he operated the film projectors and occasionally, much to his colleagues' amusement, he even swapped his shirt and trousers for a dress, saying this was *plus aéré* [airier].[27]

Leisure

Every staff member of the Philips Pavilion was entitled to only one weekday off. At the weekends, the busiest days of the week, everyone had to stay at their posts. The only exceptions were made for the Dutchmen Theo Boesveld, Jan van Hoof and Wiel Cox, who commuted to and from the Netherlands by car or Sabena helicopter at the weekends.[28]

However, the building's spatial and technical possibilities meant they could be deployed to fend off boredom in all sorts of ways. During the day, thousands of visitors were confronted in the public area with Le Corbusier's vision of our civilization as conqueror of modern times;[29] in the evenings, this area was converted into a table-tennis venue. At the request of employees, a table-tennis table had been purchased; it was kept out of sight behind the balustrade in the public area, next to the projection lanterns, lights and bass speakers. When the last notes of *Le poème électronique* had died away, the table-tennis table was often brought out for an hour of ping-pong.[30]

In 1957, Philips acoustics technician Dick Raaijmakers had adapted the march music 'Colonel Bogey March' from the war film *Bridge on the River Kwai*, transforming it into the electronic composition 'Colonel Bogey'.[31] In the weeks during which the Philips Pavilion remained closed following the opening of the World's Fair, pavilion manager Simon de Bruin passed the time by developing an executive program to play this composition over the loudspeakers in the pavilion. Late one summer afternoon, a heavy thunderstorm passed over the grounds of the World's Fair. Just as a performance of *Le poème électronique* had ended it started to pour with rain, so instead of leaving the Philips Pavilion visitors took shelter in the

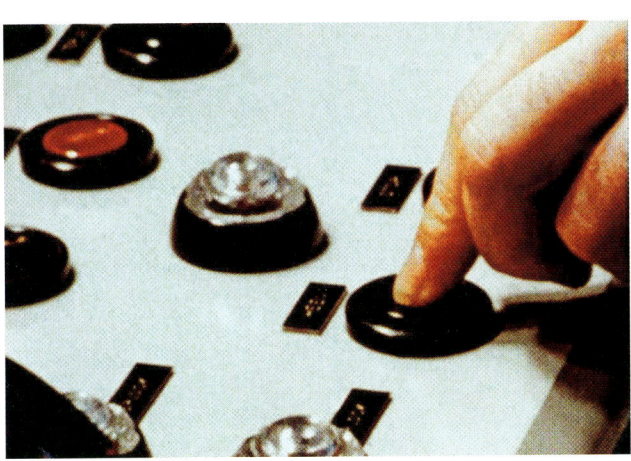

6.9
A Sabena Sikorsky S-58 helicopter, which was frequently used by technicians Theo Boesveld, Jan van Hoof and Wiel Cox to fly between Brussels and the Netherlands.

6.10
Image from an 8-mm amateur film showing technician Wiel Cox pressing the button on the control desk in the control room of the Philips Pavilion by which a performance of *Le poème électronique* was started.

public area. Simon de Bruin seized the opportunity to play his version of Dick Raaijmakers' composition: he started the audiotape and the control tape, and the sounds circulated through the loudspeaker tracks in the pavilion. The public was deeply impressed, rewarding the satisfied Simon de Bruin with loud applause.[32] The sound system was not the only equipment deployed for the staff's amusement: the film projectors in the pavilion were also put to use. In the weeks before the postponed opening of the pavilion, projectionist Max Naveaux regularly showed 35-mm films: a film about the defence of the English coast against German attacks during the Second World War, for example, was projected onto the inside walls of the Philips Pavilion.[33] Both the adapted music from *Bridge on the River Kwai* and the war film were far removed from the universal brotherhood that was one of the aspirations of this World's Fair, the first since the end of the Second World War.

Electronic music was not the only music that was to be heard in the Philips Pavilion. Technician Theo Boesveld in particular had a preference for jazz at the time. He bought a Dual record player, which was put in the coffee room on the

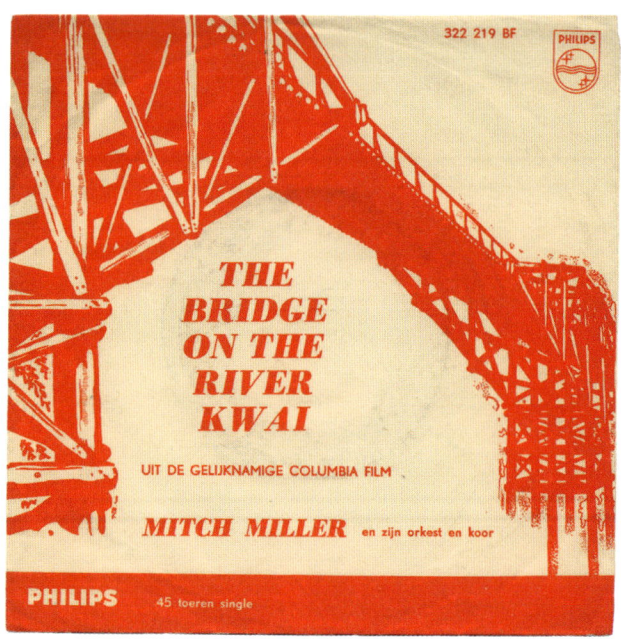

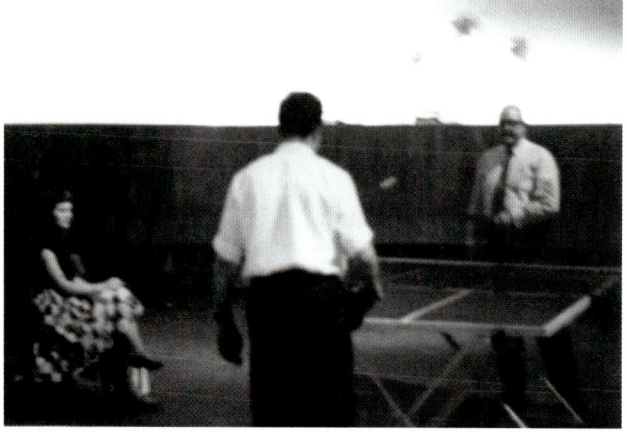

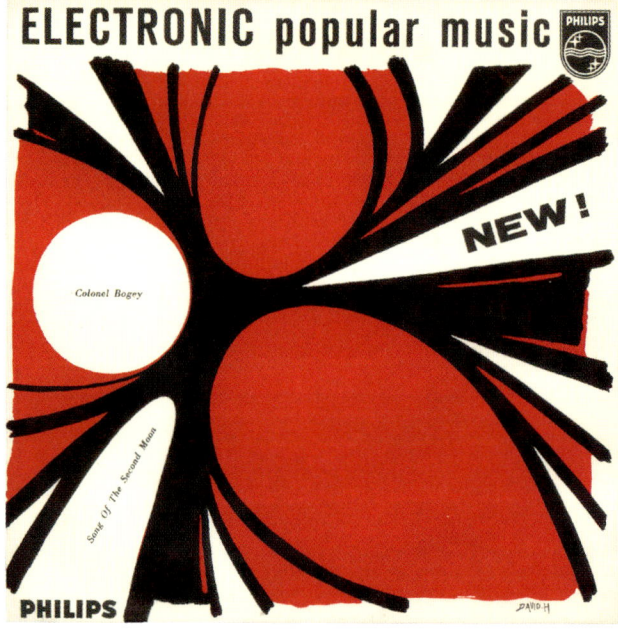

6.11
Technician Jan van Hoof, seen from behind, and pavilion manager Simon de Bruin passed some of their evenings playing ping-pong in the public area of the Philips Pavilion. Their sporting activities are watched by Nelly Oosterom, who worked as an information officer at the Dutch pavilion.

6.12
Above, the cover for the Mitch Miller orchestra's single of the 'Colonel Bogey March' from the film *Bridge on the River Kwai*. Below, the cover for a singles recording of technician Dick Raaijmakers' electronic version of the march, 'Colonel Bogey'; pavilion manager Simon de Bruin developed an executive program to play Raaijmakers' composition through the loudspeakers in the Philips Pavilion.

6.13
Time for coffee in the kitchenette with its sitting area on the first floor of the Philips Pavilion. Clockwise from the left, technician Wiel Cox, technician Jan van Hoof, Agnes Bos and Nelly Oosterom (seen from behind), respectively hostess and information officer at the Dutch pavilion.

6.14
Hidden from view in a corner of the control room, technician Theo Boesveld opens a bottle of wine while spectators enter the Philips Pavilion on the other side of the window. Nelly Oosterom, information officer at the Dutch pavilion, can be seen in the foreground.

6   Inside the Philips Pavillion

first floor. Via an amplifier, the sound was transmitted to an internal-communications loudspeaker. LPs were purchased at the Philips staff shop in Brussels at a 30% discount. The Dave Brubeck Quartet's *Jazz Goes to College* album was appreciated by everyone, but recordings of classical music, including Rachmaninov, Beethoven and Paganini, were also heard in the pavilion.[34]

One More Cup of Coffee

When the pavilion had been opened to the public, running it soon became a daily routine. Once a week there was a technical check of the equipment to ensure it was in order. Coffee was one of the small joys of life that provided a welcome break in the daily routine. Pavilion manager Simon de Bruin in particular drank copious amounts of coffee. Projectionist Max Naveaux, whose projection booth was located on the first floor next to the kitchenette, was the obvious person in the pavilion to make coffee. Simon de Bruin would therefore often call out from behind the control desk, 'Naveaux! Is the coffee ready yet?' So he would not have to keep running up and down the stairs, Max Naveaux had devised a logistical system using the lid of a round film-reel tin as a tray: he had drilled holes in three places in the raised edge of the tin, threaded a cord through them, and hung the tin on a line that was stretched between the narrow passageway on the first floor and the control desk. To everyone's amusement, he would carefully lower the tin with a cup of coffee so that it landed precisely on Simon de Bruin's control desk.[35]

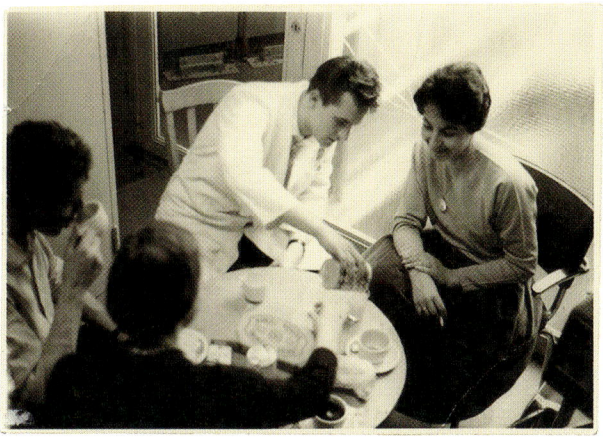

Confession

The staff at the Philips Pavilion were present during thousands of performances of *Le poème électronique*. Despite this, projectionist Paul Vancoppenolle confessed that he never really understood much of it. Technician Wiel Cox also said he did not understand most of it, partly because no one had bothered to explain the ideas behind the work to the staff: it was impressive, but the link between the various elements was unclear. Technician Theo Boesveld did realize after some time that it dealt with a vision of man's development, especially in the field of technology – after all, the performance started with the *Genesis* sequence and ended with the atom bomb and rockets. Looking back, he thought the story was presented in a rather infantile way.[36]

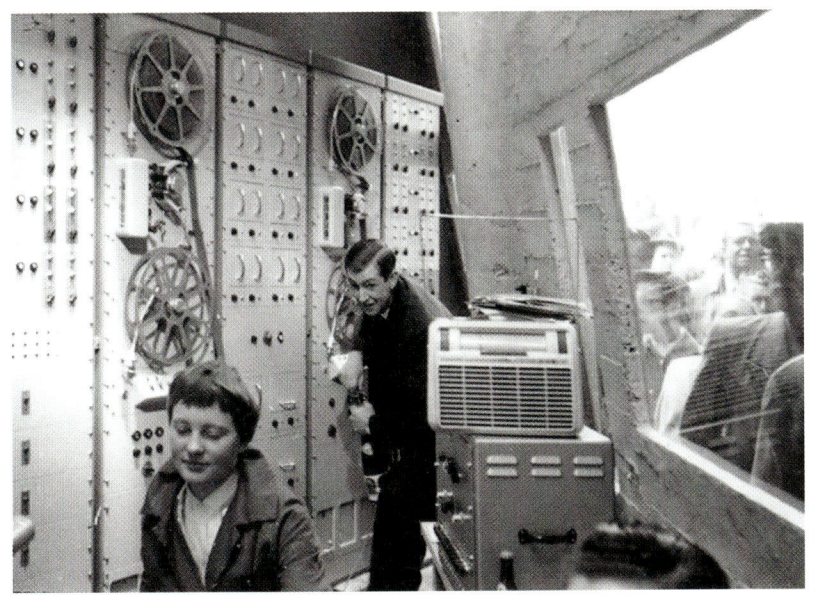

7 That's Entertainment
Publicity for the Philips Pavilion
Peter Wever

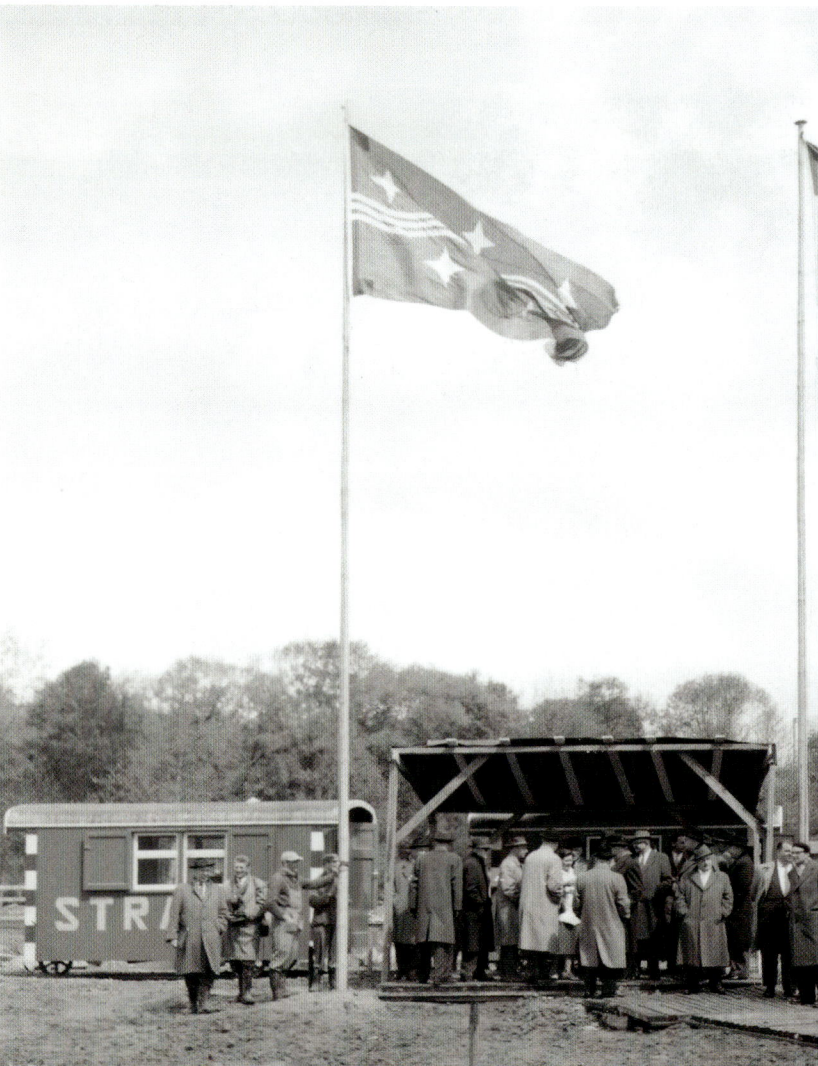

7.1
The Dutch flag and the Philips flag were raised to mark the ground-breaking ceremony for the foundation of the Philips Pavilion on 6 May 1957. Images of this ceremony were used as the opening shots in the publicity film *De bouw van het Philips paviljoen* **[The Construction of the Philips Pavilion].**

Notwithstanding the avant-garde nature of the Philips Pavilion, the Philips company would have aimed to generate as much publicity as possible for the pavilion, and various means were deployed to provide the public with information. Publisher Les Éditions de Minuit published a book about the Philips Pavilion, which was intended for sale and as a commemorative volume for visiting dignitaries. In retrospect, Frits Philips was ambivalent about whether the millions that had been expended on the pavilion were actually well spent. In any event, he proposed that the company should not participate in another World's Fair.

Publicity Film 'The Construction of the Philips Pavilion'

In the words of Louis Kalff, Philips intended the Philips Pavilion to provide 'an avant-garde display that will certainly be one of the fair's most remarkable'.[1] Philips' interest in generating as much publicity as possible for the pavilion was that much greater because virtually all the expenses relating to this display were paid for from the Algemeen Reclamebudget Eindhoven [General advertising budget Eindhoven].[2] General Advertising Director Sies Numann had sole responsibility for the publicity for the Philips Pavilion.[3]

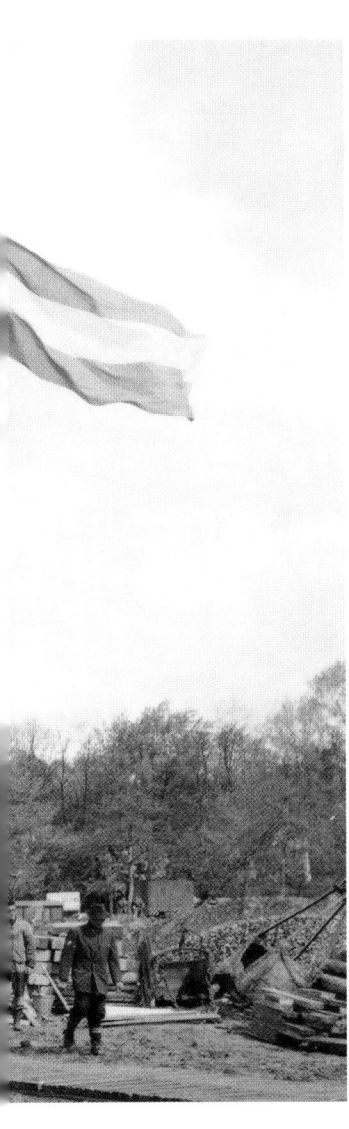

One obvious opportunity to attract publicity was the ground-breaking ceremony for the foundation of the pavilion site on 6 May 1957.[4] Numan did the honours during a violent hailstorm in the presence of senior Philips Netherlands and Philips Belgium executives, including Louis Kalff and deputy manager of Philips Belgium, Charles Spaens, as well as several newspaper reporters. The Dutch tricolour and the Philips flag were raised in honour of the event. Film images of this ceremony appear as the opening shots in the publicity film *De bouw van het Philips paviljoen* [The Construction of the Philips Pavilion]. This eleven-and-a-half minute, black-and-white film then shows images of load tests on a scale model of the pavilion; the construction of the concrete tiles for the pavilion's walls in a Brussels warehouse; Le Corbusier and Iannis Xenakis' 15 April 1957 visit to the Philips truck garage at the Strijp III premises in Eindhoven, which had been converted into a test workshop and studio;[5] and finally, the construction of the pavilion within the precincts of the World's Fair.[6] The film was made by producer Jan Daudey of Philips' General Advertising Division and the company's in-house film maker Jan Bijvank, who together had made many company films in the past.[7] *De bouw van het Philips paviljoen* was included in the film archive of the Philips Film Library.[8]

Philips Spatiorama

At the 1958 Brussels World's Fair, national pavilions such as the one for the Netherlands simply bore the name of their country. Pavilions belonging to national and international companies, such as the Coca-Cola Pavilion, usually bore the company name.[9] With this in mind, Louis Kalff wrote in September 1957 that he believed 'effective publicity will ensure that the pavilion will become known as the Philips Pavilion without the need to stridently announce its name'.[10] Nevertheless, in October 1957 a competition was announced in the weekly Philips staff newspaper, the *Philips Koerier*, inviting readers to think of a name for the pavilion. Surprisingly, the competition was announced in an article headed

'Wie weet naam voor Philips paviljoen?' [Who knows name for Philips pavilion?], suggesting that the building was already known under that name. The winner of the competition was promised a trip to Brussels for two, including several nights' accommodation and a visit to the Philips Pavilion. Submissions would be accepted until 1 November.[11]

In the weeks that followed, the *Philips Koerier* received 7,204 suggestions from 3,023 readers from at least three continents – one Philips employee submitted 75 names. Many readers' imaginations led them to names that were derived from the company name – Philutopia, Philifiction, Philektron, Philispace, Philiscoop, Philatrium, Philidrome, Philips Elektrópolis and even Philips Apocalyps. The frequently submitted Philirama made use of 'rama', a popular suffix at the time: it was used in the American widescreen film systems Cinerama (an anagram of American) and Walt Disney's Circarama, and in their Soviet counterpart Kinopanorama, all three of which were presented to the public at the 1958 Brussels World's Fair.[12] The same suffix was used in the Spatiorama submission and the frequently submitted Futurama, although the latter had already been used during the 1939–1940 New York World's Fair for the incredibly successful diorama of the future created by Norman Bel Geddes for the General Motors Corporation Pavilion.[13] Other suggestions that were not derived from the word Philips included Poëtron, Autavision and Kosmovitron.[14]

Although readers of the *Philips Koerier* were informed on 9 November that the jury still had not reached a decision,[15] Kalff suggested the name Philips Spatiorama to Le Corbusier during a working visit on 15 November 1957.[16] Le Corbusier's '*c'est trop affreux!*' [it is too awful!] indicated his aversion to the name, and he suggested simply calling it the 'Pavillon Philips', '*un vocable qui ne fasse pas "rigoler" tout le monde*' [a word that won't make everyone laugh].[17] In January 1958 the *Philips Koerier* informed its readers that both Kalff and Le Corbusier were of the opinion 'that despite the large number of submissions, *the* name has not been found'. It was foreseeable that the pavilion would, at least for the moment, and maybe even permanently, be known as the 'Philips' Paviljoen'.[18] The editors of the *Philips Koerier*, however, thought the efforts of its readers deserved to be rewarded: the promised prize was therefore awarded to the readers who had submitted Philips Elektrópolis and Spatiorama.[19]

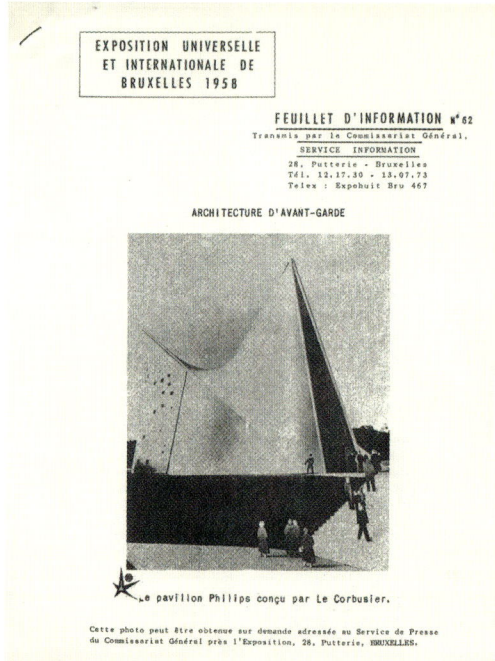

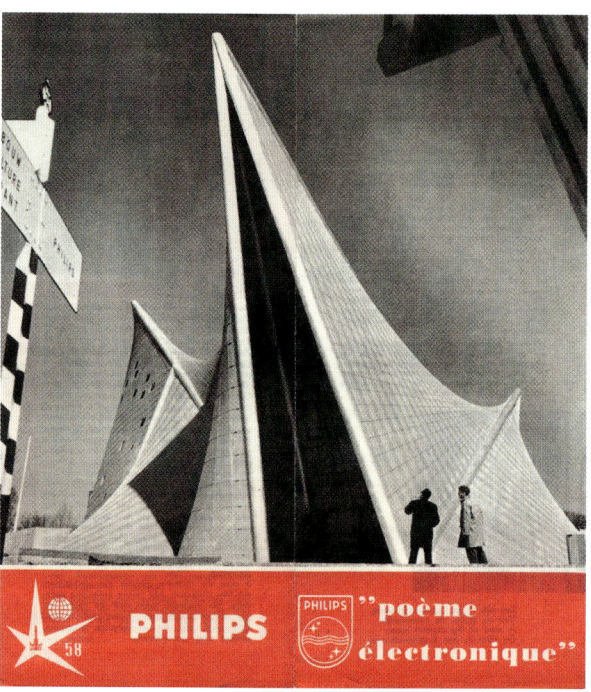

7.2
The Office of the Commissioner General of the World's Fair made the French-language information bulletin N° 62 available before the opening, which described the Philips Pavilion as an avant-garde construction within whose walls a *spectacle 'son et lumière'* [sound and light show] would take place.

7.3
The rarer red version of the simple, four-language folder that Philips provided in an attempt to give visitors an impression of what they were going to see in the Philips Pavilion.

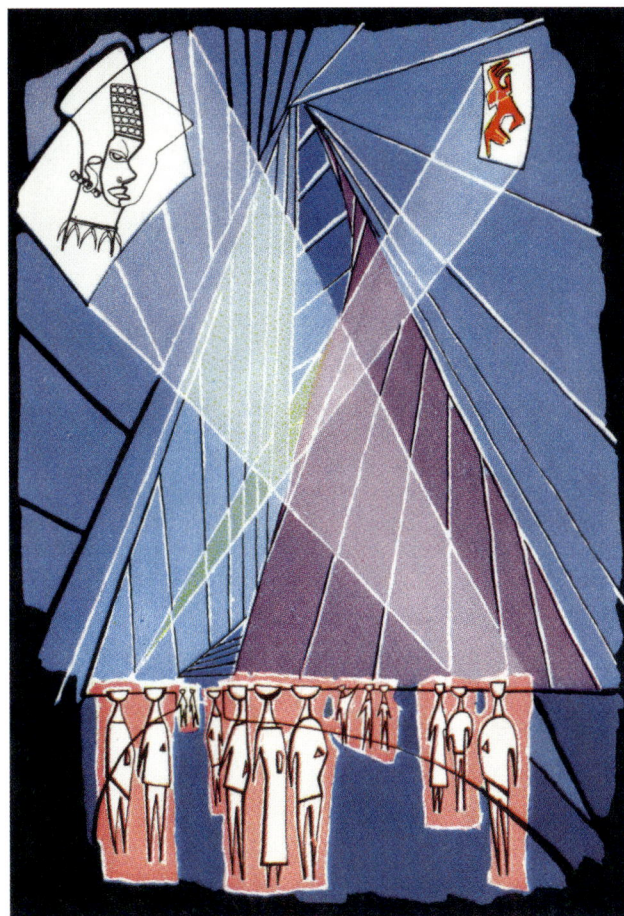

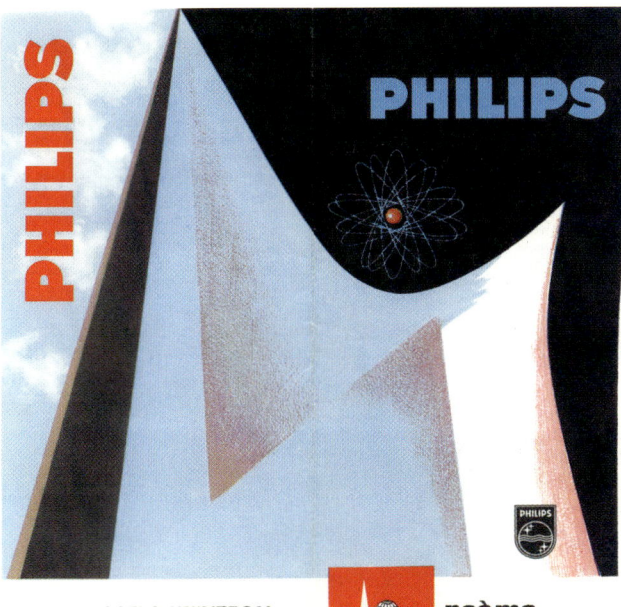

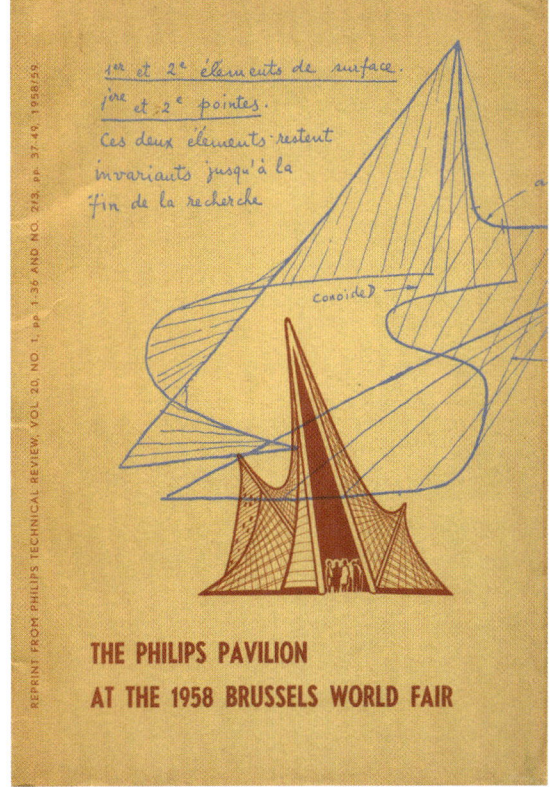

7.4
The illustration on the left shows the English version of the more detailed folder providing on the one hand general information about Philips and the company's operations at the 1958 Brussels World's Fair, and on the other hand a text about *Le poème électronique*. The top right illustration is an artist's impression of *Le poème électronique* that appeared in this brochure.

7.5
English reprint publication with a collection of articles about the Philips Pavilion that had originally appeared in the *Philips Technisch Tijdschrift* [Philips Technical Review] magazine.

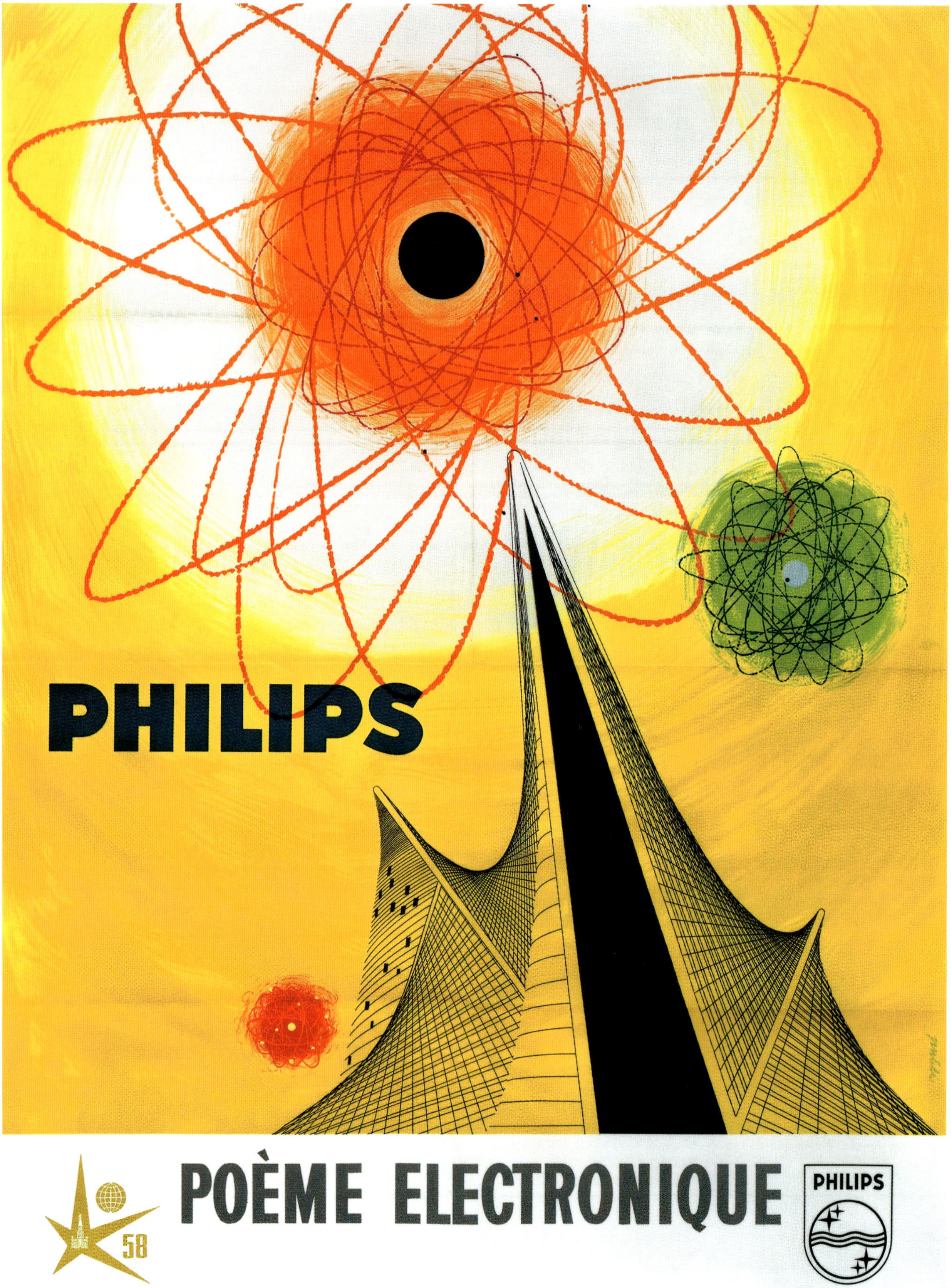

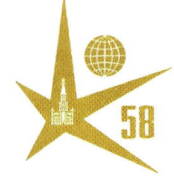
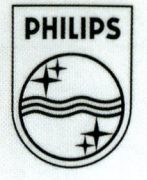

Written Information

In order to provide general information before the opening of the fair, the Office of the Commissioner General of the World's Fair supplied information bulletins in various languages about the national pavilions and the pavilions of participating organizations. The French-language information bulletin N° 62 describes the Philips Pavilion as an avant-garde architectural structure where a spectacle *'son et lumière'* [sound and light show] will take place, and it is illustrated with a photograph of a scale model of the pavilion.

Philips itself wanted to provide visitors with 'a simple folder giving people an impression of what they are going to see'.[20] A folder was therefore made, with a brief explanation in Dutch, French, German and English of the technical aspects of the performance of *Le poème électronique*. Green and, more rarely, red copies of this folder were distributed to the public. The photograph on the front page of this folder was taken by Philips' in-house film maker Jan Bijvank.[21]

A second, more detailed folder provided on the one hand general information about Philips and the company's operations at the World's Fair, which included supplying the lighting for a large number of the pavilions, and a text about the performance of *Le poème électronique* on the other. This text was illustrated with two artist's impressions of the performance that were far removed from the *ambiances* that Le Corbusier aimed to create. The folder was published in several languages, including Dutch, French and English.

To provide the international press with information, a press file about the Philips Pavilion was made available to the media in different languages.[22] Various articles in the monthly *Philips Technisch Tijdschrift* [Philips Technical Review] magazine supplied more detailed technical information about the pavilion and the performance. These articles proved to be so popular that they appeared in a special reprint publication in Dutch, French, German and English.[23]

Publicity Campaign

Philips had already recognized the importance of publicity early in its history, and a huge amount of advertising was created for the company. Starting in 1916, famous artists were regularly commissioned to make posters or other forms of advertising. In 1922, Philips employed the German Hans Oertle as its first permanent advertisement designer. Oertle illustrated printed matter and designed posters, folders and packaging. Louis Kalff started

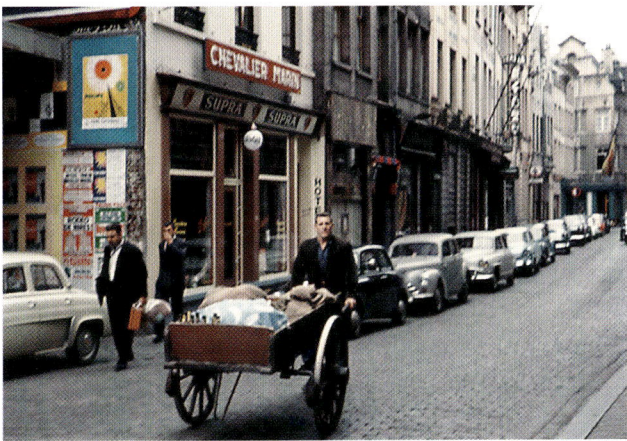

7.6
The illustration on the left shows the poster that was created to promote the Philips Pavilion, which is here surrounded by three electron clouds circling atomic nuclei. The illustration on the lower right shows the poster as it appeared in the streetscapes of Brussels.

7.7
An advertisement from the *Het Laatste Nieuws* newspaper dated 19 April 1958 urging readers to experience the World's Fair on a Philips television set at home, far from the madding crowds. The oblong in the bottom left-hand corner points out the Philips Pavilion and *Le poème électronique*.

his work as an advertisement designer for Philips in 1925, and went on to become head of the advertising department.[24]

The importance of publicity for the Philips Pavilion was also understood at an early stage, and poster advertising was considered the obvious instrument.[25] A futuristic poster was therefore created showing the Philips Pavilion against a dark yellow background, surrounded by three electron clouds circling atomic nuclei.[26] The design was in keeping with the so-called 'Expostyle' architecture with its kidney and star shapes, Atomium motif and colourful geometric details as formal elements.[27] The poster also incorporated the five-pointed star designed by the Belgian Lucien de Roeck that, in line with the Expostyle, served as the general logo for the World's Fair.[28] The poster can be seen in photographs taken of Brussels street scenes and the hospitality centre that Philips Belgium set up for the occasion at its offices at Anderlechtstraat 37 in Brussels.[29]

Before and during the World's Fair, small informative oblongs about the Philips Pavilion and *Le poème électronique*, complete with a picture of De Roeck's five-pointed star, were added to advertisements for Philips products in Belgian newspapers, magazines and brochures.[30]

From about 1900, picture postcards were Philips' first known form of advertising.[31] Picture postcards of the Philips Pavilion were therefore also regarded as a form of publicity, and Philips initially considered printing these postcards itself.[32] In the end, however, three external firms sold the postcards of the pavilion. The Belgian Egicarte company was the exclusive licence-holder for the World's Fair and it printed hundreds of colour and black-and-white postcards of the event, several of which included views of the Philips Pavilion. Because the photographs for these postcards had been taken before the opening of the World's Fair, construction works within the fair precincts can still be seen on many of the cards. The Hague bookseller W.P. van Stockum & Zoon N.V. printed a series of black-and-white postcards

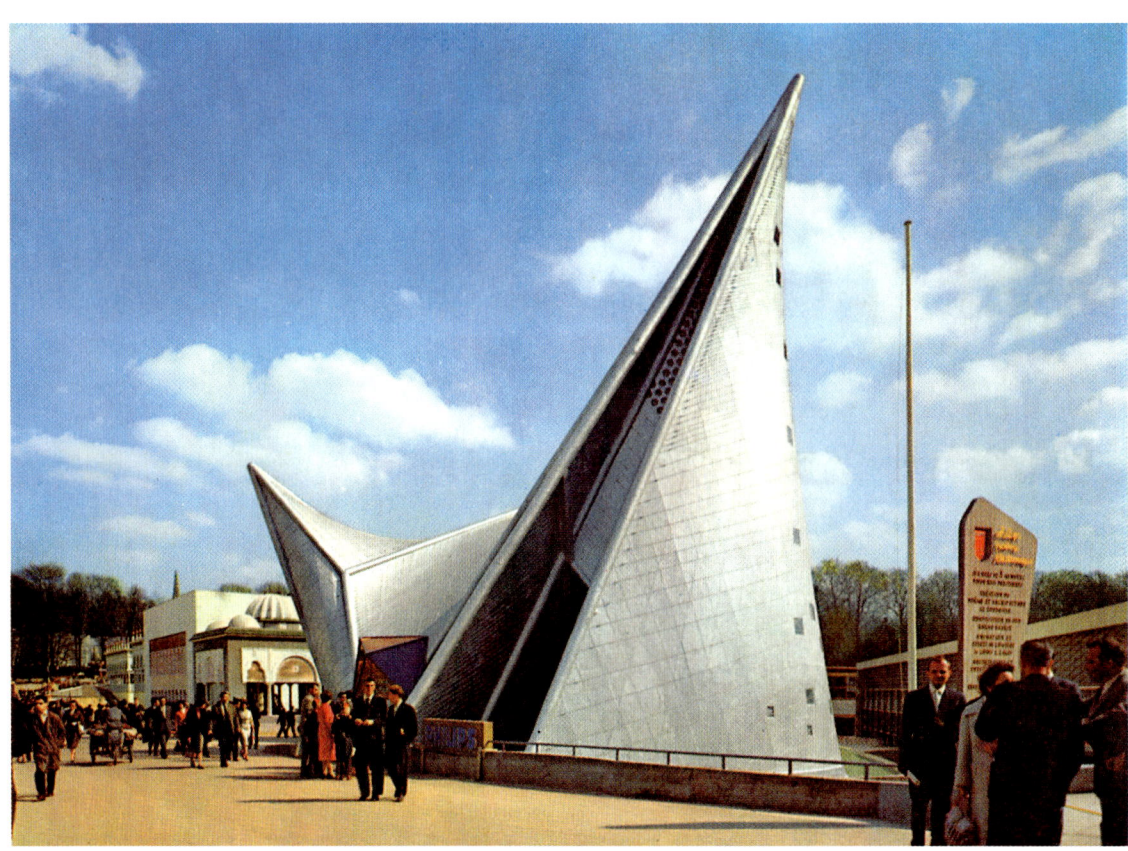

of the Dutch pavilion as well as a card of the Philips Pavilion. The Rotterdam publisher Gebr. Spanjersberg N.V. also printed a small series of black-and-white postcards that included pictures of the Dutch pavilion and the Philips Pavilion.[33]

Perhaps the most famous of all the publicity photographs that were taken of the Philips Pavilion shows Le Corbusier, Varèse and Kalff in conversation, the pavilion in the background, during their visit on 7 February 1958.[34] The weather that day was miserable,[35] which probably contributed to Le Corbusier and Varèse getting the flu a few days later.[36]

Les Cahiers Forces Vives

In a letter to Kalff dated 17 August 1957, Le Corbusier hinted at a possible Les Éditions de Minuit book about the Philips Pavilion. The Paris publishing house Les Éditions de Minuit was set up as a clandestine operation in 1941 during the German occupation. It published the *Les Cahiers Forces Vives* series, which focused on the problems of modern architecture and provided Le Corbusier in particular with a platform.[37] When Le Corbusier again raised this issue with Kalff during a meeting in Paris on 12 September, Kalff proposed that Numann consider the publication,[38] arguing that the book would be 'the only thing left' after the pavilion had been dismantled.[39]

The editor of *Les Cahiers Forces Vives* was Jean Petit, who had also collaborated with Le Corbusier to gather together the photographic documentation using Le Corbusier's scenario for *Le poème électronique*.[40] In a discussion

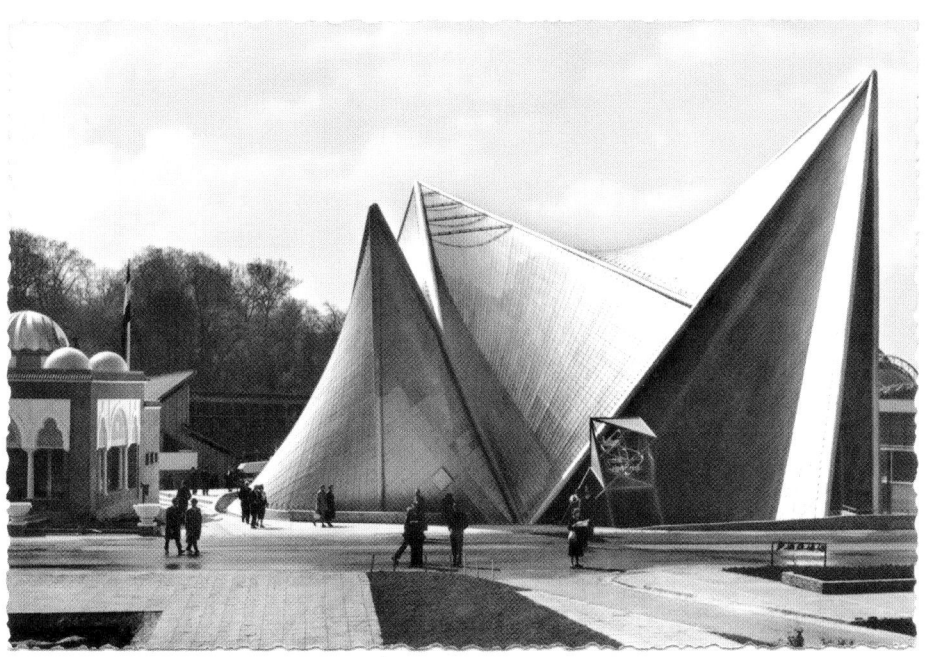

7.8
Picture postcard of the Philips Pavilion printed by the exclusive licence-holder for the World's Fair, the Belgian Egicarte company. 'PHILIPS' has been added in blue lettering to the concrete balustrade in front of the pavilion, around which part of the temporary wooden boarding is still visible.

7.9
The Philips Pavilion on a picture postcard printed by the Hague bookseller Boekhandel W.P. van Stockum & Zoon N.V.

with Kalff on 15 November, Petit took responsibility for the book's editing and typography. The book would deal with the pavilion's inception, the scenario, and the public's reaction. The initial aim was to print a minimum of 10,000 copies of the French and Dutch editions,[41] to be sold or presented as commemorative volumes to visiting dignitaries.[42]

Le Corbusier's handwritten draft contribution for the book dated from 29 March 1958, three weeks before the opening of the World's Fair.[43] The final publication, a 244-page, hardback French-language volume with a dust jacket, did not appear until two months after the end of the World's Fair, in December 1958. The book, *Le poème électronique. Le Corbusier*, included contributions by Kalff, Petit, Le Corbusier, Michel Butor, Iannis Xenakis, Professor Cornelis Vreedenburgh, Hoyte Duyster and Edgard Varèse. Besides a large number of black-and-white photographs and design drawings, the publication also included a colour section with illustrations of several of the images selected by Le Corbusier for *Le poème électronique*. It was emphasized that this visual depiction did not aspire to be a reproduction of *Le poème électronique*, 'which is a unity of sounds, of light variations, of images, of rhythm, and of colours, housed in an architectural construct whose volume is naturally linked to the universe'. On the dust jacket is Le Corbusier's drawing of an open hand, made specially for the book.[44] This drawing also appears on a supplementary sheet that accompanied the book, next to a text by Le Corbusier:

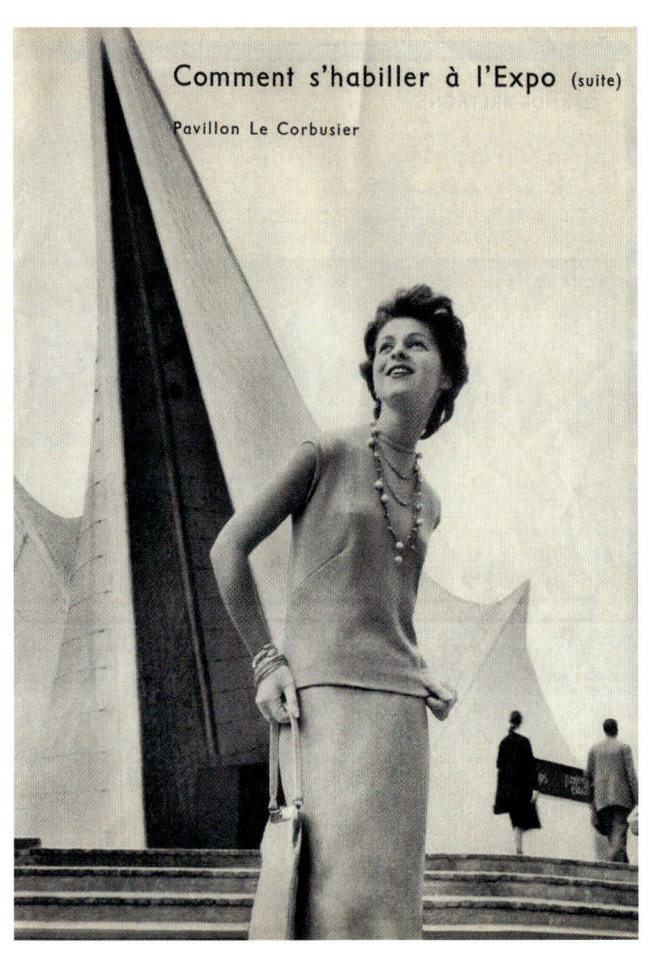

Reconnais cette main ouverte,
    la main ouverte
        dressée
            comme
un signe de réconciliation
    ouverte pour recevoir
    ouverte pour donner[45]

7.10
The Philips Pavilion served as the backdrop for a fashion special for *Elle*, the trend-setting French magazine.

7.11
A publicity photograph on the front page of the Dutch *Radio Bulletin* monthly, showing Edgard Varèse and acoustics technician Jan de Bruyn in the Philips truck garage that had been converted into a studio.

7.12
Publicity photograph taken on 7 February 1958, showing Louis Kalff, Le Corbusier and Edgard Varèse at the Philips Pavilion. Several days later, Le Corbusier and Varèse were ill with the flu.

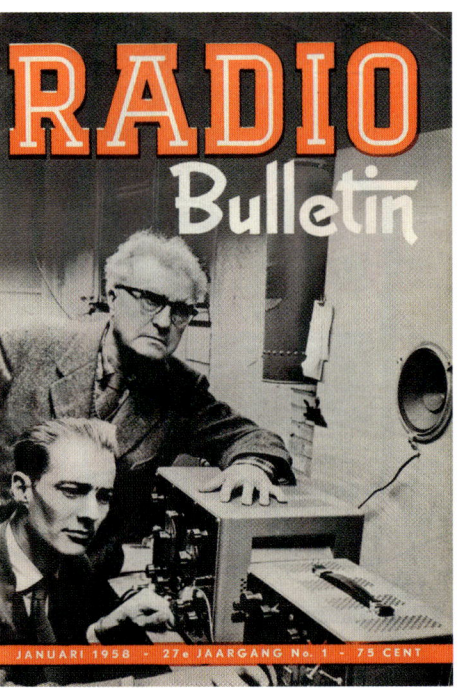

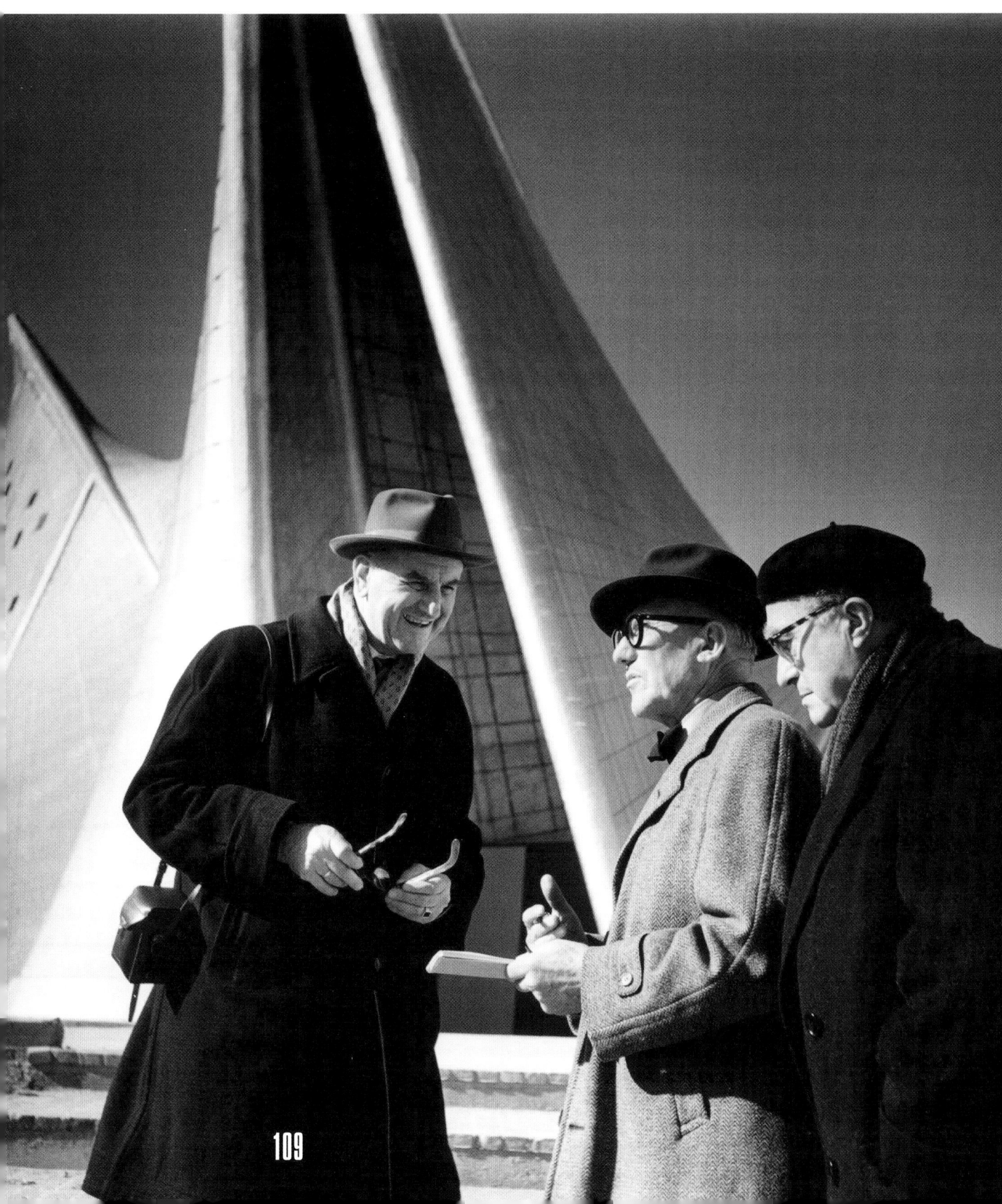

These sentences were also part of the so-called *paroles*, a component of *Le poème électronique* that was never realized. The *paroles* included a text that, according to the *minutage définitif*, was to be pronounced by Le Corbusier in the fifth sequence, *How time moulds civilization*.[46] The open hand is a recurring motif in Le Corbusier's work, about which he would say: 'The open hand is the only political act of my life. (. . .) The hand is open to give and receive. It's a sign of optimism in this world of catastrophe.'[47] This vision culminated in the 14-metre-high, 50-ton 'Open hand monument' that was the crowning glory of his work in Chandigarh, India, and that is used as the city's official logo.[48] A photograph of a plaster model of the 'Open hand monument' is also one of the images in *Le poème électronique*'s concluding seventh sequence, *To all mankind*,[49] and it appears in the colour section of Petit's book.[50]

At Kalff's request, Le Corbusier signed fifty copies of the book, which were to be given to Philips employees who had helped realize *Le poème électronique*.[51] Le Corbusier himself had also written a list of people whom Petit was to send the book to – it included the name of the French

7.13
The illustration on the left shows the dust jacket of the book about the Philips Pavilion in the *Les Cahiers Forces Vives* series published by Les Éditions de Minuit. The illustration on the right shows a page from the colour section of the book, which contained visual depictions of several images selected by Le Corbusier for *Le poème électronique*.

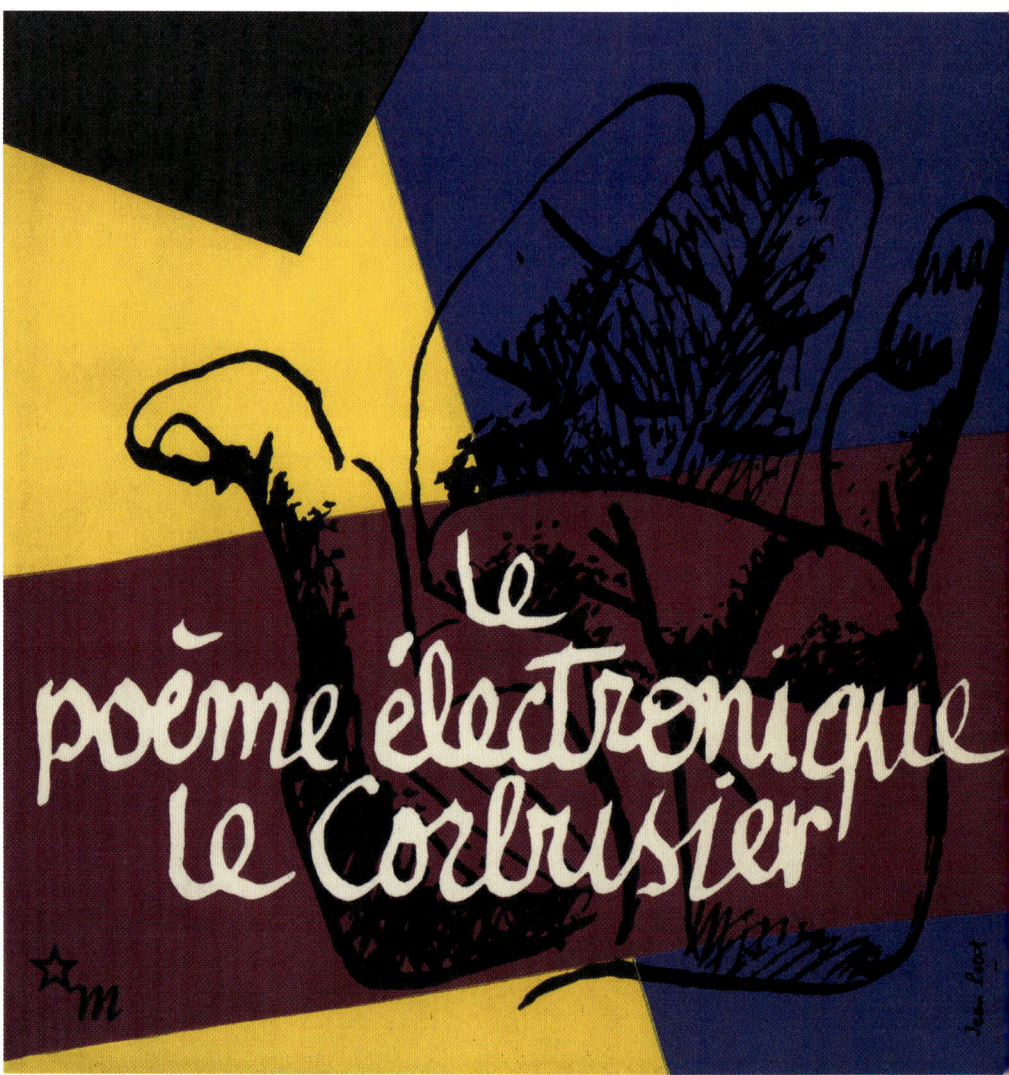

president, Charles de Gaulle.⁵² The number of copies of this luxury edition probably totalled no more than 1,000.⁵³

The *poème* Saleswoman

The publication of the hardcover edition of Petit's book in December 1958 was preceded in mid-June by the appearance of two shorter paperback editions that were considered 'excerpts'.⁵⁴ The two editions differed from each other in length (one was 124 pages long, the other 72), as one had the colour section, while the other did not. The 124-page edition appeared in French and Dutch, while the 72-page edition appeared in French, Dutch, English, German and Spanish. In total, therefore, there were eight different versions of the book.⁵⁵

At first, the book – probably the 72-page version⁵⁶ – was sold at the pavilion for 30 Belgian francs. Sales of the book were probably disappointing, something suggested by a reduction in price to 10 Belgian francs at the end of August, 'aimed at improving distribution'.⁵⁷ Pepita de Nerée tot Babberich, a descendant of a prominent Dutch Catholic family, was appointed to sell the book at the Philips Pavilion. She was later assisted by the Belgians Annie de Potter and Robert Sterneberg. Described as an 'extremely cultured young lady', whose conduct was 'very courteous', and 'a delight',⁵⁸ the 23-year-old Pepita de Nerée tot Babberich more or less carried out the duties performed by 'hostesses' at the

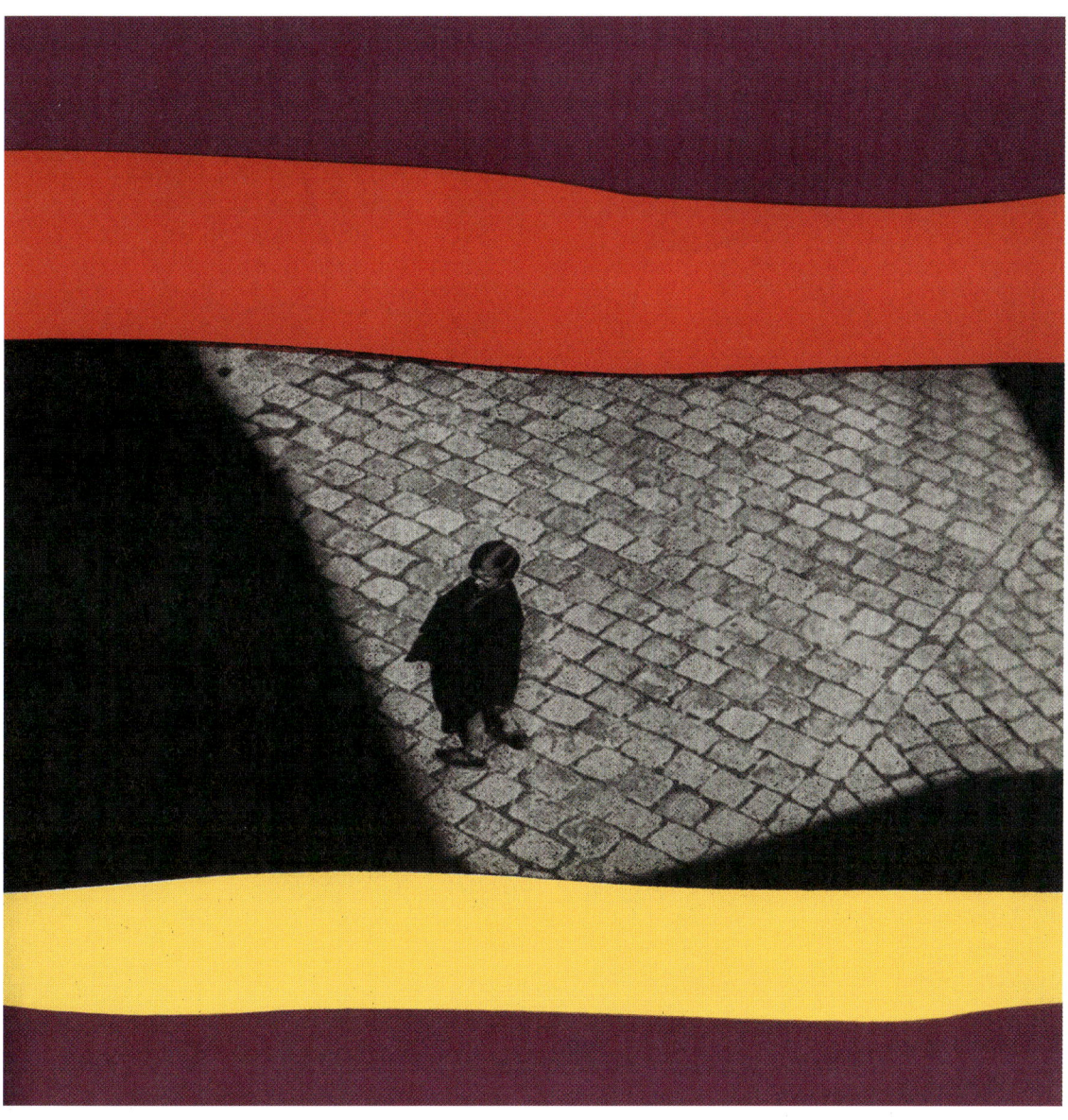

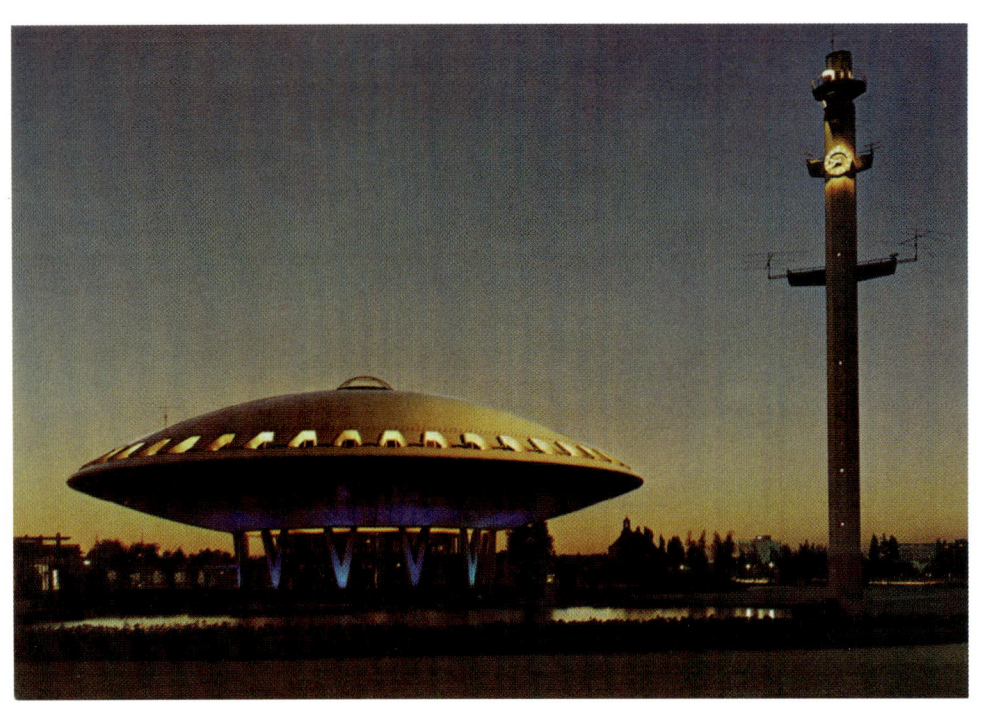

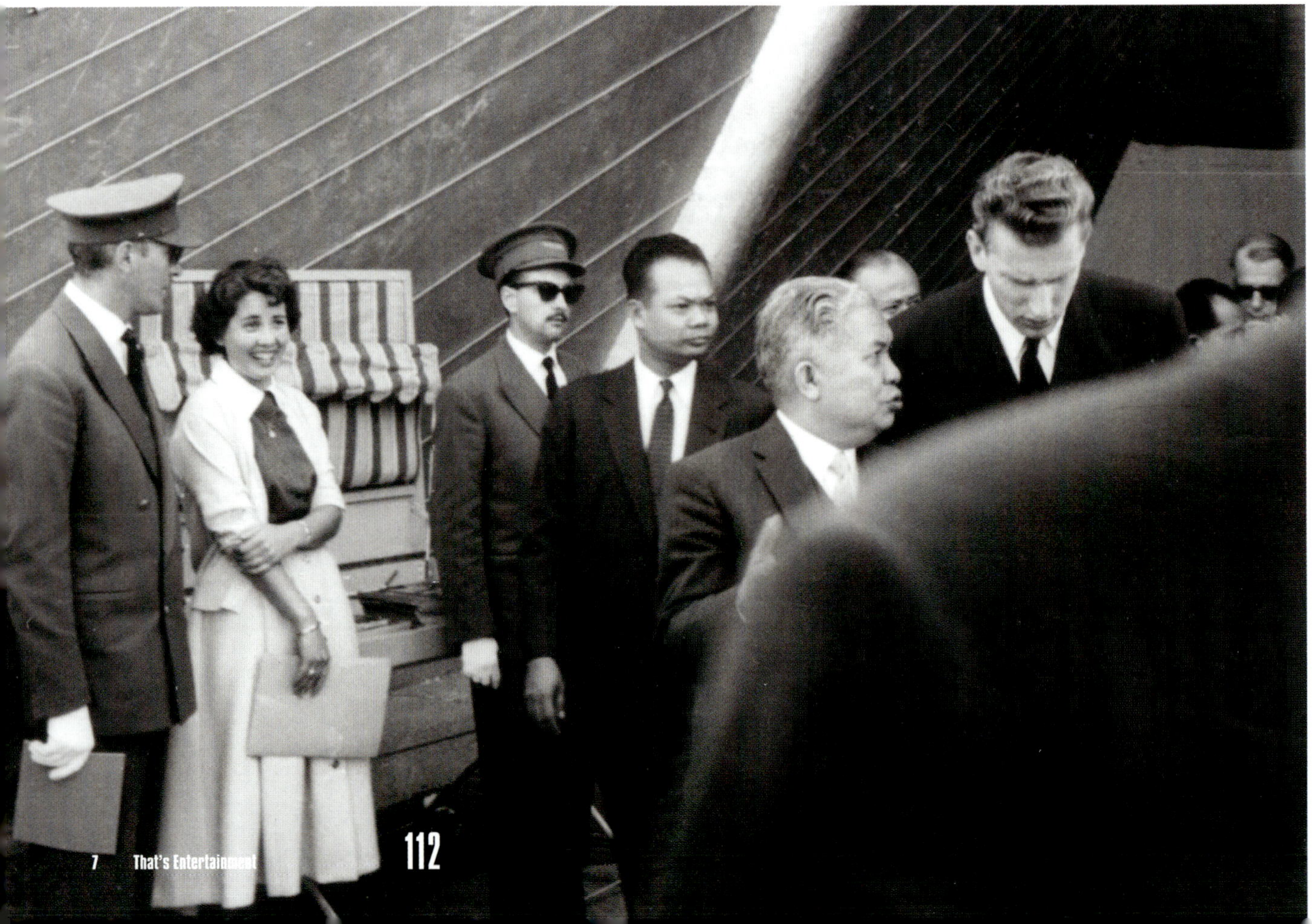

7 That's Entertainment   112

other pavilions.[59] The hostesses at the World Fair's various pavilions were a new phenomenon: 'the "hostess", a strange, until then unknown word for a new profession for women. A new job for the female, an institutionalized western geisha. Hospitality, helpfulness and obligingness were now united in a single person, who was specially appointed for this purpose and who was therefore expected to be "helpful" and "friendly" as part of the job.'[60]

The book was sold at a folding bookstall with an awning just in front of the cord next to the entrance, where the public stood and waited for the next performance. If a dignitary was visiting (known as a *séance spéciale*) the bookstall could be moved to the immediate entrance, which was used as the exit by visiting dignitaries, since they walked through the pavilion in reverse direction. Official guests were presented with a copy of the book to commemorate their visit.[61]

The Balance Sheet

As far as Philips' press office was concerned, the publicity efforts proved effective: 'The press, radio, film and television all found special effects to their taste.' Presumably, the remarkable shape of the Philips Pavilion meant that, together with the Atomium, it was among the most photographed objects at the World's Fair. And around the world thousands of newspaper and magazine articles were apparently written about the pavilion.[62]

In 1957 Philips' profits amounted to more than 173 million Dutch guilders.[63] Initially, a total budget of one million guilders was set aside for the Philips Pavilion[64] but by 31 March 1958 the anticipated cost had already risen to 1.9 million guilders, and further costs were expected.[65] Kalff later estimated that the total cost of the Philips Pavilion divided by the number of visitors resulted in a figure of less than two guilders per visitor, which he considered reasonable; in his opinion, the results of the Philips Pavilion were satisfactory.[66] Frits Philips, however, found it difficult to decide, in retrospect, to what extent the millions that had been expended on the pavilion were well spent. He proposed that Philips should not participate in a World's Fair again: the money this would save could be used for a permanent exhibition building in Eindhoven. This led to the opening of the Evoluon, which was designed by Kalff, on 24 September 1966 to celebrate Philips' 75th anniversary.[67]

7.14
Picture postcard of Philips' permanent Evoluon exhibition centre in Eindhoven. The Evoluon was partly built as a result of Frits Philips' doubts as to whether the millions of guilders that had been expended on the Philips Pavilion in 1958 had been well spent.

7.15
An unidentified guest leaving the Philips Pavilion via the entrance following an official reception. On the left, between pavilion attendants Julien Huyghe and Raymond Médard, is Pepita de Nerée tot Babberich, who worked as publicity officer and presented publicity material during official receptions. Behind her is the folding bookstall with its awning, where the books by Jean Petit were displayed.

Text Box II

The 'Electronic Poem' in the Philips Pavilion
A Rich and Rare Experience of a World of Wonder

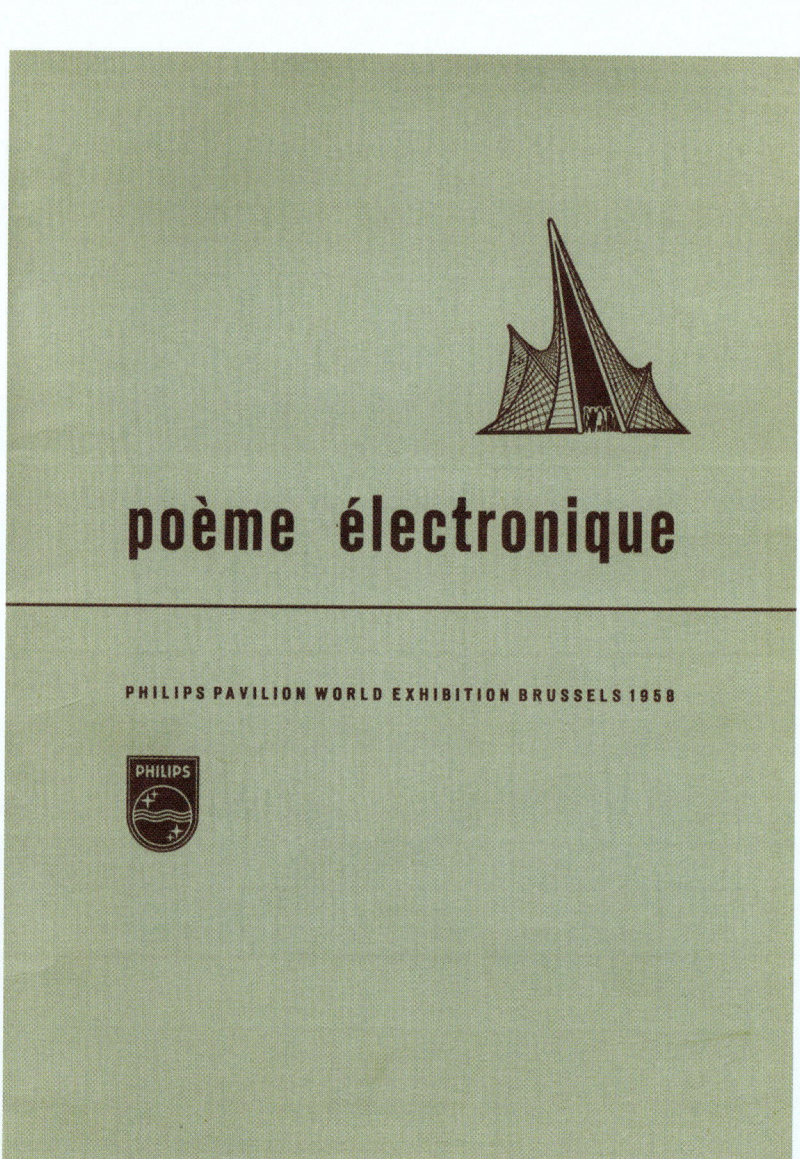

II.1
Front cover of the English press file for the Philips Pavilion.

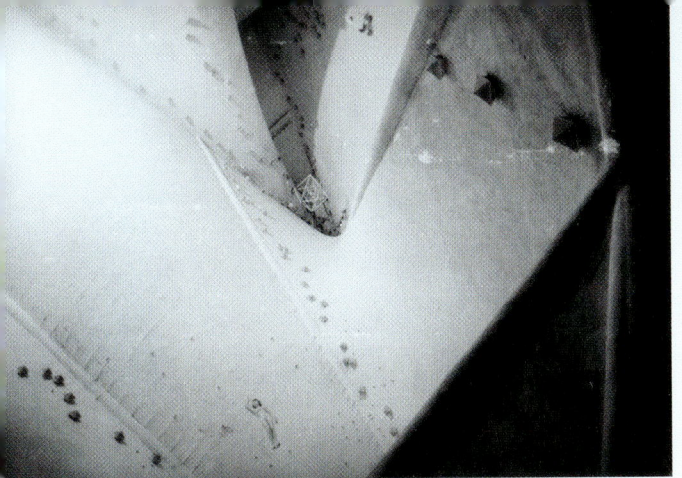

To provide the international press with information, a press file about the Philips Pavilion was distributed. The press file included a general text about the pavilion, with the above title. This text, which is reproduced in full below, illustrates Philips' expectations of how visitors would experience Le poème électronique.[1]

The silvery and lustrous Philips Pavilion looms before the visitor to the Brussels' International Exhibition like a giant shell of bizarre shape from some exotic sea-bed. Involuntarily, the visitor is struck and his attention captured by the gently curving surfaces of this highly remarkable building with its pointed peaks rising to height of some 70 feet. The building, as well as the 'Electronic Poem' performed in it, is the creation of Le Corbusier, the celebrated French-Swiss architect.[2] The Poem is the Pavilion's only exhibit and in its synthesis of art and the latest scientific and technical achievements, it is one show at the 'Expo 1958' that is really unique. Every day thousands upon thousands of visitors stream into the Philips Pavilion which, not only for its daring design and extraordinary construction, but also for the strange and extravagant light-and-sound show given inside of it, has become one of the most discussed attractions of the Exhibition.

The visitor walks into an almost empty enclosure bounded by bare and lofty walls that curve over his head into saddle surfaces finally sweep up to three apices, thus forming narrowing chimneys, as it were. Surprised, he gazes about him, seeking a central point; but the underlying idea is difficult to grasp. Peering into the semi-obscurity above, in one of the apices he suddenly recognises the large-scale model of an atom, hanging by a scarcely visible thread. His glance wanders to a second apex, and there he discovers a nude figure.[3] To start off with, the visitor is only half aware of what he sees, for the deathly quiet interior does not yield up its secret at first glance. At this stage he wonders whether the model and the figure are meant to symbolise Matter and Mind. Is it a question of human defencelessness facing the threat of danger? While the observer, his head full of all that he has seen in other pavilions, is still asking himself what is going to happen, the 'Poem' starts; a wave of images, sounds, light and colour breaks over him.

It only lasts eight minutes, this cataract of optical and acoustic effects that, changing second by second and at even shorter intervals, fills up the space that a moment ago was quite lifeless, penetrating into its furthest corners. Gigantic pictures appear on the asymmetric curved walls that converse above one's head. There are birds, fishes, reptiles, masks, skeletons, idols, girls looking anxiously upward, buildings and steel

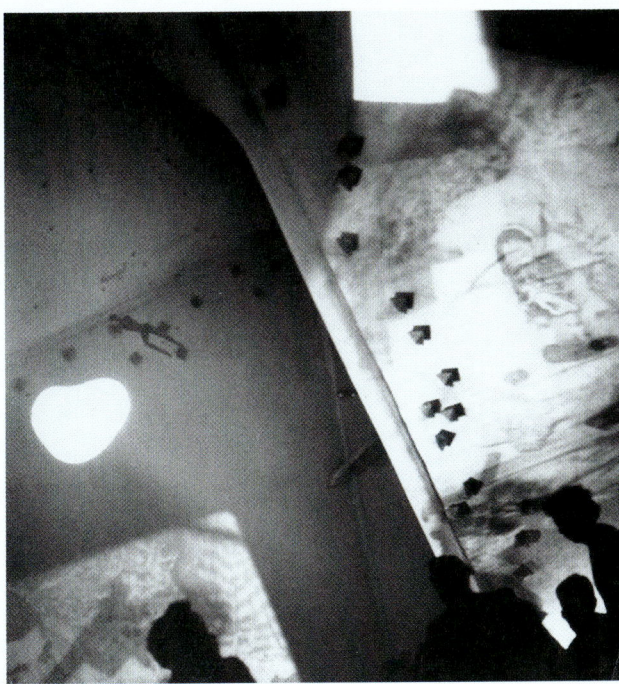

II.2
'In one of the apices he suddenly recognises the large-scale model of an atom, hanging by a scarcely visible thread. His glance wanders to a second apex, and there he discovers a nude figure.' Le Corbusier had originally indicated that a mannequin could be used for the female figure, but he later decided to use a figure he had designed himself. The photograph at the top was probably taken before the opening of the pavilion, and and at the lower side, a naked mannequin with feet, arms, breasts and half-length hair can be discerned. The geometric object is visible in the centre. The top-left of the photograph at the bottom, which was taken during a performance of Le poème électronique, shows the more abstract female figure that replaced the mannequin. Lucien Hervé photographs, 1958.

115

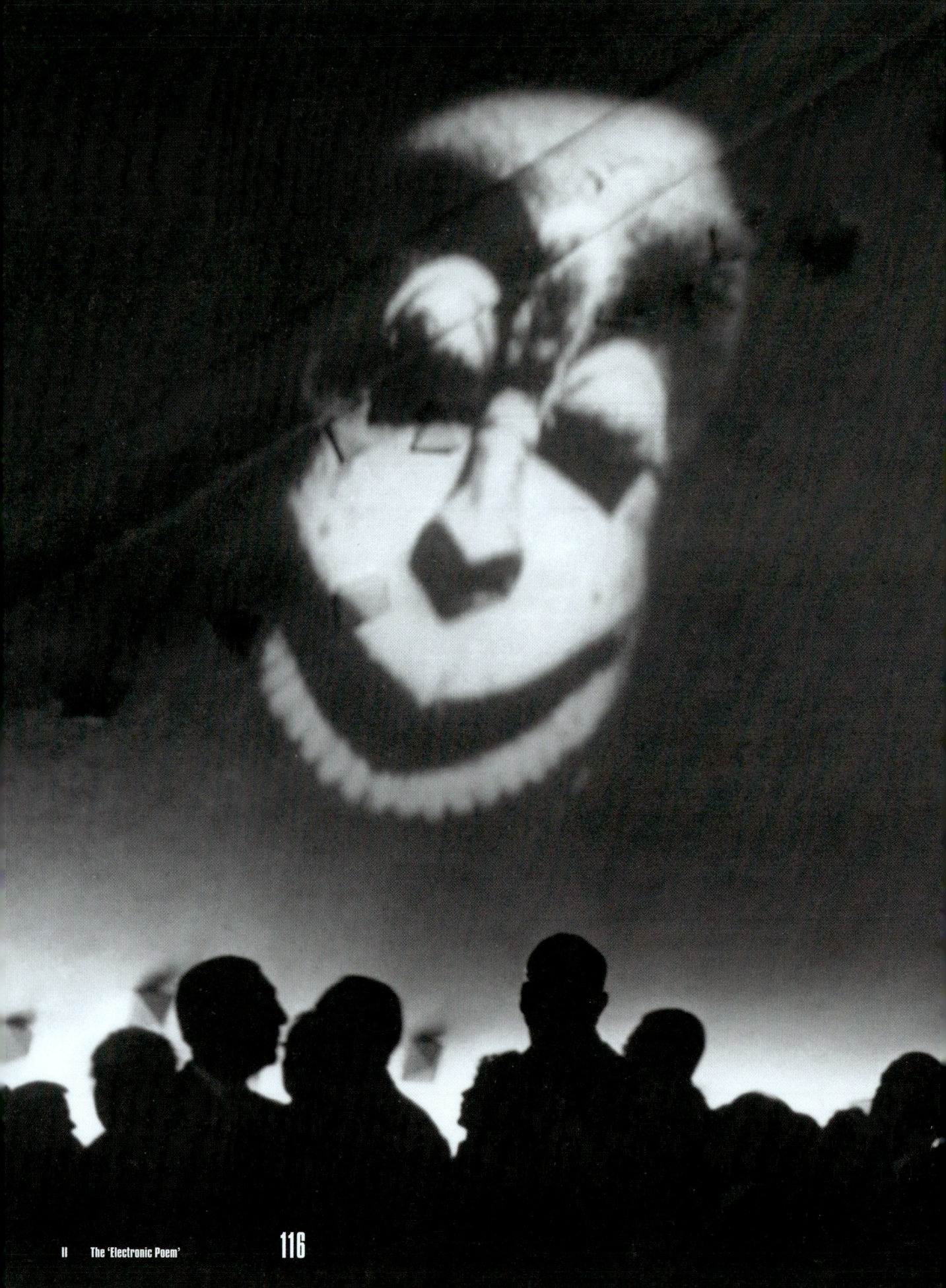

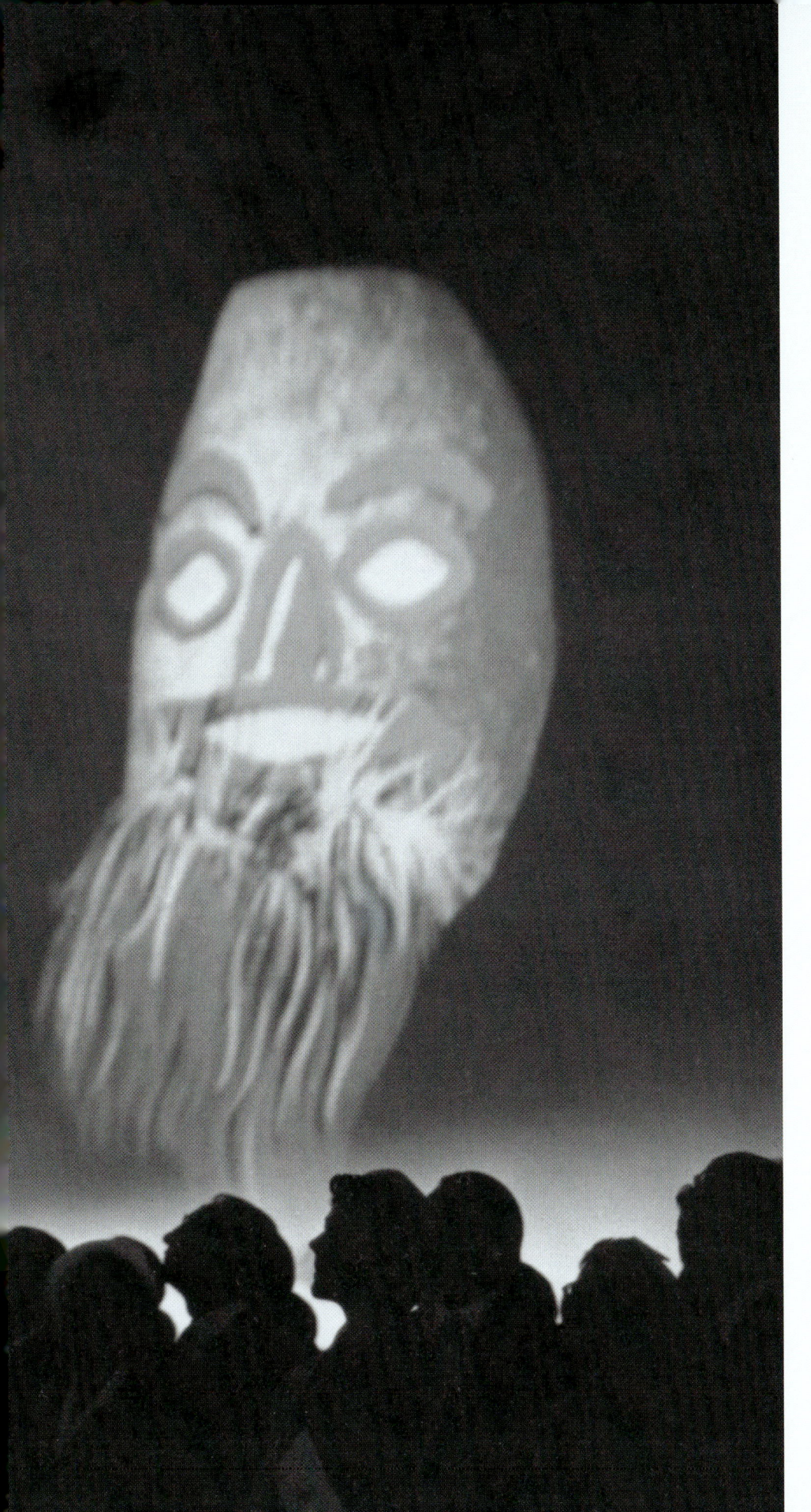

II.3
'Gigantic pictures appear on the asymmetric curved walls.'

structures are askew, mushroom explosions and ruins, crippled children, but also film-stars, inventors, tools and many other symbols or abstract compositions symbolizing whole epochs. All this is intended to represent the dramatic story of mankind's development right up to the present day. It is necessarily a somewhat sketchy account, but the overall effect of this selection of pictures is to make it clear how, since its creation, humanity has struggled for harmony and happiness and defended itself against sorrow and catastrophe, how it has been torn back and forth between love and hate, between the elevated and unattainable ideal and the inevitable irritations of everyday life.

Le Corbusier's scenario comprises seven pictorial sequences, namely 'The Formation of the Earth', 'Matter and Mind', 'Out of the Depths into the Dawn', 'Man made unto himself Gods', 'Men build their World', 'Harmony' and 'The Heritage of Posterity'.[4] The apotheosis of the 'Electronic Poem' concerns the mission of humanity: the task of preserving what has been acquired and of handing it on to posterity is symbolized by the gesture of a hand that receives and bestows.

If there were nothing to see in the pavilion but these black and white images, they would not be anything out of the ordinary; they would be a sort of picture book, nothing more and nothing less. It is only the auxiliary elements provided by electroacoustics and electronic control techniques that – strange as it may seem – really bring the kaleidoscope to life. One half would be pointless without the other, and the two things together would be nothing if the whole were not taking place inside that mystical architectural shape. It is only by virtue of the place where it is staged that the 'Electronic Poem' is an instrument of allusion, interpretation and pronouncement that is as keen as a surgeon's scalpel, and as mordant as many an unpalatable truth.

On entering the Pavilion, the visitor notices certain dark patches on the walls; they obviously have a purpose, but what it is he is unable to guess. They prove to be loudspeakers, from which electronic music is now pouring forth. Heard for the first time by a willing and attentive listener, it all sounds extremely odd and yet, at the same time, this music takes you into a world of wonder; it is rather like a trip to another planet, which makes you frightened but curious. On the other hand, the indifferent visitor hears nothing but highly remarkable sound effects in this piece of electronic music, for which Le Corbusier left the French composer Edgar Varèse a free hand. It is made up of rattling and whistling sounds, it is threatening and plaintive by turns, it thunders and it roars.

At one point a human voice is imitated; it is somewhat like a coloratura and,[5] like the other sounds, it moves about within the enclosed space, from left to right and back, upwards and down again. So palpably does it swing hither and thither that the audience tries to follow its path. You can see their heads moving. At another point – when the picture of the atomic explosion appears – a thunderous roar fills the Pavilion. There are about 400 loudspeakers, and when the din from all of them at once starts to verge on the intolerable, the visitor really has a sense of being in the middle of things, and almost believes he can feel the air trembling. Like the images, the sounds are constantly changing, scarcely leaving the listener time to reflect. The human ear is exhausted by the great number of unusual impressions it has to respond to. The volume varies between 40 and 130 Phon. The aesthetic scale of these electronic sounds ranges from muted music of the spheres (illustrating the birth of human hope) to crashing dissonance (when a catastrophe enters into the plot of the drama).

To the pictorial and acoustic components are added light and colour. The picture-and-sound sequences are accompanied by luminous effects conjured up out of several hundred red, blue, green, violet and yellow fluorescent lamps. At other times immense patches of light of complementary or clashing colours are projected by ingenious systems of mirrors on to the walls around the big film pictures at the same time, coloured stripes move round the walls; these stripes are images of a rotating disc projected by an epidiascope.[6] Once or twice there is darkness for a split second and, in the two hollows in the roof, the atom model and the naked figure become visible; irradiated with invisible ultra-violet light, they now shine forth and exercise their spell on all. But then comes a burst of light from the colour organ; the radiance dies away and swells again, or dissolves into flashes that hurt the eyes.

For this complicated interplay of space, image, sound, light and colour intended to convey a message and not merely to astonish the visitor, it is necessary that scene should follow scene with almost unimaginable exactitude. The light and sound show adheres to a time-table of seconds and fractions of a second. Le Corbusier called this time-table 'minutage', but it would be apter to call it 'secondage'. During intervals as brief as before-mentioned, such and such a picture must be screened, certain sounds must be heard, and the prescribed light and colour accompaniments must be in action. A moment later the scene has changed, but all the components of the spectacle still fit together as if made to measure. And so it all continues right up to the 'final chord'. Compressed in this manner, the message that Le Corbusier is trying to convey demands of the visitor much attention and concentration and even a certain mental attitude. But the rapid changes of scene are necessary if any impression is to be made upon the audience, who are tired out from their wanderings around the Exhibition, and whose heads are still full of the Atomium, sputniks, Circarama and the thousand other technical wonders they have witnessed. The sensations registered on the faces of visitors are various. The scale of feelings ranges from profound shock to hilarity, from admiration to scepticism. However, they all agree on one point: the 'Electronic Poem' is fascinating and astonishing, and must not be missed.

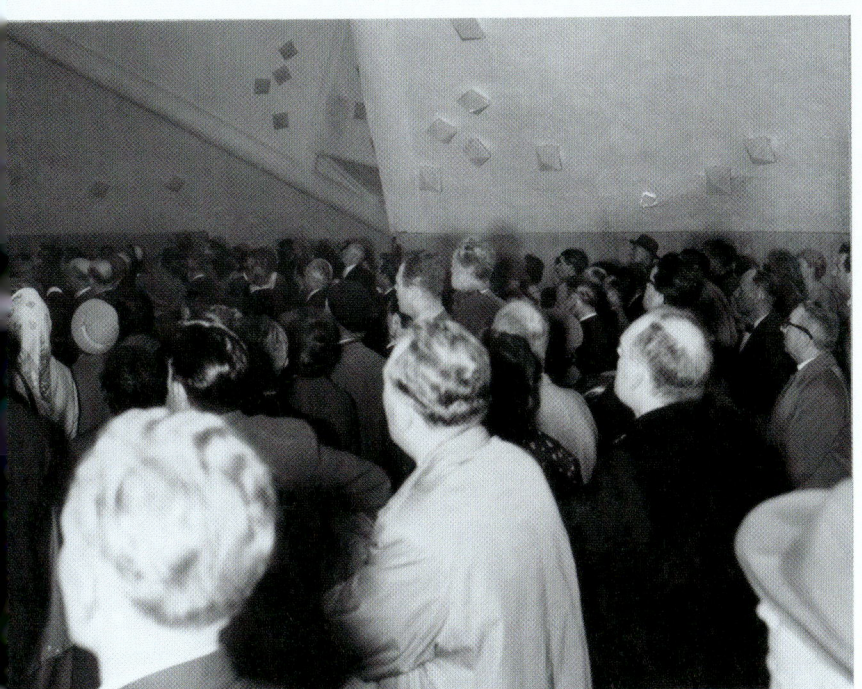

II.4
'On entering the Pavilion, the visitor notices certain dark patches on the walls.'

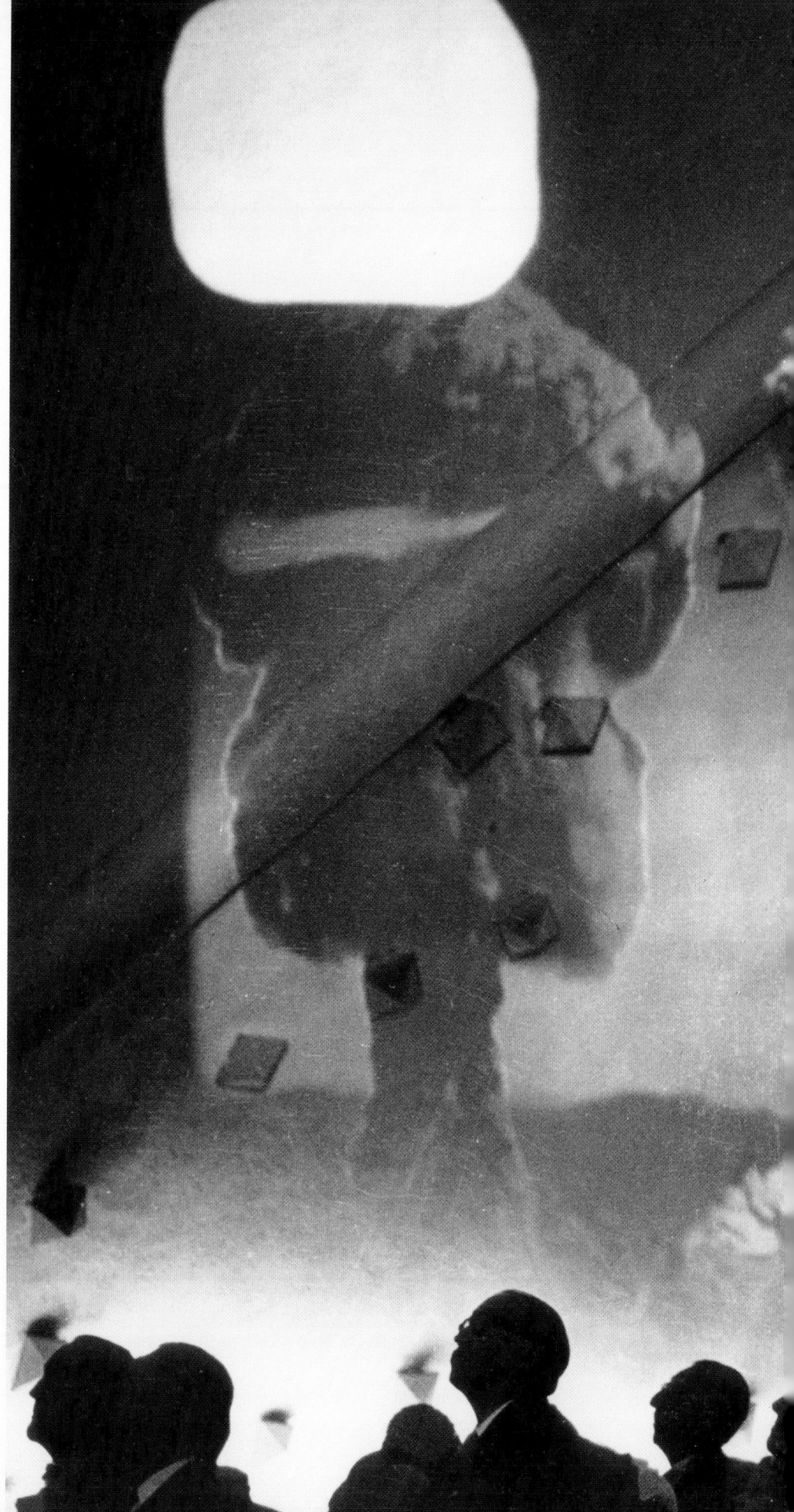

II.5
'The picture of the atomic explosion appears.'

14 The 'Electronic Poem'

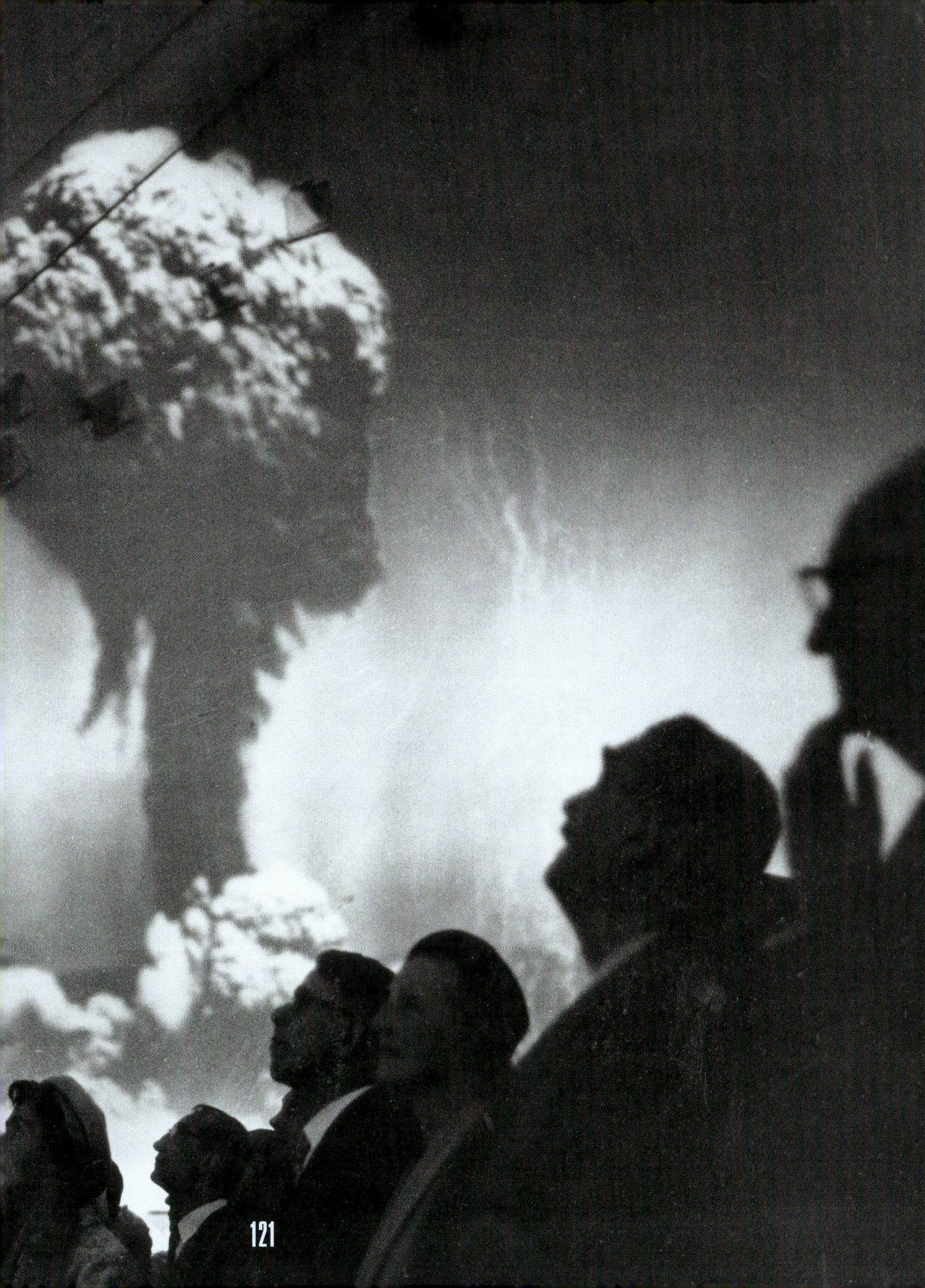

8 Like Ants in a Hurricane
One and a Half Million Visitors to the Philips Pavilion

Peter Wever

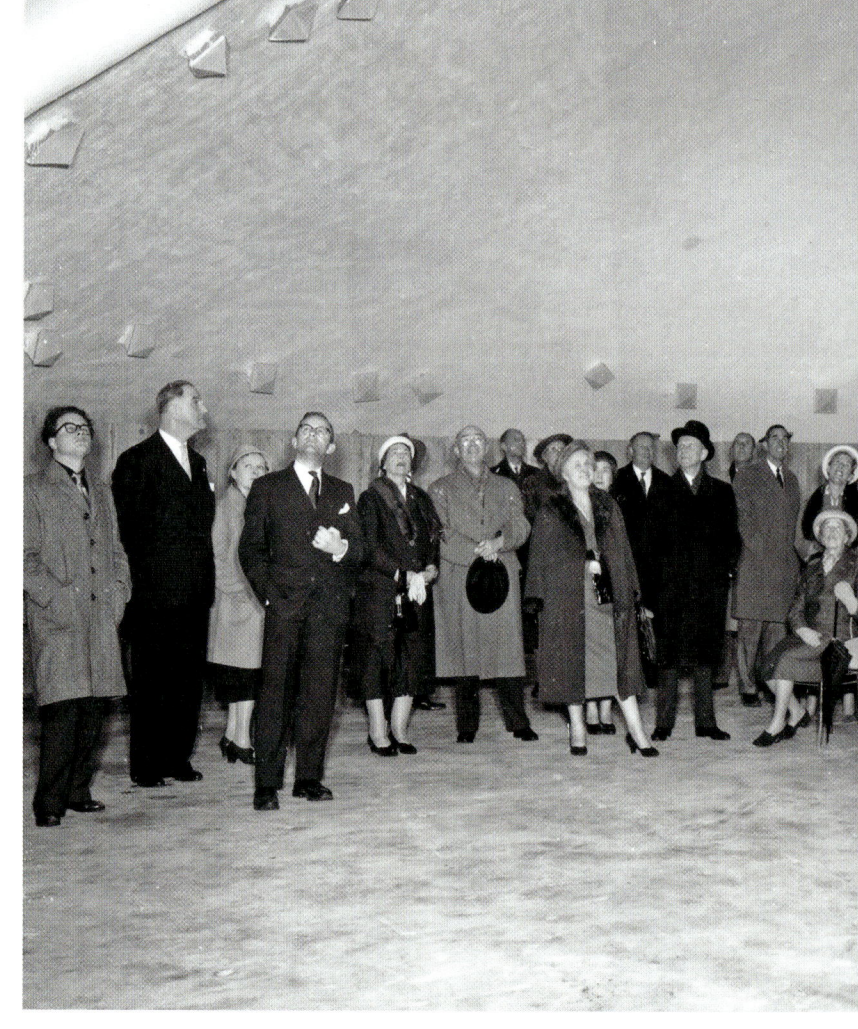

8.1
Executives from Philips Netherlands and Philips Belgium visited the Philips Pavilion with their wives on 18 April 1958, when the first unofficial performance of *Le poème électronique* **took place. The second man from the left is Louis Kalff. To the left of the seated woman in the middle is Frits Philips. To his left, wearing a hat, is Frans Otten.**

The public that attended the performances of *Le poème électronique* at the Philips Pavilion ranged from royalty and fellow architects and musicians to everyday World's Fair visitors. Attending a performance was a particularly intense experience. Le Corbusier intended visitors to feel as if they had entered a slaughterhouse, received a blow to the head and been taken away. The pavilion and the performance were a success, although the majority of spectators may not have understood it all.

Official Opening of the Pavilion

A total of 3,013 performances of *Le poème électronique* were attended by an estimated one and a half million visitors.[1] The first guests were received at the pavilion on 18 April, one day after the opening of the 1958 Brussels World's Fair.[2] Top executives from Philips Netherlands and Philips Belgium, including President of the Board of Directors Frans Otten, Vice-president Frits Philips, General Art Director Louis Kalff and the deputy manager of Philips Belgium Charles Spaens and their wives visited the Dutch and Philips pavilions. Several speeches were given, as well as what is considered the first performance of *Le poème électronique* for visitors to the Philips Pavilion. The guests concluded their visit with a luncheon at the restaurant in the Atomium's top-most sphere.[3]

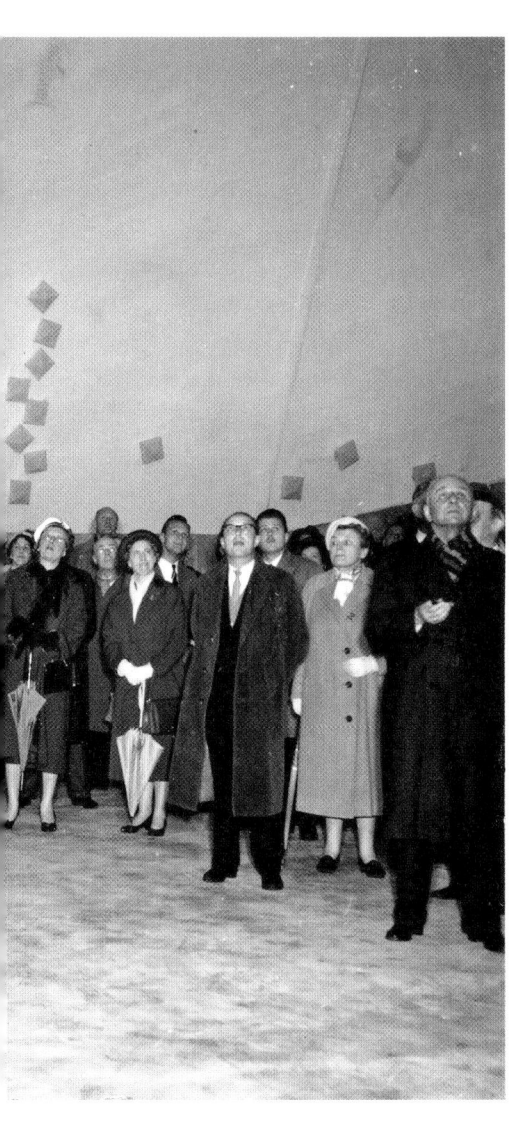

On 22 April, at eleven o'clock in the morning, the Philips Pavilion and *Le poème électronique* were presented to 175 local and foreign journalists from all over the world. Philips considered this the first official performance and the company was therefore again represented by Frans Otten, Frits Philips, Louis Kalff and Charles Spaens.[4] Edgard Varèse was also present at the performance and at the end he acknowledged the audience's applause with a courteous bow.[5] Le Corbusier himself was not present.[6] Following the performance and a tour of the pavilion, a number of speeches were given during drinks and a luncheon at the Canadian pavilion's restaurant.[7] Dutch newspaper reactions varied, from 'modern nightmare' and 'inconsolable loneliness in this concrete space' (*Eindhovens Dagblad*) to 'a dignified symbol (. . .) of the prestige of this international company' (*De Telegraaf*), and 'one of the strangest pavilions and events at the 1958 World's Fair' (*Het Vrije Volk*).[8]

That same day, at six o'clock in the evening, a second performance of *Le poème électronique* was given for a large number of guests from the Belgian government and establishment. This was followed by a cocktail party at the Dutch pavilion. And finally, a midday performance was given on 23 April for the Commissioner General of the 1958 Brussels World's Fair, Baron Moens de Fernig, which Philips considered the official inauguration.[9] The Philips Pavilion was closed again immediately after these ceremonial events for adjustments to the performance, not opening to the public until 20 May.[10]

Into the Slaughterhouse and Bang . . .

From 20 May until 19 October visitors could attend a performance of *Le poème électronique* every twenty minutes from ten o'clock in the morning until seven in the evening.[11] The pavilion could accommodate approximately 500 people per performance. The free performance attracted large crowds. The waiting public gathered in front of a long, low-hanging cord under the watchful eye of two pavilion attendants. Although virtually everything in the Philips Pavilion was automatic, the time of the next performance was indicated on a clock whose hands had to be moved by one of the attendants using a long stick. When it was time for the next performance, both attendants removed the cord and visitors were led down to the pavilion entrance by a third attendant. In the vestibule, visitors could look through the windows in the wall and see the technical equipment in the control room. Under the supervision of a fourth attendant, the public passed through opened doors into the public area.

The public area was dimly lit, with indirect white light illuminating the rising walls from behind the balustrade. When everyone was in the public area, the doors were shut. Two attendants remained with the public. In theory, the doors were not allowed to be opened until the performance had ended. Closing the doors caused a switch on one of the doors to turn on a light, which indicated to the technician at the control desk that the performance could start. While the indirect lighting was still on, Iannis Xenakis' *Interlude sonore* began, which served as intermission music and lasted almost two minutes. Then all the lights went out and the public area became pitch black. The tension among visitors rose. An introductory text to *Le poème électronique* appeared on the walls of the pavilion. Next, the piercing sound of one of Delft's Oude Kerk bells announced the start of the eight-minute-long *Le poème électronique*.[12] At the end of the performance, one of the attendants opened the doors at the back of the pavilion, while the other attendant ensured that everyone left the public area. When the public area was empty, the exit doors were closed, and the entrance doors were opened again to admit visitors for the next performance.[13] This meant that the flow of visitors in the Philips Pavilion came close to Le Corbusier's vision articulated in 1956: 'Just like an oesophagus, that's how they go in and how they go out. (. . .) It must feel as if they're entering a slaughterhouse. In: bang, a blow to the head, and out.'[14]

A *carte de priorité* [priority ticket] was introduced at Le Corbusier's request to ensure that invited guests would not have to wait too long to enter the pavilion. This bright orange ticket was made available to

8.2
Programme for the first official performance of *Le poème électronique* in the Philips Pavilion for 175 local and international journalists on the morning of 22 April 1958.

8.3
Invitation to the evening performance of *Le poème électronique* at the Philips Pavilion on 22 April 1958 for members of the Belgian government and establishment.

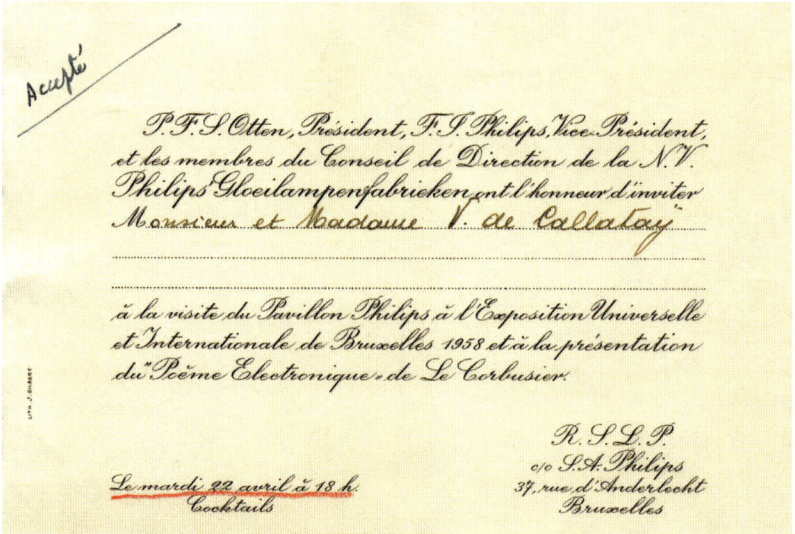

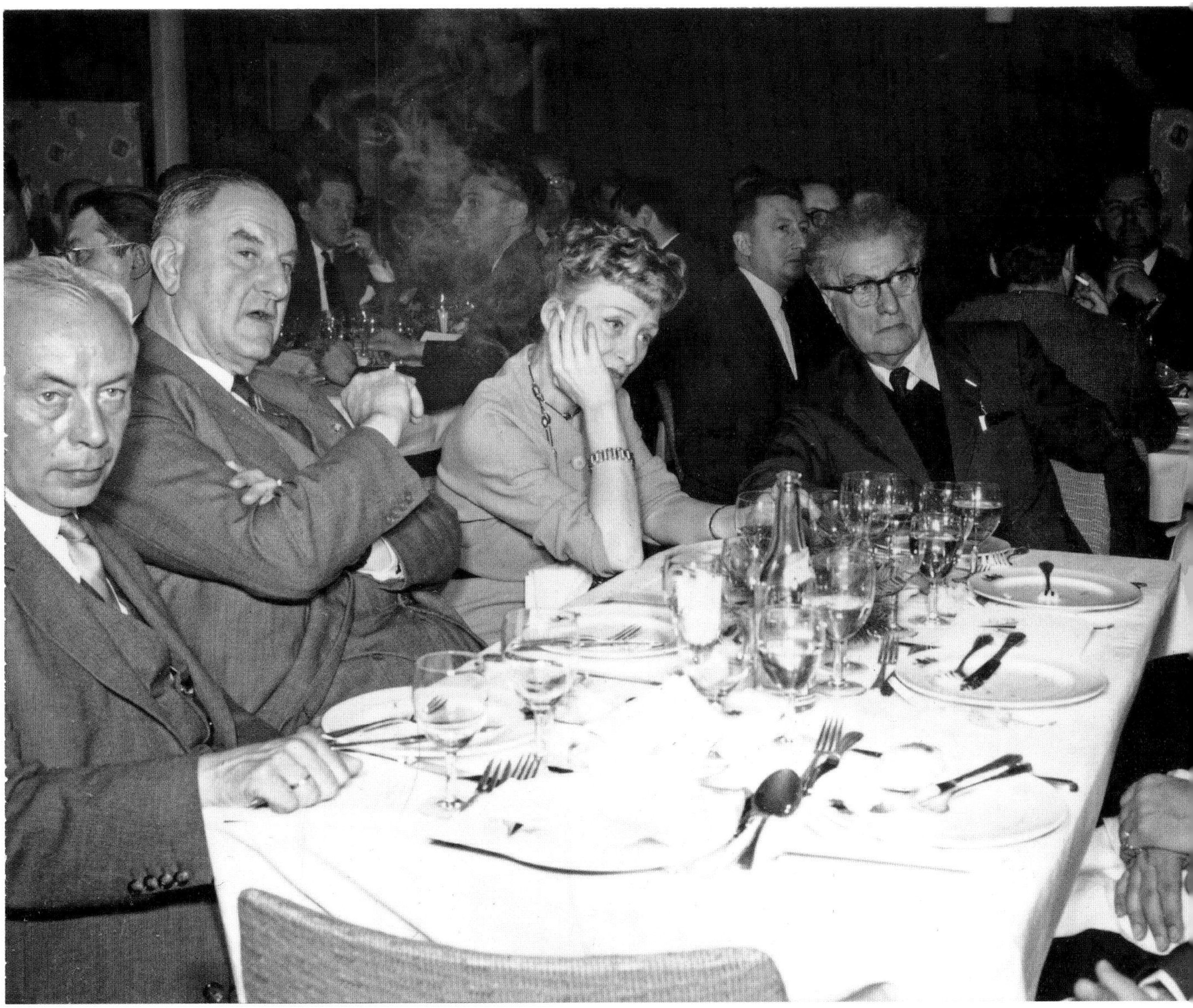

8.4
Left Louis Kalff and right Edgard Varèse in the company of an unidentified woman during drinks and a luncheon at the Canadian pavilion's restaurant following the first official performance of *Le poème électronique* on the morning of 22 April 1958.

8.5
Evening reception at the Philips Pavilion on 22 April 1958 for guests invited from the ranks of the Belgian government and establishment. In the foreground from left to right Frits Philips, Charles Spaens, Anna Otten-Philips, Frans Otten and an unidentified guest. In the control room at the back are left technician Wiel Cox and right technician Jan Brouwer.

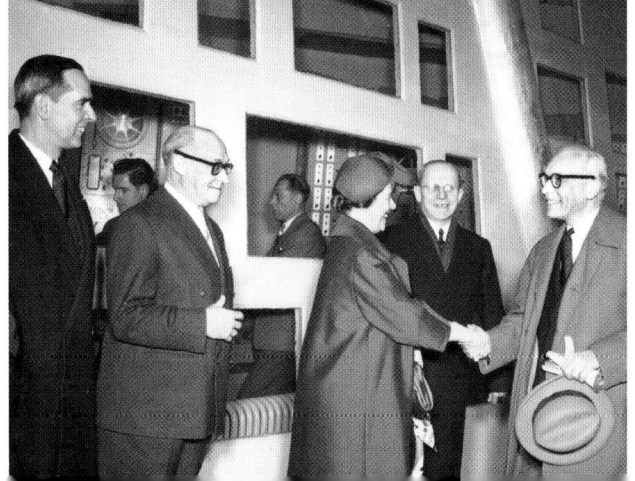

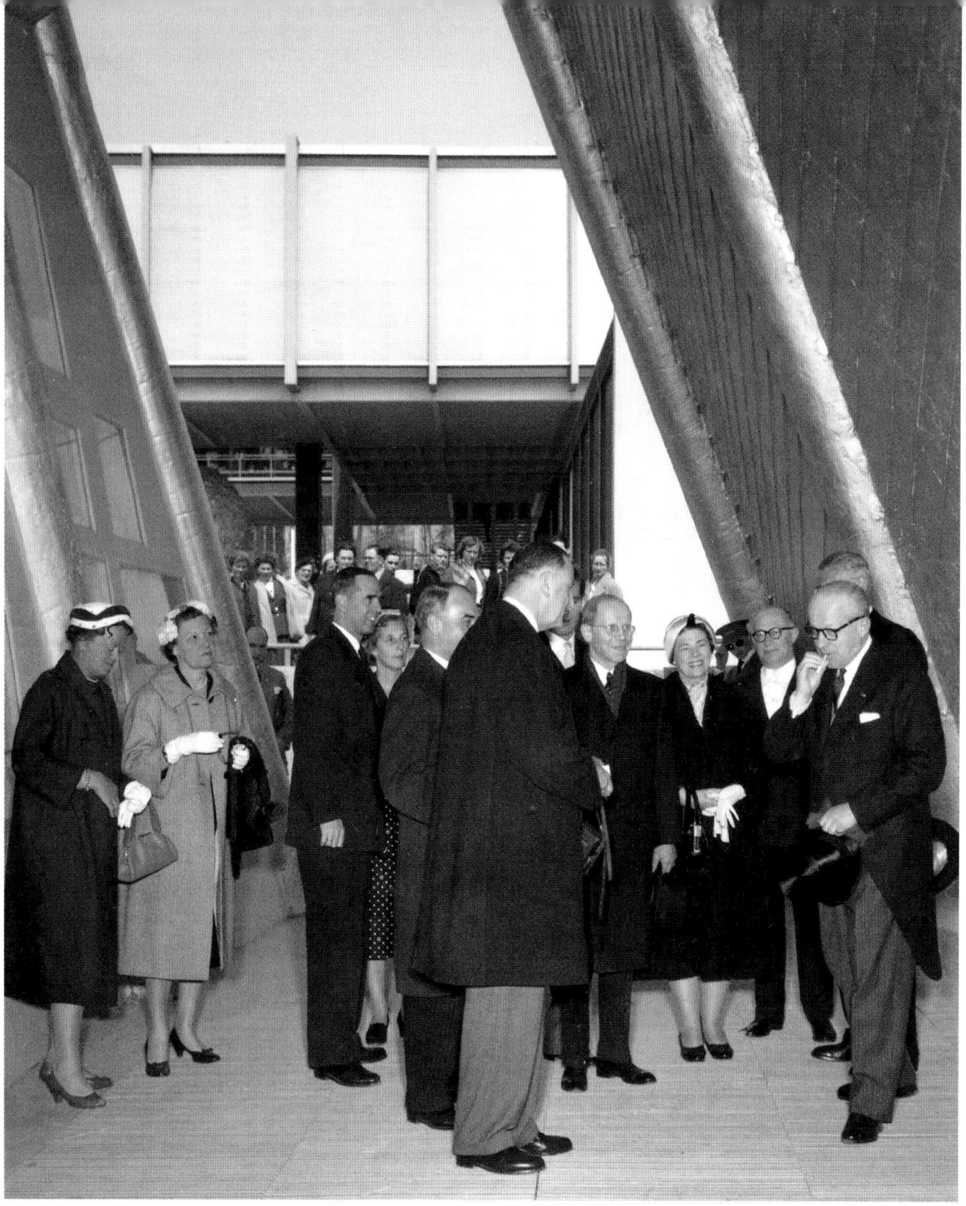

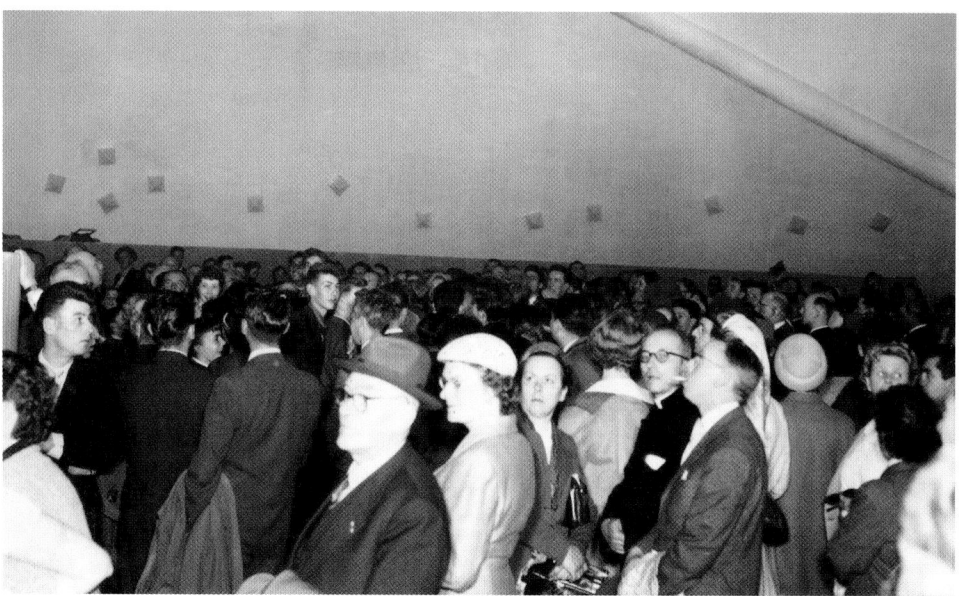

8.6
Welcoming Baron Moens de Fernig, Commissioner General of the 1958 Brussels World's Fair, to the official inauguration of the Philips Pavilion on 23 April 1958. The first man on the left is Frits Philips, the third man on the left is Louis Kalff, next to him on the right are Frans Otten, Anna Otten-Philips and Charles Spaens. Baron Moens de Fernig is to the right, holding a cigarette.

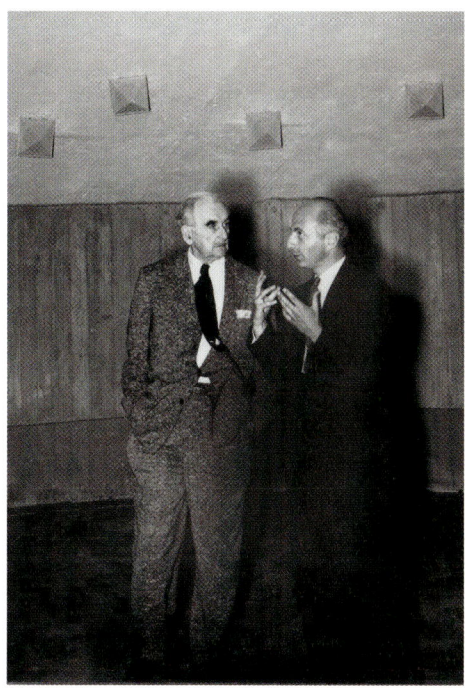

guests invited by, for example, Le Corbusier, Varèse and Philippe Agostini.[15]

Le Corbusier's Visits

Le Corbusier visited the Philips Pavilion twice after it was opened. On 26 June 1958 he flew to Brussels in a helicopter to give a speech in the auditorium of the French pavilion about architecture and urbanism.[16] This speech was given between five and seven o'clock in the evening.[17] Either before or after that Le Corbusier visited the Philips Pavilion together with Guillaume Gillet, the architect of the French pavilion. Le Corbusier stayed the night at the famous Hotel Metropole at Brussels' Place de Brouckère.

In the Philips Pavilion's visitors' book, which was called the *Gulden Boek* [Golden Book] because of its gold-coloured inlay,[18] Le Corbusier wrote: *'Merci à tous amis de Philipp's Le Corbusier 26/6/58'* [Thanks to all friends of Philipp's Le Corbusier 26/6/58]. It is telling that he spelled the name of his client incorrectly.

Le Corbusier's second visit to the Philips Pavilion was occasioned by a disagreement. Le Corbusier expected Philips to pay for an excursion to Brussels for everyone who had worked on realizing the pavilion and *Le poème électronique*. Philips apparently failed to meet his demand, upon which Le Corbusier accused the Philips management of ingratitude. On 22 July 1958 he wrote to Kalff that he had never received a word of thanks for his unstinting efforts regarding the pavilion. He pointed out to Kalff that when an architect delivers a building, the client treats him to a lamb chop or steak, and smiles, even if the smile is forced. In his written response, dated 28 July, Kalff indicated that in view of what had been achieved, there was no question of a smile but rather a heartfelt laugh, and certainly not a forced one at that. In addition, he wrote that the delayed opening and the problems relating to the performance meant there had been no opportunity to organize a fitting opening for those involved. On behalf of Philips, he

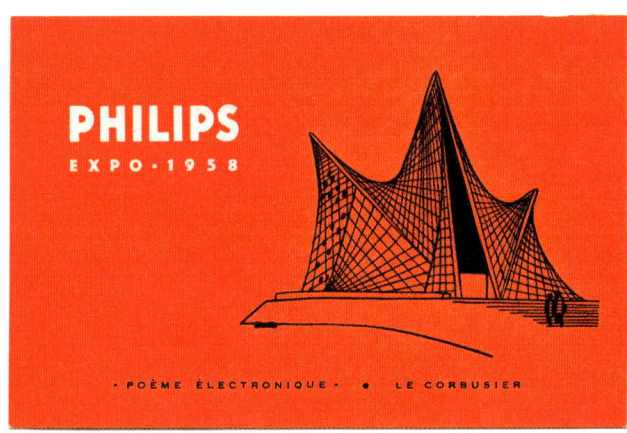

8.7
Architect Richard Neutra, seen on the left, visited the Philips Pavilion on 9 May 1958 to attend a trial performance of *Le poème électronique*.

8.8
Spectators filled with expectation, waiting for the first public performance of *Le poème électronique* on 20 May 1958. The public area in the Philips Pavilion could accommodate about 500 people.

8.9
Front and back of the priority ticket for the Philips Pavilion, which was made available to guests invited by, for example, Le Corbusier, Edgard Varèse and Philippe Agostini.

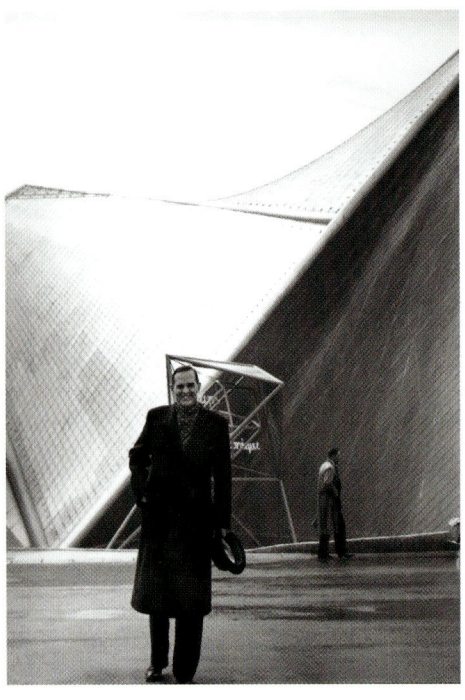
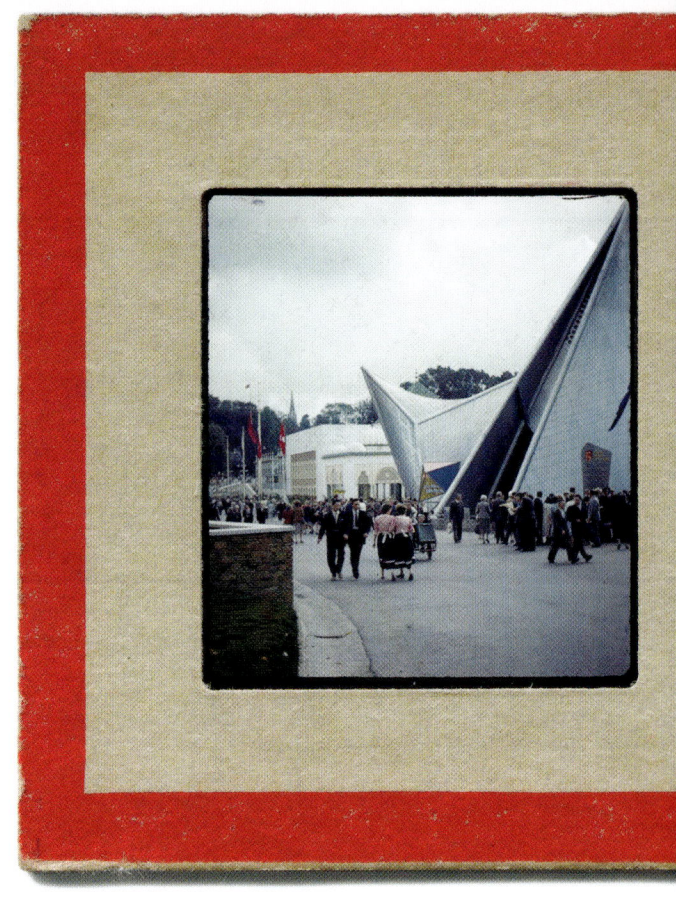
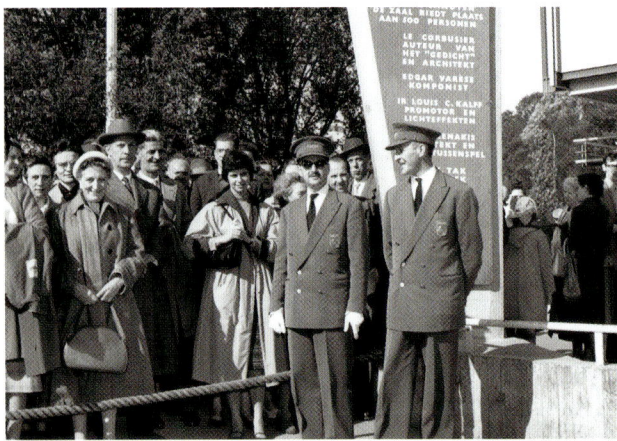
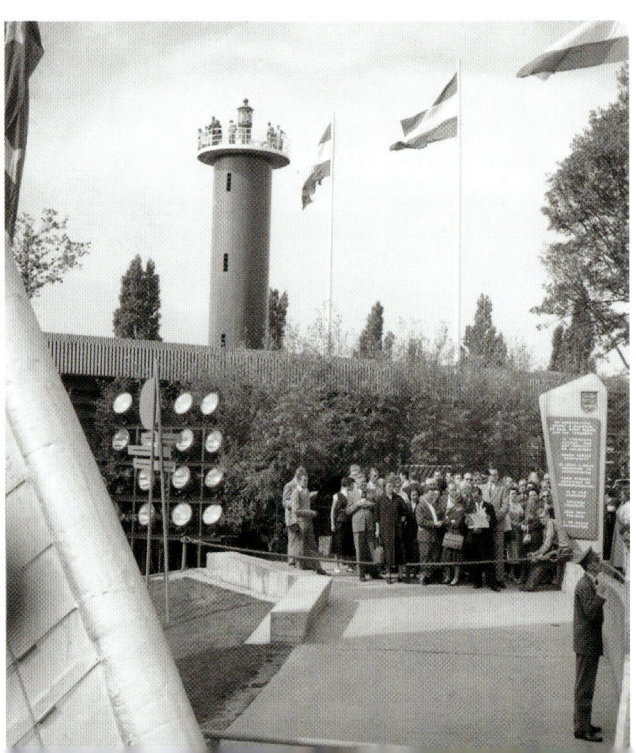

8.10
Philips' Vice-president Frits Philips stands on the Avenue de l'Europe in front of the Philips Pavilion.

8.11
The public waiting for the next performance in the Philips Pavilion gathered in front of a long, low-hanging cord under the watchful eye of two pavilion attendants.

8.12
Stereo photograph of the Philips Pavilion showing waiting visitors.

8.13
Visitors entering the Philips Pavilion under the supervision of the pavilion attendants for a performance of *Le poème électronique.*

KODACHROME STEREO TRANSPARENCIES
PROCESSED BY KODAK

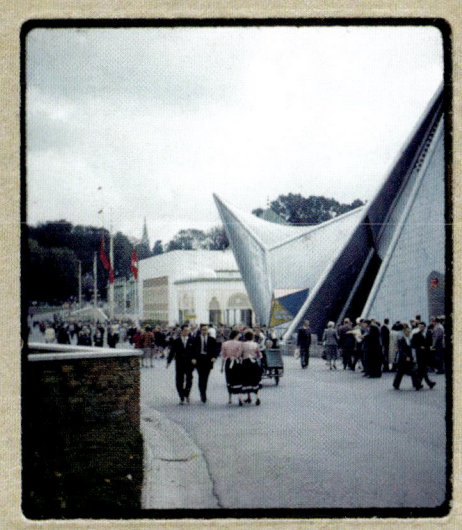

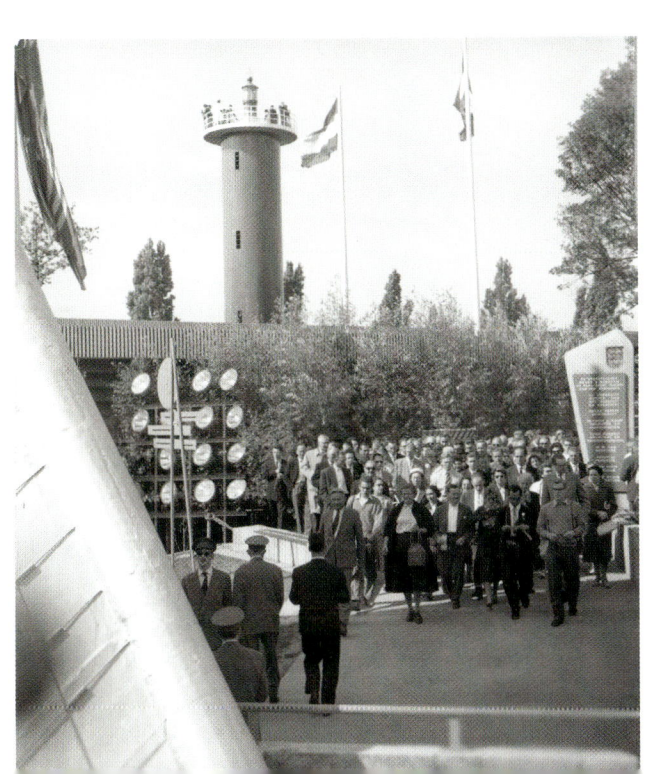
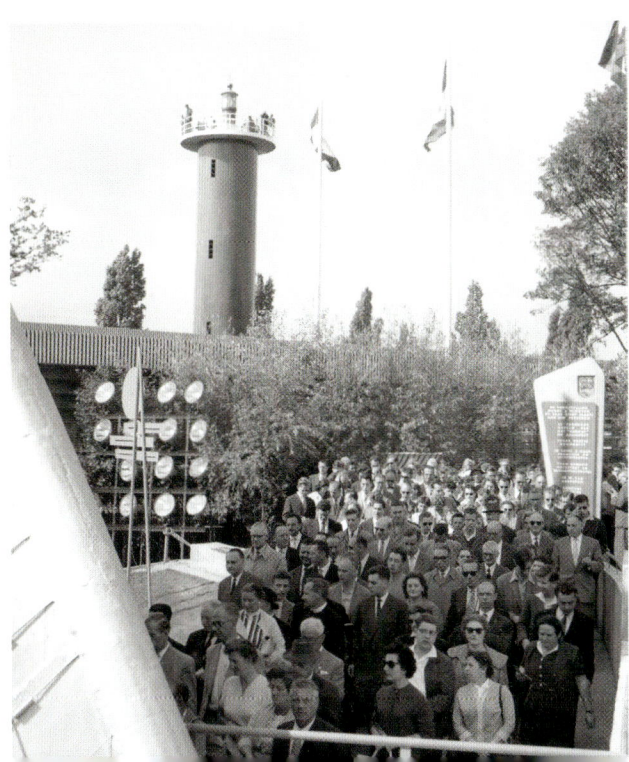

invited Le Corbusier together with Iannis Xenakis, Jean Petit and Philippe Agostini to a dinner of lamb chops in Brussels in September.[19]

On 29 September Le Corbusier attended the Philips Pavilion for an afternoon *séance spéciale* for Paul Meyers, the Belgian Minister of Public Works and Reconstruction. He spent the night in room 1102 at the Hotel Metropole. On 30 September, less than three weeks before the conclusion of the 1958 Brussels World's Fair on 19 October, a number of ceremonies took place that may or may not have been intended as inaugural events for those who had worked on realizing the pavilion and *Le poème électronique*. These events were attended by Le Corbusier, Iannis Xenakis and top executives from Philips Netherlands and Philips Belgium. In the Philips Pavilion, Philips staff were presented with an envelope by Frans Otten that probably contained a financial reward for their efforts. A reception was then held at the Dutch pavilion. The Dutch hostess Beatrijs Mendes de Leòn-van Liebergen asked Le Corbusier for his autograph, upon which he replied, 'God, I've already had to shake 150 hands, and now this on top of it all.' She decided

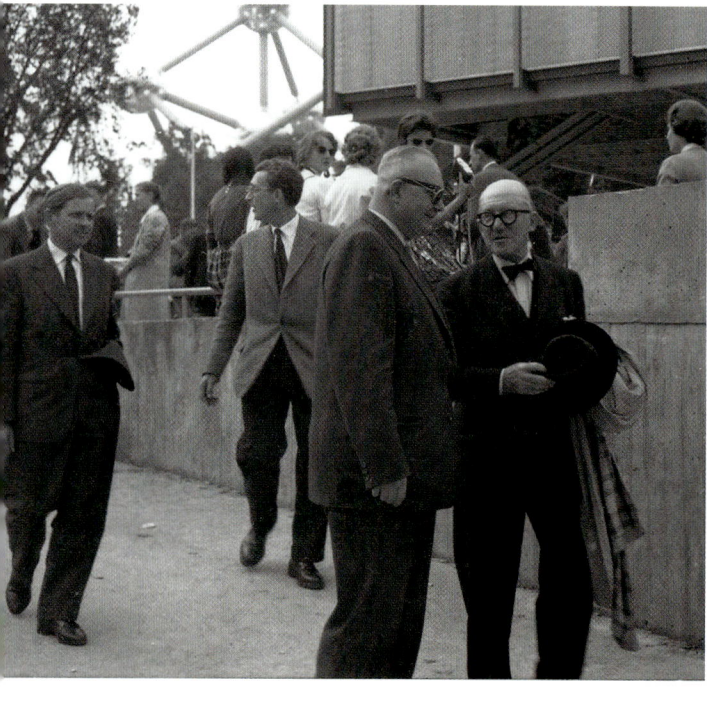

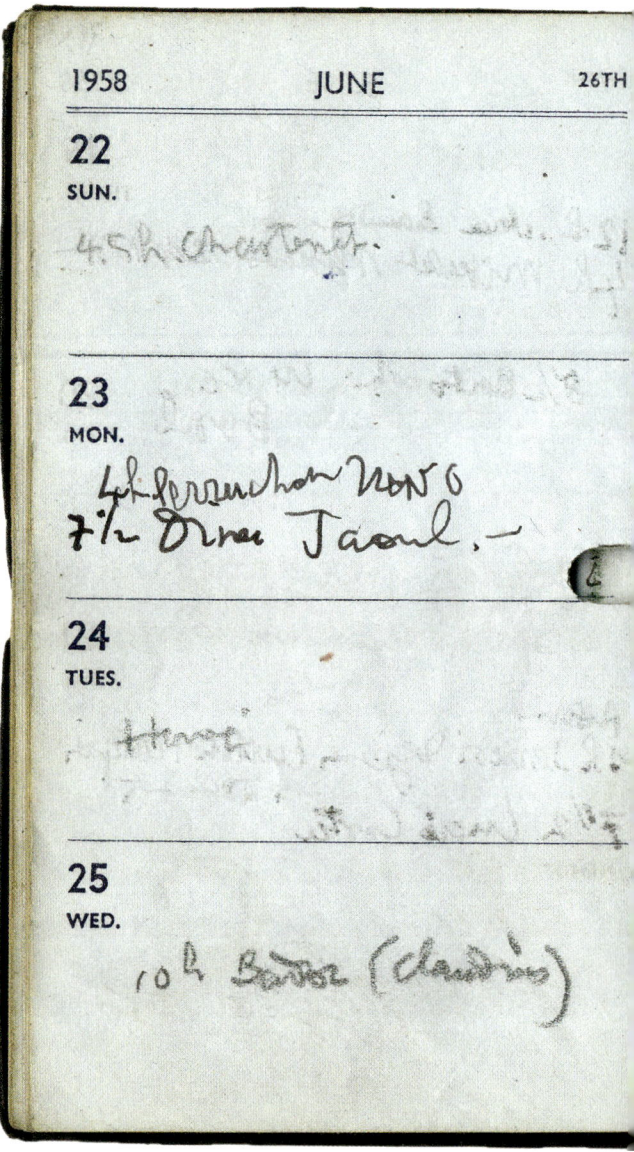

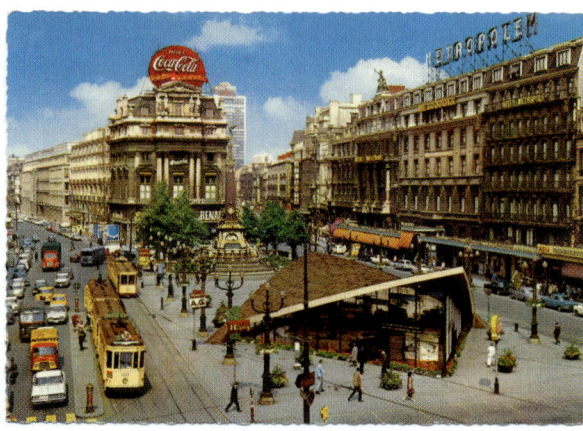

8.14
Le Corbusier, accompanied by pavilion manager Simon de Bruin on his right, attended the Philips Pavilion on 26 June 1958. The man with spectacles behind Simon de Bruin is Guillaume Gillet, the architect of the French pavilion.

8.15
Le Corbusier's diary entry mentioning his visit to Brussels on 26 and 27 June 1958, when he stayed at the Hotel Metropole at Place de Brouckère.

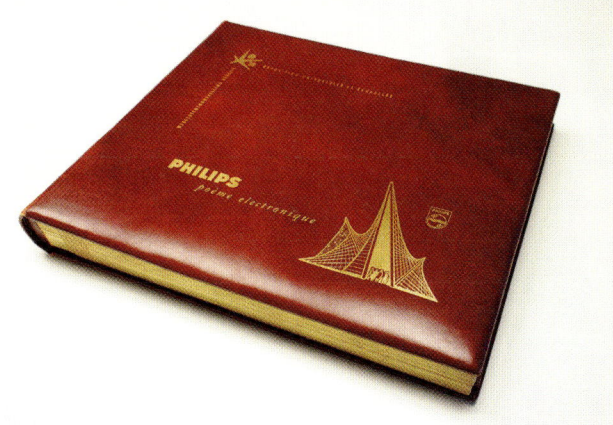

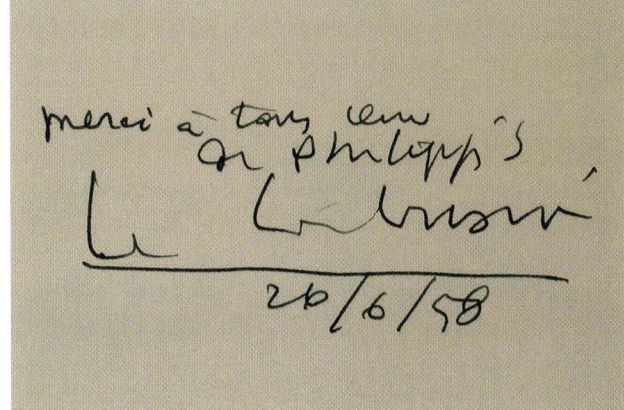

8.16
Picture postcard of Place de Brouckère in Brussels with the Hotel Metropole on the right, where Le Corbusier stayed during his visits to the Philips Pavilion in June and September 1958. On the square in front of the hotel is the 1958 Brussels World's Fair information centre, which, like the Philips Pavilion, incorporated a hyperbolic paraboloid (saddle-shaped) roof construction.

8.17
The Philips Pavilion's visitors' book, which was called the *Gulden Boek* [Golden Book] because of its gold-coloured inlay (top), was signed and dated by Le Corbusier on 26 June 1958 (middle) watched by pavilion manager Simon de Bruin (bottom).

131

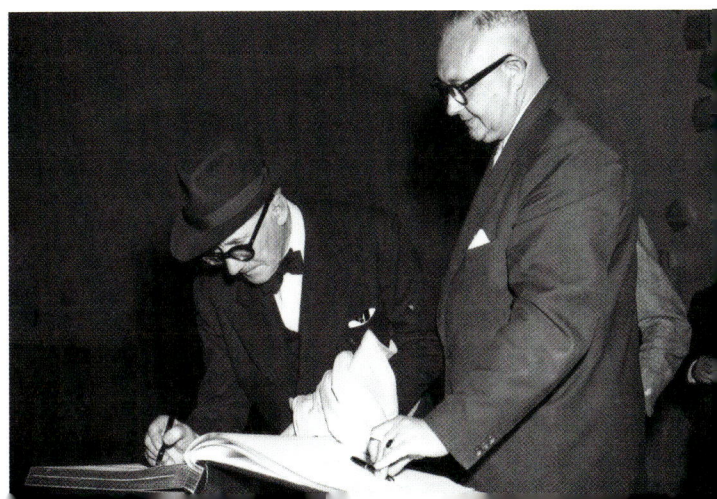

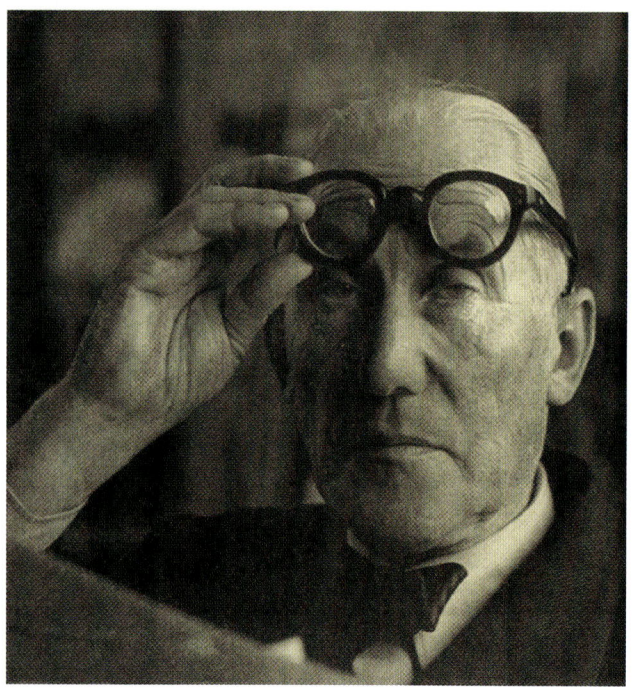

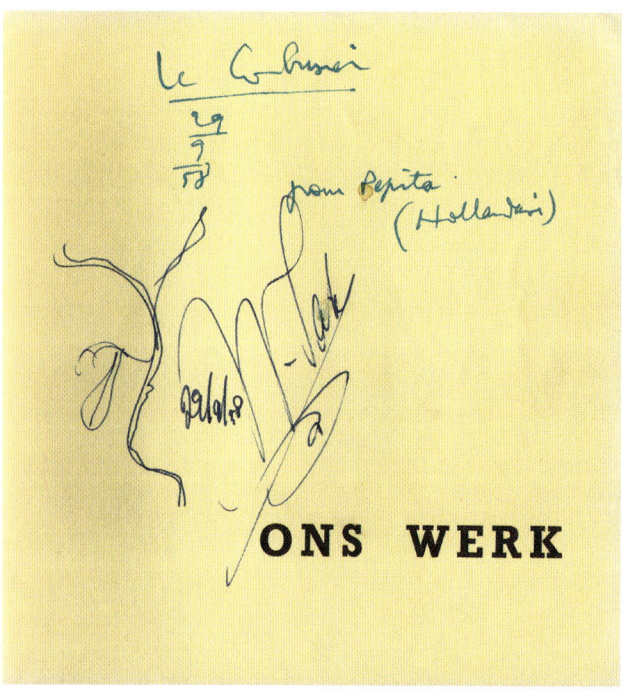

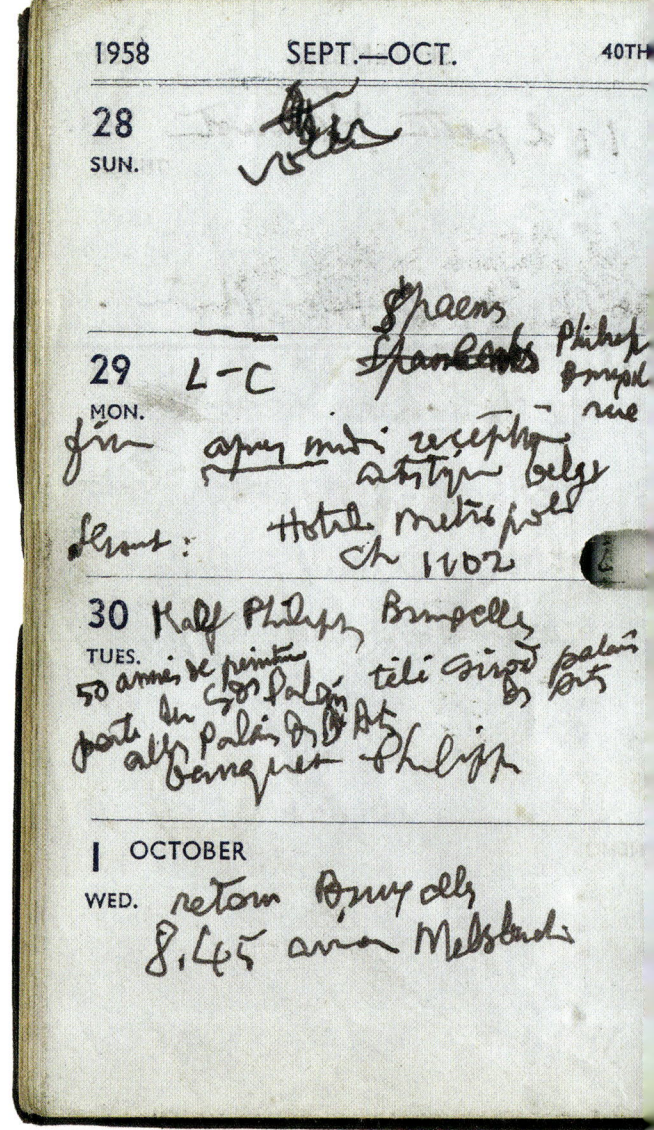

8.18
At the request of publicity officer Pepita de Nerée tot Babberich, on 29 September 1958, Le Corbusier and acoustics expert Willem Tak signed a copy of the book *Le poème électronique*. Le Corbusier opposite a page with a portrait picture of Le Corbusier. To the left of his signature, Tak drew a branch as his surname means 'branch' in Dutch.

8.19
Le Corbusier's diary, which indicates that he was in Brussels from 29 September to 1 October and that he stayed in room 1102 at the Hotel Metropole, Place de Brouckère.

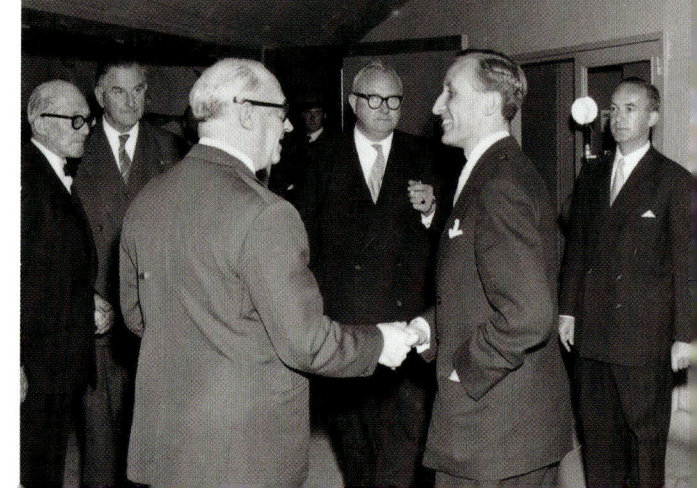

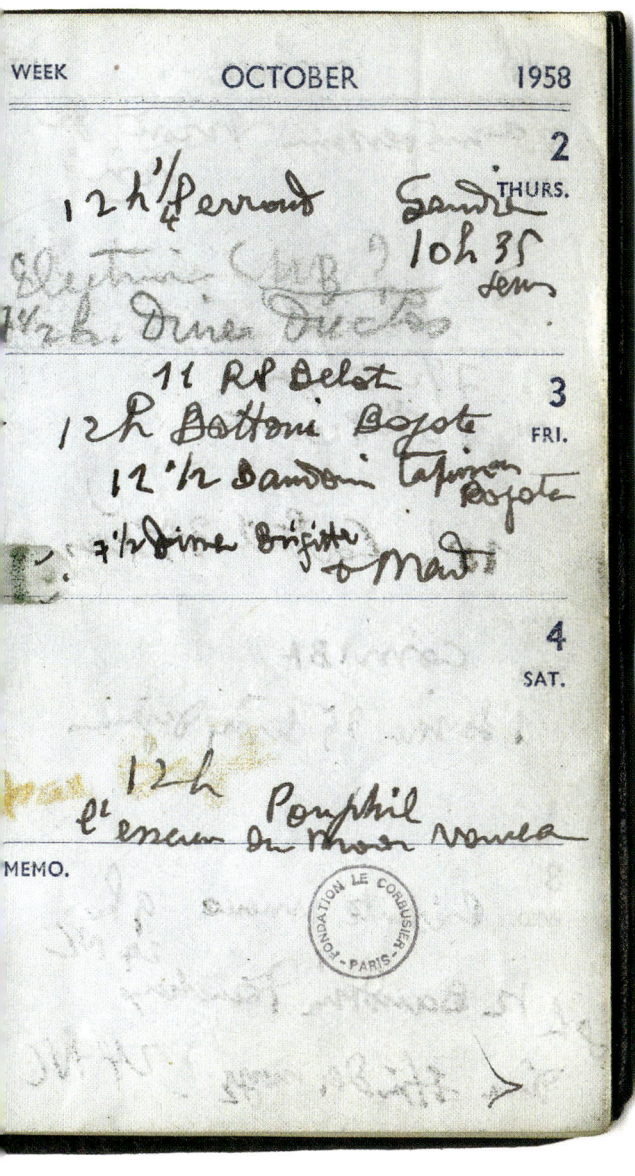

not to press him: '(...) if he'd been a really good-looking man, I'd have persisted, but he was just a little old man – small, bespectacled, grey, half bald: nothing to write home about.'[20] A banquet took place later at the Swiss pavilion's restaurant, where Frans Otten and Le Corbusier gave speeches. That day, Le Corbusier also visited the '50 Years of Modern Art' [50 jaar Moderne Kunst] exhibition at the International Hall of Fine Arts in Brussels. He left Belgium on the morning of 1 October, flying out from the airport at Melsbroek.[21]

Like an Ant in a Hurricane

Official receptions at the Dutch pavilion, which were usually reserved for royalty and other dignitaries, were concluded with a *séance spéciale* in the Philips Pavilion. A *séance spéciale* took place 164 times, during which the pavilion was closed to the public. Top Philips executives sometimes came from Eindhoven to attend receptions - Frans Otten, for example, attended the visit by Queen Juliana and Prince Bernhard on 16 June 1958. The Queen was apparently very interested in 'the intentions of the artists Le Corbusier and Varèse', and Prince Bernhard was deeply impressed by the 'avant-garde experiment'.[22] Visiting dignitaries ended their tour of the Dutch pavilion at the exit of the Philips Pavilion, where they entered and walked through the pavilion in reverse order. And whereas the public had to watch the performance standing, during a *séance spéciale* chairs were placed in the public area for guests. Dignitaries were requested to sign the *Gulden Boek*.[23] A silver and blue-enamelled paperweight in the shape of the Philips Pavilion could be presented as a commemorative gift.[24]

The Philips Pavilion was also visited by distinguished colleagues of Le Corbusier and Edgard Varèse. The Austro-American architect Richard Neutra visited the pavilion

8.20
Front left Charles Spaens of Philips Belgium shaking hands with Paul Meyers, the Belgian Minister of Public Works and Reconstruction, who visited the Philips Pavilion on 29 September 1958 in the afternoon. Between the two men is pavilion manager Simon de Bruin. Back left are Le Corbusier and Louis Kalff.

8.21
Le Corbusier in conversation with Louis Kalff on his right and acoustics expert Willem Tak on his left during a reception at the Dutch pavilion on 30 September 1958.

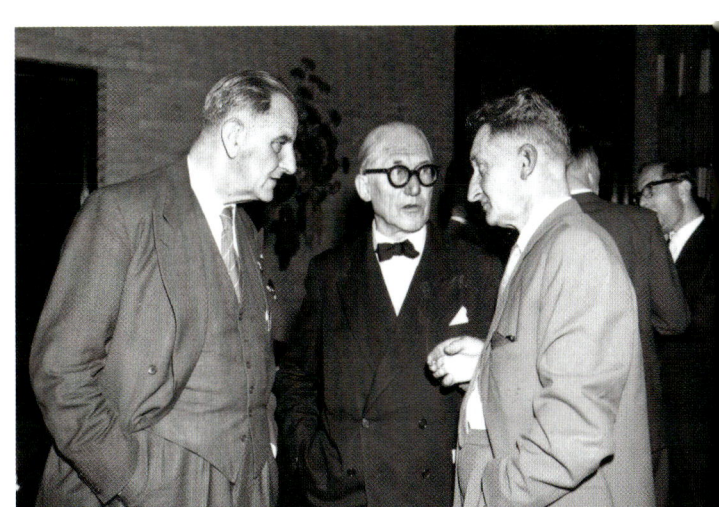

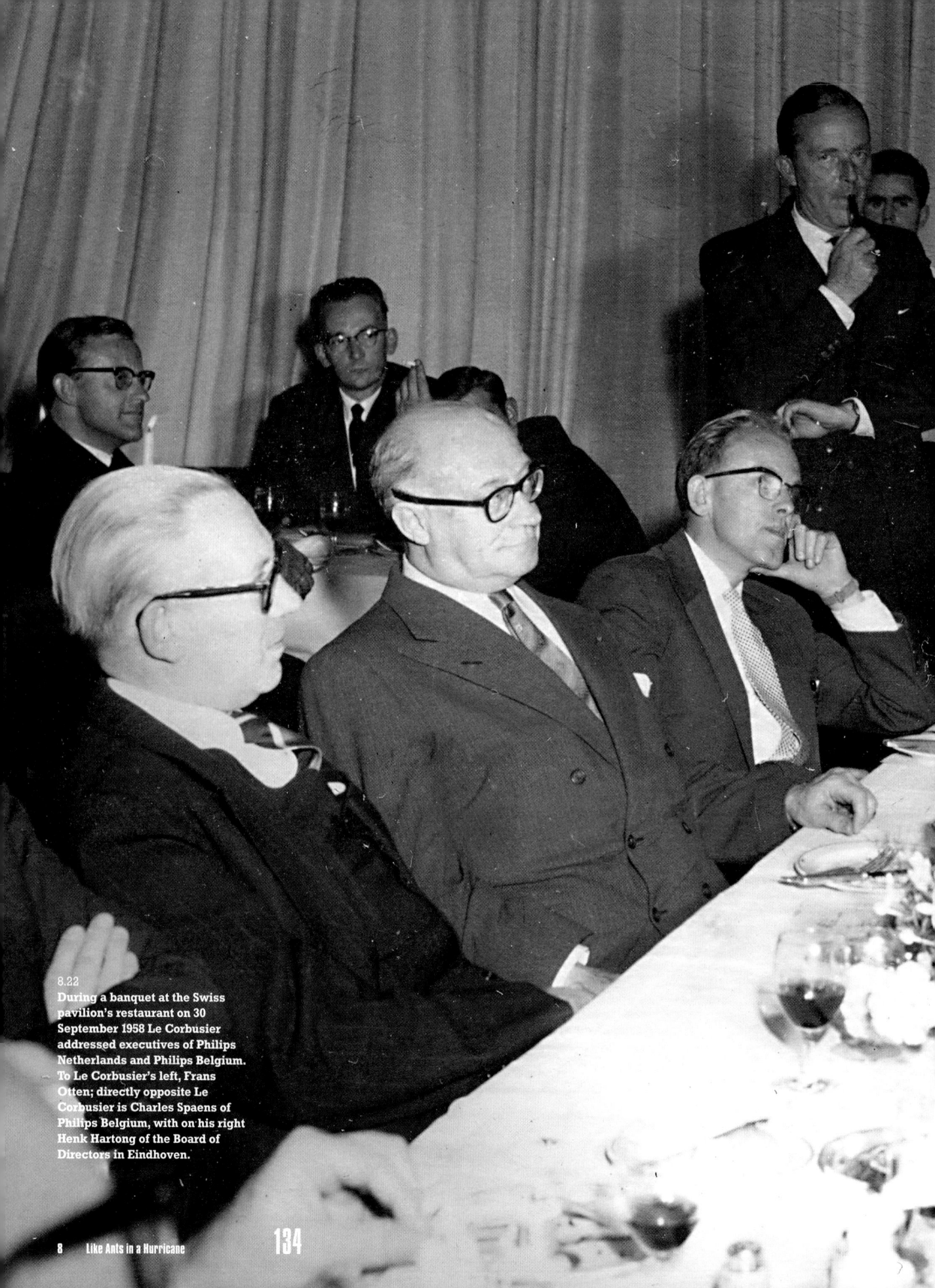

8.22
During a banquet at the Swiss pavilion's restaurant on 30 September 1958 Le Corbusier addressed executives of Philips Netherlands and Philips Belgium. To Le Corbusier's left, Frans Otten; directly opposite Le Corbusier is Charles Spaens of Philips Belgium, with on his right Henk Hartong of the Board of Directors in Eindhoven.

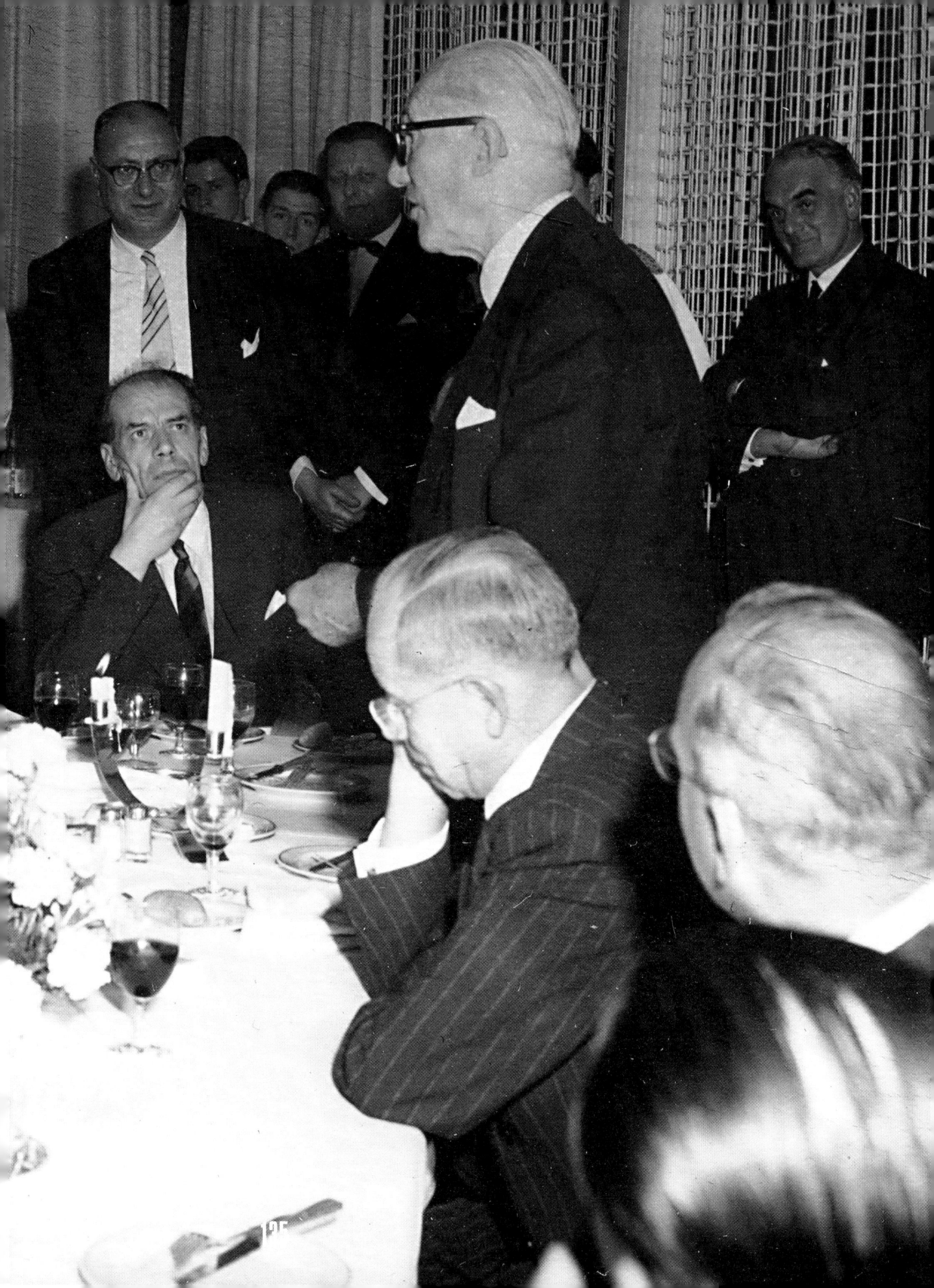

on 9 May to attend a trial performance of *Le poème électronique*.[25] Famous visitors from the world of music included Malcolm Arnold, Stefan Askenase, Yehudi Menuhin, Isaac Stern and Leopold Stokowski. The latter visited the pavilion with his friend Varèse for a *séance spéciale*.[26]

Most of the visitors to the Philips Pavilion were not treated to a *séance spéciale*. They were part of what was considered a 'mixed public mostly interested in – superior – fair-ground entertainment' – the performance in the Philips Pavilion might even have been so successful precisely because it was described with words such as 'horror show' and 'frightening and barbaric'.[27] During the performance, 'speechlessness, apathy, disbelief, wonder, superior ridicule, enthusiasm, even rage' alternated on the visitors' upturned faces.[28] Some people panicked. 'When a group went in, the doors were shut. Then images, coloured surfaces, exploded from all sides, projected above, below, left and right. On top of all that, there were the sounds. Some members of the public became very agitated and had to be calmed.'[29] In a foresighted act, 'lighting for panic cases' had been installed in several places in the pavilion, which could be lit from the control desk if necessary.[30]

Various descriptions illustrate the intensity with which *Le poème électronique* was let loose on the visitors. The performance was described as 'an intense physical experience' during which 'it felt as if you were walking *through* the sound', and the spectator felt like 'an ant in a hurricane'.[31] *Le poème électronique* was also described as a 'storm of light, images, colour and sound', or 'a terrifying natural disaster' that 'overwhelmed' the visitor.[32] Visitors were so affected by the performance that they 'constantly laughed, giggled, or suppressed their startled cries' and 'they felt they were suffocating, gasping for air'.[33] In view of the criticism of one visitor to the Philips Pavilion, it is doubtful whether most visitors understood Le Corbusier's intentions: 'It is impressive, but do I understand it? No, not really.'[34] But even the culturally engaged Willem Sandberg, the then director of the Stedelijk Museum in Amsterdam, had unanswered questions following his visit to the Philips Pavilion. He incorporated his questions in a review about the pavilion that was published in the *Museumjournaal*:

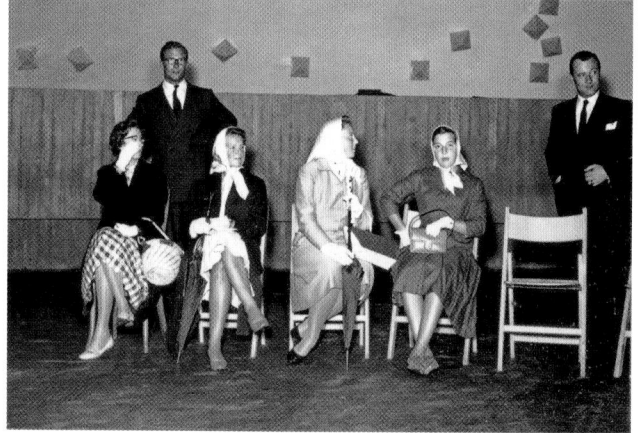

8.23
From left to right, wearing scarves, are the Dutch princesses, Irene, Beatrix and Margriet, waiting incognito on 25 August 1958 for a performance of *Le poème électronique*. Chairs were only placed in the public area of the Philips Pavilion during a *séance spéciale*.

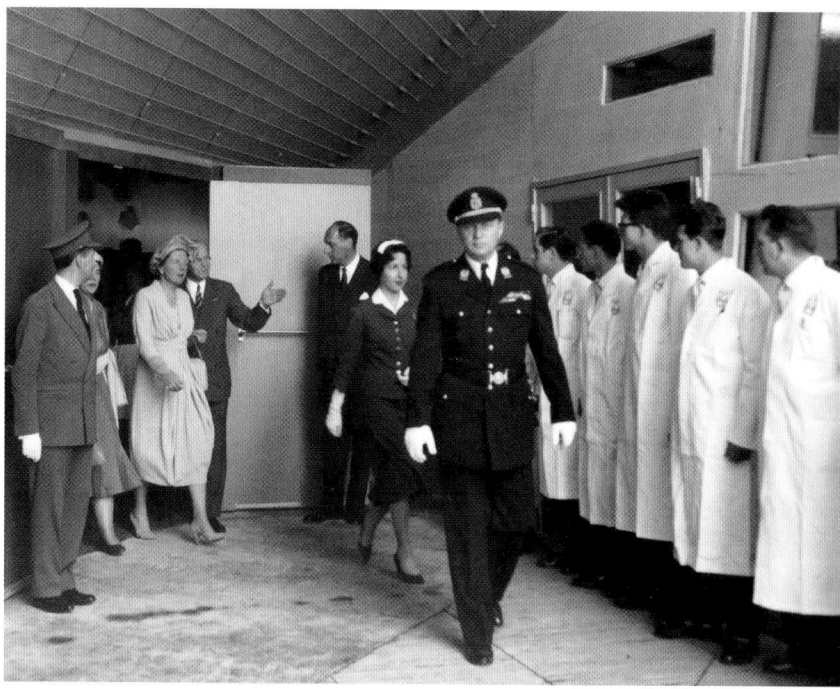

8.24
Queen Juliana leaving the Philips Pavilion via the entrance on 16 June 1958, passing the control room and the pavilion's staff. During official receptions, guests walked through the pavilion in reverse direction.

*boys play in the forest during the holidays:
they cut off a couple of strong branches,
stick them in the ground,
throw their raincoats over them and crouch
in their new tent,
their imagination completely fulfilled.*

*perhaps le corbusier had something like
that in mind
when he designed the philips pavilion for
the brussels world's fair.
then the builders, engineers, and experts
came along
and his rarefied invention was petrified
into a strong prestressed
concrete construction*

*the result looks like a pevsner sculpture
enlarged
only: it doesn't give the impression that it
can be only this way
and no other
does it satisfy le corbusier's imagination?
does it satisfy ours?
i don't know...*[35]

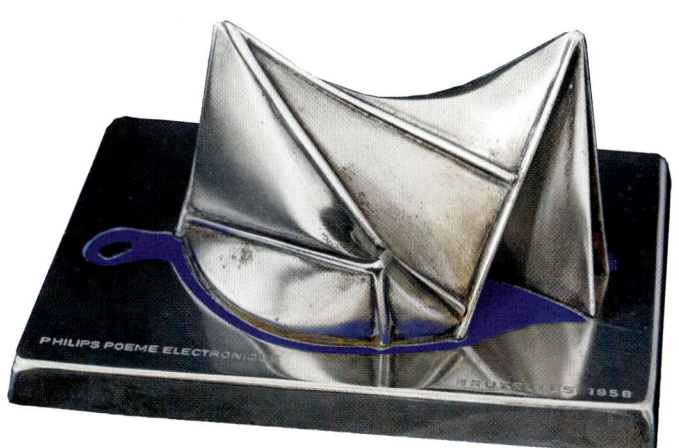

8.25
Paperweight in the shape of the Philips Pavilion, which could be presented as a commemorative gift.

8.26
Cover of the May 1959 issue of the Dutch *Museumjournaal* monthly in which Willem Sandberg, the director of the Stedelijk Museum in Amsterdam, reviewed the Philips Pavilion.

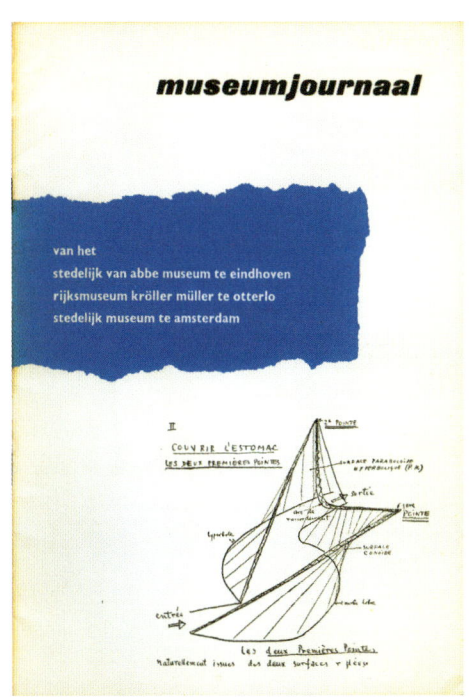

9 Beyond the Final Performance
Demolition of the Philips Pavilion

Peter Wever and Kees Tazelaar

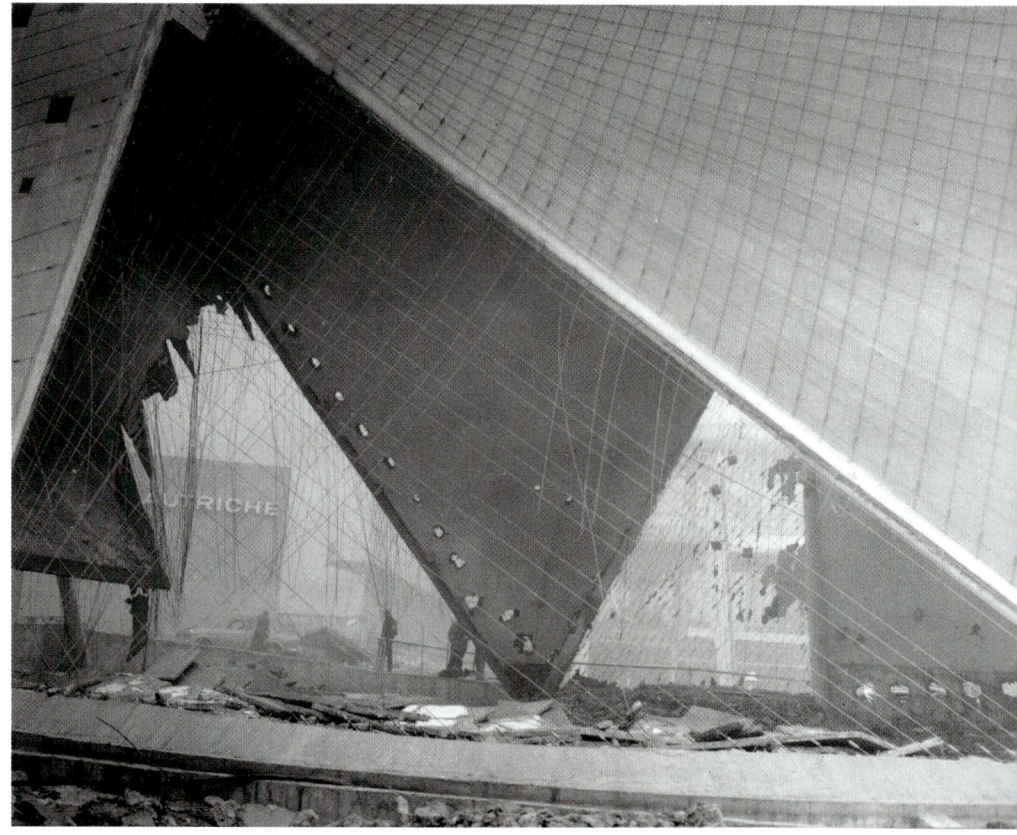

9.1
The partly-dismantled Philips Pavilion, with bracing wires dangling loose.

Towards the end of the 1958 Brussels World's Fair, several attempts were made to preserve the Philips Pavilion. That the building would be torn down, however, was inevitable. Louis Kalff wanted to turn the demolition into a publicity stunt, leading to some spectacular scripts, which were scrapped as being too dangerous. The partly-dismantled pavilion was blown up with dynamite on 2 February 1959. Since then, objects linked to it have found their way into collections and archives all over the world. In the absence of the physical context of the pavilion, several reconstructions have been made of the performance of *Le poème électronique*. In addition, some have looked into the possibility of rebuilding the Philips Pavilion. Largely unaware of this renewed interest, five Belgian and Dutch former employees at the Philips Pavilion revisited the grounds where they had dedicated over five months of their lives to *Le poème électronique* – more than fifty years later.

The Final Performance

At twenty to seven on the evening of Sunday, 19 October 1958, the projectionist Paul Vancoppenolle and co-worker Michel Cools heard their superior, Simon de Bruin, calling over the speaker in their projection booth 'Lanterns on!' for the last time. There were fewer than five hundred people in the public area. When the performance was finished, the two men shook hands without saying a word. It was all over. The film reels were put away and the projectors cleaned. Everything looked neat and tidy. Simon de Bruin called everyone into the control room for some brief words of farewell. It was a simple occasion, without much emotion. There was no wine. *Le poème électronique* had finished.

Paul Vancoppenolle was asked to report to the pavilion at eight o'clock the next morning. He passed dozens of people heading home, in varying stages of inebriation. They had spent the night celebrating the end of the World's Fair at *La Belgique Joyeuse*, the picturesque village built on the grounds, financed by Belgian brewers. When Paul Vancoppenolle arrived at the pavilion, he saw no one he knew. The other Dutch and Belgian employees had to return to their previous jobs at Philips. The pavilion was to be dismantled by a group of new technicians, to which Paul Vancoppenolle was seconded. The camaraderie had evaporated. He was given a pair of pliers and told to cut through all the wires attached to the relay boxes, which his former associates had worked on for hours, to prepare them for transport. Two of the four Philips FP56 projectors from the pavilion were sold to the cinema and party venue Pax in the village of Erpe to the west of Brussels.[1] Paul Vancoppenolle helped to install them in the projection booth there. Soon afterwards, on 31 January 1959, his temporary job at Philips Brussels was terminated, after a period of ten months.[2]

Plans for Preservation

The 'Foundation World Exhibition Brussels 1958 Netherlands Section' had a contractual obligation to restore the grounds of its entry, which included the Philips Pavilion, to their original state.[3] This was because the pavilions had been built in the Royal Gardens, which had been made available only for the duration of the World's Fair.[4] Louis Kalff had already told Le Corbusier back in October 1956 that there was a legal obligation to demolish the Philips Pavilion after the World's Fair.[5] Even so, several attempts were made to preserve it as the event drew to a close. The Brussels architect Stanislas Jasinski, president of the Belgian Society of Architects,[6] was deeply impressed with the pavilion. He approached Le Corbusier, offering to try to ensure that the structure was preserved.[7] On 26 September, Jasinski submitted a written request to this effect to Charles Spaens, the deputy manager of Philips Belgium. In consultation with Jasinski, Le Corbusier proposed setting up an international testing laboratory for electronic games in the Philips Pavilion. The idea was to make the pavilion available to people with innovative minds, who could produce brief performances (5 to 15 minutes long) with its equipment, and if appropriate broadcast them on the radio.[8] Le Corbusier had already realized in July 1956 that *Le poème électronique*, which had yet to be written, would be the first ever *jeu électrique*, combining light, design, colour, movement and concepts into a surprising whole, which would be accessible to the masses.[9] Le Corbusier wanted to ask the Belgian government to accept the Philips Pavilion as a gift.[10] With this in mind, he sent the correspondence between Jasinski and himself to Paul Meyers, the Belgian Minister of Public Works and Reconstruction, on 8 October. They had met a week before then, during a visit to the Philips Pavilion on 29 September, and had already discussed the possibility of preserving the building.[11] On 9 October, however, just one day after he had forwarded the letters, Spaens informed Jasinsky that after discussing the matter with the Philips directors, they had decided that the building could not be preserved on the grounds of the World's Fair.[12] The Philips directors briefly considered demolishing the pavilion and rebuilding it in Eindhoven for use as an industrial museum or a music studio, but the projected expenses soon led them to abandon the idea.[13] In November 1958, the Brussels lawyer Freddy Caliouw made a fresh enquiry about the possibility of preserving the pavilion. Philips replied that he could have it free of charge if he could get consent to leave the building on the

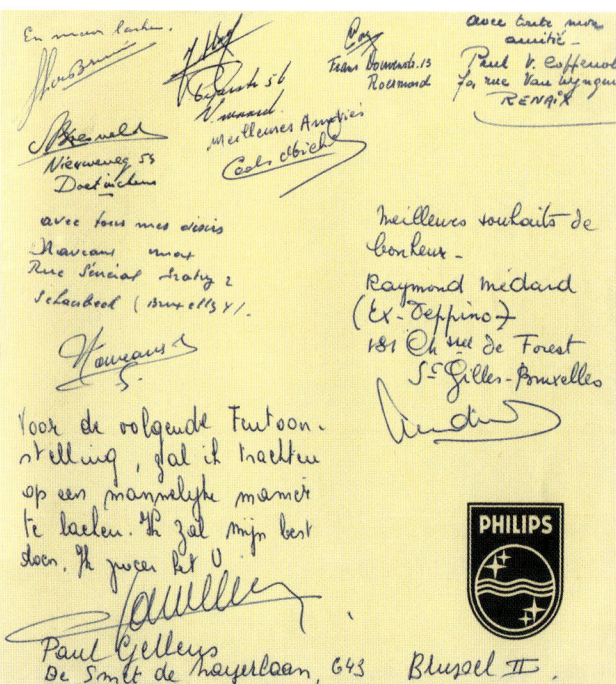

9.2
When the 1958 Brussels World's Fair ended, publicity officer Pepita de Nerée tot Babberich asked each of her fellow employees at the Philips Pavilion to write a dedication in a copy of the book *Le poème électronique*. Le Corbusier.

9.3
Loudspeaker cabinet from the Philips Pavilion which one of the employees took home after the end of the World's Fair.

9.4
A wooden crate used to transport the projector head of an FP56 projector from the Philips truck garage on the Strijp III premises in Eindhoven to the Philips Pavilion in Brussels. The words 'DE GARAGE' are printed on the crate.

exhibition grounds. However, Brussels city council rejected the request out of hand.[14]

Another – equally important, perhaps – factor that made the demolition of the Philips Pavilion inevitable had to do with the building's construction. In line with the prevailing concept of exhibition architecture, the pavilion had not been built to last much longer than the duration of the World's Fair. The walls were too thin to protect the electronic equipment from frost, the roof was not built to withstand the pressure of snow, the seams might freeze and crack, and the bracing wires might corrode. The demolition of the Philips Pavilion was unavoidable. Even Louis Kalff, who had taken the initiative for the pavilion and wanted to leave it standing so that other modern composers, such as Karlheinz Stockhausen and Henk Badings, could experiment with it, seemed to be resigned to the fact that the structure had to be taken down.[15]

Demolition of the Philips Pavilion

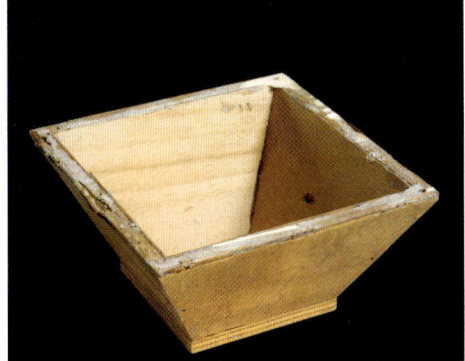

Although the commission for the building of the Philips Pavilion had been given to the Belgian contractors Société de Travaux & Béton et Dragages (known as 'Strabed'), with the Dutch civil engineer Hoyte Duyster assuming primary responsibility,[16] Philips had not made any binding agreements, either with Strabed or with anyone else, for the pavilion's demolition. On 6 November 1958, however, at a meeting with an employee of Philips' Office of Lighting Advice, Duyster said that getting in a different firm to pull the building down might be extremely dangerous, since it would know too little about the construction, as a result of which dismantling the bracing wires, in particular, might be fraught with risks. Another problem was that the building contained several solutions for the assembly of the bracing wires that had been patented by Strabed and could not be used by third parties to slacken them.[17] All this meant that hiring Strabed to demolish the building was the only viable option. Accordingly, at the beginning of December 1958, Strabed and Philips signed a contract for the demolition of the Philips Pavilion, the removal of the rubble, and the levelling of the site.[18]

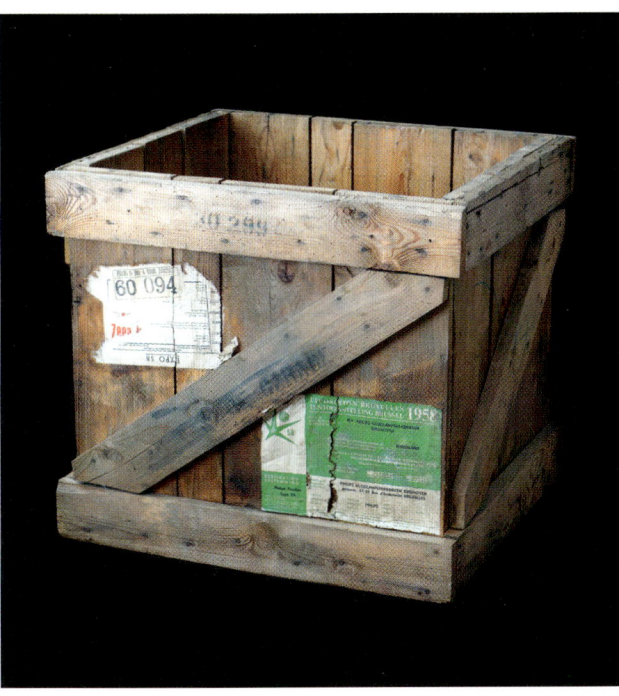

Strabed was free to choose the demolition method. But Kalff did urge that a spectacular mode of demolition was chosen, to take advantage of the ensuing publicity.[19] Several spectacular options were considered. Since the bracing wires had to be slackened first, it was not possible to simply blow up the entire building in one go.[20] Even so, Kalff suggested placing a hydrogen-filled balloon in the pavilion and exploding it, so that the excess pressure would cause the wires to snap. Another plan that was soon abandoned was to conduct a high-voltage electric current through the bracing wires, so that the wires would become red-hot and the pavilion would cave in like a pudding. Duyster, on the other hand, proposed hacking holes in the pavilion's concrete shell, and then more holes in between these holes, and to carry on in this way until the whole structure buckled and collapsed.[21]

On 30 January 1959 a company of engineers, with Kalff among them, visited the former exhibition grounds. That afternoon, between two and four o'clock, the Philips Pavilion was to be razed to the ground. Several of the pavilion's walls had already been dismantled in pieces, exposing a jumble of dangling wires. Workers leant ladders against the

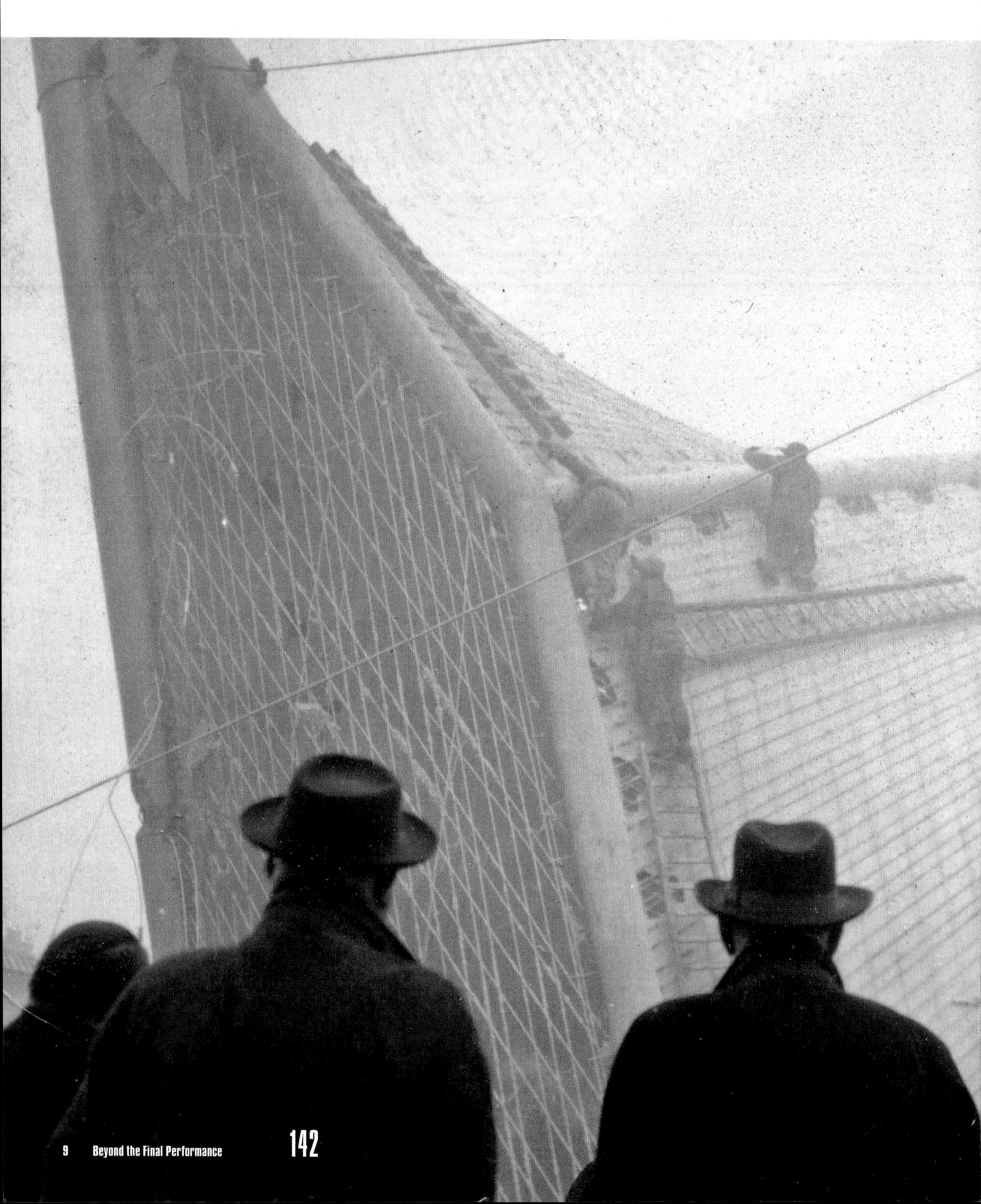

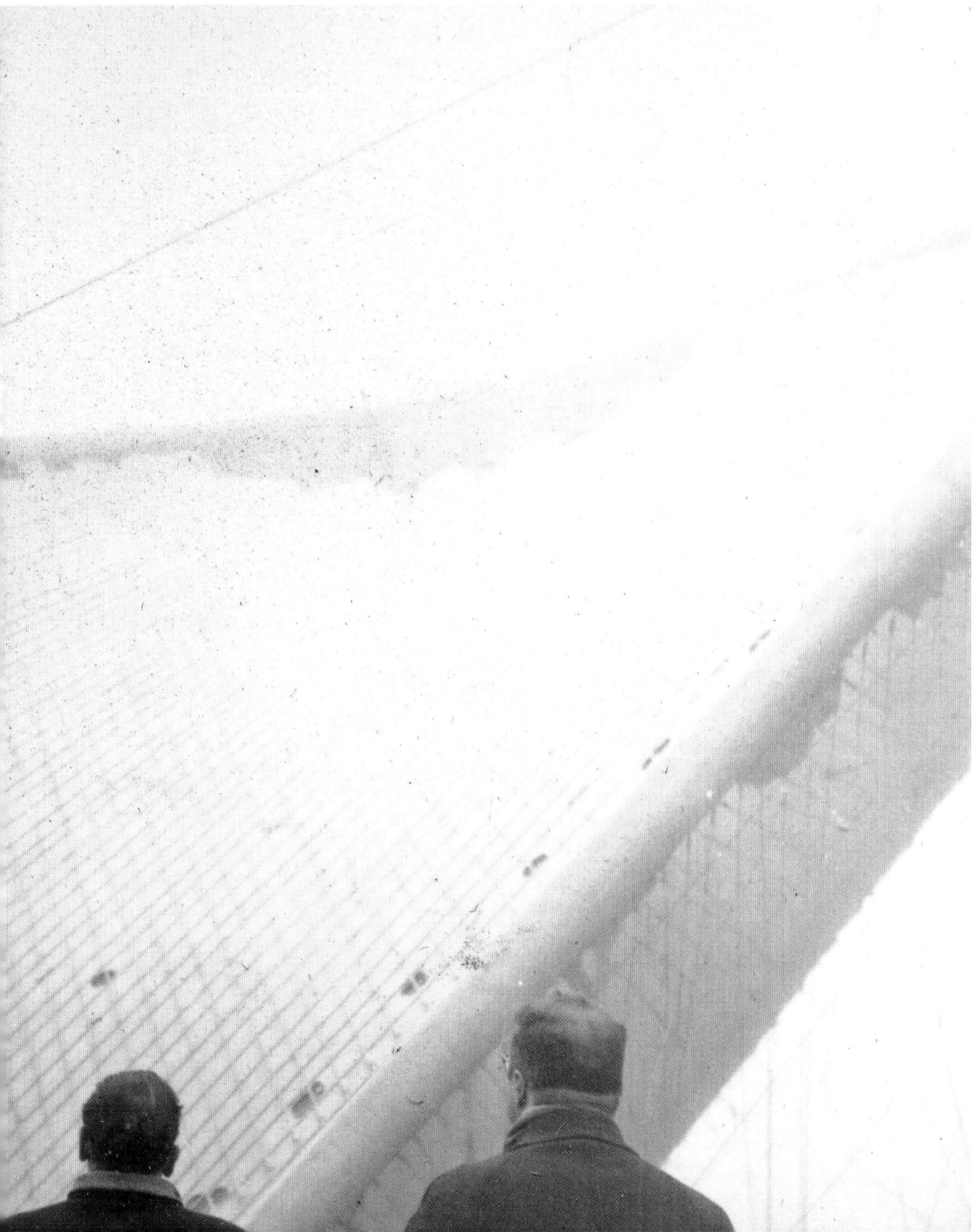

remaining walls and climbed up, regardless of the risks, to cut through the bracing wires, to cause the building to collapse. Tremendous creaking sounds ensued, but the structure somehow remained standing.[22] After his visit, Kalff informed Le Corbusier of the progress of the demolition and the feelings it stirred. 'It is a task which makes us a bit sad; nevertheless, it is necessary since the avant-garde creations at the exposition are only remarkable for a very short time. Already, to see again the few pavilions remaining on the site of the exposition gives us very little pleasure.'[23] In the end, it was decided to use dynamite after all.[24] On 2 February 1959, almost 19 months after the first posts had been driven into the ground,[25] the Philips Pavilion was blown up.[26] In June 1959, long after the scheduled date of 15 February 1959,[27] an official report was drawn up, affirming that the site had been returned in its original state.[28]

Towards Archives and Collections

After the dismantling of the Philips Pavilion, the *Objet mathématique* was the only structural element of the building to be preserved. It is currently owned by the Art Committee of Eindhoven University of Technology, and stands on the campus, on the grass outside the university auditorium.[29]

As far as the performance of *Le poème électronique* is concerned, its script and its audiovisual components have been preserved in full. The original hand-coloured loose-leaf version of the *minutage définitif* of *Le poème électronique* belongs to the collection of the Fondation Le Corbusier in Paris. Jean Petit had a number of hand-coloured copies (reportedly twenty in total) produced in book form, at least three of which have been preserved: in the collections of the Getty Research Institute in Los Angeles (Johan Jansen's personal copy), Philips Company Archives in Eindhoven, and a private collection.[30]

When the World's Fair closed, the projectionist Max Naveaux was given permission to take the 35-mm films with the final versions of the *écran* and *tri-trous* home with him. Through the mediation of Paul Vancoppenolle, both films came into the possession of the first author of this chapter in 2009. They were handed over for storage in the repository of the EYE Film Institute Netherlands, in Amsterdam, which had the *tri-trous* film digitized by Cineric film laboratory in

9.6
The *Objet mathématique* is the only structural element of the Philips Pavilion that has been preserved. It belongs to the Art Committee of Eindhoven University of Technology and stands on the grass outside the university auditorium. The original neon light tubes have been removed and the words 'poème électronique' are currently displayed in blue LED lighting. The word 'philips' has gone.

9.7
The picture at the top shows the sleeve of the LP *Memories aux Bruxelles: The Official Music of the Brussels World's Fair*, released in 1959, including a fragment of Varèse's *Le poème électronique* that was probably recorded during a performance in the Philips Pavilion, using recording equipment placed in the public area. The illustration in the middle shows the sleeve of the LP *Varèse* with the full *Le poème électronique*, released in 1960 by Philips' own record label. The image at the bottom shows the sleeve of the LP *Music of Edgar Varèse*, released in 1960 by Columbia Records, with exactly the same tracklist as the LP produced by Philips.

9.8 (next pages)
Images from the reconstruction of *Le poème électronique*, based on the *minutage définitif* and commissioned by the Stichting Elektronische Gedichten.

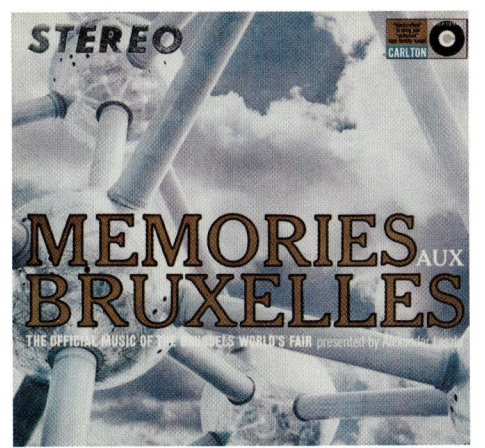

New York. This colour film had acquired a reddish tinge over the years, typical of the ageing process, and the original colours were restored as well as possible in the digitization process. The EYE Film Institute Netherlands has also possessed for some time a Philips film collection, which includes a 35-mm negative copy and a positive copy of the *écran* film. In addition, the *écran* images were incorporated (as a 16-mm film) into the film database of the Philips Film Library. Finally, the first author of this chapter possesses several strips deriving from the 35-mm rush print of the *écran* film from Joop Geesink's Dollywood Studios. This is the first positive copy of the original camera negative, including film images of blackboards on which the numbers of various scenes were chalked in.[31]

The original sound tracks of *Le poème électronique* are on audiotapes that are preserved in the archives of the Institute of Sonology of the Royal Conservatoire in The Hague, in the Netherlands.[32] Varèse's collage-like score for *Le poème électronique* is preserved (although incomplete) along with other sketches in the collection of the Paul Sacher Foundation in Basel.

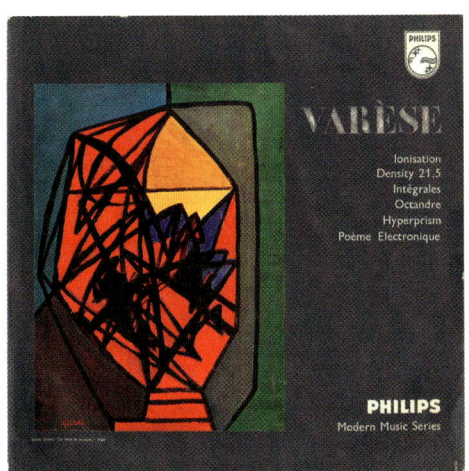

As far as the colour elements of *Le poème électronique* are concerned, the Art Committee of Eindhoven University of Technology and the Getty Research Institute have preserved a number of the coloured glass slides that were used, with projectors, to create parts of the *ambiances*.[33]

Discography of Varèse's *Le poème électronique*

After the closure of the 1958 Brussels World's Fair, Varèse's *Le poème électronique* proved to have a *raison d'être* as an independent piece of music. That same year – in November 1958 – a concert was staged in New York, at which *Le poème électronique* was played to the audience in stereo.[34] In 1959, the first LP was released, with at least part of a recording of Varèse's composition. The LP was entitled *Memories aux Bruxelles: The Official Music of the Brussels World's Fair*, and was released by Carlton Record Corporation, an American recording label.[35] It consists of a collection of twelve pieces of music played at different national pavilions at the World's Fair 'as recorded in actual performances – presented as it was to those who were there'. This suggests that the recording was made during a performance in the Philips Pavilion, with recording equipment placed in the public area. The fragment, which lasts 3 minutes and 59 seconds and therefore represents only part of *Le poème électronique*, is described on the sleeve of the album as 'Electronic Music from the Netherlands Pavilion (Varese)'. It is most probably an unofficial recording.

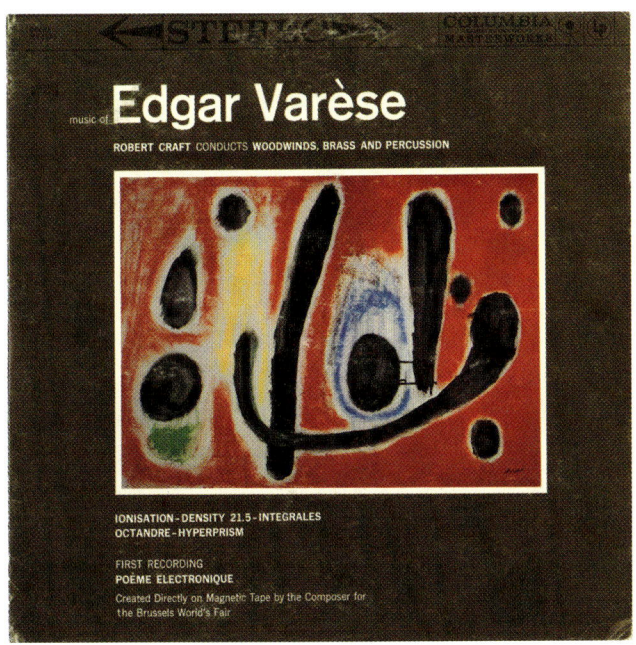

In 1960, the Philips recording label and the American label Columbia Records released identical LPs containing *Le poème électronique* in its entirety.[36] Columbia Records had an exchange agreement with the Philips label giving Columbia exclusive rights to sell recordings made by Philips' Phonographic Industries in its contract region.[37] The two albums have different sleeves: the Philips LP is called *Varèse* whereas the one released by Columbia Records bears the title *Music of Edgar Varèse*. Both LPs are labelled: 'FIRST RECORDING POÈME ELECTRONIQUE: Created Directly on Magnetic Tape by the Composer for the Brussels World's Fair.'

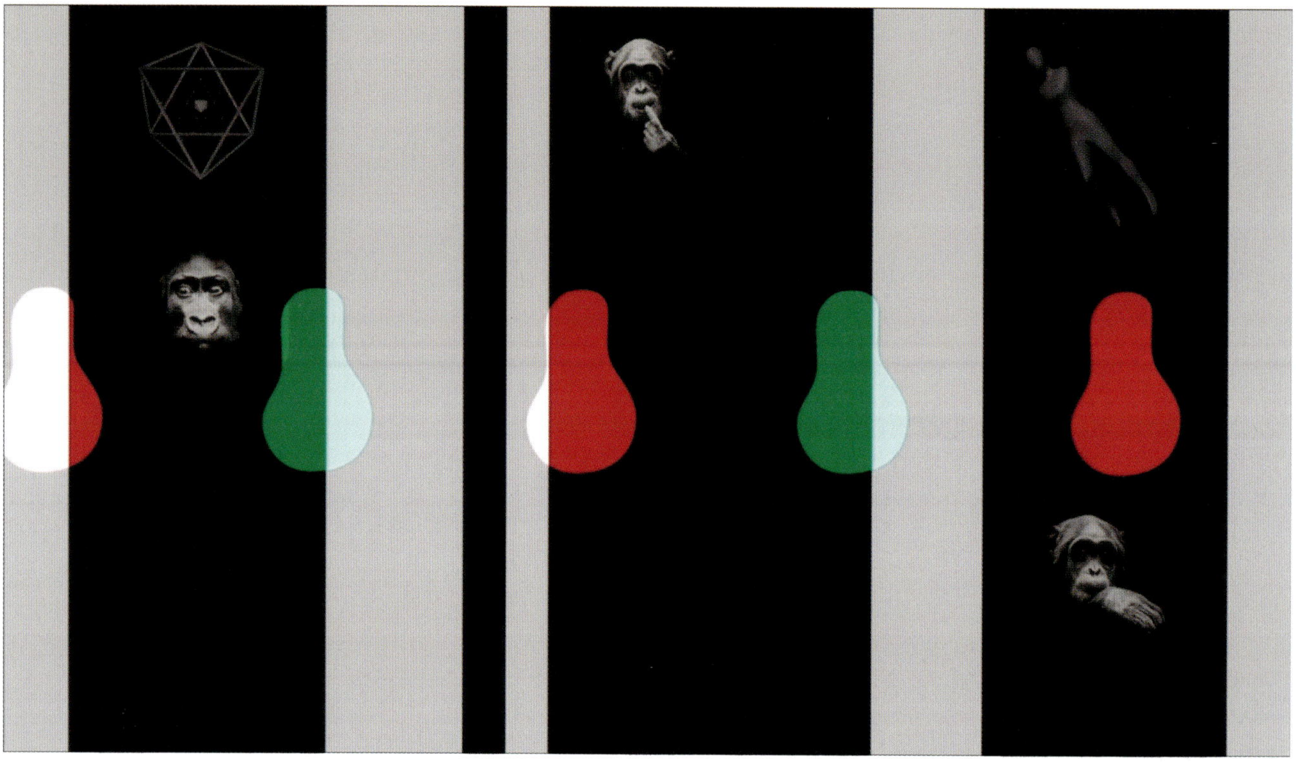

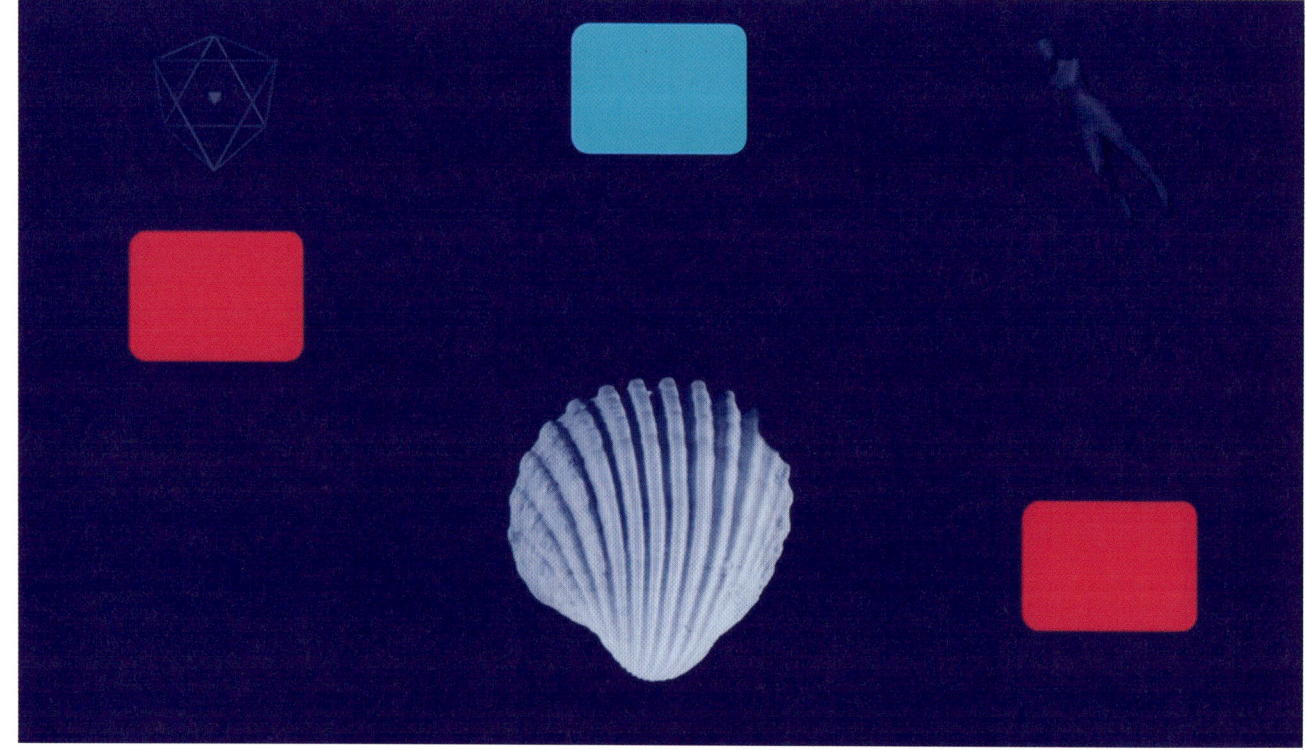

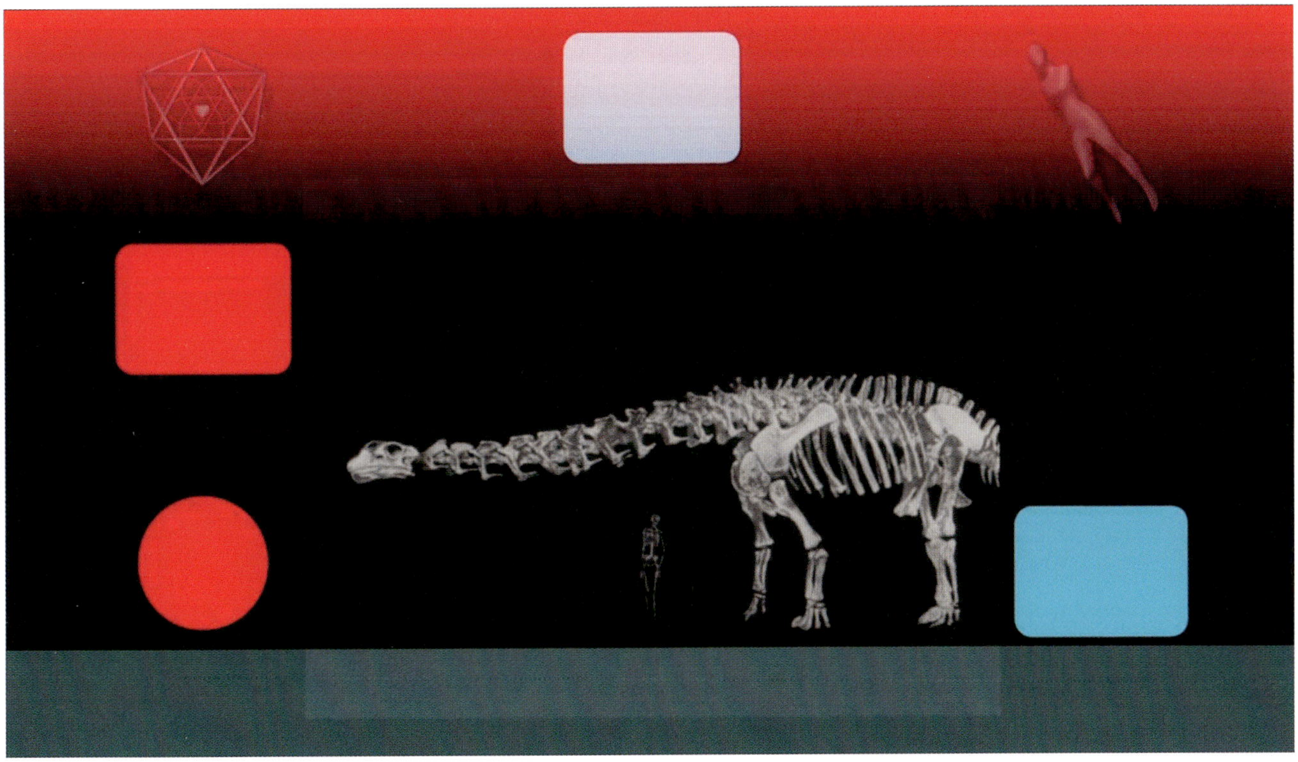

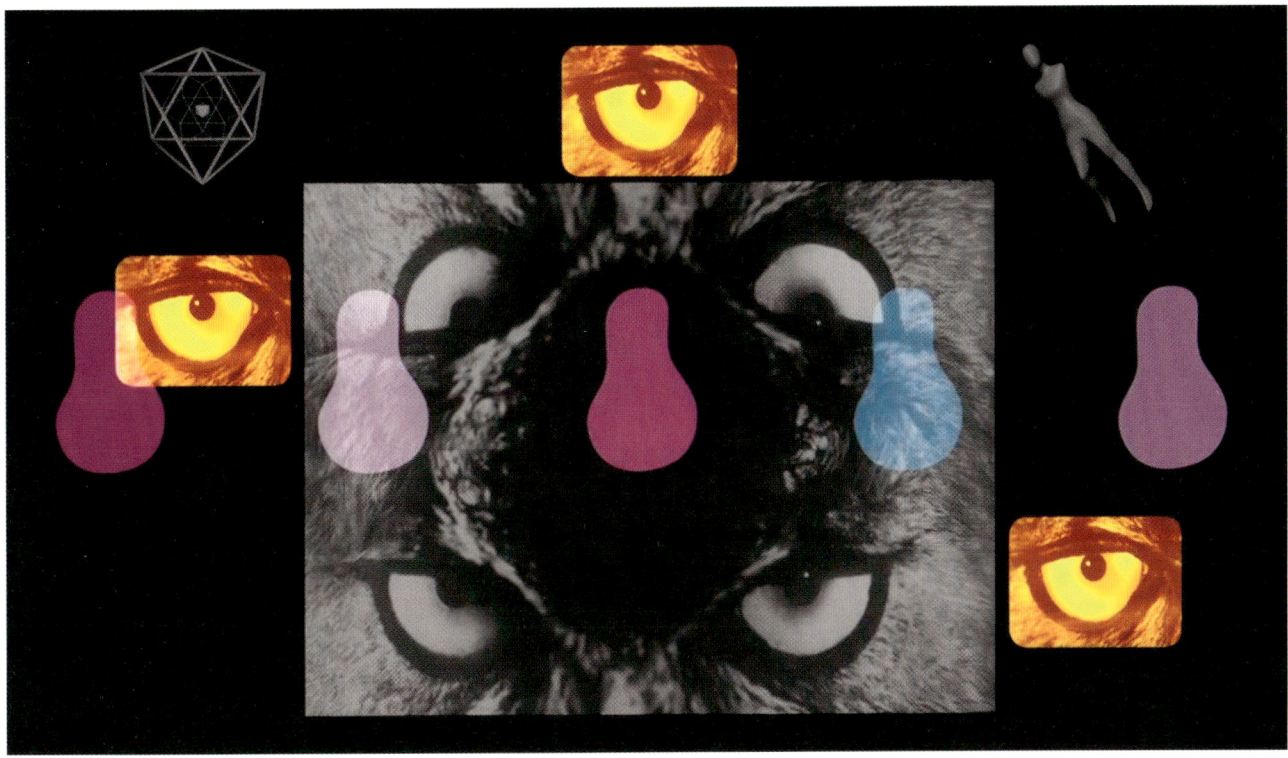

In 2000, Kees Tazelaar, searching the archives of the Institute of Sonology, found three mono audiotapes, one stereo audiotape, and a three-track perfo tape, which together constitute the original recording of *Le poème électronique* and Xenakis' *Interlude sonore*. He used these tapes to reconstruct the music of these compositions. They were released in stereo in 2001 by the CD-label BVHAAST, on the CD *His Master's Noise: The Institute of Sonology*.[38]

Reconstruction of *Le poème électronique* and the Philips Pavilion

Around New Year's Day 1959, Eindhoven's cinemas were showing *Kroniek van Eindhoven* [Chronicle of Eindhoven], which looked back over the previous year at events relating to the city. The film included shots of the Philips Pavilion, and as the cameras followed people entering the pavilion, they also recorded part of *Le poème électronique*.[39]

In 1998, Willem Hering and Hank Onrust made a documentary for Dutch television entitled *Het elektronisch gedicht: Edgard Varèse in Nederland* [The Electronic Poem: Edgard Varèse in the Netherlands], for which they combined the *écran* film with coloured *ambiances* on the basis of Le Corbusier's script.

More recently, advances in fields such as graphic programmes have made it possible to make a digital reconstruction of *Le poème électronique*. In 2003, Piet Lelieur of the Architecture and Urban Development Department of the University of Ghent produced a filmic reconstruction of the Philips Pavilion and *Le poème électronique*, focusing on the situation in the pavilion.[40] In 2005, an international partnership integrated all the elements of *Le poème électronique* that were available up to then to make the *Virtual Electronic Poem* in what was described as an 'immersive virtual reality installation'. The user wears headphones and a stereoscopic helmet shielding the eyes, and consequently sees only a computer image. The sound and images respond to the user's movements, giving the user the illusion that he is actually present during a performance of *Le poème électronique* in the Philips Pavilion.[41]

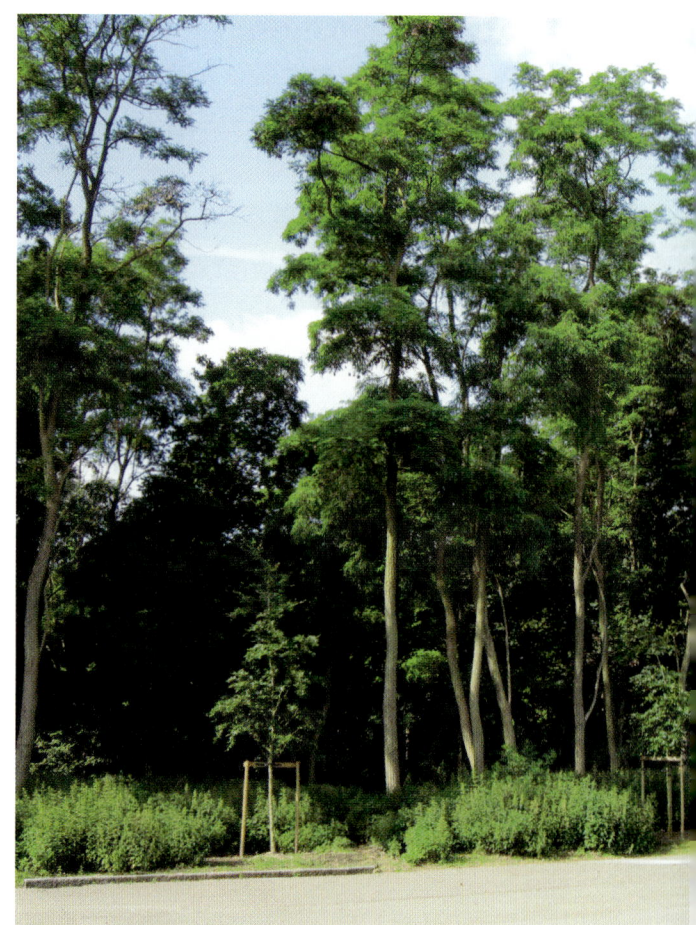

In 2009 the Stichting Elektronische Gedichten [Electronic poems foundation] staged a reconstruction of *Le poème électronique* in the Netherlands for full-dome digital planetariums, based on the *minutage définitif*. This reconstruction sought to capture the essence of the performance as envisaged by Le Corbusier, regardless of the technical restrictions of the day.[42] In 2014, a version of the full-dome reconstruction was produced for 'flat' projection.

In June 2006, the Alice Foundation held an international symposium in Eindhoven entitled 'Make it New: Le poème électronique', on the rebuilding of the Philips Pavilion on one of Philips' old industrial sites in Eindhoven. The plan enjoys widespread support, and is deemed internationally to be of great cultural significance.[43] Even so, the pavilion's reconstruction has yet to materialize.[44] In 2013, the Foundation for the Reconstruction of the 1958 Philips Pavilion, which took over the project from the Alice Foundation, presented a feasibility study that could provide a new basis for subsequent decision-making.[45] An important problem in the pavilion's reconstruction is the question of authenticity. An authentic reconstruction would mean re-creating a pavilion that would have only a brief life span, just as the one in 1958.

Fifty Years Beyond

Largely unaware of the renewed interest in the Philips Pavilion, a number of men who had worked at the Philips Pavilion revisited the grounds where they had dedicated over five months of their lives to Le poème électronique – just over fifty years after the event had closed down. In the afternoon of 26 August 2009, the Belgian projectionists Paul Vancoppenolle and Max Naveaux, the Belgian technicians Michel Cools and Michel Soete, and the Dutch technician Wiel Cox congregated in a restaurant next to the Atomium that had served as the pavilion of the Courtrai Roof Tiles Bureau [Kortrijks Dakpannenkantoor] during the World's Fair. Some of them had not seen each other since the event. Judging by the comment, 'It was a great technological feat for the benefit of a load of hogwash',[46] opinions on the performance Le poème électronique were if possible even fiercer fifty years later than they had been during the World's Fair itself.

The former employees visited the site on the former Avenue de l'Europe where the Philips Pavilion had stood. Today, the place is completely overgrown with bushes and trees. Aside from the nearby, futuristic Atomium, nothing remains to recall the avant-garde pavilion of 1958. Wiel Cox expressed the group's general sentiments when he said: 'our home was the pavilion.'[47]

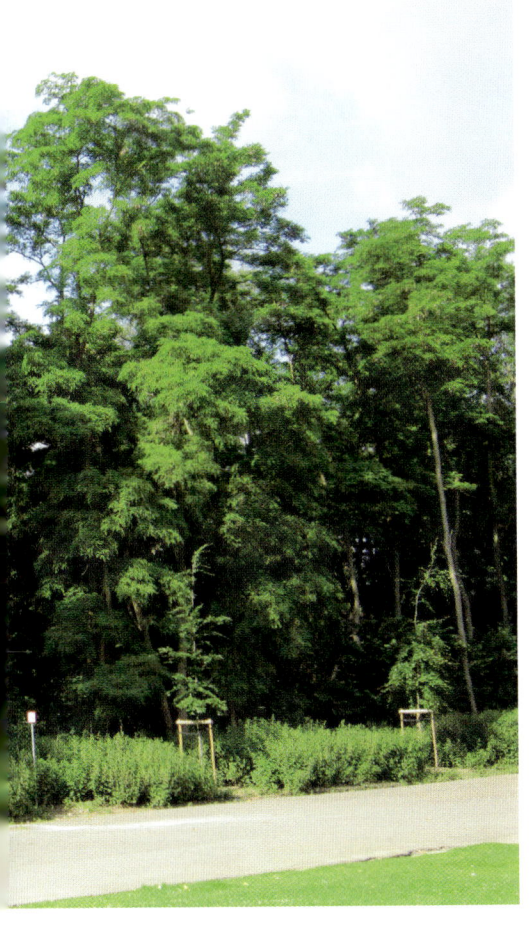

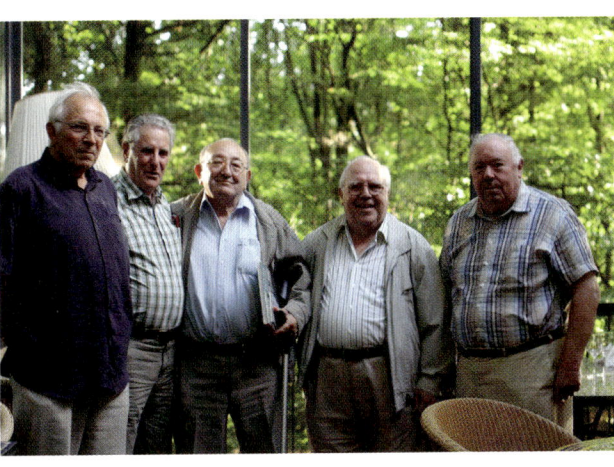

9.9
The location beside the former Avenue de l'Europe where the Philips Pavilion stood during the 1958 Brussels World's Fair. Nothing remains today to recall the avant-garde pavilion that once stood on this site.

9.10
The five former employees of the Philips Pavilion at their reunion on 26 August 2009, just over 50 years after the pavilion's closure, on the former site of the 1958 Brussels World's Fair. From left to right, technician Michel Cools, technician Wiel Cox, projectionist Max Naveaux, technician Michel Soete, and projectionist Paul Vancoppenolle.

Notes
Bibliography
Image Credits
Name Index
Credits

Notes

1 Pavilion without a Façade
Le Corbusier Versus Gerrit Rietveld

1. This chapter has been adapted from Wever 2008, 112–127.
2. See: Everts 1960, 3–26.
3. See: National Archives, The Hague, archives of the Foundation World Exhibition Brussels 1958 Netherlands Section (NA Brussels 1958), Inv. No. 11: Participation of Philips Lightbulb Factories Ltd. [Deelneming Philips Gloeilampenfabrieken], letter from Kalff to Everts, dated 23 March 1956. This letter can be interpreted as a concrete request to Rietveld to provide the exterior of the pavilion.
4. See: NA Brussels 1958, Inv. No. 2: Meetings of the governing board (minutes), minutes of the 9th meeting of the governing board, dated 24 April 1956.
5. See: Het Nieuwe Instituut, Rotterdam, G.Th. Rietveld archive [Het Nieuwe Instituut Rietveld archives], Inv. No. 671: Correspondence, 1956–1958, letter from Kalff to Rietveld, dated 7 January 1957.
6. See: NA Brussels 1958, Inv. No. 8: Team architects and supervisors correspondence, memo concerning the dispute between Philips and the Foundation, dated 14 January 1957.
7. See: NA Brussels 1958, Inv. No. 8: Team architects and supervisors correspondence, letter from Rietveld to Everts, dated 28 April 1956.
8. See: Getty Research Institute, Los Angeles, Special Collections, L.C. (Louis Christiaan) Kalff materials relating to the Philips Pavilion at the Brussels Universal and International Exhibition, 1955–1958 (GRI Kalff), Inv. No. 870438-2: Kalff correspondence, January–May 1956, letter from d'Aboville to Kalff, dated 23 May 1956.
9. See: NA Brussels 1958, Inv. No. 11: Participation of Philips Lightbulb Factories Ltd., letter from Rietveld to the Foundation World Exhibition Brussels 1958 Netherlands Section, dated 13 December 1956.
10. See: Bibeb 1958 [A], 79.
11. See: GRI Kalff, Inv. No. 870438-3: Kalff correspondence, June–Sept. 1956, letter from Rietveld to Kalff, dated 10 June 1956.
12. See: NA Brussels 1958, Inv. No. 11: Participation of Philips Lightbulb Factories Ltd., letter from Rietveld to the Foundation World Exhibition Brussels 1958 Netherlands Section, dated 13 December 1956.
13. See: Bibeb 1958 [A], 80.
14. Initially it was assumed that Rietveld had made his sketches of the Philips Pavilion on a sandwich wrapper, and that these sketches had been lost. See: Mens 1985, 84. But in the Rietveld Schröder archives of the Centraal Museum, under Inv. No. 167 A 001, is a sketch for the roof of the pavilion. In 2006, the author found a sketch design for the front of the pavilion in Het Nieuwe Instituut Rietveld archives, Inv. No. 668: Drawings of pavilions and stands, 1956, 1957, and s.a. In recent inventory of a donation, it turned out the Centraal Museum Utrecht is in possession of the 'small sketch model' that Rietveld was referring to in his letter to the Foundation World Exhibition Brussels 1958 Netherlands Section, dated 13 December 1956 (see note 9). This is a model in watercolour and ink on paper on a glass surface with Inv. No. 31245. See: Küper en Van Zijl 1992, 291–292; Van Thoor 1998, 173–176; and in particular Van Thoor 2010, 159–167, where Rietveld's design is described in detail.
15. See: Majorick 1961, n.p.
16. See: Bos en Van Lier 2004, 102. In 1948, Rietveld and Bons worked together on the design of the Jaarbeurs in Utrecht. In 1950, Bons made wall ornaments for houses by Rietveld and a wall for the Holland Fair in Philadelphia, USA. In 1952, this was followed by the mural for the exhibition *Así es Holanda*. See: 'Jan Bons, affiches' 1975, n.p.
17. See: Everts 1960, 93.
18. See: NA Brussels 1958, Inv. No. 12: Interior Architects, Designers, Artists, unaddressed letter Architect Group Brussels 1958, dated 23 April 1956.
19. See: NA Brussels in 1958, Inv. No. 8: Team architects and supervisors correspondence, memo concerning the dispute between Philips and the Foundation, dated 14 January 1957.
20. See: Treib 1996, 5.
21. See: Het Nieuwe Instituut Rietveld archives, Inv. No. 671: Correspondence, 1956–1958, letter from Kalff to Le Corbusier, dated 18 July 1956.
22. See: NA Brussels 1958, Inv. No. 11: Participation of Philips Lightbulb Factories Ltd., letter from Kalff to Bakema, dated 16 October 1956.
23. See: NA Brussels 1958, Inv. No. 11: Participation of Philips Lightbulb Factories Ltd., letter from Everts to Kalff, dated 23 October 1956. The Foundation had apparently not understood, or had not been adequately informed, that the exterior of the Philips Pavilion would be the result of its content (i.e. a sound and light show with specific technical and artistic demands on the building), so that the interior and exterior would coincide, and that the exterior would thus not need to be designed.
24. See: GRI Kalff, Inv. No. 870438-4: Kalff correspondence, October 1956, letter from Kalff to Le Corbusier, dated 13 October 1956.
25. See: Treib 1996, 27–37.
26. See: Het Nieuwe Instituut Rietveld archives, Inv. No. 671: Correspondence, 1956–1958, letter from Kalff to Le Corbusier, dated 31 October 1956.
27. See: NA Brussels 1958, Inv. No. 3: Correspondence Head Office, letter from Van Hoorn to Van Walsem, dated 7 November 1956. This suggests that the Architect Group Brussels 1958 had much less resistance than the supervising architects and the Foundation to the idea that Le Corbusier would also provide the exterior of the pavilion.
28. See: NA Brussels 1958, Inv. No. 2: Meetings of the governing board (minutes), minutes of the 15th meeting of the governing board, dated 9 November 1956; and the minutes of the 16th meeting of the governing board, dated 12 December 1956.
29. See: Het Nieuwe Instituut Rietveld archives, Inv. No. 671: Correspondence, 1956–1958, letter from Van Walsem to Kalff, dated 18 December 1956. That 'an open rectangular skeleton' meant an actual physical construction, and not a virtual demarcation, is made clear in a letter from Kalff to Rietveld, in which he wrote that '[one wanted] to force Le Corbusier to squeeze his pavilion into a skeleton of metal columns and beams'. See: Het Nieuwe Instituut Rietveld archives, Inv. No. 671: Correspondence, 1956–1958, letter from Kalff to Rietveld, dated 7 January 1957.
30. See: Mens 1985, 66.
31. See: Het Nieuwe Instituut Rietveld archives, Inv. No. 671: Correspondence, 1956–1958, letter from Kalff to Rietveld, dated 7 January 1957.
32. See: NA Brussels 1958, Inv. No. 11: Participation of Philips Lightbulb Factories Ltd., letter from Rietveld to the Foundation World Exhibition Brussels 1958 Netherlands Section, dated 13 December 1956.
33. See: NA Brussels 1958, Inv. No. 8: Team architects and supervisors correspondence, undated report from a 1 March 1956 discussion in The Hague between several members of the Foundation's governing board and the architects.
34. See: Het Nieuwe Instituut Rietveld archives, Inv. No. 671: Correspondence, 1956–1958, letter from Kalff to Van Walsem, dated 27 December 1956.
35. Ibid. Kalff referred twice in his letter to 'the drawing with the rectangle, as proposed by the Dutch architect'. Unfortunately, this drawing could not be found in the examined archival material.
36. See: Het Nieuwe Instituut Rietveld archives, Inv. No. 671: Correspondence, 1956–1958, letter from Van Walsem to the architects, dated 5 January 1957.
37. See: Het Nieuwe Instituut Rietveld archives, Inv. No. 671: Correspondence, 1956–1958, letter from Kalff to Van Walsem, dated 27 December 1956. The construction contract was finally awarded to the Belgian contractor Société de Travaux en Béton et Dragages (Strabed) under the direction of the Dutch Dr. Ir. Hoyte Duyster, who wanted to build the pavilion as a largely self-supporting slab of pre-stressed concrete. See: Xenakis s.a., 6.
38. See: NA Brussels 1958, Inv. No. 2: Meetings of the governing board (minutes), minutes of the 17th meeting of the governing board, dated 9 January 1957.
39. Ibid.
40. See: NA Brussels 1958, Inv. No. 8: Team architects and supervisors correspondence, letter from Merkelbach to Van Walsem, dated 11 January 1957.
41. See: Fondation Le Corbusier, Parijs (FLC), Inv. No. J2-19-517-518: Pavillon Philips - Exposition Internationale 1956 – 1964 Belgique Bruxelles, Documents divers, Lettre B. Merkelbach / L.C. - 15/01/1957, letter from Merkelbach to Le Corbusier, dated 15 January 1957.
42. See: NA Brussels 1958, Inv. No. 8: Team architects and supervisors correspondence, letter from Van Walsem to Merkelbach, dated 14 January 1957.
43. See: 'Nederlands inzending Brussel '58 versoberd' ['Dutch entry Brussels '58 toned down'] 1957.
44. See: NA Brussels 1958, Inv. No. 8: Team architects and supervisors correspondence, letter from Merkelbach to Van Walsem, dated 11 January 1957.
45. See: GRI Kalff, Inv. No. 870438-6: Kalff correspondence, Jan.–Feb. 1957,

letter from Heilbuth to Kalff, dated 11 January 1957.
46 See: NA Brussels 1958, Inv. No. 11: Participation of Philips Lightbulb Factories Ltd., memo of a 19 January 1957 discussion in Brussels, dated 24 January 1957.
47 See: NA Brussels 1958, Inv. No. 8: Team architects and supervisors correspondence, memo concerning the dispute between Philips and the Foundation, dated 14 January 1957.
48 See: NA Brussels 1958, Inv. No. 8: Team architects and supervisors correspondence, letter to Peutz, dated 21 January 1957.
49 See: NA Brussels 1958, Inv. No. 11: Participation of Philips Lightbulb Factories Ltd., memo of a 19 January 1957 discussion in Brussels, dated 24 January 1957.
50 Ibid. The maximum height of the pavilion was 20.25 meters, which considerably exceeded the limit of 15 meters that had been agreed upon in the spring of 1956, and the limit of 13 meters that had been imposed in December 1956 with the open rectangular skeleton construction. The distance from the Dutch pavilion had to be at least 9 meters. The exterior of the pavilion was to be realized in an aluminium or copper colour (see also Chapter 2).
51 See: NA Brussels 1958, Inv. No. 8: Team architects and supervisors correspondence, letter to Peutz, dated 21 January 1957.
52 See: NA Brussels 1958, Inv. No. 11: Participation of Philips Lightbulb Factories Ltd., memo of a 19 January 1957 discussion in Brussels, dated 24 January 1957.
53 See: GRI Kalff, Inv. No. 870438-6: Kalff correspondence, Jan.–Feb. 1957, letter from Heilbuth to Kalff, dated 11 January 1957.
54 See: NA Brussels 1958, Inv. No. 8: Team architects and supervisors correspondence, letter from Van Walsem to Bakema, dated 24 January 1957.
55 See: NA Brussels 1958, Inv. No. 8: Team architects and supervisors correspondence, letter from Van Walsem to supervisors and architects, dated 22 January 1957.
56 See: NA Brussels 1958, Inv. No. 8: Team architects and supervisors correspondence, letter from Oud to Van Walsem, dated 23 January 1957.
57 See: NA Brussels 1958, Inv. No. 8: Team architects and supervisors correspondence, letter from Van Walsem to Oud, dated 1 February 1957.
58 See: NA Brussels 1958, Inv. No. 8: Team architects and supervisors correspondence, letter from Oud to Van Walsem, dated 6 February 1957.
59 See: Mens 1985, 19–28.
60 See: Mens 1985, 52.
61 See: Mens 1985, 54–56; and Provoost 2003, 36.
62. See: Het Nieuwe Instituut Rietveld archives, Inv. No. 671: Correspondence, 1956–1958, letter from Peutz to the Foundation World Exhibition Brussels 1958 Netherlands Section, dated 16 January 1957.
63 See: Het Nieuwe Instituut Rietveld archives, Inv. No. 671: Correspondence, 1956–1958, undated letter from Peutz to the Foundation World Exhibition Brussels 1958 Netherlands Section.
64 See: NA Brussels 1958, Inv. No. 8: Team architects and supervisors correspondence, letter to Peutz, dated 21 January 1957.
65 See: NA Brussels 1958, Inv. No. 8: Team architects and supervisors correspondence, letter from Everts to Peutz, dated 4 December 1957. Oud asked Peutz in November of 1957 to communicate in writing to the Foundation that he had to withdraw from the Architect Group Brussels 1958 because of pressured circumstances. With a view to the payment of the architect's fee, the retention of Peutz had become unjust. Peutz had only participated in a few of the meetings of the architects, and was the only architect who had not submitted his own design for the Dutch pavilion. See: NA Brussels 1958, Inv. No. 2: Meetings of the governing board (minutes), minutes of the 26th meeting of the governing board, dated 20 November 1957.
66 See: NA Brussels 1958, Inv. No. 8: Team architects and supervisors correspondence, letter from Van Walsem to supervisors and architects, dated 7 March 1957.
67 See: NA Brussels 1958, Inv. No. 11: Participation of Philips Lightbulb Factories Ltd., letter from Kalff to Everts, dated 25 April 1957.
68 See: NA Brussels 1958, Inv. No. 11: Participation of Philips Lightbulb Factories Ltd., letter from Everts to Kalff, dated 26 April 1957.
69 See: Everts 1960, 14.
70 See: Bibeb 1958 [A], 80.
71 See: NA Brussels 1958, Inv. No. 21: Awards, letter from Schurmans to Van Walsem, dated 23 September 1959.

1 Woman's Hairpins Help to Build Architecture of the Future
An Unlikely Tale of the Conception of the Philips Pavilion

1 See: Robb, undated. Almost exactly the same column was published, untitled, on 22 April 1958, in the *Reading Eagle*, a newspaper for the city of Reading, Pennsylvania, and on 23 April, 1958, under the headline 'Dutch building puzzler at fair' in the *Deseret News*, a newspaper for the city of Salt Lake City, Utah.
2. The term Euclid refers to the Greek mathematician Euclid, who is considered one of the founders of geometry.
3 It is evident that the incident described here never took place. The actual first scale model of the Philips Pavilion was produced by Iannis Xenakis, at the request of Le Corbusier. The ribs, in which different surfaces of the pavilion intersect each other, are represented in this model by piano wire. The surfaces of the pavilion itself are visualized by strings tightened between the piano wire. See: Xenakis s.a., 2–8; and Lootsma 1984 [A], 13.

2 Colour in the Philips Pavilion
Le Corbusier's Use of *Types Couleurs*

1 The photographs of the Philips Pavilion that have been published until now consist mainly of black and white photographs taken by the Philips' Photo Technical service [Fototechnische dienst]. In Marc Treib's standard work from 1996, *Space calculated in seconds: The Philips Pavilion, Le Corbusier, Edgard Varèse*, there are only four colour photographs of the Philips Pavilion. Yet in recent years, particularly from private collections, several original colour photographs, colour slides, and colour cine-films of the pavilion have surfaced. In particular, a roughly five-minute colour cine-film by projectionist Paul Vancoppenolle should be mentioned. These image carriers have yielded important information for this chapter.
2. See: De Heer 2009, 189.
3 See: NA Brussels 1958, Inv. No. 11: Participation of Philips Lightbulb Factories Ltd., memo of a 9 January 1957 meeting in Brussels, dated 24 January 1957.
4 See: NA Brussels 1958, Inv. No. 11: Participation of Philips Lightbulb Factories Ltd., suggestions of Mr. Van Walsem for an agreement between the Foundation and Philips, dated 15 January 1957.
5 See: NA Brussels 1958, Inv. No. 11: Participation of Philips Lightbulb Factories Ltd., memo of a 9 January 1957 meeting in Brussels, dated 24 January 1957.
6 See: GRI Kalff, Inv. No. 870438-9: Kalff correspondence, May–June 1957, report of a 1 June 1957 conversation, between Kalff and Le Corbusier, dated 3 June 1957.
7 See: Duyster s.a., 35.
8 See: 'The "electronic poem" in the Philips Pavilion' 1958.
9 See: Taubman, undated.
10 See: 'Brüsseler Spitzen' ['Brussels spikes'] undated.
11 See: GRI Kalff, Inv. No. 870438-14: Kalff correspondence, March 1958, letter from Xenakis to Kalff, dated 11 March 1958; and Philips Company Archives, Eindhoven (PCA), letter from Kalff to those concerned, dated 24 April 1958. The first letter specifically mentions painting the sprayed asbestos layer white ['*peints en blanc*'], whereas the second letter states 'that all of the discussed repairs to the walls will be carried out, and repainted white'.
12. See: PCA, report of a 15 November 1957 trip to Paris by Kalff, dated 18 November 1957.
13 See: GRI Kalff, Inv. No. 870,438-13: Kalff correspondence, Jan.-Feb. 1958, questions to architect Le Corbusier, dated January 1958. This colour proposal probably came from Philips. In a report of a 15 January 1957 meeting in Eindhoven, at which Le Corbusier and Kalff were present, it can already be read that 'the preference from our [Philips] side goes to a deep-blue for the entrance and a warm-yellow for the exit'. See: GRI Kalff, Inv. No. 870,438-8:. Kalff correspondence, April 1957, undated report of 15 April 1957 talks at the scale model.
14 See: GRI Kalff, Inv. No. 870438-13: Kalff correspondence, Jan.–Feb. 1958, letter from Kalff to Le Corbusier, dated 18 February 1958.
15 See: GRI Kalff, Inv. No. 870438-14: Kalff correspondence, March 1958, letter from Xenakis to Kalff, dated 11 March 1958.

16 See: GRI Kalff, Inv. No. 870438-14: Kalff correspondence, March 1958, letter from Kalff to Xenakis, dated 13 March 1958.
17 See: De Franclieu 1982, figure 108, n.p. The author's interpretation of Le Corbusier's handwriting differs from the interpretation presented in the source document. The undated sketch is located in sketchbook M53. On the front of this sketchbook is written 'PHILIPP magnetophone MAI.58 (?) TOURETTE'. If the dating of the sketchbook is correct, then the colours of the entrance and exit of the Philips Pavilion were only determined after the opening of the 1958 Brussels World's Fair on 17 April, 1958. The question mark may indicate that there are doubts about the dating of the sketchbook.
18 The scale model of the Philips Pavilion has a scale of 1:25, and is located in the collection of the Stichting tot Behoud van Historische Philips Producten [Foundation for the Preservation of Historical Philips Products] in Eindhoven. The model has been loaned to the Rijksmuseum in Amsterdam for permanent exhibition at the 20th-Century Galleries. There is a small plate attached to the model with the text 'NV Philips. Eindhoven. Plastics [Kunststoffen] Laboratory', which suggests that it may refer to the division within Philips where the model was created. The model's colour palette for the pavilion's entrance and exit includes the colours yellow, red, blue, and green. For every colour that is applied to a specific surface area on the model, confirmation has been found in various original colour photos, colour slides, and colour cine-films that this colour was also in fact used in the realized pavilion.
19 The author assumes that the colours yellow, red, blue, and green correspond respectively to the *types couleurs* n° 2 *jaune vif*, n° 4 *rouge*, n° 12 *bleu foncé*, and n° 14 *vert vif*.
20 See: De Heer 1986, 21–23; and De Heer 2009, 165–189.
21 See: PCA, report of a 15 November 1957 trip to Paris by Kalff, dated 18 November 1957. The exact wording in the travel report reads: 'If Pevsner does not come, then the mathematical sculpture that he [Le Corbusier] strongly desires can be placed in the water'. By 'Pevsner', Kalff was referring to Antoine Pevsner's statue *Phoenix*. Under consideration was the idea of installing a cast of this statue by the entrance to the Philips Pavilion. This did not take place, because it proved impossible to have the casting ready in time. See: Lootsma 1984 [B], 25. On the floor plan PHIL LC 5528 'Plan du parc' (FLC, archive number 28598), dated 19 June 1957, both Pevsner's statue (indicated as PEV) and the *Objet mathématique* (indicated as MATH) are drawn in. It was suggested in the design that Pevsner's sculpture would be installed in the pond behind the low concrete wall on the street-facing side of the Philips Pavilion, where the *Objet mathématique* was later placed. In the design drawing PHIL LC 5528, the *Objet mathématique* itself was drawn several meters further to the left, along the tiles on the street-facing side of the pavilion.
22 See: Treib 1996, 89. It has been suggested that the sculpture was meant to serve as 'a beacon to the entrance'. See: Le Corbusier - 'Object Mathematique' s.a. But because, on the floor plan PHIL LC 5528 'Plan du parc', the *Objet mathématique* has been somewhat moved away from the entrance, it seems unlikely that the sculpture was intended to serve this role in Le Corbusier's original design.
23 See: GRI Kalff, Inv. No. 870438-13: Kalff correspondence, Jan.–Feb. 1958, letter from Kalff to Le Corbusier, dated 18 February 1958.
24 See: Treib 1996, 92–93. The design sketch has the FLC archive number 30622.
25 The five colours from the *types couleurs* palette that were used in the *Objet mathématique* are mentioned in a letter that Xenakis sent to Kalff, presumably together with the design drawings. These are the *types couleurs* n° 2 *jaune vif* (yellow), n° 4 *rouge* (red), n° 8 *gris foncé* (grey), n° 12 *bleu foncé* (blue), and n° 14 *vert vif* (green). See: FLC, Inv. No. J2-19-272: Pavillon Philips - Exposition Internationale 1956 – 1964 Belgique Bruxelles, Correspondence diverses entreprises, Société Philips / L.C. - 13/10/1956 – 09/04/1958, letter from Xenakis to Kalff, dated 4 March 1958. The design drawings of the *Objet mathématique* have the numbers PHIL.-L.C. 5547, 5548, and 5549 (respectively FLC archive numbers 28599, 28591, and 28592). On the design drawing PHIL.-L.C. 5549 is written that the words 'philips' and 'poème électronique' should be realized in, respectively, bright blue (*bleu vif*) and red (*rouge*) neon light tubes. Yet colour photos of the realized *Objet mathématique* show that the word 'philips' was executed in a pink-red neon light tube, and the words 'poème électronique' in light blue neon light tubes. The *Objet mathématique* was very similar to the geometric object made of metal tubes that hung in one of the apices inside the pavilion (see Text Box II). In design drawings PHIL.-L. C. 5547 and 5550 (FLC archive number 28593), there are also designs for, respectively, a *'petite flèche de l'entrée'* [small arrow of the entrance] and a *'grande flèche à la sortie'* [large arrow at the exit]. Yet Kalff informed Xenakis that he wanted to keep the small arrow on hold, because he hoped that an information pillar would also be placed at the entrance. This pillar was indeed placed there, and the available photographic material indicates that the small arrow was not installed. The large arrow, though, was installed, to the right of the exit, and pointed visitors who had left the Dutch pavilion via the textile section or the agriculture section to the entrance of the Philips Pavilion on the street-facing side. A colour cine-film shows that the words 'philips', 'poème électronique', and 'ENTREE' had been written on the large arrow, using red letters on a black background. In accordance with the *Objet mathématique*, the words 'philips' and 'poème électronique' were realized in the handwriting of Le Corbusier, while the word 'ENTREE' was written in block letters. Although the intention was to realize these words in neon tubes, Philips chose not to do so for technical reasons. According to the design drawing, the large arrow was four meters and 74 centimetres long. See: GRI Kalff, Inv. No. 870438-14: Kalff correspondence, March 1958, letter from Kalff to Xenakis, dated 13 March 1958.
26 See: GRI Kalff, Inv. No. 870438-14: Kalff correspondence, March 1958, letter from Kalff to Xenakis, dated 13 March 1958; and Treib 1996, 89. Kalff wrote that the *Objet mathématique* would be manufactured in their own factory. In agreement with this, Treib wrote that the *Objet mathématique* had been produced in the 'Philips machine shop in Eindhoven'. This may be a reference to the department of Electronic Company Mechanization [Elektrische Bedrijfsmechanisatie] of the Main Industrial Division Products for Industrial Applications [Hoofdindustriegroep Produkten voor Industriële Toepassingen], where equipment was made for Philips' own production lines, and where some of the equipment for the Philips Pavilion also came from (see also Chapter 6).
27 See: http://library.tue.nl/catalog/FullBB.csp?WebAction=ShowFullBB&RequestId=16528052_20&Profile=KC&OpacLanguage=dut&NumberToRetrieve=50&StartValue=9&WebPageNr=1&SearchTerm1=1958.43.912&SearchT1=&Index1=Index4301&SearchMethod=Find_1&ItemNr=9, last consulted on 3 October 2012.
28 The *Objet mathématique* was preserved after the 1958 Brussels World's Fair, and for years was located at Philips Lighting in Eindhoven. The sculpture is currently in the possession of the Arts Committee of the Eindhoven University of Technology, and is located on the lawn in front of the university's auditorium. See: Le Corbusier - 'Object Mathematique' s.a.

3 The Decorators
Creation of the Light Effects in *Le poème électronique*

1 See: NA Brussels 1958, Inv. No. 11: Participation of Philips Lightbulb Factories Ltd., letter from Kalff to Everts, dated 23 March 1956.
2 See: Lootsma 1984 [B], 20–26.
3 See: Kalff, Tak and De Bruin s.a., 37–42; and Tazelaar 2009, 5.
4 See: Lootsma 1984 [B], 20.
5 See: Kalff, Tak and De Bruin s.a., 37–42; and Tazelaar 2009, 5.
6 See: Petit 1958 [A], n.p.
7 See: Lootsma 1984 [B], 23–24.
8 See: Treib 1996, 100.
9 See: 'Dollywood tekent een wereldtaal' ['Dollywood draws a global language'] 1958. The name 'Dollywood' was coined because of the many dolls' films that were commissioned *inter alia* by Philips for advertising purposes.
10 See: PCA, report of a 15 November 1957 trip to Paris by Kalff, dated 18 November 1957.
11 See: Treib 1996, 112.
12 See: Tazelaar 2009, 10; and Lootsma 1984 [B], 22.
13 See: GRI Kalff, Inv. No. 870438-9: Kalff correspondence, May–June 1957, report of a 1 June 1957 meeting between Kalff and Le Corbusier, dated 3 June 1957.
14 See: GRI Kalff, Inv. No. 870438-15: Kalff correspondence, April–Dec. 1958, letter from Le Corbusier to Kalff, dated 26 October 1956; and Kalff, Tak and De Bruin s.a., 37–42.
15 See: PCA, report of a 15 November 1957 trip to Paris by Kalff, dated 18 November 1957; and GRI Kalff, Inv. No. 870438-12: Kalff

correspondence, Dec. 1957, Kalff's notes, dated 9 December 1957.
16 See: FLC, Inv. No. J2-19-368: Pavillon Philips - Exposition Internationale 1956–1964 Belgique Bruxelles, Poème électronique, Présentation, notes, dated 5 November 1957.
17 See: GRI Kalff, Inv. No. 870438-13: Kalff correspondence, Jan.–Feb. 1958, questions to architect Le Corbusier, January 1958.
18 See: PCA, letter from Kalff to those concerned, dated 24 April 1958.
19 See: Kalff, Tak and De Bruin s.a., 37–42. The description of the mirror construction and the *tri-trous* projection is based on photographs from Philips Belgium, Corporate Communication & Public Affairs, Brussels, Philips Pavilion archives (CCPA archives); and photographs from the collection of the FLC. With thanks to Kees Tazelaar, who was the first to note the mirror construction in the extant photographic material.
20 Based on: 'Dag and nacht waren teams van specialisten bezig' ['Experts worked day and night'] 1958; and email messages from Paul Vancoppenolle to Peter Wever, dated 4 July and 7 July 2012.
21 There are significant differences in the sequence of film images between the two copies in the archives of EYE Film Institute Netherlands, however. The existence of different versions can be explained by Le Corbusier's comment on 13 April 1958 that 'a number of drastic changes' would have to be made to the script of *Le poème électronique*. In a letter of 24 April, Kalff referred to 'the two copies in Brussels'. These copies were probably shown at the first, ceremonial, presentations of *Le poème électronique* in the Philips Pavilion on 18, 22 and 23 April. In the same letter, Kalff also stated that changes would have to be made to the [*écran*] film, after which 'the final films' would be delivered on 29 or 30 April. Besides modifications to the the film images, these changes included the insertion of a multilingual introductory text and some final words. On 23 May, Kalff and the acoustics expert Willem Tak visited the Philips Pavilion, which by then was open to the public. They found the same flawed version of the *écran* film being shown as had been used in April. The final film, complete with introductory text and final remarks, was eventually delivered, as is clear from a photograph in the collection of FLC that shows the introductory text being projected in the *écran* film, in Dutch and English, on the walls of the Philips Pavilion. The negative copy of the *écran* film in the archives of the EYE Film Institute Netherlands is a version of the final film, while the positive copy is the version that was shown in April and May. Based on: Tazelaar 2009, 9; 'Philips-paviljoen opende zijn deuren nog niet' ['Philips Pavilion has not opened its doors yet'] 1958; GRI Kalff, Inv. No. 870438-15: Kalff correspondence, April–Dec. 1958, letter from Kalff to Xenakis, dated 9 April 1958 (see also Chapter 8); PCA, letter from Kalff to those concerned, dated 24 April 1958; GRI Kalff, Inv. No. 870438-15: Kalff correspondence, April–Dec. 1958, report prepared by Kalff on his 23 May 1958 visit to the Philips Pavilion, dated 28 May 1958; and email message from Kees Tazelaar to Peter Wever, dated 12 October 2012.
22 See: Tazelaar 2009, 10.
23 See: GRI Kalff, Inv. No. 870438-17: Kalff script for *Le poème électronique*. In this document, the column 'Tritrous' contains the printed word 'bleu', while the word 'rouge' is both printed and added in handwriting; the words 'jaune', 'vert' and 'violet' are added only in handwriting. The times at which specific colours appear in the *tri-trous* film do not correspond precisely to the *minutage définitif*. Given the degree of discoloration in the original film material of the *tri-trous*, the assertions made about the colours used in the film should be read with some reservations.
24 Ibid. This document labels the seven sequences in French: *Genese, D'argile et d'esprit, Des profondeurs à l'aube, Des dieux faits d'hommes, Ainsi forgent les ans, Harmonie* and *Et pour donner à tous*. The English names for the seven sequences that are used here have been derived from the original *écran* film in the archives of the EYE Film Institute Netherlands.
25 See: GRI Kalff, Inv. No. 870438-17: Kalff script for *Le poème électronique*.
26 Various reconstructions have been made of *Le poème électronique*: they include the one by Piet Lelieur of the University of Ghent, Belgium (2003), the international *Virtual Electronic Poem* project (2005), and the one by Kees Tazelaar of the Royal Conservatoire in The Hague, the Netherlands, on behalf of the Electronic Poems Foundation [Stichting Elektronische Gedichten; 2009]. See: Tazelaar 2009, 9–10 (see also Chapter 9).
27 See: Lootsma 1984 [B], 21.
28 See: Treib 1996, 158.
29 See: GRI Kalff, Inv. No. 870438-17: Kalff script for *Le poème électronique*.
30 See: Petit 1958 [A], n.p.
31 See: GRI Kalff, Inv. No. 870438-17: Kalff script for *Le poème électronique*. The *minutage définitif* states 'Les images du taureau et du toréador n'ont pas de liaison avec les singes des tritrous.'
32 Based on: Kalff, Tak and De Bruin s.a., 37–42; Lootsma 1984 [B], 24–25; and GRI Kalff, Inv. No. 870438-15: Kalff correspondence, April–Dec. 1958, report drawn up by Jansen on a 26 August 1958 meeting held in Brussels, dated 27 August 1958 (see also Text Box II).
33 Based on: Lootsma 1984 [B], 24; Treib 1996, 163; and Petit 1958 [A], 24.
34 See: Kalff, Tak and De Bruin s.a., 37–42.
35 Based on: email message from Paul Vancoppenolle to Peter Wever, dated 4 July 2009; and on photographs from the collection of the FLC.
36 See: Kalff, Tak and De Bruin s.a., 37–42. The current passing through the fluorescent light tubes behind the balustrade could be adjusted using thyratrons.
37 See: Kalff, Tak and De Bruin s.a., 37–42; and Treib 1996, 96.
38 See: GRI Kalff, Inv. No. 870438-17: Kalff script for *Le poème électronique*. Although the GRI regards the copy of the *minutage définitif* as the former property of Louis Kalff, the author believes that this copy belonged to Johan Jansen, primarily because his name is written on the front, in his own handwriting.
39 Based on: Kalff, Tak and De Bruin s.a., 37–42; Petit 1958 [B], 209; and email messages from Paul Vancoppenolle to Peter Wever, dated 4 October 2012 and 25 October 2012.
40 See: GRI Kalff, Inv. No. 870438-17: Kalff script for *Le poème électronique*.
41 See: GRI Kalff, Inv. No. 870438-15: Kalff correspondence, April–Dec. 1958, report drawn up by Jansen on a 26 August 1958 meeting held in Brussels, dated 27 August 1958.
42 See: GRI Kalff, Inv. No. 870438-17: Kalff script for *Le poème électronique*, 870438-18: Kalff copies of notes relating to *Le poème électronique*, undated sketch-like floor plan of the Philips Pavilion, indicating the light sources and projectors; and Petit 1958 [B], 209.
43 Based on: Petit 1958 [B], 206–209; email message from Hans Michael Wörwag to Peter Wever, dated 26 October 2012; and personal observations of Peter Wever at Eindhoven University of Technology, dated 28 August 2012. With thanks to Jan de Heer, who ascertained that the projectors described here were made by the manufacturer Reiche & Vogel.
44 Personal observations of Peter Wever at Eindhoven University of Technology, dated 28 August 2012, and the GRI, dated 5 and 6 September 2012.
45 See: GRI Kalff, Inv. No. 870438-17: Kalff script for *Le poème électronique*.
46 Personal observations of Peter Wever at Eindhoven University of Technology, dated 28 August 2012, and the GRI, dated 5 and 6 September 2012.
47 Email message from Paul Vancoppenolle to Peter Wever, dated 7 July 2012.
48 Email message from Paul Vancoppenolle to Peter Wever, dated 15 November 2012.
49 Based on: personal observations of Peter Wever at Eindhoven University of Technology, dated 28 August 2012, and the GRI, dated 5 and 6 September 2012; and email message from Sally McKay to Peter Wever, dated 27 November 2012.
50 See: Lootsma 1984 [B], 24. The archive material studied did not yield any evidence to confirm, however, that the figurative patterns on the fan-shaped glass slides were designed by Le Corbusier.
51 See: Treib 1996, 158.
52 See: GRI Kalff, Inv. No. 870438-17: Kalff script for *Le poème électronique*, 870438-18: Kalff copies of notes relating to *Le poème électronique*, undated sketch-like floor plan of the Philips Pavilion showing the places of light sources and projectors; and Petit 1958 [B], 209.
53 Email message from Rob Oey to Peter Wever, dated 7 November 2012.
54 See: GRI Kalff, Inv. No. 870438-17: Kalff script for *Le poème électronique*, 870438-18: Kalff copies of notes relating to *Le poème électronique*, undated sketch-like floor plan of the Philips Pavilion showing the places of light sources and projectors; and Petit 1958 [B], 204.
55 See: photographs from the collection of the FLC.
56 See: GRI Kalff, Inv. No. 870438-18: Kalff copies of notes relating to *Le poème électronique, Minutage* drawn up by Jansen for the lighting of *Poème Electronique*, dated 24 June 1958.
57 See: Kalff, Tak and De Bruin s.a., 37–42; and NA Brussels 1958, Inv. No. 18: Commemorative volume, Kalff text entitled 'De Philips' inzending op de Wereldtentoonstelling in Brussel 1958' ['The Philips entry for the 1958 Brussels World's Fair'], dated 5 August 1959.
58 See: GRI Kalff, Inv. No. 870438-15: Kalff correspondence, April–Dec.

1958, report prepared by Kalff on his 23 May 1958 visit to the Philips Pavilion, dated 28 May 1958.
59 See: GRI Kalff, Inv. No. 870438-17: Kalff script for *Le poème électronique*.
60 See: GRI Kalff, Inv. No. 870438-18: Kalff copies of notes relating to *Le poème électronique*, undated plan of the light effects for *Le poème électronique*; and *Minutage* drawn up by Jansen for the lighting of *Poème Electronique*, dated 24 June 1958. The former document states under *ambiance* no. 10 'only red, scrap green, scrap sun', while the latter indicates for this *ambiance* 'red fluorescent lighting'.
61 See: GRI Kalff, Inv. No. 870438-17: Kalff script for *Le poème électronique*.
62 Ibid.; and GRI Kalff, Inv. No. 870438-18: Kalff copies of notes relating to *Le poème électronique*, *Minutage* drawn up by Jansen for the lighting of *Poème Electronique*, dated 24 June 1958.
63 See: photos from the CCPA archives.
64 See: GRI Kalff, Inv. No. 870438-15: Kalff correspondence, April–Dec. 1958, report drawn up by Jansen on a 26 August 1958 meeting held in Brussels, dated 27 August 1958.
65 See: de Franclieu 1982, fig. 159, n.p. Sketchbook M54 contains an undated note by Le Corbusier on the omitted *ambiances*. It appears on a page following a page that is dated 29 September 1958, on which date Le Corbusier had visited the Philips Pavilion (see also Chapter 8). Le Corbusier wrote: *'Les ambiances sont supprimées hélas!'* (Unfortunate that they left out the *ambiances*!).
66 See: NA Brussels 1958, Inv. No. 18: Commemorative volume, Kalff text entitled 'De Philips' inzending op de Wereldtentoonstelling in Brussel 1958' ['The Philips entry for the 1958 Brussels World's Fair'], dated 5 August 1959.

4 Shadowplay
Pierre Arnaud's Replacement Show for the Philips Pavilion

1 Pierre Arnaud was born on 6 November 1921, in Asnières-sur-Seine, a suburb of Paris. During the German occupation of France in 1941, as part of a substitute civilian service, he was in charge of the musical theatre group *les Chantiers de Jeunesse*, which was derived from the *le Jeune France* organization. He came to the attention of Pierre Schaeffer, a co-founder of *Jeune France*, and in 1942 became his assistant. This was about the time that Schaeffer founded the *Studio d'Essai de la Radio Diffusion Française*. In the *Studio d'Essai* (later called *Club d'Essai*), Pierre Arnaud was given responsibility for broadcasts of vaudeville performances that he wrote and presented, in which many subsequent stars debuted. In 1948, Pierre Arnaud made a twice-daily broadcast for *Radio France Inter* based on the so-called 'Music while you work' concept. In October of the same year, Pierre Arnaud co-founded the studio *la Diffusion Magnétique Sonore* (*la D.M.S.*), where recordings were made for *Radio France Inter* and which was also rented out to businesses and shops. *La D.M.S.* was thereby the world's first publisher of audio tapes. At the same time, Pierre Arnaud was involved, in varying functions (presenter, author, pianist, actor, and composer), in broadcasts on *Radio la Française* and on radio stations for France from abroad ('*les radios périphériques*'). Under the pseudonym Pierre Arnaud de Chassy-Poulay, he also became famous for the radio serial *Signé Furax* [Signed Furax], which he made for the radio station *Europe 1* between 1957 and 1960. He also wrote the music for several theatrical plays that were performed in Paris. At *la D.M.S.*, in 1953, the second *'spectacle Son et Lumière'* [sound and light spectacle] was produced for the Grosbois Castle near Paris. Partly with the support of Philips France, Pierre Arnaud then made a hundred sound and light spectacles for, amongst others, Compiègne, Chenonceau, Azay-le Rideau, Tours, Vézelay, Toulouse, Paris (Hôtel des Invalides), Milan, Athens (Acropolis), Karnak in Egypt, and Persepolis in Iran. Based on: email messages from Pierre Arnaud to Peter Wever, dated 21 May 2010, 22 May 2010, 31 May 2010, and 3 June 2010. See also: http://fr.wikipedia.org/wiki/Pierre-Arnaud_de_Chassy-Poulay, last accessed on 14 June 2010.

2 The trail that led to Pierre Arnaud began with an overview of the budgetary developments regarding the Philips Pavilion, dated 11 April 1958, which came from the PCA (this document has not been made available for publication by the PCA). This overview contains an expense item for a 'Reserve program P. Arnoud (special budget)' of 54,000 guilders. It was notable that these costs were not included in a calculation dated 26 February 1957, but they were included in the expected expenditures, dated 31 March 1958. The term 'Reserve program' suggested that a replacement show for *Le poème électronique* may have been made, which included more than merely the eponymous piece of replacement music composed by the French composer and conductor Henri Tomasi, which had already been known. For the piece of music by Tomasi, see e.g.: Lootsma 1984 [B], 26; Treib 1996, 194–195; Blanken 2002, 3–4; and Mattis 2006, 315. In a telephone call dated 3 May 2009, Kees Nijsen, the former publicity manager of the Main Industrial Division Electroacoustics of Philips Nederland, told Peter Wever that the misspelled name P. Arnoud in the expense item was a reference to the Frenchman Pierre Arnaud, with whom he had previously worked on a regular basis. An Internet search led to the contact information for Pierre Arnaud's son, Jean-François Arnaud, with whom telephone contact was made on 13 May 2009. Jean-François Arnaud presented the questions about the contents of the replacement program to his father. This led Pierre Arnaud to decide to break his silence, and to tell his story in writing. Important considerations here were that Pierre Arnaud had then reached an advanced age, and wanted to prevent the events coming to light without him being able to tell the story in his own words; that coming out with the story could no longer do any harm to the reputations of the now deceased Le Corbusier and Varèse; and to show respect for the competence and discretion of the involved parties from Philips Nederland and his friend Henri Tomasi. The story of Pierre Arnaud was received via email on 18 May 2009. A second and third version, each with several changes to the content, were received via email on 21 May 2010 and 1 September 2010. This chapter includes the text of Pierre Arnaud, edited by Peter Wever, and supplemented by notes that place the story in a broader context. The chapter also relies on oral communications from Pierre and Jean-François Arnaud to Peter Wever at a personal meeting, dated 16 October 2009, in Paris, and a number of additional email communications from Pierre Arnaud to Peter Wever. It also made use of a letter, dated 15 February 1958, in which Pierre Arnaud explained to the persons concerned the elements that the replacement show consisted of, and a letter, dated 27 October 1958, in which he informed Kalff about a performance of the replacement show in the Philips Pavilion shortly after the conclusion of the World's Fair. Pierre Arnaud expressly required that the publication of his story could only take place with the consent of Philips Nederland. This consent was obtained from the PCA on 23 September 2009. The original French text by Pierre Arnaud is also intended to be included in his memoir, with the planned title *Et qui la mise en ondes?* [And who made the radio broadcast?].

3 *Studio la D.M.S.* was located on 15 Rue Saussier Leroy, in the seventeenth arrondissement of Paris. *La D.M.S.* was co-founded in 1948 by Pierre Arnaud, and was acquired by Philips France on 6 November 1957. Pierre Arnaud was thereby appointed as *Président Directeur Général*, which position he held until 1967. Email messages from Pierre Arnaud to Peter Wever, dated 21 May 2010 and 22 May 2010. Claude Dejacques, the artistic director of Philips France, described *la D.M.S.* in his book *Piégée, la chanson . . . ?* as '*une arrière salle de jeux clandestins, à un garage pour cinq bagnoles*' [a back room for illegal gambling, in a garage for five cars]. Nevertheless, the studio was used by several of Philips' French celebrities, such as Johnny Hallyday, Georges Brassens, and Barbara. See: http://francois.faurant.free.fr/stud/studios.htm#saussier, last accessed on 23 May 2010.

4 On 1 May 1946, Jack Haver Droeze was appointed as general manager of S.A. Philips Éclairage et Radio, in which capacity he functioned to the great satisfaction of the Board of Directors in Eindhoven. See: Blanken 2002, 210.

5 From a position as commercial director of the Main Industrial Division Machinery [Hoofdindustriegroep Apparaten], Henk Hartong joined the Board of Directors in Eindhoven on 1 January 1957, where he bore a commercial responsibility. See: Blanken 2002, 21, 33, 348. Hartong had already been involved in the realization of the Philips Pavilion and *Le poème électronique* at an early stage, as evidenced by his presence at a 17 January 1956 meeting about Philips' participation in the World's Fair. See: GRI Kalff, Inv. No. 870438-2: Kalff correspondence, January–May 1956, report of a discussion about the participation in the 1958 Brussels World's Fair, dated 17 January 1956.

6 Because Pierre Arnaud indicated that the first contact with Hartong took place at the time of the discussions surrounding the sale of *la D.M.S.*, one can surmise that this must have been before 6 November 1957. The Kalff archives of the GRI indeed contain an internal communication from Hartong to Kalff, dated 27 August 1957, in which Hartong indicates

having met 'a certain Mr. Pierre Arnaud' in Paris. Hartong included Pierre Arnaud's business card along with the message, and suggested that Kalff find out whether it would be useful to hire Arnaud for the 'production of the image and light script' for the Philips Pavilion. However, it is unlikely that Hartong was already implicitly referring to a replacement show at this point, because the letter concludes with the expectation that Arnaud would be exactly the type of person 'to form the right *trait d'union*' with Le Corbusier. It is more likely that the idea for a replacement show arose after Varèse had arrived in Eindhoven on 2 September 1957, to work on the musical part of *Le poème électronique*. In this context, at a 24 September 1957 meeting between Kalff and Ir. Ferdinand van Stekelenburg of Philips Technical Services Department [Technische Dienstverlening], the question 'how long do we have to keep hoping for a favourable outcome of Varèse?' was already being asked. See: GRI Kalff, Inv. No. 870438-10:. Kalff correspondence, July-Sept. 1957, internal communication from Hartong to Kalff, dated 27 August 1957; and a report of a discussion between Kalff and Stekelenburg, dated 24 September 1957. Sometime later, the Philips' Board of Directors, and in particular Vice-president Frits Philips, expressed scepticism about *Le poème électronique,* with the music of Varèse being the main point of concern. After listening to a piece of music by Varèse, Frits Philips said in a 16 December 1957 meeting of the Board of Directors, that he found the piece to be a paragon 'of the confusion of the spirits of our time'. See: Blanken 2002, 3-4.
7   An initial meeting between the German Chancellor Konrad Adenauer and the French President Charles de Gaulle took place on 14 September 1958.
8   In the calculation dated 26 February 1957, a total budget of 1.5 million Dutch guilders had been allocated to the Philips Pavilion. Taking into account the varying exchange rates, this corresponds to about 150 million French francs. In the expected expenditures dated 31 March 1958, this amount had risen to 1.9 million Dutch guilders, which is equivalent to about 190 million French francs. See: PCA, budget developments Philips Pavilion, dated 11 April 1958.
9   No documents were found in the examined archival materials that refer to this clause. Several sources do mention a fee of 10 million French francs for Le Corbusier's work. This corresponds to a sum of about 100,000 Dutch guilders. See: GRI Kalff, Inv. No. 870438-3:. Kalff correspondence, June-Sept. 1956, letter from Le Corbusier to Kalff dated 14 September 1956; Inv. No. 870438-4:. Kalff correspondence, October 1956, letter from Kalff to Le Corbusier, dated 13 October 1956; and PCA, overview of fees, dated 15 July 1958.
10 Contrary to what is suggested here, Le Corbusier was indeed responsible for the content of the film. For the production of this film, he was supported by Jean Petit and Philippe Agostini. Petit helped Le Corbusier in the collection of the photographic documentation for the film, while the production of the film was contracted out to Agostini. See: PCA, report of a 15 November 1957 trip to Paris by Kalff, dated 18 November 1957. As far as the exchange of information is concerned, both Le Corbusier and Varèse expressed their views on the undesirability of having the music correspond to the projected images. See: Tazelaar 2009, 5.
11 Varèse arrived in Eindhoven with his wife on 2 September 1957. See: Tazelaar 2009, 7. The period of eight months that is referred to would place Pierre Arnaud's first visit to Eindhoven in May of 1958, and is therefore incorrect. From a chronological point of view, it is most likely that this visit took place one or two months after Varèse's arrival in Eindhoven.
12 The warehouse referred to was the Philips truck garage on the Strijp III premises in Eindhoven; this garage had been temporarily converted into a test workshop and studio, where Varèse worked on his music. See: Tazelaar 2009, 5 (see also Chapter 5).
13 Ir. Willem Tak was working for Philips Nederland at the time as an acoustics expert (see also Chapter 5).
14 The fee of two and a half million French francs corresponds to approximately 25,000 Dutch guilders, and represents about half of the total costs incurred for the replacement show.
15 Contrary to what is suggested here, Le Corbusier's *Le poème électronique* did indeed have a theme, which he himself phrased as follows: 'The Electronic Poem seeks to show, in the midst of an anguishing tumult, our civilisation out to conquer modern times'. See: Petit 1958 [C], n.p. The 'civilisation' and 'modern times' that Le Corbusier refers to can be seen as the result of, among other things, 'the evolution of man and technology' that Pierre Arnaud referred to in

his show. In that sense, the themes of the performances by Le Corbusier and Pierre Arnaud are in fact not very different from each other.
16 On the way back from Eindhoven to Paris, Pierre Arnaud visited the construction site of the Philips Pavilion to take a look at the technical possibilities. Oral communication from Pierre Arnaud to Peter Wever, dated 16 October 2009.
17 On the basis of photographs, Pierre Arnaud confirmed, when asked, that the cybernetic structure in question was the work 'CYSP 1' by Nicolas Schöffer. Oral communication from Pierre Arnaud to Peter Wever, dated 16 October 2009. The name CYSP 1 was composed of the first two letters of the words cybernetic and spatio-dynamic. CYSP 1, a 1956 spatial work by Schöffer made of iron and duralumin, was constructed on a base, inside of which was a so-called electronic brain developed by Philips. Four wheels were attached to the underside of the base. One part of the artwork consisted of 16 rotating multi-coloured plates. Built-in photoelectric cells and a microphone captured variations in colour, light, and sound, which set the structure in motion. The colour blue, for example, caused CYSP 1 to roll forward, and set the coloured plates in motion, while the colour red brought the artwork to a stop. Likewise, silence or darkness set CYSP 1 in motion, whereas sound or bright light brought it back to a resting state. Because these phenomena were continuously variable, the reaction of CYSP 1 was also continuously variable and unpredictable. See: Habasque and Ménétrier 1963, 50. Shortly after Pierre Arnaud had created the replacement show for the Philips Pavilion, CYSP 1 became an object of interest in the Netherlands. At the opening of the auditorium (designed by the architect and furniture designer Gerrit Rietveld) of the National Academy of Fine Arts [Rijksacademie van Beeldende Kunsten] in Amsterdam, an ensemble was performed on 21 March 1958 under the name *Geluid van de werkelijkheid* [The Sound of Reality] that consisted of experimental poetry, electronic music, and dance. In a décor designed by Gerrit Rietveld, texts taken from the poetry of the Dutch-Belgian literary movement known as '*Vijftigers*' were recited by Hélène Oosthoek, André van den Heuvel, and Ramses Shaffy. Between the recited texts, CYSP 1 'danced' to electronic music that Henk Badings had produced for the occasion at the Philips Research Laboratories in Eindhoven. Light and colour effects were the only other movable elements in the performance, for which Leo Verboon had compiled the script. This *Gesamtkunstwerk* depicted the struggle between man and machine, with suggestions of the threat of war, confusion, disarray, degeneration, and decadence. In thematic terms, *Geluid van de werkelijkheid* was therefore not much different from *Le poème électronique*. See: 'Philips-robot danst op elektronische muziek' ['Philips robot dances to electronic music'] 1958; and 'Geluid van de werkelijkheid' ['Sound of reality'] 1958.
18 Together with the film footage and the audio tapes, a letter dated 15 February, 1958 was delivered in Eindhoven; in this letter, Pierre Arnaud explains point by point to Hartong, Kalff, Tak, Tomasi, Schöffer, and Meyerstein (presumably a reference to Georges Meyerstein-Maigret of Philips France) the elements from which the replacement show was constructed. See: collection of Claude Tomasi, letter from Arnaud to Hartong and others, dated 15 February 1958. This letter also contains the written instructions for the light projections during the replacement show which were to be realized on site at the pavilion in Brussels. Oral communication from Pierre Arnaud to Peter Wever, dated 16 October 2009.
19 The 1958 Brussels World's Fair opened on 17 April 1958.
20 Without any citation, Lootsma indicates that the music of Tomasi was performed in the spring of 1958 by an orchestra and a choir, in the presence of Le Corbusier and Xenakis, among others. See: Lootsma 1984 [B], 26. Treib indicates that he could not find any mention of this performance in the archive materials that were available to him. See: Treib 1996, 266. When asked, Pierre Arnaud indicated that he had no knowledge of any such performance taking place in the spring of 1958, and doubts whether that performance actually took place. Email message from Pierre Arnaud to Peter Wever, dated 27 May 2010.
21 See: collection of Claude Tomasi, letter from Arnaud to Kalff, dated 27 October 1958. In this letter, Pierre Arnaud writes that he had been in Brussels on the previous Thursday ['*jeudi dernier*']. Most likely he was referring to 16 October 1958, which was the last Thursday of the 1958 Brussels World's Fair, and not Thursday, 23 October. On that date, the dismantling work in the Philips Pavilion had already begun, for which projectionist Paul Vancoppenolle was to report on 20 October at eight o'clock in the morning (see also Chapter 9). At that time, within the

22. General Advertising Division of Philips in Eindhoven, John Hafkemeijer was responsible (among other things) for the publicity for the Philips Pavilion (see also Chapter 7).
22. At the request of Philips France, Ir. Chris van Lummel also worked for some time at *la D.M.S.* Email message from Pierre Arnaud to Peter Wever, dated 21 May 2010. In 1962, Van Lummel also worked with Nicolas Schöffer on the project *Mur Lumière*, which was presented at the exhibition *L'Artiste et l'Objet* in the Musée des Arts Décoratifs in Paris. See: Habasque and Ménétrier 1963, 143; and http://www.olats.org/schoffer/biograph.htm, last accessed on 19 October 2010.
23. It is still unknown on what date Henri Tomasi's *Le poème électronique* was broadcast on the radio. In the mid-1980s, Claude Tomasi (the son of Henri Tomasi) and Pierre Arnaud made a partial reconstruction, on audio tape, of Henri Tomasi's musical work *Le poème électronique*, which now also exists in a digitized version. On 20 February 1991, the copyrights for the track were granted to Claude Tomasi and Pierre Arnaud by the *Société des Auteurs et Compositeurs Dramatiques* in Paris. Claude Tomasi and Pierre Arnaud recently renamed the piece of music *Trajectoire*. Email messages from Claude Tomasi to Peter Wever, dated 6 January 2010 and 7 June 2010; and an undated written communication, by letter, from Claude Tomasi to Peter Wever.
24. This assertion is confirmed by the mention of appointments with 'M. Arnaud' in Le Corbusier's agenda on 7 March, 17 March, 20 March, and 4 April 1958. See: FLC, Inv. No. F3-11-5: Agendas – Carnets de notes et d'adresses 1956 – 1961, Agendas, 1958. The content of the interview is still unknown. In the second, slightly modified version of Pierre Arnaud's story, he wrote about '*le texte de présentation de Le Corbusier*'. It is therefore possible that this refers to the recordings of the so-called *paroles*. This is the spoken text that Le Corbusier had planned to include with *Le poème électronique*, but that was ultimately not included in the performance. Le Corbusier corresponded about this with e.g. Varèse in a letter dated 18 February 1958. See: Cohen and Benton 2008, 632.
25. Xenakis' piece of music was called *Interlude sonore*, but received more attention in a slightly modified version under the name *Concret PH*. See: Tazelaar 2009, 8. Treib has indicated that Xenakis made use of a Philips laboratory in Paris for the recordings of the *Interlude sonore*. See: Treib 1996, 208. Given that *studio la D.M.S.* had at that time already been acquired by Philips France, this claim is correct. Xenakis refers to his visit to Pierre Arnaud's studio in a letter to Kalff: '*J'ai commencé avec Arnaud qui a fait bonne impression. On a fait la prise de son du charbon, c'est très bien*' [I have started with Arnaud, who made a good impression. A sound recording was made using [char]coal, it is very good]. See: GRI Kalff, Inv. No. 870438-14: Kalff correspondence, March 1958, letter from Xenakis to Kalff, dated 11 March 1958.
26. The existence of the replacement show for the Philips Pavilion is confirmed by the expense item 'Reserve program P. Arnoud (special budget)' listed on the overview of the budgetary developments for the Philips Pavilion, dated 11 April 1958; by the sheet music for soloists and choirs for Henri Tomasi's musical work *Le poème électronique* as part of the replacement show; by the letter dated 15 February 1958, in which Pierre Arnaud explains point by point to the concerned parties the elements that the replacement show consisted of; and by the letter dated 27 October 1958, in which Pierre Arnaud informs Louis Kalff about attending a performance of the replacement show in the Philips Pavilion.

5 An Austrian in Eindhoven
Anton Buczynski and the Recording of *Le poème électronique*

1. This chapter is largely based on the interview with Anton Buczynski that the author conducted in Baarn on 19 February 2004. The illustrations are photographs taken either by him or with his camera in 1958.
2. See also Chapter 4.
3. It may already have been clear at that point that Buczynski would be working in the Austrian pavilion at the 1958 Brussels World's Fair.
4. The NRU technician Arie Brandon had gained experience with the use of electronic sounds in radiophonic productions while working in the studios in Hilversum. In 1956 he had played an important part in the creation of Henk Badings's electronic composition *Kaïn en Abel* [Cain and Abel] in the acoustics department of Philips Research Laboratories.
5. Although Buczynski was unable to recall the precise date, he was certain that he had arrived on Ash Wednesday, since he recalled gaping in astonishment at people emerging from church, their foreheads marked with ashes in the shape of a cross. Ash Wednesday fell on 19 February in 1957.
6. See: Tazelaar 2013, 144–146.
7. On 24 March 1958, Varèse's wife Louise wrote in her diary that Jan de Bruyn had admitted over dinner that he had been following Tak's instructions. See: Paul Sacher Foundation, Basel, Edgard Varèse collection, Louise Varèse's diaries.
8. See: De Beer 1984. Tak told De Beer that he had 'been led to understand that he was to take part in the composing process'. Tak had prepared a large number of sounds, which Varèse rejected.
9. Varèse lived in Turin from 1893 until approximately 1900 (i.e. from the age of ten to seventeen).
10. The Strijp III premises were only five kilometres away from Welschap military airbase (today Eindhoven Airport), and it was not unusual for fighter jets to fly over the Strijp III premises when coming in to land.
11. See: De Beer 1984. Deutekom told De Beer that this recording was made in the truck garage on the Strijp III premises, whereas Buczynski recalled that it was made in the Catherinakerk [St Catherine's Church] in Eindhoven.
12. The Dutch name for the Philips Research Laboratories is 'Philips Natuurkundig Laboratorium', commonly abbreviated to NatLab.
13. This in contrast to the 'physical' movements of sounds along the audio routes, which consisted of large numbers of loudspeakers positioned along the most important lines of the pavilion's structure.

6 Inside the Philips Pavilion
Personal Stories from the People Who Operated *Le poème électronique*

1. Peter Wever personally contacted the following former employees of the Philips Pavilion: Pepita de Nerée tot Babberich († 2009), Theo Boesveld († 2014), Michel Cools, Wiel Cox, Max Naveaux, Michel Soete, and Paul Vancoppenolle. He also personally contacted Sonja Bootz's sister, Stef Niamonitakis' († 2011) grandson, and the widows of Therus van Andringa de Kempenaer († 2003), Frans Heukensfeldt Jansen († 1989), and Jan van Hoof († 2000).
2. See: Lesage 2008, 263.
3. A Dutch inscription still had to be added to the information pillar at the entrance to the pavilion, as well as a cord in front of which spectators were to wait, and a clock to indicate when the next performance would start. On the outside of the pavilion, the vents in the building's apices still had to be finished. Inside the pavilion, repairs had to be carried out to the walls, which then had to be touched up in white. The projection openings in the projection booths still had to be sealed off with double-glazed projection windows. And, lastly, the installation of the fluorescent lighting behind the balustrade still had to be finished off. See: PCA, letter from Kalff to those concerned, dated 24 April 1958.
4. Ibid. The audiotapes for Iannis Xenakis' *Interlude sonore* were not ready yet either.
5. See: 'Philips-paviljoen opende zijn deuren nog niet' ['Philips Pavilion has not opened its doors yet'] 1958.
6. See: 'Elektronisch gedicht een fascinerend epos' ['Electronic poem a fascinating epos'] 1958; and Everts 1960, 62 (see also Chapter 8).
7. Others who were sent to Brussels to get the performance ready included lighting expert Johan Jansen (described as 'overall trouble-shooter' in Treib 1996, 96; lighting technicians J. van Eeghen en J.A.M. Binnendijk from the Office of Lighting Advice [Lichtadviesbureau], and technician Jan Brouwer from the Main Industrial Division Electroacoustics. Based on: photographs in Theo Boesveld's collection; oral communication from Theo Boesveld to Peter Wever, dated 27 March 2009; 'Dag en nacht waren teams van specialisten bezig' ['Experts worked day and night'] 1958; and PCA, letter from Kalff to those concerned, dated 24 April 1958.
8. Email message from Paul Vancoppenolle to Peter Wever, dated 24 June 2009.
9. Based on: email message from Paul Vancoppenolle to Peter Wever, dated 24 June 2009; 'Philips' Electronisch gedicht en de Expo-bezoekers' ['Philips' Electronic poem and the Expo visitors'] 1958; and NA Brussels 1958, Inv. No. 18: Commemorative volume, text by Philips' press office entitled 'Drieduizend séances in Philips Paviljoen' ['Three thousand séances in Philips Pavilion'], unpublished concept text for Everts 1960, dated 1959.
10. Both Lootsma 1984 [B], 29; and Treib 1996, 113, refer to 2 May 1958 as

the opening date for the public. Kalff's letter dated 24 April 1958, referred to in note 3 also refers to 2 May as the intended opening date. However, there are a number of reasons to assume that performances for the public started at a later date. The Austro-American architect Richard Neutra visited the Philips Pavilion on 9 May 1958 and thanked Le Corbusier in a letter dated 10 May, for being allowed to attend a 'trial production' of *Le poème électronique*. See: photographs from the CCPA archive; and Cohen and Benton 2008, 640. On 10 May 1958 Le Corbusier wrote a letter to Kalff proposing the introduction of priority tickets for guests invited by the staff at the Philips Pavilion: Le Corbusier wrote, *'Cette carte serait à établir à partir du moment où le Poème Electronique fonctionnerait normalement'* [This ticket should be made available from the time *Le poème électronique* functions normally], implying that *Le poème électronique* was not ready at that date. See: PCA, letter from Le Corbusier to Kalff, dated 10 May 1958. The fact that Everts 1960, 62, indicated that the performances for the public started on 18 May 1958 is even more important, while the CCPA archive includes photographs with the caption *'Succès de Foule au Pavillon PH lors de la Ière admission du Public pour entendre le Poème Electronique – 20/5/58'* [An enthusiastic crowd at the Philips Pavilion during the first opportunity for the public to hear *Le poème électronique* on 20 May 1958]. Based on these sources, it seems most probable that public performances in the Philips Pavilion started on either 18 May or 20 May 1958. The correct chronology of most of the photographs in the CCPA archive book leads the author to consider 20 May 1958 as the likeliest date for the opening of the pavilion to the public.

11 Their stature led colleagues to nickname Simon de Bruin 'Dikke De Bruin' ['Fatty De Bruin'] and Jan de Bruyn 'Dunne De Bruyn' ['Skinny De Bruyn'] (see also Chapter 5). Oral communication from Theo Boesveld to Peter Wever, dated 27 March 2009. The equipment that was necessary for realizing *Le poème électronique* had already been manufactured in Eindhoven under Simon de Bruin's supervision. See: 'Zij leggen gewicht in de schaal' ['They carry some weight'] 1958.

12 Based on: oral communication from Theo Boesveld to Peter Wever, dated 27 March 2009; oral communication from Wiel Cox to Kees Tazelaar and Peter Wever, dated 28 July 2009; email message from Paul Vancoppenolle to Peter Wever, dated 24 June 2009; and 'Spel van klank en kleur, licht en leven' ['Play of sound and colour, light and life'] 1958. As head of the department of Electronic Company Mechanization, Jan de Zeeuw was responsible for the manufacture of a considerable part of the equipment and the control desks. Email message from Theo Boesveld to Peter Wever, dated 17 January 2011.

13 Email message from Paul Vancoppenolle to Peter Wever, dated 24 June 2009.

14 Email messages from Paul Vancoppenolle to Peter Wever, dated 14 June 2009 and 9 July 2009; and oral communication from Paul Vancoppenolle to Peter Wever, dated 20 July 2010.

15 Email message from Paul Vancoppenolle to Peter Wever, dated 12 June 2009.

16 Oral communication from Marijke Heukensfeldt Jansen to Peter Wever, dated 16 November 2010.

17 John Hafkemeijer's presence in Brussels is referred to in notes in the personal scrapbooks belonging to Beatrijs Mendes de Leòn-van Liebergen, a hostess at the Dutch pavilion.

18 Oral communication from Theo Boesveld to Peter Wever, dated 27 March 2009; and oral communication from Rosita Bootz to Peter Wever, dated 20 May 2009.

19 Email message from Paul Vancoppenolle to Peter Wever, dated 8 July 2009.

20 The description of the work areas in the Philips Pavilion is based on photographs in Theo Boesveld's and Peter Wever's collections; oral communication from Theo Boesveld to Peter Wever, dated 27 March 2009; email message from Paul Vancoppenolle to Peter Wever, dated 24 June 2009; oral communication from Paul Vancoppenolle to Peter Wever, dated 28 June 2009; email message from Theo Boesveld to Peter Wever, dated 27 November 2010; 'Het Philips-paviljoen' ['The Philips Pavilion'] 1958, 213; and Kalff, Tak and De Bruin s.a., 37–49 (see also Chapter 3).

21 Based on: email messages from Paul Vancoppenolle to Peter Wever, dated 24 June 2009, 12 October 2012, and 17 October 2012.

22 See: 'Technical realization' 1958.

23 Based on: email message from Paul Vancoppenolle to Peter Wever, dated 24 June 2009.

24 See: 'Philips' Electronisch gedicht en de Expo-bezoekers' ['Philips' Electronic poem and the Expo visitors'] 1958.

25 Email message from Paul Vancoppenolle to Peter Wever, dated 4 July 2009. There is doubt as to whether the interlock system functioned and whether it was even actually installed in the pavilion. Technician Theo Boesveld is convinced that the interlock system did not work. Email message from Theo Boesveld to Peter Wever, dated 17 January 2011. Lootsma 1984 [B], 28, considers *Le poème électronique* a complete failure, partly because the interlock system was never installed, leading to problems in synchronizing the different components of the performance. This contradicts Paul Vancoppenolle's statement, which is confirmed by images of the interlock system on an 8-mm amateur film that he shot in the Philips Pavilion. Paul Vancoppenolle was, however, unable to say with certainty whether the driving motors for the perfotape machines were also controlled by the interlock system: 'I think that the driving motors for the perfotape machines were also linked to the interlock system.' In Kalff, Tak and De Bruin, s.a., 44, this was, however, suggested: 'Each of the tapes was scanned in a special scanning device (. . .) and activated by a quick-starting synchronous motor.' As far as the film projection was concerned, Paul Vancoppenolle also explained that each of the four projectors in the pavilion had their own original motors that were controlled by the projectionist. However, a second driving motor was mounted on each of the projectors. The projectionist had no control over this second motor; it was switched on and off by the interlock system in the following order: a button was pressed that connected the extra driving motors with the interlock system; they were then started by pressing another button, the actual start button. This explanation is consistent with the description of the operation of *Le poème électronique* given by François Vanderschrick in the *Eindhovens Dagblad* newspaper: he also indicated that two buttons had to be pressed one after the other. See: 'Philips' Electronisch gedicht en de Expo-bezoekers' ['Philips' Electronic poem and the Expo visitors'] 1958. When Pierre Losange called *'Continuez à la main . . .'* through the loudspeakers, he meant that the original motors for the projectors had to be used.

26 In Jean Petit's book *Le poème électronique. Le Corbusier*, Le Corbusier wrote about 'the light, the colour, the rhythm, the sound, the image, as merged phenomena'. See: Petit 1958 [A], 28.

27 Based on: oral communication from Theo Boesveld to Peter Wever, dated 27 March 2009; and email messages from Paul Vancoppenolle to Peter Wever, dated 24 June 2009 and 4 July 2009. The description of the ventilation in the public area is partly based on a longitudinal section and floor plans of the Philips Pavilion that were published in the July 1958 issue of *Forum*. See: 'Het Philips-paviljoen' ['The Philips Pavilion'] 1958, 211–214.

28 Email messages from Paul Vancoppenolle to Peter Wever, dated 4 July 2009 and 5 July 2009; and email message from Theo Boesveld to Peter Wever, dated 17 January 2011.

29 See: Petit 1958 [A], n.p.

30 Based on: oral communication from Theo Boesveld to Peter Wever, dated 27 March 2009.

31 See: Schönberger 2008, 350. Dick Raaijmakers was known under the pseudonym 'Kid Baltan', an anagram of 'Dik NatLab', Raaijmakers' nickname.

32 Based on: email message from Paul Vancoppenolle to Peter Wever, dated 24 June 2009. The technicians at the Philips Pavilion used the technical resources at their disposal for a variety of purposes, for example, to make copies for each other of the audio-tapes that were present in the pavilion. Oral communication from Paul Vancoppenolle to Peter Wever, dated 28 June 2009. Some of these copies survive, including recordings of Edgard Varèse's *Le poème électronique*, Iannis Xenakis' *Interlude sonore*, Dick Raaijmakers' 'Song of the Second Moon' and 'Colonel Bogey', and an unidentified electronic composition referred to as *Ondes martenot électroniques*.

33 Based on: Kees Tazelaar's transcript of a discussion between Paul Vancoppenolle, Max Naveaux, Michel Cools, Michel Soete, Wiel Cox, Kees Tazelaar and Peter Wever, dated 26 August 2009; and oral communication from Paul Vancoppenolle to Peter Wever, dated 20 July 2010.

34 Email message from Theo Boesveld to Peter Wever, dated 27 November 2010.

35 Based on: email message from Paul Vancoppenolle to Peter Wever, dated 24 June 2009; and 'Philips' Electronisch gedicht en de Expo-bezoekers' ['Philips' Electronic poem and the Expo visitors'] 1958.

36 Based on: email message from Paul Vancoppenolle to Peter Wever, dated 24 June 2009; email message from Wiel Cox to Peter Wever, dated 6 December 2010; and email message from Theo Boesveld to Peter Wever, dated 6 December 2010.

7 That's entertainment
Publicity for the Philips Pavilion

1. See: NA Brussels, Inv. No. 11: Participation of Philips Lightbulb Factories Ltd., report of Kalff's trip to Paris, dated 18 December 1956.
2. See: PCA, budget developments Philips Pavilion, dated 11 April 1958.
3. See: GRI Kalff, Inv. No. 870438-8: Kalff correspondence, April 1957, report of 8 April 1957 talks between Kalff, Naber, Thijssen and De Bruin, dated 9 April 1957.
4. See: NA Brussels 1958, Inv. No. 11: Participation of Philips Lightbulb Factories Ltd., letter from Kalff to Everts, dated 25 April 1957.
5. See: GRI Kalff, Inv. No. 870438-8: Kalff correspondence, April 1957, report of 8 April 1957 talks between Kalff, Naber, Thijssen and De Bruin, dated 9 April 1957; and undated report of 15 April 1957 talks at the scale model.
6. Based on digitized version of the film *De bouw van het Philips paviljoen* [The Construction of the Philips Pavilion] in the EYE Film Institute Netherlands archive.
7. See: Smit 1985, 41; and GRI Kalff, Inv. No. 870438-8: Kalff correspondence, April 1957, undated report of 15 April 1957 talks at the scale model.
8. Email message from Wim Langenhoff to Peter Wever, dated 14 July 2009.
9. See: Everts 1960, 55; and Souvenir of your visit to the Coca-Cola Pavilion 1958.
10. See: GRI Kalff, Inv. No. 870438-10: Kalff correspondence, July–Sept. 1957, report concerning various talks on 11, 12 and 13 September in Paris, dated 18 September 1957.
11. See: 'Wie weet naam voor Philips paviljoen?' ['Who knows name for Philips pavilion'] 1957.
12. See: Sterken 2008 [A], 53–54.
13. See: Rydell 1993, 132–135.
14. See: '7000 namen voor Philips Paviljoen' ['7,000 names for Philips Pavilion'] 1957.
15. Ibid.
16. See: PCA, report of a 15 November 1957 trip to Paris by Kalff, dated 18 November 1957.
17. See: GRI Kalff, Inv. No. 870438-11: Kalff correspondence, Oct.–Nov. 1958, letter from Le Corbusier to Kalff, dated 19 November 1957.
18. At Philips itself, the name of the pavilion was written inconsistently: in the Dutch-language publicity material and the company's own publications about the pavilion, the name was usually written as 'Philips Paviljoen' or 'Philips paviljoen', but 'Philips' Paviljoen', 'Philips' paviljoen', 'Philipspaviljoen' and 'Philips-paviljoen' are also found.
19. See: 'Nog geen naam voor Philips' Paviljoen' ['No name yet for Philips' Pavilion'] 1958.
20. See: GRI Kalff, Inv. No. 870438-6: Kalff correspondence, Jan.–Feb. 1957, undated preliminary calculation 1958 Brussels World's Fair Philips Pavilion.
21. See: 'Introduction' 1958, 81. This photograph is undated but on the back cover of a copy in the NA Brussel 1958 are the words *'Het Philipspaviljoen vlak voor de opening'* [The Philips Pavilion just before the opening].
22. See Text Box II for a description of the Philips Pavilion press file.
23. See: Het Philipspaviljoen op de Wereldtentoonstelling te Brussel 1958 [The Philips Pavilion at the 1958 Brussels World's Fair] s.a.; and Peter Wever's collection.
24. See: Wilbrink 2005, 7–63.
25. See: GRI Kalff, inv. nr. 870438-6: Kalff correspondence, Jan.–Feb. 1957, undated preliminary calculation 1958 Brussels World's Fair Philips Pavilion.
26. The poster is 100 cm long and 65 cm wide, and costed about 15 Belgian francs. See: GRI Kalff, Inv. No. 870438-6: Kalff correspondence, Jan.–Feb. 1957, undated report of a 20 February meeting in Brussels. (This meeting almost certainly took place on 20 February 1958 and the report was then mistakenly filed in the wrong section of the archive.) It is still not known who designed the poster.
27. See: Devos 2008, 19.
28. See: Scheerlinck, Wever and Lucas 2008, n.p.
29. Based on: photographs in Peter Wever's collection and the CCPA archive. See also: NA Brussels 1958, Inv. No. 11: Participation Philips Lightbulb Factories Ltd., announcement concerning the World's Fair in Brussels, Nr. 01, dated 18 February 1958.
30. Peter Wever's collection includes examples of such advertisements that appeared in the following Belgian publications: the *Le Soir* newspaper, the *Goed Nieuws voor de Vrouw* [Good News for Women] magazine, and a folder for Philips ventilators.
31. See: Wilbrink 2005, 7–63.
32. See: GRI Kalff, inv. nr. 870438-6: Kalff correspondence, Jan.–Feb. 1957, undated report of a 20 February meeting in Brussels (see also note 29).
33. Based on: Peter Wever's collection.
34. See: photographs in the CCPA archive. The photographer who took this photograph is still unidentified.
35. Photographs in the CCPA archive show that on 7 February 1958 people were dressed in winter coats and scarves because it was so cold. The weather conditions that day were described as 'miserable'. See: Treib 1996, 112.
36. See: GRI Kalff, Inv. No. 870438-13: Kalff correspondence, Jan.–Feb. 1958, recapitulation, dated 15 February 1958; and Treib 1996, 112.
37. See: GRI Kalff, Inv. No. 870438-10: Kalff correspondence, July–Sept. 1957, letter from Le Corbusier to Kalff, dated 17 August 1957; and http://www.lesedtionsdeminuit.com/f/index.php?sp=page&c=7, last consulted on 28 April 2013.
38. See: GRI Kalff, Inv. No. 870438-10: Kalff correspondence, July–Sept. 1957, report concerning various talks on 11, 12 and 13 September in Paris, dated 18 September 1957.
39. See: PCA, report of a 15 November 1957 trip to Paris by Kalff, dated 18 November 1957.
40. See: GRI Kalff, Inv. No. 870438-10: Kalff correspondence, July–Sept. 1957, report concerning various talks on 11, 12 and 13 September in Paris, dated 18 September 1957 (see also Chapter 3).
41. See: PCA, report of a 15 November 1957 trip to Paris by Kalff, dated 18 November 1957. The intention was to print 6,000 French and 4,000 Dutch copies, costing between 300 and 400 French francs (between three and four Dutch guilders) per copy.
42. See: GRI Kalff, Inv. No. 870438-10: Kalff correspondence, July–Sept. 1957, report concerning various talks on 11, 12 and 13 September in Paris, dated 18 September 1957.
43. See: FLC, Inv. No. J2-19-579: Pavillon Philips - Exposition Internationale 1956 – 1964 Belgique Bruxelles, Poeme electronique, Texte manuscrit chapitre IV : Comment c'est arrivé...., Le Corbusier's text for Chapter 4, dated 29 March 1958.
44. See: Petit 1958 [B]. The date of publication is determined as December 1958, which date appeared on a supplementary sheet accompanying the book. Michel Butor was a novelist whose work was published by Les Éditions de Minuit. It is unclear what his relationship with the Philips Pavilion was. See: http://www.leseditionsdeminuit.eu/f/index.php?sp=livAut&auteur_id=1388, last consulted on 28 April 2013. Professor Cornelis Vreedenburgh of the Delft University of Technology was involved in developing scale-model tests for the Philips Pavilion. See: Lootsma 1984 [A], 14.
45. See: accompanying supplementary sheet for Petit 1958 [B].
46. See: GRI Kalff, Inv. No. 870438-17: Kalff script for *Le poème électronique*.
47. See: http://www.youtube.com/watch?v=UmcR9jU6SPw (Le Corbusier's interview on the philosophy behind the Open Hand Monument), last consulted on 28 April 2013.
48. See: Weber 2008, 641; and http://www.chandigarh.co.uk/tourist-attractions/open-hand.html, last consulted on 28 April 2013.
49. See: Weber 2008, 711.
50. See: Petit 1958 [B], n.p.
51. See: GRI Kalff, Inv. No. 870438-15: Kalff correspondence, April–Dec. 1958, letter from Kalff to Le Corbusier, dated 29 November 1958.
52. See: FLC, Inv. No. J2-19-557-558: Pavillon Philips - Exposition Internationale 1956 – 1964 Belgique Bruxelles, Poeme electronique, Envoi du livre : 'Le Poème Electronique', letter to Petit, dated 13 October 1958.
53. Based on: NA Brussels 1958, Inv. No. 11: NA Brussels 1958, Inv. No. 11: Participation of Philips Lightbulb Factories Ltd., announcement concerning the World's Fair in Brussels, Nr. 01, dated 18 February 1958, which refers to a *'luxe album over het werk van Le Corbusier en in het bijzonder over het Philips Paviljoen'* [a luxury edition about Le Corbusier's work and the Philips Pavilion in particular], with a total of *'1000 exemplaren'* [1,000 copies].
54. See: GRI Kalff, Inv. No. 870438-6: Kalff correspondence, Jan.–Feb. 1957, undated report of a 20 February meeting in Brussels (see also note 29) which indicates that the paperback edition would be ready in mid-June.

55 Based on: Peter Wever's collection.
56 Because a single retail price is mentioned but there were two paperback editions of varying lengths, the author assumes that the 72-page edition was intended for sale and the 124-page edition served as a commemorative gift for visiting dignitaries.
57 See: NA Brussels 1958, Inv. No. 11: Participation of Philips Lightbulb Factories Ltd., letter from Hafkemeijer to Van Hoorn, dated 30 August 1958.
58 Email messages from Paul Vancoppenolle to Peter Wever, dated 14 June 2009 and 4 July 2009. When the World's Fair ended, publicity officer Pepita de Nerée tot Babberich asked her colleagues at the Philips Pavilion to write a short note in a copy of *Le poème électronique. Le Corbusier*. In his note, pavilion attendant Jaak Derijcke called Pepita *'mijn kleine poème verkoopster'* [my little *poème* saleswoman].
59 In a telephone conversation with the author dated 17 June 2008, Pepita de Nerée tot Babberich introduced herself as *'hostess van het Philips paviljoen'* [hostess of the Philips Pavilion].
60 See: de Kuyper 1992, 147.
61 The description of the folding bookstall is based on photographs in the CCPA archive and Theo Boesveld's collection. Images on the 8-mm amateur film made by Paul Vancoppenolle suggest that the books were also sold under the canopy ceiling of the Philips Pavilion exit.
62 See: NA Brussels 1958, Inv. No. 18: Commemorative volume, text by Philips' press office entitled 'Drieduizend séances in Philips Paviljoen' ['Three thousand séances in Philips Pavilion'], unpublished concept text for Everts 1960, dated 1959.
63 See: Wie wat waar? ['Who what where?'] 1958, 151.
64 See: NA Brussels 1958, Inv. No. 11: Participation of Philips Lightbulb Factories Ltd., letter from Kalff to Everts, dated 23 March 1956.
65 See: PCA, budget developments Philips Pavilion, dated 11 April 1958.
66 See: NA Brussels 1958, Inv. No. 18: Commemorative volume, Kalff text entitled 'De Philips' inzending op de Wereldtentoonstelling in Brussel 1958' ['The Philips entry for the 1958 Brussels World's Fair'], dated 5 August 1959.
67 See: Philips 1979, 332–336.

7 The 'Electronic Poem' in the Philips Pavilion
A Rich and Rare Experience of a World of Wonder

1 See: 'The "electronic poem" in the Philips Pavilion' 1958. It is known that there were Dutch and English versions of the press file for the Philips Pavilion but it is likely that a French and possibly a German version were also distributed. The text, reproduced complete and unabridged in this chapter, was probably written by Philips' press office. The notes accompanying the text were added by Peter Wever. The press file also included texts about the technical realization of the pavilion, its structural principles, a text by Iannis Xenakis about the pavilion and *Le poème électronique*, a page from the *minutage*, a schematic reproduction of the equipment in the pavilion, a page from Varèse's score, various photographs of the pavilion, illustrations showing design sketches, a colour picture-postcard of the pavilion, and a brochure about the use of Philips equipment at the World's Fair.
2 This text completely ignores Iannis Xenakis' role in designing the pavilion (see also Chapter 1).
3 The 'model of an atom' and 'nude figure' referred to here concern the two *volumes*. The *volumes* were among the light effects in *Le poème électronique* outlined by Le Corbusier (see also Chapter 3). They consisted of a female figure and a geometric object constructed out of metal tubes that hung opposite each other in the apices of the pavilion. Both *volumes* were painted with fluorescent paint. When ultraviolet light was shone on them, the female figure lit up red, and the geometric object became greenish blue. The female figure symbolized matter and the geometric object the spirit. The *volumes* were used at the beginning of the performance, at the end of the fourth sequence (*Man-made Gods*), and at the end of the performance. The geometric object displayed many similarities to the *Objet mathématique* that was situated at the entrance to the Philips Pavilion. See: Kalff, Tak and De Bruin, s.a., 37–42; and Lootsma 1984 [B], 25. Le Corbusier had initially indicated that a mannequin could be used for the female figure. Probably in March 1957, he made a note in his sketchbook about this: 'hang from the ceiling a Galeries Lafayette bare mannequin with pretty eyes or a standard mannequin with neither eyes nor hands'. In a 1 June 1957 discussion with Kalff, Le Corbusier still indicated that he had a mannequin painted white in mind, and not a specially sculpted image. On 11 February 1958, however, Le Corbusier wrote to Iannis Xenakis: 'I will take care of the story of the mannequin myself. It must be made by the tinsmith quickly with a wire chosen for its small scale.' See: Treib 1996, 110–111, 261; and GRI Kalff, Inv. No. 870438-9: Kalff correspondence, May–June 1957, report of a 1 June 1957 meeting between Kalff and Le Corbusier, dated 3 June 1957. In photographs taken by Lucien Hervé in the FLC collection, two different female figures are visible in the Philips Pavilion. Archive section L1(3)84 contains several contact prints in which a naked mannequin with feet, arms, breasts and half-length hair can be seen hanging in the pavilion. A ladder can also be seen on one of these contact prints, as well as an employee who is carrying out work. This suggests that these photographs were taken before the opening of the Philips Pavilion. Archive sections L1(3)53, L1(3)55–L1(3)59 and L1(3)63 include a series of photographs in which a more abstract female figure can be seen hanging in the pavilion. It is most probable that these photographs were taken after the opening of the pavilion because visitors and film images are also visible. It is clear that the mannequin was replaced at some stage by the more abstract female figure. This would agree with technician Theo Boesveld's memory that a naked female mannequin stood in one of the pavilion's work areas until the end of the World's Fair. Oral communication from Theo Boesveld to Peter Wever, dated 27 March 2009.
4 In an original *écran* film in the archive of the EYE Film Institute Netherlands, the seven successive sequences of *Le poème électronique* are introduced in English as *Genesis*, *Spirit and Matter*, *From darkness to dawn*, *Man-made Gods*, *How time moulds civilization*, *Harmony*, and *To all mankind*.
5 This soprano solo was recorded by the still unknown Dutch coloratura soprano Cristina Deutekom. See: Oskamp 1995 (see also Chapter 5).
6 The projection lantern that was used for projecting the coloured glass slides in the Philips Pavilion was incorrectly referred to here as an epidiascope. An epidiascope can project both solid flat objects and transparent images. It would have been more correct to refer to the device in question as a diascope.

8 Like Ants in a Hurricane
One and a Half Million Visitors to the Philips Pavilion

1 See: Kalff, Tak and De Bruin s.a., 48; Philips rapport annuel 1958 [Philips annual report 1958] 1959, n.p.; and Everts 1960, 62. The estimate of one and a half million visitors was probably based on three performances an hour spread over seven hours a day, over a five-month period and attracting 500 visitors per performance. However, the pavilion was temporarily closed during important receptions, and sometimes there were fewer than 500 visitors for a performance – one visitor remembers being one of a group of only sixty visitors who entered the pavilion. See: Van Dijk 2008, 110. It is therefore likely that the real number of visitors was smaller than the number suggested here.
2 The first performance of *Le poème électronique* was meant to take place on 15 April 1958 during a visit by Dutch officials and the press to the Dutch and Philips pavilions. But no matter what, the performance had to be ready by 17 April for the opening of the 1958 Brussels World's Fair. See: GRI Kalff, Inv. No. 870438-15: Kalff correspondence, April–Dec. 1958, letter from Kalff to Xenakis, dated 9 April 1958. However, *Le poème électronique* was not ready to be performed on either occasion. See: 'Philips-paviljoen opende zijn deuren nog niet' ['Philips Pavilion has not opened its doors yet'] 1958.
3 The description of this 18 April 1958 visit is based on photographs in the CCPA archive; and GRI Kalff, Inv. No. 870438-15: Kalff correspondence, April–Dec. 1958, letter from Kalff to Xenakis dated 9 April 1958. Projectionist Paul Vancoppenolle indicated that a *séance spéciale* took place during the visit by members of the Board of Directors of Philips Netherlands and Philips Belgium. Email message from Paul Vancoppenolle to Peter Wever, dated 24 June 2009.
4 See: 'Elektronisch gedicht een fascinerend epos' ['Electronic poem a fascinating epos'] 1958; and Peter Wever's collection, Programme de la presentation du pavillon Philips a l'Exposition Universelle et Internationale de Bruxelles 1958.

5   See: 'Philips' Expo-paviljoen: wonderlijk "elektronisch gedicht" in licht' ['Philips' Expo-pavilion: curious "electronic poem" in light'] undated. Varèse was also in Brussels because he and Man Ray were part of the jury for the Internationale Wedstrijd voor de Experimentele Film [International Competition for Experimental Film], which was held from 21–27 April 1958, on the occasion of the World's Fair. See: Het officieel gedenkboek [The official commemorative volume] 1960, 135–137.
6   Kalff had indicated to Xenakis that Le Corbusier's presence at the Philips Pavilion on 22 April would be greatly appreciated. See: GRI Kalff, Inv. No. 870438-15: Kalff correspondence, April–Dec. 1958, letter from Kalff to Xenakis, dated 9 April 1958. However, nothing in the available material suggests that Le Corbusier was present on 22 April, nor does his diary mention that he was in Brussels on that date. See: FLC, Inv. No. F3-11-5: Agendas - carnets de notes et d'adresses 1956–1961, Agendas, 1958.
7   See: Peter Wever's collection, Programme de la presentation du pavillon Philips a l'Exposition Universelle et Internationale de Bruxelles 1958.
8   See: 'Dingen uit de vijf ringen' ['Things from the five rings'] 1958; 'Verbijsterend modern gedicht overspoelt de Expo-bezoeker' ['Bewildering modern poem overwhelms the Expo visitor'] 1958; and 'Philips' Expo-paviljoen: wonderlijk "elektronisch gedicht" in licht' ['Philips' Expo-pavilion: curious "electronic poem" in light'] undated.
9   The description of the performances of Le poème électronique on the evening of 22 April and on 23 April is based on photographs in the CCPA archive; the invitation for the performance on 22 April; and 'Elektronisch gedicht een fascinerend epos' ['Electronic poem a fascinating epos'] 1958.
10 See note 10, Chapter 6.
11 The opening times and frequency of three performances per hour are printed on the priority ticket. Occasionally there were four performances an hour, for example, following a *séance spéciale* for dignitaries. Email message from Paul Vancoppenolle to Peter Wever, dated 24 June 2009. The initial aim was for six performances an hour. See: PCA, letter from Kalff to those concerned, dated 24 April 1958. However, this would not have been realistic because Xenakis' Interlude sonore and Le poème électronique with its introduction together lasted more than ten minutes.
12 In Willem Hering and Hank Onrust's 1998 documentary Het elektronisch gedicht: Edgard Varèse in Nederland [The electronic poem: Edgard Varèse in the Netherlands], Dick Raaijmakers indicated that the bell in question was Delft's Oude Kerk emergency bell, which may only be used on special occasions, such as the funerals of members of the Dutch royal family. Email message from Kees Tazelaar to Peter Wever, dated 21 December 2010.
13 The description of the flow of visitors in the Philips Pavilion is based on email messages from Paul Vancoppenolle to Peter Wever, dated 24 June 2009 and 4 July 2009; and Tazelaar 2013, 153.
14 See: Bibeb 1958 [A], 79. Other words used by Le Corbusier for his design of the Philips Pavilion were 'stomach' and 'bottle'. See: Lootsma 1984 [A], 11.
15 See: PCA, letter from Le Corbusier to Kalff, dated 10 May 1958.
16 The description of Le Corbusier's 26 and 27 April 1958 visit to Brussels is based on photographs in the CCPA archive; Benton 2009, 117–125, 220–243; and mentions in Le Corbusier's diary on 26 and 27 April 1958. See: FLC, Inv. No. F3-11-5: Agendas - carnets de notes et d'adresses 1956 – 1961, Agendas, 1958.
17 Le Corbusier's speech in the auditorium of the French pavilion was meant to be broadcast on radio but, under the pretext of technical problems, this did not happen. According to Benton 2009, 117, the radical nature of the speech's content and the informal presentation possibly played a role in censoring the broadcast. Benton 2009, 235–243, reproduces the complete text of Le Corbusier's 58-minute speech, which was finally broadcast on 3 March 1995 by the France Culture radio station.
18 Email message from Paul Vancoppenolle to Peter Wever, dated 24 June 2009. The Gulden Boek is in the possession of the CCPA archive.
19 See: Treib 1996, 113–114.
20 See: Bibeb 1958 [B]. Beatrijs Mendes de Leòn-van Liebergen later described Le Corbusier as 'an insufferably arrogant fellow'. Oral communication from Beatrijs Mendes de Leòn-van Liebergen to Peter Wever, dated 29 May 2011.
21 The description of Le Corbusier's visit to Brussels from 29 September to 1 October 1958 is based on photographs in the CCPA archive; and references in Le Corbusier's diary on 29 and 30 September and 1 October 1958. See: FLC, Inv. No. F3-11-5: Agendas - carnets de notes et d'adresses 1956 – 1961, Agendas, 1958.
22 See: 'Koningin en Prins geboeid door het "Poème Electronique"' ['Queen and Prince fascinated by "Poème Électronique"'] 1958.
23 The description of the official receptions is based on Philips rapport annuel 1958 [Philips annual report 1958] 1959, n.p.; photographs in the CCPA archive, Theo Boesveld's and Peter Wever's collections; and email message from Paul Vancoppenolle to Peter Wever, dated 24 June 2009.
24 Oral communication from Theo Boesveld to Peter Wever, dated 27 March 2009. There are both silver (with Dutch silver marks) and silver-plated copies of the paperweight. The ponds around the Philips Pavilion were incorporated into the paperweight as blue enamel. The manufacturer of the paperweight is still unknown.
25 See: Cohen & Benton 2008, 640.
26 Oral communication from Theo Boesveld to Peter Wever, dated 27 March 2009; and email message from Paul Vancoppenolle to Peter Wever, dated 24 June 2009.
27 See: 'Teleurstelling en verrassing in de hedendaagse muziek' ['Disappointment and surprise in contemporary music'] undated; and Veltman, undated.
28 See: Maelstaf 1958, 158.
29 See: Oskamp 1995.
30 See: Kalff, Tak and De Bruin, s.a., 37–42.
31 See: Oskamp 1995.
32 See: 'Philips' Electronisch gedicht en de Expo-bezoekers' ['Philips' Electronic poem and the Expo visitors'] 1958; Bosman, undated; and 'Verbijsterend modern gedicht overspoelt de Expo-bezoeker' ['Bewildering modern poem overwhelms the Expo visitor'] 1958.
33 See: 'Teleurstelling en verrassing in de hedendaagse muziek' ['Disappointment and surprise in contemporary music'] undated; and Veltman, undated.
34 See: 'Elektronisch gedicht van Philips overweldigt de Expo-bezoekers' ['Electronic poem overwhelms the Expo visitors'] 1958.
35 See: Sandberg 1959, 179.

9 Beyond the Final Performance
Demolition of the Philips Pavilion

1   The projectors from the Philips Pavilion have been identified from film material as Philips FP56 projectors. The two projectors that were sold to the Pax centre in Erpe (now the municipality of Erpe-Mere) were used there for many years, and were later resold elsewhere. See: De Schamphelaere 2006.
2   The description of the final performance of Le poème électronique in the Philips Pavilion is based on email messages from Paul Vancoppenolle to Peter Wever, dated 24 June 2009, 8 July 2009, and 6 September 2009.
3   See: Everts 1960, 84.
4   See: Lootsma 1984 [A], 17.
5   See: GRI Kalff, Inv. No. 870438-4: Kalff correspondence, October 1956, letter from Kalff to Le Corbusier, dated 13 October 1956.
6   See: Kint 2001, 225.
7   See: Treib 1996, 226–228.
8   See: FLC, Inv. No. J2-19-506-507: Pavillon Philips - Exposition Internationale 1956 – 1964 Belgique Bruxelles, Documents divers, Correspondence sur la conservation Pavillon - 22/09/1958 – 15/10/1958, letter from Le Corbusier to Jasinksi, dated 3 October 1958.
9   See: GRI Kalff, Inv. No. 870438-3: Kalff correspondence, June–Sept. 1956, letter from Le Corbusier to Kalff, dated 3 July 1956.
10 See: FLC, Inv. No. J2-19-506-507: Pavillon Philips - Exposition Internationale 1956 – 1964 Belgique Bruxelles, Documents divers, Correspondence sur la conservation Pavillon - 22/09/1958 – 15/10/1958, letter from Le Corbusier to Jasinski, dated 3 October 1958.
11 See: FLC, Inv. No. J2-19-508: Pavillon Philips - Exposition Internationale 1956 – 1964 Belgique Bruxelles, Documents divers, Correspondence sur la conservation Pavillon - 22/09/1958 – 15/10/1958, letter from Le Corbusier to Meyers, dated 8 October 1958.
12 See: Treib 1996, 226–228; and Sterken 2008 [B], 93.
13 Ibid.
14 See: Sterken 2007, 63–68.
15 See: Lootsma 1984 [A], 17; and Sterken 2007, 63–68.
16 See: Xenakis s.a., 6.
17 See: GRI Kalff, Inv. No. 870438-15: Kalff correspondence, April–Dec. 1958, report of a 6 November 1958 meeting between Thijssen and Duyster, dated 12 November 1958.

18 See: GRI Kalff, Inv. No. 870438-15: Kalff correspondence, April–Dec. 1958, draft contract of 9 December 1958 drawn up by Kalff.
19 Ibid.
20 See: GRI Kalff, Inv. No. 870438-15: Kalff correspondence, April–Dec. 1958, report of a 6 November 1958 meeting between Thijssen and Duyster, dated 12 November 1958.
21 The account of the different plans for the demolition of the Philips Pavilion is based on GRI Kalff, Inv. No. 870438-15: Kalff correspondence, April–Dec. 1958, report of a 6 November 1958 meeting between Thijssen and Duyster, dated 12 November 1958; a memorandum from Kalff to all those concerned, dated 8 December 1958; and 'Elektronisch gedicht op Expo weerstaat slopers...' ['Electronic poem withstands demolishers...'] 1959.
22 The description of the events of 30 January 1959 is based on photographs from the CCPA archives; and 'Elektronisch gedicht op Expo weerstaat slopers...' ['Electronic poem withstands demolishers...'] 1959.
23 See: Treib 1996, 226–228.
24 See: 'Elektronisch gedicht op Expo weerstaat slopers...' ['Electronic poem withstands demolishers...'] 1959.
25 See: NA Brussels 1958, Inv. No. 11: Participation of Philips Lightbulb Factories Ltd., letter from Kalff to Everts, dated 25 April 1957.
26 See: NA Brussels 1958, Inv. No. 22: Winding up: Demolition, sale, and transport III. Demolition: Van Eck Brothers, D. Blankevoort & Son, report of working day, Brussels, dated 3 February 1959. The report states: 'The Philips Pavilion was pulled down yesterday.' Both Treib 1996, 226–228; and Sterken 2007, 63–68, wrongly state that the pavilion was demolished on 30 January 1959. Lootsma 1984 [A], 17, wrongly states that the pavilion was blown up using dynamite in the autumn of 1958.
27 See: Kint 2001, 225.
28 See: Sterken 2007, 63–68.
29 The neon light tubes of the *Objet mathématique* have been removed and the words 'poème électronique' are currently displayed using blue LED lighting. The word 'philips' has gone (see also note 28 to Chapter 2).
30 Email message from Kees Tazelaar to Peter Wever, dated 22 February 2012.
31 For which Emiel de Jong is acknowledged.
32 See: Tazelaar 2009, 10.
33 Several employees with a technical background retained objects from the Philips Pavilion for their own personal use. These were items like a fluorescent light tube, a tape recorder, loudspeaker cabinets, and a crossover separating high from low tones. Because of the difficult economic situation, projectionist Paul Vancoppenolle converted some of the pavilion's bracing wires into tools like a screwdriver. Employees also took press files and press photos along with them as mementos. Some were given a silverplated and blue-enamelled Philips Pavilion paperweight as a gift. Furthermore, the collections of the Fondation Le Corbusier in Paris, Het Nieuwe Instituut in Rotterdam and the Foundation for the Preservation of Historical Philips Products [Stichting tot Behoud van Historische Philips Producten] in Eindhoven contain original structural models and scale models of the Philips Pavilion. The scale model in the collection of the latter foundation is on long-term loan to the Rijksmuseum in Amsterdam for permanent exhibition in the 20th-Century Galleries. The display in the Rijksmuseum is accompanied by a reconstruction, made by Kees Tazelaar, of the music of *Le poème électronique*. Correspondence, notes, floor plans and other paper documents relating to the Philips Pavilion and *Le poème électronique* can be found in the Philips Company Archives in Eindhoven, the Getty Research Institute in Los Angeles, the Fondation Le Corbusier, the Iannis Xenakis Archives of the Bibliothèque nationale de France in Paris, the Edgard Varèse Collection of the Paul Sacher Foundation in Basel, the Expo 58 archival collection of the Ministry of Economic Affairs in Brussels, and the archives of the 'Foundation World Exhibition Brussels 1958 Netherlands Section' at the National Archives in The Hague. A book containing photographs of the pavilion, and the Philips visitors' book known as the Golden Book, are preserved at Corporate Communication & Public Affairs of Philips Belgium in Brussels. Photographs of the Philips Pavilion made by Lucien Hervé, who recorded the architecture of Le Corbusier, Marcel Breuer and Alvar Aalto, among others, can be found in the collection of the Fondation Le Corbusier. See: Andrieux, Bajac, Richard and Sbriglio 2011, 264–275. The Nederlands Fotomuseum in Rotterdam has the photographs that Hans de Boer made of the Philips Pavilion under its curatorship.
34 See: Tazelaar 2009, 9.
35 See: http://www.bsnpubs.com/nyc/carlton/carltonlps.html, last consulted on 7 April 2012. The Carlton Record Corporation album has the catalogue number STLP 12/112.
36 Email message from Kees Tazelaar to Peter Wever, dated 5 April 2012. The Philips' Phonographic Industries album has the catalogue number A 01494 L and the Columbia Records album has the catalogue number ML 5478.
37 See: Blanken 2002, 73.
38 The catalogue number of the BV HAAST CD is 06/0701.
39 See: '*Poème electronique* in stadsjournaal' ['*Poème electronique* in city journal'] 1959.
40 See: Tazelaar 2009, 9.
41 See: Lombardo 2007, 89–91; and Lombardo 2009, 24–47.
42 See: Tazelaar 2009, 9. The first performance of the reconstruction of *Le poème électronique* for full-dome digital planetariums took place on 12 June 2009 in the planetarium of Amsterdam's zoo, Artis, as part of a Varèse symposium held during the Holland Festival.
43 See: De Jonge 2007, 11–19.
44 See: Scholtes 2009.
45 See: Stichting Reconstructie Philips Paviljoen 1958 [Foundation for the Reconstruction of the 1958 Philips Pavilion] 2013, 31.
46 The quotation comes from Kees Tazelaar's transcript of a discussion between Paul Vancoppenolle, Max Naveaux, Michel Cools, Michel Soete, Wiel Cox, Kees Tazelaar and Peter Wever, dated 26 August 2009.
47 Ibid.

Bibliography

'7000 namen voor Philips Pavilioen', *Philips Koerier*, 9 November 1957.
Andrieux, B., Q. Bajac, M. Richard, and J. Sbriglio, *Le Corbusier Lucien Hervé: Contacts*, Paris 2011.
Beer, R. de, 'En Varèse deed "kwè-kwè"', *De Volkskrant*, 27 January 1984.
Benton, T., *The Rhetoric of Modernism: Le Corbusier as a lecturer*, Basel 2009.
Bibeb [A], *Bibeb in Holland*, Utrecht 1958.
Bibeb [B], 'Fair hostess: zij maakte de hele Expo mee', *Vrij Nederland*, 1 November 1958.
Blanken, I.J., *Geschiedenis van Koninklijke Philips Electronics N.V. Een industriële wereldfederatie*, Zaltbommel 2002.
Bos, B., and F. van Lier, *De appels van Jan Bons. Affiches voor toneelgroep De Appel*, Hoorn 2004.
Bosman, A., 'Elektronisch gedicht een fascinerend epos', *Algemeen Dagblad*, undated cutting.
'Brüsseler Spitzen', *Frankfurter Allgemeine Zeitung*, undated cutting.
Cohen, J-L., and T. Benton, *Le Corbusier le grand*, London 2008.
'Dag en nacht waren teams van specialisten bezig', *Philips Koerier*, 19 April 1958.
Devos, R., '"Voor een humaner wereld". Moderne architectuur op Expo 58' in: A. Koch, *Dichtbij klopt het hart der wereld. Nederland op de Expo 58*, Schiedam 2008, 13–33.
Dijk, M. van, 'De mislukte padvinderstent' in: A. Koch, *Dichtbij klopt het hart der wereld. Nederland op de Expo 58*, Schiedam 2008, 110–111.
'Dingen uit de vijf ringen', *Eindhovens Dagblad*, 24 April 1958.
'Dollywood tekent een wereldtaal', *Philips Koerier*, 12 April 1958.
Duyster, H.C., 'De constructie van het paviljoen in voorgespannen beton' in: *Het Philipspaviljoen op de Wereldtentoonstelling te Brussel 1958* (reprint from *Philips Technisch Tijdschrift*), s.a., 27–36.
'Elektronisch gedicht een fascinerend epos', *Philips Koerier*, 26 April 1958.
'Elektronisch gedicht op Expo weerstaat slopers...', *Het Vrije Volk*, 31 January 1959.
'Elektronisch gedicht van Philips overweldigt de Expo-bezoekers', *Limburgsch Dagblad*, 23 August 1958.
Everts, F.E.C., *Nederland op de Wereldtentoonstelling Brussel 1958*, The Hague 1960.
Franclieu, F. de, *Le Corbusier sketchbooks 4. 1957–1964*, New York 1982.
'Geluid van de werkelijkheid', *Philips Koerier*, 29 March 1958.
Habasque, G., and J. Ménétrier, *Nicolas Schöffer*, Neuchâtel 1963.
Heer, J. de, 'Aarde en zon. Kleurgebruik in de architectuur van Le Corbusier' in: J. de Heer, *Kleur en architectuur*, Rotterdam 1986, 10–23.
Heer, J. de, *The Architectonic Colour: Polychromy in the Purist Architecture of Le Corbusier*, Rotterdam 2009.
Het officieel gedenkboek van de Algemene Wereldtentoonstelling te Brussel 1958. De kunsten, Brussels 1960.
'Het Philips-paviljoen', *Forum*, 13(1958)6, 211–214.
Het Philipspaviljoen op de Wereldtentoonstelling te Brussel 1958 (reprint from *Philips Technisch Tijdschrift*), s.a.
http://francois.faurant.free.fr/stud/studios.htm#saussier
http://fr.wikipedia.org/wiki/Pierre-Arnaud_de_Chassy-Poulay
http://library.tue.nl/catalog/FullBB.csp?WebAction=ShowFullBB&RequestId=16528052_20&Profile=KC&OpacLanguage=dut&NumberToRetrieve=50&StartValue=9&WebPageNr=1&SearchTerm1=1958.43.912&SearchT1=&Index1=Index4301&SearchMethod=Find_1&ItemNr=9
http://www.bsnpubs.com/nyc/carlton/carltonlps.html
http://www.chandigarh.co.uk/tourist-attractions/open-hand.html
http://www.leseditionsdeminuit.com/f/index.php?sp=page&c=7
http://www.leseditionsdeminuit.eu/f/index.php?sp=livAut&auteur_id=1388
http://www.olats.org/schoffer/biograph.htm
http://www.youtube.com/watch?v=UmcR9jU6SPw
'Introduction', *International Lighting Review*, 1958.
'Jan Bons, affiches', *Fodor*, 1975.
Jonge, W. de, 'Het Philips-paviljoen: van 1958 naar 2008? Haalbaarheidsonderzoek voor reconstructie' in: Stichting Alice, *Make it New: Le poème électronique. Onderzoek voor de reconstructie van het Philips-paviljoen uit 1958 in Eindhoven*, Eindhoven 2007, 11–19.
Kalff, L.C., W. Tak, en S.L. de Bruin, 'Verwezenlijking van het "elektronisch gedicht" in het paviljoen' in: *Het Philipspaviljoen op de Wereldtentoonstelling te Brussel 1958* (reprint from *Philips Technisch Tijdschrift*), s.a., 37–49.
Kint, J., *Expo 58 als belichaming van het humanistisch modernisme*, Rotterdam 2001.
'Koningin en Prins geboeid door het "Poème Electronique"', *Philips Koerier*, 21 June 1958.
Küper, M., and I. van Zijl, *Gerrit Th. Rietveld (1888–1964). Het volledige werk*, Utrecht 1992.
Kuyper, E. de, *Grand Hotel Solitude. Taferelen uit de adolescentiejaren*, Nijmegen 1992.
'Le Corbusier - "Object Mathematique"' in: J. Milchers, K. Overdijk, and G. Verhoogt, *Ensemble. De kunstcollectie van de Technische Universiteit Eindhoven*, Eindhoven s.a., 20–21.
Lesage, A., *Expo '58. Het wonderlijke feest van de fifties*, Antwerp 2008.
Lombardo, V., 'Het Virtual Electronic Poem project (VEP-project)' in: Stichting Alice, *Make it New: Le poème électronique. Onderzoek voor de reconstructie van het Philips-paviljoen uit 1958 in Eindhoven*, Eindhoven 2007, 89–91.
Lombardo, V., A. Valle, J. Fitch, K. Tazelaar, S. Weinzierl, and W. Borczyk, 'A virtual-reality reconstruction of Poème Électronique based on philological research', *Computer Music Journal*, 33(2009)2, 24–47.
Lootsma, B. [A], 'Een ode van Philips aan de vooruitgang. Het paviljoen van Le Corbusier, Xenakis en Varèse op de Brusselse wereldtentoonstelling', *Wonen-TA/BK*, 12(1984)2, 10–17.
Lootsma, B. [B], '*Le Poème Electronique*. Het verlangen naar synthese', *Wonen-TA/BK*, 12(1984)2, 20–31.
Maelstaf, R., 'Het Electronisch Poëem', *La Fenêtre Ouverte/Op de Uitkijk*, 39–40 (October–December 1958), 157–159.
Majorick, B., 'Genesis van een compositie', *Kwadraat-blad*, 1961.
Mattis, O., 'From bebop to poo-wip: jazz influences in Varèse's *Poème électronique*' in: F. Meyer, and H. Zimmermann, *Edgard Varèse: Composer, sound sculptor, visionary*, Woodbridge 2006, 309–317.
Mens, R., 'Documenten rondom Le Corbusier, 1920–1965' in: R. Mens, B. Lootsma, and J. Bosman, *Le Corbusier en Nederland*, Utrecht 1985, 9–84.
'Nederlands inzending Brussel '58 versoberd', *De Telegraaf*, 11 January 1957.
'Nog geen naam voor Philips' Paviljoen', *Philips Koerier*, 11 January 1958.
Oskamp, J., 'Een haperend voorschot op de toekomst', *de Volkskrant*, 13 October 1995.
Petit, J. [A], *Le poème électronique. Le Corbusier* (extended Dutch-language paperback edition), Paris 1958.
Petit, J. [B], *Le poème électronique. Le Corbusier* (French-language hardcover edition), Paris 1958.
Petit, J. [C], *Le poème électronique: Le Corbusier* (English-language paperback edition), Paris 1958.
'Philips' Electronisch gedicht en de Expo-bezoekers', *Eindhovens Dagblad*, 16 August 1958.
'Philips' Expo-paviljoen: wonderlijk "elektronisch gedicht" in licht', *Het Vrije Volk*, undated cutting.
Philips, F., *45 jaar met Philips*, Rotterdam 1979.
'Philips-paviljoen opende zijn deuren nog niet', *Algemeen Handelsblad*, 19 April 1958.
Philips rapport annuel 1958, Brussels 1959.
'Philips-robot danst op elektronische muziek', *Philips Koerier*, 15 March 1958.
'"Poème electronique" in stadsjournaal', *Philips Koerier*, 17 January 1959.
Provoost, M., *Hugh Maaskant. Architect van de vooruitgang*, Rotterdam 2003.
Robb, I., 'Woman's hairpins help to build architecture of the future', *New York World-Telegram and the Sun*, undated cutting.
Rydell, R.W., *World of Fairs: The Century-of-Progress Exhibitions*, Chicago 1993.
Sandberg, W., 'Nabeschouwing over het philipspaviljoen op de expo '58 te brussel', *Museumjournaal*, series 4 no. 10 (May 1959), 179–182.
Schamphelaere, S. De, 'Filmexploitatie in Erpe-Mere', *Mededelingen van de Heemkundige Kring van Erpe-Mere*, 46(2006)2, 21–35.
Scheerlinck, K., P. Wever, and R. Lucas, *58 affiches voor Expo 58*, Brussels 2008.
Scholtes, P., 'Paviljoen Corbusier van de baan', *Eindhovens Dagblad*, 6 June 2009.
Schönberger, E., 'Dick Raaymakers: composer of bodiless sounds' in: A. Mulder, and J. Brouwer, *Dick Raaymakers: A Monograph*, Rotterdam 2008, 347–356.
Smit, R., K. Nijsen, L. Nouwen, and B. Postema, *Filmhistorie in Eindhoven. 1897–1985*, Eindhoven 1985.
Souvenir of your Visit to the Coca-Cola Pavilion: Brussels World's Fair 1958, information brochure.
'Spel van klank en kleur, licht en leven', *Philips Koerier*, 19 April 1958.

Sterken, S., 'Biografie van het Philips-paviljoen 1953–1959' in: Stichting Alice, *Make it New: Le poème électronique. Onderzoek voor de reconstructie van het Philips-paviljoen uit 1958 in Eindhoven*, Eindhoven 2007, 63–68.

Sterken, S. [A], 'Het *Poème Electronique* van Le Corbusier op de Wereldtentoonstelling van Brussel' in: J. Kint, and J. Stuyck, *Resten van de toekomst. Expo 58 vijftig jaar later*, Louvain 2008, 47–59.

Sterken, S. [B], 'Reconstructing the Philips Pavilion, Brussels 1958. Elements for a critical assessment' in: D. van den Heuvel, M. Mesman, W. Quist, and B. Lemmens, *The Challenge of Change: Dealing with the Legacy of the Modern Movement: Proceedings of the 10th International Docomomo Conference*, Amsterdam 2008, 93–98.

Stichting Reconstructie Philips Paviljoen 1958, *Reconstructie Philips-paviljoen 1958. Samenvatting haalbaarheidsonderzoek*, Eindhoven 2013.

Taubman, H. 'Fairgoers hear electronic poem', *The New York Times*, undated cutting.

Tazelaar, K., 'Poème électronique' in: *Varèse symposium Holland Festival 2009* (programme), Amsterdam 2009, 3–11.

Tazelaar, K., *On the Threshold of Beauty: Philips and the Origins of Electronic Music in the Netherlands 1925–1965*, Rotterdam 2013.

'Technical realization' in: *Poème électronique: Philips Pavilion World Exhibition Brussels 1958* (press file), 1958.

'Teleurstelling en verrassing in de hedendaagse muziek', *Trouw*, undated cutting.

'The "electronic poem" in the Philips Pavilion. A rich and rare experience of a world of wonder' in: *Poème électronique: Philips Pavilion World Exhibition Brussels 1958* (press file), 1958.

Thoor, M.T.A. van, *Het gebouw van Nederland. Nederlandse paviljoens op de wereldtentoonstellingen 1910–1958*, Zutphen 1998.

Thoor, M.T.A. van, 'Factoren van het Zichtbare. Rietvelds ideeën over de vernieuwing van de architectuur' in: R. Dettingmeijer, M.T.A. van Thoor, and I. van Zijl, *Rietvelds universum*, Rotterdam 2010, 154–173.

Treib, M., *Space Calculated in Seconds: The Philips Pavilion, Le Corbusier, Edgard Varèse*, Princeton 1996.

Veltman, J., 'Een <<elektronische>> klap in het gezicht', *Het Nieuws van den Dag*, undated cutting.

'Verbijsterend modern gedicht overspoelt de Expo-bezoeker', *De Telegraaf*, 24 April 1958.

Weber, N.F., *Le Corbusier. A life*, New York 2008.

Wever, P.C., 'Le Corbusier versus de Nederlandse architecten. "De gedeukte fluitketel van Philips" slaat een deuk in het Nederlandse prestige' in: A. Koch, *Dichtbij klopt het hart der wereld. Nederland op de Expo 58*, Schiedam 2008, 113–127.

Wie wat waar? Jaarboek 1959, Leiden 1958.

'Wie weet naam voor Philips paviljoen', *Philips Koerier*, 19 October 1957.

Wilbrink, F., *Kunst in de Philips-reclame 1891–1941*, Eindhoven 2005.

Xenakis, Y., 'Het architectonische ontwerp van Le Corbusier en Xenakis voor het paviljoen' in: *Het Philipspaviljoen op de Wereldtentoonstelling te Brussel 1958* (reprint from *Philips Technical Review*), s.a., 2–8.

'Zij leggen gewicht in de schaal', *Philips Koerier*, 19 April 1958.

Image Credits

Aloi, R., *Esposizioni architetture allestimenti*, Milan 1960, 29, 31: *2.8, 6.7*.
Art Committee of the Eindhoven University of Technology, Eindhoven, the Netherlands: *3.18b–e, 3.21a–b, 3.22b–d, 9.6* (photos by Peter Wever).
Centraal Museum Utrecht, Utrecht, the Netherlands: *1.1b*.
Elle, 23 June 1958, 37: *7.10*.
Everts, F.E.C., *Nederland op de Wereldtentoonstelling Brussel 1958*, The Hague 1960, 15: *1.3*.
Fondation Le Corbusier, Paris, France: *1.7, 1.9, 2.4, 2.7, 3.1b, 4.8, 8.15, 8.19* (© FLC/Pictoright, 2015).
Fondation Le Corbusier, Paris, France: front flyleaf, *3.6, 3.19, 3.22a–c, II.2a–b,* back flyleaf, *back cover* (© FLC/Pictoright, 2015; © J. Paul Getty Trust, photographs by Lucien Hervé, The Getty Research Institute, Los Angeles (2002.R.41)).
Fondation Le Corbusier, Paris, France: *3.14* (© FLC/Pictoright, 2015; © Royal Philips).
Het Nieuwe Instituut, Rotterdam, the Netherlands: *1.1a, 1.6a*.
Het Rotterdamsch Parool, 12 October 1957, 9: *1.4*.
International Lighting Review, 1958 (3–4), 147, 127: *3.13, 3.26*.
John Donat/RIBA Library Photographs Collection, London, United Kingdom: *2.6b*.
Le Soir, 27 February 1958, 18: *6.2*.
Liberaal Archief, Ghent, Belgium: *7.7*.
Majorick, B., 'Genesis van een compositie', *Kwadraat-blad* 1961, n.p.: *1.5, 1.6b*.
Malraux, G.A., *Le musée imaginaire de la sculpture mondiale*, Paris 1952, n.p.: *3.4a*.
Museumjournaal, May 1959 (series 4 no. 10), cover: *8.26*.
Nederlands Fotomuseum, Rotterdam, the Netherlands: *6.1* (photo by Hans de Boer).
Paul Sacher Foundation, Edgard Varèse Collection, Basel, Switzerland: *5.4*.
Petit, J., *Le poème électronique. Le Corbusier*, Paris 1958, cover, 87: *7.13a–b*.
Philips Belgium, Corporate Communication & Public Affairs, Brussels, Belgium: introduction *d–e–f,* 3.5, 3.23, 7.1, II.4, 8.1, 8.4, 8.5, 8.6, 8.7, 8.8, 8.10, 8.11, *8.13a–b–c, 8.14, 8.17a–b–c, 8.20, 8.21, 8.22, 8.23, 9.1a–b, 9.5* (photos *8.17a–b* by Kees Tazelaar).
Philips Company Archives, Eindhoven, the Netherlands: front endpaper, *4.5, 7.6a, 8.9a–b* (© Royal Philips).
Philips Koerier, 12 April 1958, 5: *3.4b* (photo provided by the Philips Company Archives, Eindhoven, the Netherlands).
Philips Koerier, 19 April 1958, 3: *3.20* (photo provided by the Philips Company Archives, Eindhoven, the Netherlands).
Philips Pavilion press file: *cover insert, back cover inserts*.
Photo Jean-Pierre Leloir, Paris, France: *2.3*.
Private collection Pierre Arnaud, Poissy, France: *4.1, 4.7*.
Private collection heirs of Theo A. Boesveld-Oosterom, Bergen/Utrecht, the Netherlands: *6.4a–b, 6.5, 6.9, 6.11, 6.13, 6.14, 7.15*.
Private collection Bill Cotter, Mission Hills, California, United States of America: *2.6a*.
Private collection Leendert de Jong, Wassenaar, the Netherlands: *7.3*.
Private collection Wim Langenhoff, Eindhoven, the Netherlands: *3.4d*.
Private collection Eléonore de Lavandeyra-Schöffer, Paris, France: *4.6* (© Société des Auteurs dans les Arts Graphiques et Plastiques).
Private collection Mies Roos-Hartong, Apeldoorn, the Netherlands: *4.4*.
Private collection Kees Tazelaar, Nootdorp, the Netherlands: *5.1, 5.2, 5.3, 5.5, 6.12b, 9.7b–c, 9.8a–b–c–d, 9.10* (photos *5.1, 5.2, 5.3, 5.5* by Anton Buczynski or from his camera).
Private collection Ger Voorsteegh, The Hague, the Netherlands: *1.12*.
Private collection Peter Wever, Rosmalen, the Netherlands: *cover,* contents, *1.2,* 1.8, *1.10,* 1.11, 1.13, 2.2, *2.9, 3.7, 3.28, 4.3, 6.3, 6.6, 6.8a–b, 6.12a, 7.2, 7.4a–b, 7.6b, 7.8, 7.9, 7.12, 7.14, II.1, II.3, II.5, 8.2, 8.3, 8.12, 8.16, 8.18a–b, 8.24, 8.25, 9.2a–b, 9.3, 9.4, 9.7a, 9.9,* back endpaper (photos *3.7,* 8.12, *8.25,* 9.3, 9.4 by Kees Tazelaar; photo 9.9 by Peter Wever).
Private collection Peter Wever, Rosmalen, the Netherlands/EYE Film Institute Netherlands, Amsterdam, the Netherlands: *3.2, 3.12a–b–c, 6.10*.
Private collection Peter Wever, Rosmalen, the Netherlands/EYE Film Institute Netherlands, Amsterdam, the Netherlands: preface *a–b–c–d–e–f,* 3.3, 3.4c, *3.8a–b–c–d, 3.9a–b, 3.10a–b–c–d–e–f–g–h–i–j–k–l–m–n* (© Royal Philips).
Private collection Frans Wilbrink, Son, the Netherlands: *2.1*.
Radio Bulletin, January 1958, cover: *7.11*.
Rijksmuseum, Amsterdam, the Netherlands, on loan from Philips International B.V.: introduction *a–b–c,* 2.5a–b (photos by Rijksmuseum).
The Getty Research Institute, Los Angeles (870438): *3.11a–b–c, 3.15, 3.17a–b–c, 3.18a–c–d–f–g–h, 3.24, 3.25a–b, 4.2*.
The Philips Pavilion at the 1958 Brussels World's Fair (reprint from *Philips Technical Review*), s.a., 41, cover: *3.27, 7.5*.
The Philips Pavilion at the 1958 Brussels World Fair (reprint from Philips Technical Review), s.a., 4: *1.1* (© J. Paul Getty Trust, photograph by Lucien Hervé, The Getty Research Institute, Los Angeles (2002.R.41)).
Treib, M., *Space Calculated in Seconds: The Philips Pavilion, Le Corbusier, Edgard Varèse*, Princeton 1996, 159: *3.16*.
Zodiac, 1958 (2), cover: *3.1a*.

Name Index

Aalto, Alvar, 162n
Adenauer, Konrad, 75, 156n
Agostini, Philippe, 50, 127, 130, 156n
Andringa de Kempenaer, Therus van, 93, 157n
Arnaud, Jean-François, 155n
Arnaud, Pierre, 4, 6, 12, 75-76, 78, 79, 81, 155n-157n
Arnold, Malcolm, 136
Askenase, Stefan, 136
Badings, Henk, 87, 141, 156n, 157n
Bakema, Jaap, 15, 18, 21, 25, 26, 29, 151n, 152n
Barbara, 155n
Beatrix, H.R.H. Princess of the Netherlands, 136
Beethoven, Ludwig van, 99
Bel Geddes, Norman, 102
Bernhard, H.R.H. Prince of the Netherlands, 133
Binnendijk, J.A.M., 52, 66, 68, 92, 157n
Boer, Hans de, 162n
Boesveld, Theo, 4, 5, 7, 91-93, 97-99, 157n-161n
Boks, Joost, 15, 18, 32
Bons, Jan, 19-21, 151n
Bootz, Sonja, 93, 157n
Bos, Agnes, 98
Bossche, Vanden (pavilion attendant), 93
Brandon, Arie, 157n
Brassens, Georges, 155n
Breuer, Marcel, 162n
Britten, Benjamin, 83
Broek, Jo van den, 15, 21, 25
Brouwer, Jan, 92, 94, 125, 157n
Brubeck, Dave, 99
Bruin, Simon de, 52, 70, 91, 93-95, 97-99, 130-133, 153n, 154n, 158n, 159n
Bruyn, Jan de, 87, 92, 93
Buczynski, Anton, 82, 83, 85-88, 157n
Butor, Michel, 108, 159n
Bijvank, Jan, 101, 105
Caliouw, Freddy, 140
Carré, John le, 75
Chottin, Georges, 81
Coolen, Jan, 50
Cools, Michel, 5, 90, 93, 95, 97, 139, 149, 157n, 158n, 162n
Cox, Wiel, 4, 5, 90-94, 97-99, 125, 149, 157n-159n, 162n
Damaz, Paul, 37
Daudey, Jan, 101
Dejacques, Claude, 155n
Derijcke, Jaak, 93, 160n
Desqueper, Marcel, 93
Deutekom, Cristina, 87, 157n, 160n
Disney, Walt, 85, 102
Duyster, Hoyte, 108, 141, 151n, 162n
Eeghen, J. van, 52, 66, 92, 157n
Faure, Élie, 50
Gaulle, Charles de, 75, 111, 156n
Geesink, Joop, 50, 51, 145
Gellens, Paul, 93
Giedion, Sigfried, 32
Gillet, Guillaume, 127, 130
Goethem, Marcel van, 29, 37

Hafkemeijer, John, 80, 93, 157n, 158n, 160n
Hallyday, Johnny, 155n
Hartong, Henk, 75-77, 79, 80, 134, 155n, 156n
Haver Droeze, Jack, 75, 155n
Hering, Willem, 11, 148, 161n
Hervé, Lucien, 160n, 162n
Heukensfeldt Jansen, Frans, 93, 157n
Heuvel, André van den, 156n
Hoof, Jan van, 91, 93, 97, 98, 157n
Huyghe, Julien, 93, 113
Irene, H.R.H. Princess of the Netherlands, 136
Jansen, Johan, 58, 60, 62, 68-71, 144, 154n, 155n, 157n
Jasinski, Stanislas, 140, 161n
Juliana, H.M. Queen of the Netherlands, 133, 136
Kalff, Louis, 11, 15, 18, 21, 25, 29, 37, 38, 41, 42, 49, 50, 69, 71, 76, 79, 80, 101, 102, 105, 107, 108, 110, 113, 122, 123, 125-127, 133, 139-141, 143, 151n-162n
Karajan, Herbert von, 87
Kleiboer, Jac., 18
Le Corbusier, passim
Lelieur, Piet, 148, 154n
Losange, Pierre, 90, 91, 93, 96, 162n
Lummel, Chris van, 80, 157n
Malraux, André, 50, 51
Man Ray, 161n
Margriet, H.K.H. Princess of the Netherlands, 136
Médard, Raymond, 93, 113
Mendes de Leòn-van Liebergen, Beatrijs, 130, 158n, 161n
Menuhin, Yehudi, 136
Merkelbach, Ben, 15, 21, 25, 28, 29, 151n
Meyers, Paul, 130, 133, 140, 156n, 161n
Meyerstein-Maigret, Georges, 156n
Miller, Mitch, 98
Moens de Fernig, Georges, 123, 126
Mozart, Wolfgang, 87
Naveaux, Max, 4, 5, 54, 68, 93, 94, 98, 99, 144, 149, 157n, 158n, 162n
Nerée tot Babberich, Pepita de, 4, 5, 93, 111, 113, 132, 140, 157n, 160n
Neutra, Richard, 127, 133, 158n
Niamonitakis, Stef, 93, 157n
Nijsen, Kees, 155n
Numann, Sies, 101, 111
Oertle, Hans, 105
Onrust, Hank, 11, 148
Oosterom, Nelly, 5, 98
Oosthoek, Hélène, 156n
Otten, Frans, 93, 122, 123, 125, 126, 130, 133, 134
Otten-Philips, Anna, 125, 126
Oud, J.J.P., 15, 21, 24, 25, 28, 29, 32, 152n
Paganini, Niccolò, 99
Petit, Jean, 50, 107, 108, 110, 111, 113, 130, 144, 154n, 156n, 158n, 159n
Peutz, Frits, 15, 32, 152n
Pevsner, Antoine, 137, 153n
Philips, Frits, 101, 113, 122, 123, 125, 126, 128, 156n
Potter, Annie de, 93, 111
Raaijmakers, Dick (Kid Baltan), 97, 98, 158n, 161n

Rachmaninov, Sergei, 99
Rietveld, Gerrit, 9, 13-15, 18-21, 24, 25, 32, 33, 151n, 156n
Robb, Inez, 35
Roeck, Lucien De, 106
Sandberg, Willem, 13, 136, 137
Schaeffer, Pierre, 155n
Schöffer, Nicolas, 78-80, 156n, 157n
Shaffy, Ramses, 156n
Soete, Michel, 5, 93, 149, 157n 158n, 162n
Spaendonck, Barend van, 25, 29
Spaens, Charles, 101, 123, 125, 133, 134, 140
Stekelenburg, Ferdinand van, 156n
Stern, Isaac, 136
Sterneberg, Robert, 93, 111
Stockhausen, Karlheinz, 141
Stokowski, Leopold, 136
Tak, Willem, 69, 76, 80, 85-87, 91, 92, 132, 133, 154n, 156n, 157n
Tazelaar, Kees, 6, 11, 148, 154n, 158n, 161n, 162n
Tomasi, Claude, 156n, 157n
Tomasi, Henri, 78-80, 155n-157n
Vancoppenolle, Paul, 4, 5, 54, 93-96, 96, 99, 139, 144, 149, 152n, 157n-162n
Vanderschrick, François, 93, 95, 158n
Varèse, Edgard, 6, 10, 11, 49, 75, 76, 80, 83, 85-88, 93, 95, 107, 108, 118, 123, 125, 127, 133, 136, 144, 145, 155n-158n, 160n-162n
Varèse, Louise, 157n
Verboon, Leo, 156n
Vreedenburgh, Cornelis, 108, 159n
Walsem, Herman van, 21, 28, 29, 32, 37, 151n, 152n
Wright, Frank Lloyd, 20, 35
Xenakis, Iannis, 6, 9-11, 21, 25, 28, 29, 34, 37, 41, 42, 80, 81, 83, 101, 108, 124, 130, 148, 152n-158n, 160n, 161n
Zeeuw, Jan de, 158n

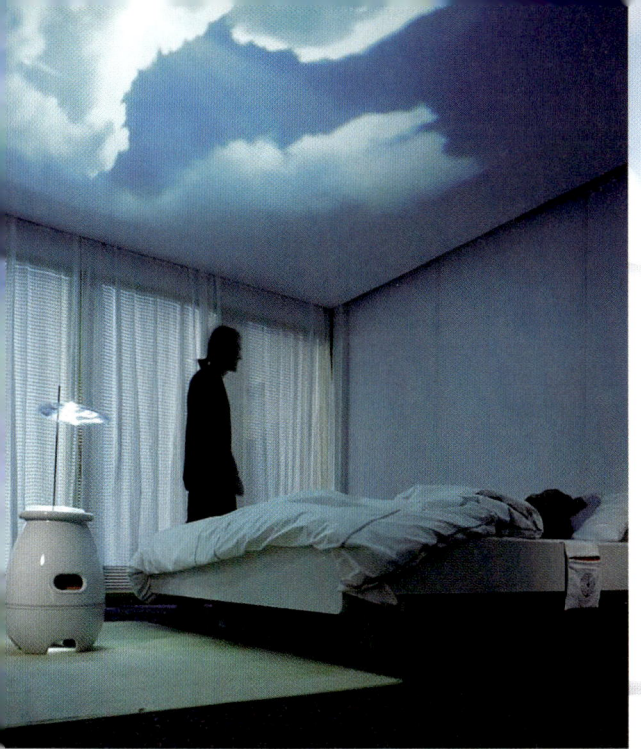
Nebula (2000)

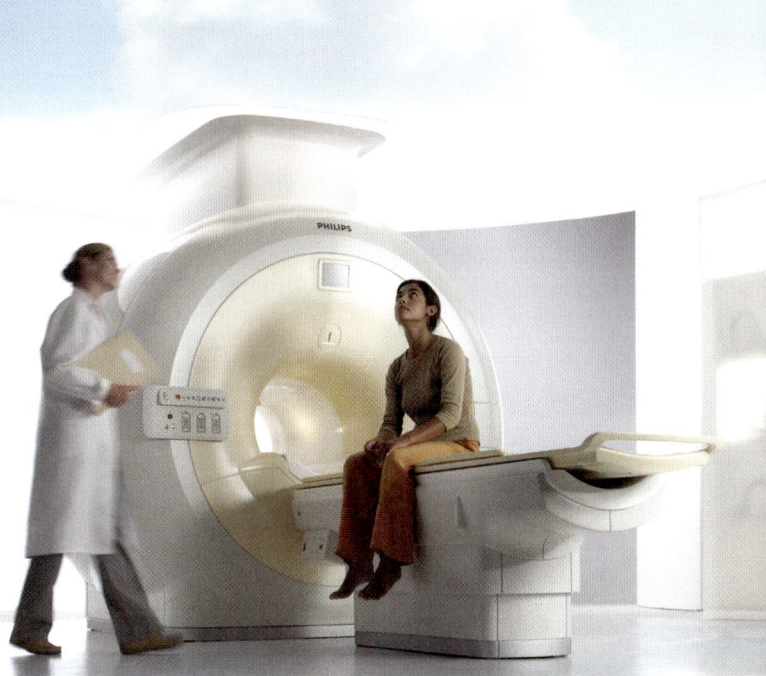
Ambient Experience (2003)

Philips Design
experiences

Since the 1958 Brussels exhibition, Philips Design has continued to explore and innovate around multi sensorial experiences.

For example, in 2000 the team embarked on a research and development program to explore how new technologies could provide people with interactive experiences that enrich their daily activities in simple and intuitive ways. This led to a prototype called Nebula which explored how using interactive projection systems could enrich the experience of going to bed. The aim was to research how multimedia and ambience could help create an atmosphere in the bedroom that encourages and enhances rest, reflection, intimacy, imagination and play, sleeping and waking up.

Such future thinking also helped to create what has now become a successful design driven proposition from Philips in the healthcare domain called Ambient Experience. The design process focuses on the values and needs of both patients and medical staff, addressing the total experience flow. It integrates architecture and technology to create an environment that the patient can personalize, improving the patient experience and quality of care, while increasing operational effectiveness.

Today Philips Design is one of the largest design groups in the world with over 500 designers globally. In 2015 the group celebrates their 90th year in using design to improve people lives.

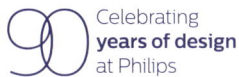

Credits

Texts: Peter Wever, Ludo van Halem, Pierre Arnaud and Kees Tazelaar
Image research: Peter Wever
Image editing: Anneliek Holland
Copy editing: Auke van den Berg, Bookmakers, Nijmegen
Translation: Douglas Heingartner – Chapter 1, 2 and 4; Beverley Jackson – Chapter 3, 5 and 9; Vivien Reid – Introduction, Chapter 6, 7 and 8
Design: Joseph Plateau graphic designers, Amsterdam
Lithography and Printing: Drukkerij Van Gorcum, Assen
Paper: LuxoArt Samt, 150 gr
Publisher: Marcel Witvoet, nai010 publishers

This publication was made possible by financial support from
heirs of Theo A. Boesveld-Oosterom
Stichting Charema, Fonds voor Geschiedenis en Kunst
Geoffrey Donaldson Institute
Provincie Noord-Brabant, Erfgoed Brabant, Prof. Dr. H.F.J.M. van den Eerenbeemtfonds
De Gijselaar-Hintzenfonds
Meulensteen Art Centre
Prins Bernhard Cultuurfonds

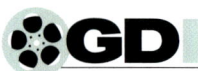

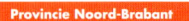

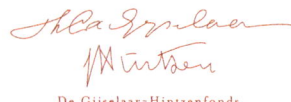

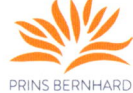

© 2015 nai010 publishers, Rotterdam. All rights reserved. No part of this publication may be reproduced, stored in a retrieval system, or transmitted in any form or by any means, electronic, mechanical, photocopying, recording or otherwise, without the prior written permission of the publisher.

For works of visual artists affiliated with a CISAC-organization the copyrights have been settled with Pictoright in Amsterdam.
© 2015, c/o Pictoright Amsterdam

Although every effort was made to find the copyright holders for the illustrations used, it has not been possible to trace them all. Interested parties are requested to contact nai010 publishers, Mauritsweg 23, 3012 JR Rotterdam, the Netherlands.

nai010 publishers is an internationally orientated publisher specialized in developing, producing and distributing books in the fields of architecture, urbanism, art and design.
www.nai010.com

nai010 books are available internationally at selected bookstores and from the following distribution partners:

North, Central and South America - Artbook | D.A.P., New York, USA, dap@dapinc.com

Rest of the world - Idea Books, Amsterdam, the Netherlands, idea@ideabooks.nl

For general questions, please contact nai010 publishers directly at sales@nai010.com or visit our website www.nai010.com for further information.

Printed and bound in the Netherlands

ISBN 978-94-6208-207-6

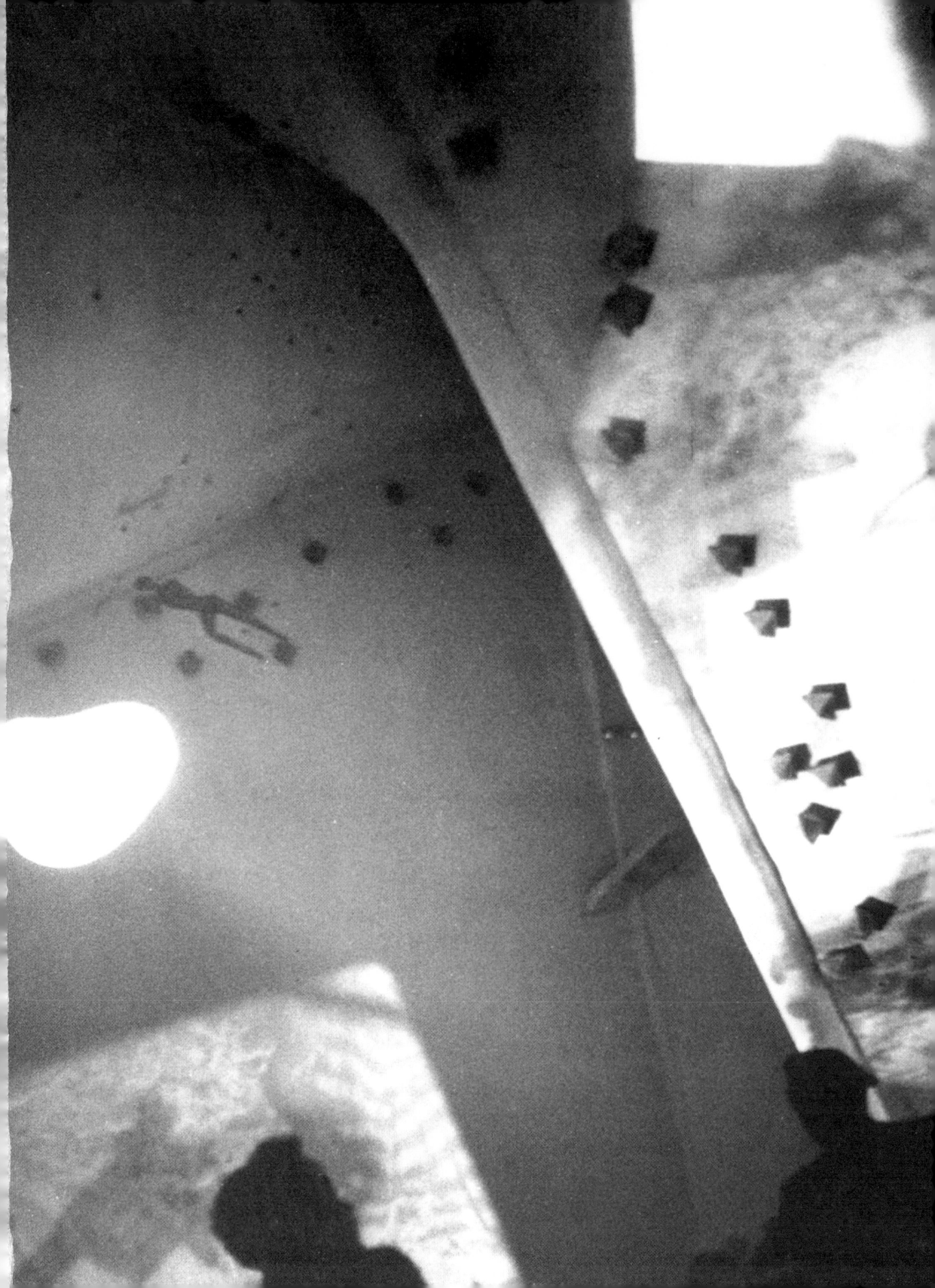

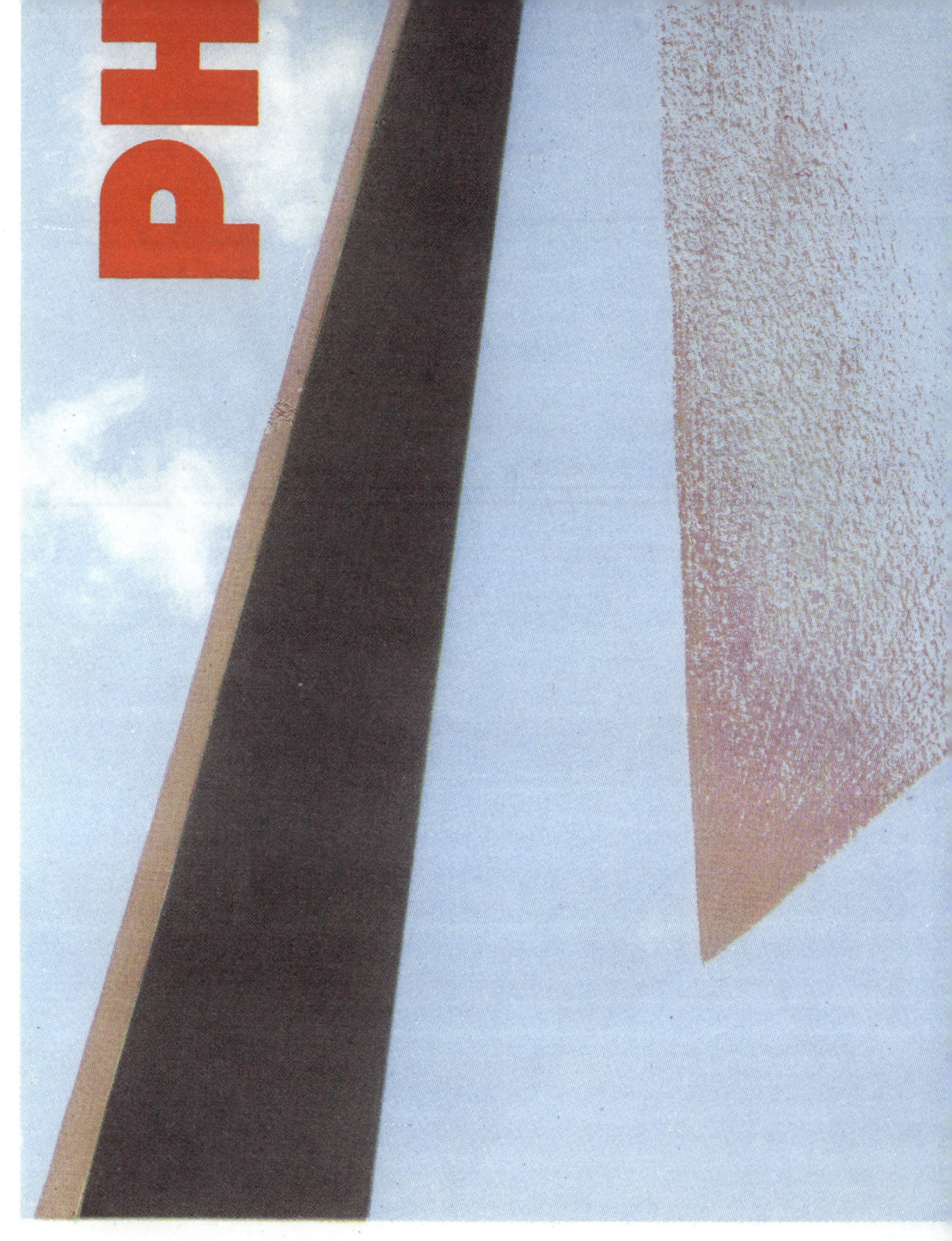